# Stirlings in Action
# with the
# Airborne Forces

# Stirlings in Action with the Airborne Forces

## Air Support for SAS and Resistance Operations during WWII

### DENNIS WILLIAMS

Pen & Sword
**AVIATION**

Published in Great Britain in 2008 by
**PEN & SWORD AVIATION**
*an imprint of*
Pen & Sword Books Ltd
47 Church Street
Barnsley
South Yorkshire
S70 2AS

ISBN 978-1-84415-648-1

A CIP catalogue record for this book is
available from the British Library.

Typeset by Concept, Huddersfield, West Yorkshire
Printed and bound in Great Britain by Biddles Ltd


*Pen & Sword Books Ltd incorporates the Imprints of*
Pen & Sword Aviation, Pen & Sword Maritime, Pen & Sword Military,
Wharncliffe Local History, Pen & Sword Select,
Pen & Sword Military Classics and Leo Cooper.




For a complete list of Pen & Sword titles please contact
**PEN & SWORD BOOKS LIMITED**
47 Church Street, Barnsley, South Yorkshire, S70 2AS, England.
E-mail: enquiries@pen-and-sword.co.uk
Website: www.pen-and-sword.co.uk

# Contents

Acknowledgements . . . . . . . . . . . . . . . . . . . . . . . . . . . .  vi

Preface . . . . . . . . . . . . . . . . . . . . . . . . . . . . . . . . . viii

Chapter 1   Two Squadrons – 190 and 620 . . . . . . . . . . . . . . . . . . . . . 1

Chapter 2   Their New Role – November 1943 to February 1944 . . . . . 13

Chapter 3   Preparing for the Second Front – March to May 1944 . . . . 35

Chapter 4   D-Day – 6 June 1944 . . . . . . . . . . . . . . . . . . . . . . . . 66

Chapter 5   Summer Nights – June to August 1944 . . . . . . . . . . . . . . 96

Chapter 6   Battle Over Arnhem – September 1944 . . . . . . . . . . . . . . 143

Chapter 7   They Also Served – The Ground Crews, 1943–6 . . . . . . . . 184

Chapter 8   Moving Eastwards – September to December 1944 . . . . . . 197

Chapter 9   Winter and Rough Weather – December 1944 to March 1945 224

Chapter 10  From Varsity to Victory – March to May 1945 . . . . . . . . . 245

Chapter 11  Keeping the Peace – June 1945 to August 1946 . . . . . . . . 281

Epilogue . . . . . . . . . . . . . . . . . . . . . . . . . . . . . . . . 311

Appendix – Roll of Honour . . . . . . . . . . . . . . . . . . . . . 313

Index . . . . . . . . . . . . . . . . . . . . . . . . . . . . . . . . . . 328

# Acknowledgements

Thisbook owes its existence to sources that are many and varied, and as far as possible, original and unpublished. I am particularly indebted to Alan White and Sue Mintram-Mason, who each provided a great deal of correspondence relating to Nos 190 and 620 Squadrons, but the gathering of information also relied on the enthusiastic support of all the following individuals, some of whom have, sadly, passed away in recent years.

Hugh Allan, Ken Back, Mrs Peggy Baker, Arthur Batten, Ron Bedford, John P. Bond, Ron Bradbury, Stan Brice, Wing Commander G.H. Briggs DFC RAF (Retd), Leonard Brock, George Chesterton, Ron Clement, Frank Cox, Tony Cramp, Peter Cutts, Eric Dane, George Dann, Brigadier M.D.K. Dauncey DSO DL, Wilf Davey, Stan Derbyshire, Arne Egner, Jim Ely, David Evans, John Everitt, Mr J. Facey, Ivan Fairfax, George Fairweather, John Fielding, Ernest Fletcher, Alan Gamble, Dennis Gibson, Ray Glass, Roy Gould, Peter Graham, Squadron Leader Hugh Grant-Dalton DFC and Bar RAF (Retd), Ken Halstead, Dr John Harrison, Bert Heald, Cec Herbert, Thomas J. Higgins, Ken Hillier, Les Hillyard, Henry Hooper, Ken Hoult, Jack Howes, John Hughes, 'Taff' Hughes, Jim Jefferies, Peter Jordan, Arthur Kempster, Ken Kendrew, Mrs Merna Kidgell, Roy Lancelott, Reg Lawton, Mrs Rosemary Lee, Gunnar Lindaas, Bill Longhurst, James Marshall, Don Mason, Malcolm Mitchell, Arthur Moody, Kenneth Morris, Reg Moss, George Neale, Eric Newbury, William Osgood, 'Dai' Owen, Rettie Palmer, Squadron Leader Joe Patient DFC RAF (Retd), Robert Powell, Bert Pryce, Philip Pryce, Charlie Randall, Ron Remfry, Elizabeth Robson, John Scott, Allan Schofield, Ray Seeley, Ron Shaw, John Shinner, Air Vice-Marshal C.L. Siegert CB CBE MVO DFC AFC RNZAF (Retd), Arthur H. Smith, Douglas Smith MBE, John R. Smith, Morgan Thomas, Eric Titterton, Donald Tranter, Douglas Venning, Joe Vinet, Jim Viney, Eric Wadman, Group Captain A.F. Wallace CBE DFC RAF (Retd), Alan Webster, Mr J.S. Welton, Fred Weston, Stan White, Howard Whitehead, 'Jock' Whitehouse and Ken Wilson.

The staffs of English Heritage's National Monuments Record at Swindon, the Imperial War Museum at Lambeth, the National Archives at Kew, and the Royal Air Force Museum at Hendon have been most courteous and helpful during my visits to their archives. I am grateful to the Imperial War Museum, the National Monuments Record, and Bombardier Aerospace (UK) Ltd of Belfast for granting permission to reproduce photographs from their collections. The 801st/492nd Bombardment Group Association kindly provided copies of photographs taken at the USAAF base at Harrington.

National Archives documents used as primary sources included Squadron, Station and Group Operations Record Books (and related appendices), Squadron

Operations Reports, and Station Watchkeeper's Logs. Short extracts from Operations Record Books AIR 28/327, AIR 28/262 and AIR 25/589 are reproduced with the permission of the National Archives. The Commonwealth War Graves Commission imparts information on all its cemeteries and register entries via its website, and this facility has proved invaluable in locating casualties' graves or places of commemoration. I am also grateful to Mrs Susan Dickinson, of the Ministry of Defence's Air Historical Branch at RAF Bentley Priory, for confirming details of accidents and operational losses involving aircraft of 190 and 620 Squadrons.

Last, but not least, I must record my respect and gratitude for the friendship and support given by the late Noel Chaffey. As a wireless operator with 620 Squadron, Noel took some fine photographs of people and planes, and his outstanding camera skills eventually led him to a successful career in photography. In the 1960s, he had the foresight to start a small aviation archive, which concentrated on 190 and 620 Squadrons. With the assistance of his wartime comrades, this soon grew into a fascinating collection of photographs, many of which are published for the first time in this book. However, I fear that with the passing of the years, the provenance of some of these photographs may have been lost. If this has happened, I offer my sincere apologies, and thanks, to contributors whose names have been omitted from the list above. Throughout the creation of this book, Noel acted as a source of enthusiastic and good-humoured advice, always being quick to forward any 'new' photos or snippets of information. Shortly before his death in 2005, he read the first illustrated version of the manuscript, and I was very grateful for his encouragement and constructive criticism at that time. Noel is still sorely missed by all who knew him, both in his native Australia and as an Honorary 'Pom' in Essex, where he lived for over fifty years.

# Preface

This book is about two Royal Air Force squadrons. At first, it seemed that to focus on just one of them might be ambitious enough. However, as research progressed, it became evident that 190 and 620 Squadrons had been so closely linked that it would be difficult, and indeed unfair, to publish the story of one without the other.

During the Second World War, 190 and 620 Squadrons flew together, from Leicester East, Fairford and Great Dunmow. They practised standards of airmanship that were second to none, and demonstrated remarkable versatility, through a wide range of air support tasks. Their Short Stirlings delivered airborne forces to Normandy on D-Day, to Arnhem in September 1944, and across the Rhine in March 1945. In addition, they took part in numerous special operations. Agents of the Special Operations Executive were parachuted into Nazi-occupied Europe, along with supplies for the Resistance organisations, while Special Air Service troops were also covertly dropped, in order to hasten the Allied victory by launching attacks far behind enemy lines.

Given the secrecy surrounding the special operations flown by 190 and 620 Squadrons, it is not surprising that some lines of enquiry turned out to be unproductive during the research for this book. On the other hand, there were a few lucky finds, the most notable of which comprised a series of Watchkeeper's Logs from the RAF stations at Fairford and Great Dunmow. These are preserved in the National Archives, among records relating to Operation 'Overlord', the invasion of Normandy, whereas equivalent documents for most other RAF stations appear to have been lost. The handwritten entries in the Watchkeeper's Logs provide a topical record of messages received by, and sent from, Fairford and Great Dunmow. They have proved especially useful in cross-checking the contents of the Operations Record Books from these stations, since errors often crept into the latter documents, in spite of the intention that they should be compiled as accurate, permanent records for the units concerned.

Valuable though they may be, official documents seldom portray the raw, human experience of the Second World War. It is therefore important to make the most of opportunities to record first-hand accounts of this conflict, before it fades from living memory. The old adage that 'there is a history in all men's lives' surely rings true in this situation, because so much information resides in personal diaries, letters, photograph albums, flying log books, and in its most fragile form, the memories of those who lived through the war. We are very fortunate that many of the people who served with 190 and 620 Squadrons have taken the trouble to contribute words and pictures that help to tell *their* wartime history. This book is dedicated to all of them.

Dennis Williams
Worcestershire
July 2007

# CHAPTER 1

# Two Squadrons

## 190 and 620

T he first British squadron to bear the number 190 was a Royal Flying Corps night-fighter training unit, which formed on 24 October 1917 at Rochford aerodrome (now Southend Airport) in Essex. Initially equipped with BE2c and BE2e biplanes, it was known as 190 (Depot) Squadron until 21 December 1917, when its full title changed to 190 (Night) Training Squadron. This unit later flew DH6 and Avro 504K aircraft and moved to Newmarket Heath in Suffolk on 14 March 1918, shortly before the founding of the Royal Air Force. A further move took place on 5 October 1918, to Upwood in Cambridgeshire, where No. 190 Squadron disbanded on 1 May 1919.

190 Squadron reappeared as a Royal Air Force unit on 1 March 1943. 210 Squadron, which operated Consolidated Catalina flying boats from Pembroke Dock, transferred surplus personnel to Shetland, where they formed the new squadron at Sullom Voe. Commanded by Wing Commander P.H. Alington DFC and equipped with nine Catalinas, 190 Squadron belonged to 18 Group, Coastal Command, whose main task was to seek and destroy German U-boats. After a period of reduced activity during the preceding winter months, these submarines were now causing such heavy losses among Allied shipping in the North Atlantic that they had to be defeated, if Britain's survival was to be assured.

The Catalina's outstanding range and endurance were demonstrated by 190 Squadron's first operational flight, on 7 March 1943. This was a patrol to the north-east of Iceland, lasting 21 hours 30 mins. 190 Squadron saw action for the first time on 26 March, when a surfaced U-boat was attacked with depth charges. Despite the difficulties of servicing the Catalinas in weather that was often appalling, the ground crews succeeded in keeping them airworthy so that the patrols could continue.

Further U-boats were located and attacked in April and May 1943. During the latter month, their losses reached a peak that corresponded to a dramatic drop in the number of Allied ships sunk. In reaching this turning point in the Battle of the Atlantic, the Coastal Command crews

No. 190 Squadron's crest: 'A cloak charged with a double headed eagle displayed'. Its motto: *Ex tenebris* (Through darkness). (*190 & 620 Sqns Archive*)

A Catalina of 190 Squadron, carrying out an air-sea rescue. (*Imperial War Museum, C 3606*)

had been helped considerably by the Anti Surface Vessel radar equipment fitted to their aircraft, and also by reliable intelligence obtained from the deciphering of coded 'Enigma' signals transmitted by the German Navy.

The fact that 190 Squadron made only sporadic contact with U-boats throughout the summer of 1943, and none at all after August of that year, was an indication of the very effective deterrent presented to the German Navy by Coastal Command. The use of 190 as a squadron number in this theatre of war came to an end when the Catalinas of 210 Squadron, now based at Hamworthy in Dorset, were dispersed to other units in December 1943, and 190 Squadron was renumbered as 210 at Sullom Voe on 1 January 1944.

On 5 January 1944, the Air Ministry authorised the re-formation of 190 Squadron, within 38 Group. This time, the squadron would be equipped with Short Stirlings and based at Leicester East. From this airfield, then Fairford, and finally Great Dunmow, 190 Squadron operated alongside 620 Squadron until after the end of the Second World War.

620 Squadron had been formed on 17 June 1943, at Chedburgh in Suffolk, and belonged to 3 Group, Bomber Command. 620 Squadron's personnel and their Stirling aircraft were made available through the rationalisation of 149 Squadron at Lakenheath, also in Suffolk, and 214 Squadron, which was already at Chedburgh. Nos 149 and 214 Squadrons were each reduced from three flights to two, thus yielding establishments of sixteen aircraft (plus four in reserve) for these existing units and the new one, 620 Squadron. In the summer of 1943, there were still eleven Stirling squadrons operating in 3 Group, with a similar number of Halifax

No. 620 Squadron's crest: 'In front of a demi-pegasus couped, a flash of lightning'. Its motto: *Dona ferentes adsumus* (We are bringing gifts). (*190 & 620 Sqns Archive*)

squadrons in 4 Group. However, by the time 620 Squadron was formed, the Stirling's days as a strategic bomber were numbered. The Avro Lancaster had become Bomber Command's first choice of aircraft, largely because its bomb load and service ceiling could not be matched by either of the other four-engined bomber types.

During the spring of 1943, the principal objective of the RAF's strategic bombing campaign had been the destruction of German manufacturing centres, mostly in the Ruhr area. From June 1943, the Commander-in-Chief of Bomber Command, Air Marshal Sir Arthur Harris, gave priority to targets associated with the German aircraft industry, especially those producing the night-fighters that presented one of the main threats to his bombers. Since 620 Squadron had a nucleus of experienced aircrews drawn from 149 and 214 Squadrons, it was able to go into action without delay. On 19 June 1943, Wg Cdr Donald Lee assumed command of 620 Squadron, and in the evening, six of its Stirlings took off under a full moon to bomb the Schneider works at Le Creusot in eastern France. This heralded the start of five months of operations, which would test the resolve and determination of the 620 Squadron aircrews and cost many of their lives.

On the night of 21/22 June, the 620 Squadron Stirlings flew to targets at Krefeld, in the Ruhr. The next night, 22/23 June, Mülheim was bombed and the squadron sustained its first casualties. Stirling EE875 'A', captained by Sgt Nicholson, failed to return and was presumed to have crashed into the North Sea, killing all members of the crew. The body of the rear gunner, Sgt Wells, was the only one recovered from the sea for burial in Holland.

620 Squadron took part in further bombing operations before the end of June 1943, as targets at Wuppertal, Gelsenkirchen and Cologne were attacked in quick succession. Stirling BK800 'Z', captained by Flt Sgt Reynolds, was lost during the first of these three operations, on 24/25 June. Only one member of the crew survived to be taken prisoner, after this aircraft was shot down by a night-fighter. The same night, BK720 'Y' was badly damaged by anti-aircraft fire. Its pilot, Sgt O'Connell, managed to get the aircraft back to Chedburgh in the early hours of the morning, but its arrival turned into a crash-landing as a tyre burst. Two members of the crew were slightly injured and the aircraft was written off.

The Stirling's poor service ceiling not only made it an easy target for searchlights and flak, but also vulnerable to bombing by Lancasters and Halifaxes flying several thousand feet higher. Ron Remfry, a Fitter II (Engines) with 620 Squadron, observed that some Stirling aircrews had very lucky escapes after being struck by 'friendly' bombs, although he and his ground crew comrades were by no means immune to danger, since Chedburgh was an obvious target for enemy aircraft:

I think the most amazing damage I saw was on an aircraft that had returned from a raid with a terrific hole in its fuselage. It must have been six feet across.

3

Short Stirling EF433 'W-Willie' of 620 Squadron at Chedburgh. (*190 & 620 Sqns Archive*)

Stirling EF433's regular crew was one of two posted to the new 620 Squadron straight from training at 1657 Heavy Conversion Unit, Stradishall: in doorway, left to right, Sergeant Lambert (mid-upper gunner) and Sergeant Gamble (wireless operator); standing, left to right, Sergeant Hill (bomb aimer), Flying Officer Hobbs (navigator), Flying Officer F.C. Macdonald (pilot), Sergeant Martin (flight engineer) and Sergeant McIlroy (rear gunner). (*190 & 620 Sqns Archive*)

It was said that a bomb from a Lancaster had gone straight through the roof and the floor without exploding. It was a good job that it had not got an impact detonator.

We had one or two intrusions by German night-fighters, and one of our aircraft was shot down on the runway as it was coming in to land. Another night, anti-personnel bomblets were scattered over the aerodrome. The next day was a bit scary. Work had to be done on the aircraft, which were at their dispersal bays all around the field. Every so often there was a bang and a whistle as the bombs were detonated and shrapnel flew around.

Tragedy struck 620 Squadron on 2 July, but this time through accident rather than enemy action. Stirlings EF394 'V' and BK724 'Y' collided to the south of Chedburgh, on their way back to the airfield after a fighter affiliation exercise with Beaufighters from Coltishall in Norfolk. Both of the bombers crashed at Stansfield, killing fifteen men in all. These fatalities included five ground crew personnel flying as passengers. One of the four survivors of this accident, Sgt Hargreaves, had been on board BK720 when it crash-landed in the early hours of 25 June, but he went on to lose his life on 20 October, in another accident involving a 620 Squadron aircraft.

On the night of 3/4 July, 620 Squadron Stirlings went to Cologne, and ten days later to Aachen. Between these operations, the crews were kept busy on various training flights, including 'Bullseye' and 'Eric' exercises. On a 'Bullseye', the bombers played the part of the enemy approaching the British air defences. This provided useful practice for the crews of night-fighters, searchlights and anti-aircraft

No. 620 Squadron personnel at Chedburgh, including one of the pilots, Flight Sergeant Ken Hoult (sitting on ground, right), with members of his crew, and Sergeant Alan Gamble (far right), sometime Keeper of the 620 Squadron Register and unit historian. (*190 & 620 Sqns Archive*)

No. 620 Squadron personnel 'under canvas' at Chedburgh. (*190 & 620 Sqns Archive*)

guns, as they sought to intercept the bombers. 'Eric' exercises similarly tested the air defences, but in daylight.

There were also many occasions when Bomber Command sent its aircraft to drop mines into German shipping lanes. Code-named 'Gardening', these operations were carried out by 620 Squadron at locations as far apart as the Frisian Islands and the Bay of Biscay, but often concentrated on the approaches to U-boat bases.

During July 1943, the Battle of the Ruhr was nearing its end, and it was time for Bomber Command to take its offensive deeper into Germany. The target was Hamburg on the night of 24/25 July. This was the first time that enemy radar was jammed by dropping aluminium foil strips, known as 'Window'. The following night's operation, on 25/26 July, was to Essen and turned out to be a disastrous one for 620 Squadron, as three of its Stirlings failed to return. These aircraft were BF511 'A', EH924 'B' and EE906 'C', captained by Sgts Patteson, Rathbone and J.R.G. Macdonald, respectively. Out of the three crews, there were twelve men killed, and nine taken prisoner.

Even though Bomber Command as a whole was suffering very heavy losses at this stage of the war, there was to be no let-up in the summer bombing campaign. When Hamburg was attacked again on the night of 27/28 July, a devastating firestorm took hold. Its flames were so persistent and widespread that the 620 Squadron crews could see the glow in the sky above Hamburg almost as soon as they became airborne the following night, 28/29 July, for a further attack on the stricken city.

On the night of 30/31 July, 620 Squadron lost two Stirlings when Remscheid was attacked. A night-fighter shot down EE905 'S', but five members of the crew survived, including the captain, Sgt Frost. This aircraft crashed in Belgium and one of the survivors evaded capture. The other 620 Squadron loss that night, EH896 'P', provided one of the rare instances of all seven members of a Stirling crew surviving after their aircraft was shot down. Although they became prisoners of war (POWs), luck had certainly been on their side, for the captain, Sgt O'Connell, and four of the others had also escaped from the crash of BK720 at Chedburgh on 25 June.

On 6 August, a single Stirling from 620 Squadron was detailed to take part in a 'Gardening' task, dropping mines into the Gironde estuary, on the Atlantic coast of France. This aircraft, BK690 'G', was shot down near Nantes on its way back. Its captain, Fg Off Rogers, was killed, along with three other members of the crew. Of the three who survived, one was taken prisoner and two evaded capture.

The bombing operations of August 1943 ranged far and wide, to targets that included Hamburg, Nürnburg, and the Italian city of Turin. On the night of the Turin operation, 12/13 August, 620 Squadron lost Stirling BK713 'E', captained by Flt Lt L.K. Williams. All on board were killed. There was bright moonlight on the night of 17/18 August, when the German rocket test establishment at Peenemünde was bombed from medium level. The enemy night-fighters were late in intercepting this raid, but they still inflicted heavy losses among the bombers, including one of 620 Squadron's Stirlings, EF457 'A', captained by Sqn Ldr Lambert DFC. Five of its eight crew members survived to become POWs.

Pilot Officer G.W. Macdonald and his crew, who failed to return from an operation to Berlin, had been posted from 214 Squadron to 620 Squadron when the latter unit was formed. (*190 & 620 Sqns Archive*)

On the night of 23/24 August, it was the turn of Berlin, a target that was to claim many aircrew lives. Out of fifty-seven bombers destroyed that night, sixteen were Stirlings, including a 620 Squadron aircraft, BK801 'X'. This was captained by Plt Off G.W. Macdonald, who was killed on what would probably have been the last operation of his tour. Of the eight crew members on board this aircraft, three survived as POWs.

Bomber Command continued to suffer heavy losses on its long-range operations, and when 620 Squadron sent eight Stirlings to Nürnburg on the night of 27/28 August, three failed to return. These were EF451 'D', BF576 'F' and EE942 'R', captained by Sgt Duroe, Sgt Eeles and Flt Sgt Nichols, respectively. This was 620 Squadron's worst bombing operation, in terms of casualties, since sixteen men were killed and only five survived as POWs. The target was Berlin again on the night of 31 August/1 September, when a further fifty bombers were lost, including EH946 'P' of 620 Squadron. This Stirling's crew, captained by Plt Off Campbell, had only been with 620 Squadron since the first week of August, when they arrived straight from training. Their bomb aimer was a New Zealander, Flight Sergeant Arthur Smith:

> We had a happy crew, with an Australian pilot – who hated us calling him 'our driver'! The crew also contained two New Zealanders, one Welshman, and one Irishman from Waterford, who went on leave in civvies as he said that the Irish would kill him if they knew he was flying and fighting for the British. On our second to last trip, to Mönchen-gladbach in the Ruhr, he started to complain of stomach pains on the way there. We had not been attacked by fighters or hit by flak so we flew on. His pains got worse and he was in agony when we landed. A waiting ambulance took him to hospital at once. He had developed appendicitis on the trip. After lunch on 31st August we saw him in hospital and that night we went to Berlin. We were hit badly by flak over Berlin and finally limped along to north-east France where fighters shot us down. There was only one other survivor out of the seven of us – our navigator. We managed to escape by parachute but were captured in the curfew some nights later and finished up in Lille prison for two weeks.
>
> Life was fast and furious in those days and casualties were very heavy on all raids, attrition at its worst. In fact, in one hut in my POW camp, among over eighty aircrew types from all over the world they had a survey one night to see what the average number of trips was before each had been shot down. It was six.

In September 1943, 620 Squadron carried out bombing operations to Mannheim, Montluçon, Modane and Hannover, and there were various 'Gardening' tasks as well. Stirling EH931 'O', captained by Flt Sgt Quayle, was lost on 5/6 September, the night of the Mannheim operation. Four out of the eight men on board this aircraft survived as POWs. During its time in Bomber Command, 620 Squadron's last operational loss of a Stirling was EH945 'H', captained by Flt Sgt Emery. This aircraft failed to return from Hannover on the night of 27/28 September. Three of the crew members were killed, and four became POWs.

During October 1943, 620 Squadron bombed factories at Kassel, Frankfurt and Hannover, and took part in further minelaying operations. The squadron suffered a fatality on the night of the Frankfurt raid, 4/5 October. Shortly after dropping its bombs on the target, Stirling EH894, captained by Flt Sgt Clark, was caught by searchlights, before being attacked by a night-fighter. The Stirling was hit by machine-gun fire and its Australian rear gunner, Sgt Langley, died when he was

A prisoner-of-war photograph of Sergeant Davies, the rear gunner in Stirling EH931, shot down on the night of 5/6 September 1943. *(190 & 620 Sqns Archive)*

wounded in the neck by a single bullet. As Clark manoeuvred his badly damaged bomber, the mid-upper gunner, Sgt Dowsett, was able to open fire on the enemy aircraft, which he claimed as destroyed. Clark then flew to Manston in Kent, where he made an emergency landing with one of the Stirling's engines shut down.

Flt Sgt Stanley Clark and Sgt Alfred Dowsett were subsequently awarded Distinguished Flying Medals for the 'great courage, skill and coolness' they displayed in the course of this action. As soon as a replacement rear gunner had joined them, Clark and his crew resumed operations with 620 Squadron. They were later posted to 115 Squadron, to fly Lancasters, but lost their lives on 4 December 1943, while taking part in an operation to Leipzig.

Stirling BK802 'Z' of 620 Squadron was destroyed in a training accident during the evening of 20 October. This aircraft was at 10,000 feet over Windsor, weaving in and out of searchlights, when heavy icing caused loss of control. Between 7,000 and 8,000 feet, all members of the crew abandoned the aircraft, except for the Canadian captain, Flt Sgt Harris, who was killed when it crashed. The navigator, bomb aimer and rear gunner were injured

Part of the plotting map used by Pilot Officer Ken Back on the night of 18/19 November 1943, showing way-points on the routes to and from the target at Ludwigshafen, plus observations of flak and marker flares. *(K.G. Back)*

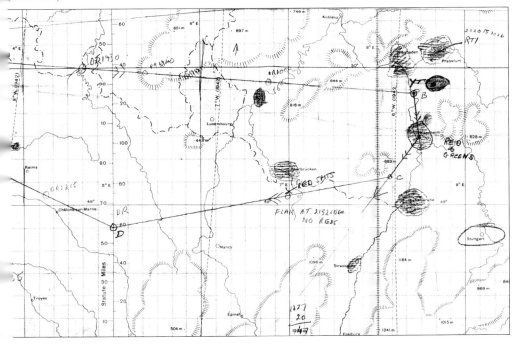

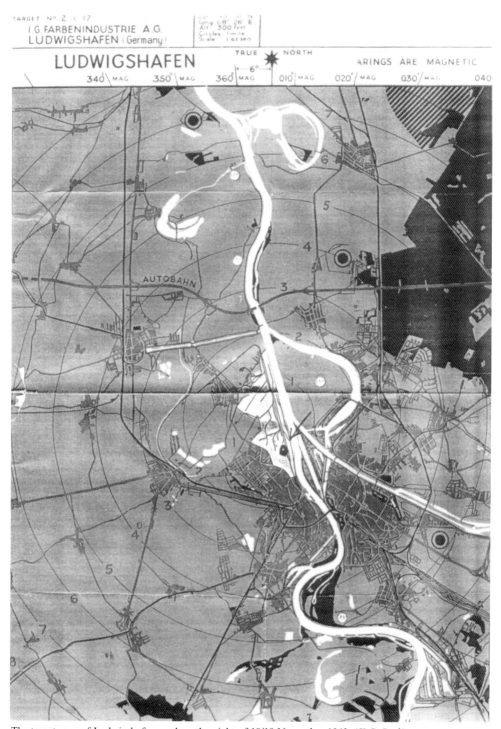

TARGET Nº 2 C 17
I.G. FARBENINDUSTRIE A.G.
LUDWIGSHAFEN (Germany)

LAT ... N
long (8° 26' E
Alt 300 feet
Circles 1 mile
Scale 1:63,360

# LUDWIGSHAFEN

TRUE NORTH

←6°→

ARINGS ARE MAGNETIC

340° MAG    350° MAG    360° MAG    010° MAG    020° MAG    030° MAG    040

The target map of Ludwigshafen used on the night of 18/19 November 1943. (*K.G. Back*)

The memorial on Chedburgh village green, commemorating the bomber crews who died while flying from RAF Chedburgh. (*190 & 620 Sqns Archive*)

as a result of baling out, but the wireless operator, Sgt Hargreaves, was killed. Although his parachute canopy opened, the harness subsequently became undone, leaving him to fall to his death.

There was then an autumn lull in 620 Squadron's operational activity. Some minelaying was carried out, but it was not until the night of 18/19 November that the squadron bombed again, at Ludwigshafen. For Plt Off Ken Back, a navigator with 620 Squadron, this operation was an eventful one:

> We lost the port outer engine and were hit by flak a few times. We dropped the bombs and (or so we thought) the photo-flash and turned for home. We got as far as Beachy Head and the starboard outer engine started to give trouble and then we were losing height, as Stirlings were not much good on three engines, let alone two. We limped along as far as Hunsdon, looking at the tree-tops through the fog and put out a 'Mayday' call. A WAAF in the control tower below saved our bacon when she nipped out and fired a signal rocket. We were now on two engines, almost out of fuel as the tanks were holed, and although the undercarriage went down for landing we could not lock it. We landed heading straight for the control tower though we didn't hit it. The undercart held but we found subsequently that the photo-flash was still hanging by its wire – if the undercart had collapsed that would have sent us up sky high.

620 Squadron's final strategic bombing operation was to Leverkusen on the night of 19/20 November. By then, it had become clear that the Stirling was experiencing an excessive loss rate on operations, compared with the other heavy bomber types. It was therefore decided to withdraw the Stirling from the main bomber force. Several of the squadrons in 3 Group would exchange their Stirlings for Lancasters, and continue to operate in the strategic bombing role. However, 196 and 620 Squadrons would retain their Stirlings, but be transferred from Bomber Command to the Allied Expeditionary Air Force, along with 1665 Heavy Conversion Unit (HCU), which trained Stirling crews at Woolfox Lodge in Rutland. In their new role, providing air support by means of parachute dropping and glider towing, 196 and 620 Squadrons would be based together at Leicester East.

As 620 Squadron prepared to leave Chedburgh, the unit was very different from the one that had formed just five months earlier. Many of the original aircrews were gone. Some, who were with 149 or 214 Squadrons before joining 620 Squadron, had completed their tours, but a considerable number had not reached that goal. The grim statistics were that eighteen of 620 Squadron's Stirlings had been destroyed on operations, and a further six written off in accidents. More importantly, the human losses amounted to ninety-three men killed and forty-five taken prisoner.

# CHAPTER 2

# Their New Role

## November 1943 to February 1944

By 1943, it had been decided that the British 6th Airborne Division would play an important part in the initial stage of Operation 'Overlord', the forthcoming invasion of Normandy, with its troops taking on the task of securing key points on the eastern flank of the beachhead. The preparations for this included a huge training programme, to provide paratroops and glider pilots in numbers that would be sufficient to achieve their objectives swiftly on D-Day, at the start the invasion. While this training was going on, the Special Operations Executive (SOE) was stepping up its assistance to the Resistance movement in occupied France, as part of its mission 'to co-ordinate all action, by way of subversion and sabotage, against the enemy overseas.' From the summer of 1943, the American Office of Strategic Services (OSS) also supported intelligence-gathering and sabotage operations by the French Resistance. These efforts yielded some notable successes against the German war machine in France, but by the end of 1943 many of the Resistance 'circuits' had become ineffective because of infiltration by the enemy. A further harsh reality was that direct attacks on the occupying forces were likely to result in fierce reprisals against the French civilian population.

Consequently, SOE developed, alongside its Special Operations counterpart within OSS, a policy of organising and arming Resistance networks that had tight security, and which would be ready to act with considerable force, but not until the Normandy landings started. By concentrating their attacks against roads and railways, the *Maquis*, as the Resistance movement became widely known, might then significantly delay the Germans' response to the invasion, by denying them easy access to the Allied beachhead. The preparation of the *Maquis* for this task called for the delivery of several thousand tons of warlike goods, as well as the deployment of many agents in the field. Although a small, dedicated fleet of surface vessels had been made available to SOE for coastal infiltration, and some submarine support was provided by the Royal Navy, increased co-operation with the RAF was going to be essential if covert operations were to be extended deep into France. Until the autumn of 1943, SOE airdrops relied on two Special Duties squadrons, flying Handley Page Halifax bombers from Tempsford in Bedfordshire, with occasional assistance from other squadrons in 3 Group, Bomber Command. The Air Ministry was loath to release further large aircraft from the strategic bombing campaign, but it had become obvious that an expansion of the RAF's air support capability could wait no longer.

When the Short Stirling was withdrawn from the RAF's main bomber force in November 1943, the opportunity was taken to retrain some of the crews for the air support role. As an interim measure they would continue to fly their existing Mk III aircraft, since these could drop supplies by parachute from their bomb-bays.

Stirlings coming off the production line were now being constructed to Mk IV standard, which meant they incorporated design changes that enabled them to tow gliders and drop both troops and supplies by parachute. A number of Halifaxes would be similarly equipped for air support work, and Armstrong Whitworth Albemarles that had been used operationally as glider tugs by 38 Wing, during the invasion of Sicily, were returning to the UK. These various aircraft types were brought together in 38 Group, which was established in October 1943 by upgrading 38 Wing when it came back from North Africa. No. 38 Group had its Headquarters at Netheravon in Wiltshire, and was commanded by Air Vice-Marshal Leslie Hollinghurst CB OBE DFC. For a short time, 38 Group formed part of the 2nd Tactical Air Force, but it became the responsibility of Headquarters Allied Expeditionary Air Force (HQ AEAF) on 15 November 1943.

Ideally, the 38 Group airfields needed to be (a) able to accommodate heavy bombers, (b) suitable for glider towing operations, and (c) within easy reach of France. Until such time that all the squadrons in 38 Group could be found sufficiently large and well-equipped airfields in the south of England, a number of others had to be utilised. One of these was RAF Leicester East, which opened on 8 October 1943. It had been intended that this station would accommodate an Operational Training Unit (OTU) belonging to 93 Group, Bomber Command, but by the end of October 1943 this plan had been cancelled, and the site, not yet complete, was downgraded to 'Care and Maintenance' status. For the time being, Leicester East was expected to operate only as a Relief Airfield, though it was being considered for possible future use by a Troop Carrier Group of the United States Army Air Force (USAAF).

On 14 November 1943, instructions were issued for Leicester East to be made ready for the arrival of two Stirling squadrons. The runways were practically finished, as were the administrative and domestic buildings, but there was still a considerable amount of work to be done before the technical facilities and dispersals could be used.

Nos 196 and 620 Squadrons learned on 15 November that they would be moving to Leicester East, and joining 38 Group, as part of the Allied Expeditionary Air Force, on 1 December. On 20 November, the personnel forming 620 Squadron's advance party left Chedburgh for Bury St Edmunds, from where they proceeded by train to Leicester. Two days later, the squadron's vehicles were driven to Leicester East, while the majority of the ground personnel made the journey by train. Those in the air party were unable to take off, because of bad weather, but the next day, 23 November, sixteen of 620 Squadron's Stirlings flew from Chedburgh to Leicester East, leaving four aircraft to be transferred later. The Stirlings of 196 Squadron were already at Leicester East, having moved from Witchford in Cambridgeshire, on 18 November.

After a temporary setback, brought about by much of the ground equipment having been delayed on the rail journey, the 620 Squadron Stirlings commenced flying from Leicester East on 25 November, and were soon busy with cross-country exercises. Some of the 620 Squadron aircrews had not made the move from Chedburgh to Leicester East, but were posted instead to Lancaster squadrons, via a short type-conversion course. The vacancies they left in 620 Squadron were filled mainly by crews from 513 Squadron, based at Witchford. The latter Stirling unit had a very brief existence in 3 Group, before it was disbanded on 21 November.

By the end of the second week of December 1943, Airspeed Horsa gliders were being delivered from Netheravon to Leicester East, to equip 'D' Squadron of the

In this photograph, taken on 30 December 1943, six Stirlings are seen at their dispersal points, close to the bomb stores at RAF Leicester East. These wartime installations have cut into the remnants of the medieval landscape in this area, with the distinctive parallel lines formed by 'ridge and furrow' ploughing clearly visible. (*English Heritage (NMR) USAAF Photography*)

Army's Glider Pilot Regiment (GPR). No. 620 Squadron's Stirling III aircraft were adapted for glider towing by means of modifications carried out on the station. The main external addition was a yoke just aft of the tailplane, to which the glider tow-rope was attached. A release mechanism, operated by a lever fitted to the right of the throttle control box, enabled the tow-rope to be jettisoned before the Stirling landed. On 19 December, most of the personnel on the station turned out to witness the start of a new era for 620 Squadron, as the CO, Wg Cdr Lee, towed a Horsa aloft for the first time. However, the airfield was still in an unfinished state and aircraft frequently became bogged down while taxiing through patches of mud. During December there were also two minor accidents involving 620 Squadron Stirlings on the ground, as one collided with a crane, and the other with a contractor's van.

No. 190 Squadron re-formed at Leicester East on 5 January 1944. In contrast to 620 Squadron, which had retained many of its aircraft and personnel after seeing action in Bomber Command, 190 Squadron was a new unit in all respects except its number. 190 Squadron's establishment was to be sixteen Stirling IV aircraft, plus four more in reserve. On 7 January the Stirlings of 196 Squadron departed for Tarrant Rushton in Dorset, to make way for the newcomers.

There was a further change for 38 Group on 10 January, when it was transferred from the Allied Expeditionary Air Force (AEAF) to the Air Defence of Great Britain (ADGB) organisation. ADGB and the 2nd Tactical Air Force had been formed in place of Fighter Command, when this disappeared from the Order of Battle in June 1943. It was agreed that HQ AEAF needed to retain control of operational matters and training in 38 Group, although it was somewhat anomalous that its Stirling, Halifax and Albemarle squadrons, which would be operating in an offensive role, should have been included

Wing Commander Graeme Harrison, Commanding Officer of 190 Squadron. (*G.H. Chesterton*)

in ADGB for administrative purposes. On 14 January, 620 Squadron received some pleasing news, as the award of the Distinguished Flying Cross to Wg Cdr Lee was gazetted.

Fresh from 1665 HCU at Woolfox Lodge, 190 Squadron's first aircrews, captained by Fg Offs Robertson, Hay, Anderson and le Bouvier, arrived at Leicester East on 15 January. They were promptly sent on seven days' leave, because there were no aircraft for them to fly. The first two Stirling IV aircraft for 190 Squadron were delivered straight from the Short and Harland factory at Belfast on 20 January, the same day that the Squadron Adjutant, Fg Off Duveen, arrived. Wg Cdr Graeme Harrison was posted from 1665 HCU to take command of 190 Squadron on 25 January, by which time a dozen more Stirlings had been delivered. Although the squadron was now close to having its full complement of aircraft, it was unable to fly them, since no ground crews had arrived yet.

Deliveries of Horsas to Leicester East were stepped up during January 1944. The 620 Squadron crews were soon learning to tow these gliders, as well as spending time on night cross-countries and practice runs over parachute Dropping Zones (DZs). Low-level cross-countries at night were particularly challenging, but the crews discovered some favourite landmarks to assist their navigation. One of these was the long, straight Bedford River, which led across the flat East Anglian landscape to Downham Market, and was often followed by the Stirlings as they flew by moonlight, sometimes at a height of only 50 feet. The navigators needed to practise traditional methods of dead reckoning, because the main radio aid they had used in Bomber Command, 'Gee', was susceptible to jamming and, at long range, was insufficiently accurate for their new role. Therefore, they reverted to compass, stopwatch and maps as the main tools of their trade. The navigators now relied on large-scale maps, rather than the 'half million' topographical sheets they had previously used on bombing operations, and they were helped in the task of map reading by their bomb aimers. Another change was the adoption of statute miles and miles per hour as units, in place of the nautical miles and knots used in Bomber Command. Flt Sgt Henry Hooper, a New Zealander, was the bomb aimer in Fg Off Murray's

620 Squadron crew, and remembered the training syllabus they followed at Leicester East:

> For a start, we did many cross country flights, which entailed flying mainly at 2,000 feet to a pinpoint, then flying on at 750 feet to a DZ. I had to concentrate on map reading using 4 miles to 1 inch maps for the main part of the flight, and for the run-in to the DZ, Ordnance maps, 1 mile to 1 inch. We had to adjust to the difference in flying heights, in Bomber Command having been at 12,000 to 15,000 feet (or as high as we could possibly get in the Stirling), but in our new role nothing more than about 2,000 feet, and it was amazing how good one's map reading at night became.
>
> Referring to my Log Book, I see we towed our first glider on 14 January 1944 and from then on there were circuits and bumps regularly, and cross country flights with gliders, followed later by squadron exercises with gliders and finally group exercises, also with gliders. Another part of bomb aimer training involved night vision classes, spending a lot of time in dark rooms until we could walk planks, climb over obstacles, etc., and also we were fed carrots!

At the end of January 1944, personnel from various ground trades were drafted to 190 Squadron from all over the country. Although Leicester East was a new station, with buildings that were only intended to last for the duration of the war, it was regarded as a pleasant posting, since it was near a big city. However, Corporal John Smith, who was posted to 190 Squadron as an electrician, soon found that the state of the domestic sites at Leicester East left a lot to be desired:

> I was posted to Leicester East from Lakenheath in January 1944. Conditions could not have been worse, as the weather was foul. The ground between the living huts was so waterlogged that duckboards were laid to enable us to walk to and fro. It was the practice of airmen to keep their best uniform trousers folded between the bedding blankets to keep the creases in. This proved to be a mistake under the terrible weather conditions at Leicester East, for we found that the exposed edges of the trousers were being gnawed, with odd holes appearing in the material. It was found out later that mice had been forced indoors by the wet conditions and had decided to eat our trousers! Although why they did not have a go at the blankets and only attacked the trousers was never explained. We had an awful job to convince the NCO in charge of the Clothing Store of the reason our clothing had been damaged.

Another electrician posted to 190 Squadron was Flight Sergeant Ivan Fairfax:

> Unable to take leave during the previous six months, I was feeling relieved to find myself standing on a railway platform, *en route* home to visit my wife and family in February 1944. Then to my chagrin, I noticed an airman running in my direction. He had instructions to tell me that I must return to the Station Adjutant immediately. I was informed that a signal marked 'Urgent' had been received and I was to proceed to RAF Leicester East. This posting meant that I had lost my acting rank of Warrant Officer, and two days later I reported to the Adjutant of 190 Squadron.
>
> The roads at Leicester East were only about six feet wide and the verges were entirely of mud. On my arrival in the dark I had noticed by the dim lights of the vehicle a line of Stirling aircraft, parked with their noses peering over the hedgerow. That evening, I slept in a Nissen hut with six aircrew members and

they informed me that they, with the Commanding Officer and Adjutant, were the only personnel of the Squadron. So why the urgency of my posting? The question was to be answered the following morning.

The Adjutant greeted me as though I had been one of his lost sheep. He informed me that the squadron was to be part of the Allied Expeditionary Air Force for the invasion of Europe and 'for starts' I was given the responsibility of setting up a squadron administrative office, and also the post office. Airmen technicians were first to arrive, so they were temporarily re-mustered to become clerks and they did an excellent job. Sleeping accommodation with its attendant furniture was arranged and every day the squadron numbers increased.

In the meantime at my own place of work – the Electrical Section – my sergeant, Ron Tyler, had been very active building up a stock of spare parts and introducing electrical technicians to the Stirling aircraft. 620 Squadron had arrived *en bloc* from Bomber Command and their air and ground crews were already experienced in their respective duties.

Although experienced personnel from Bomber Command provided the nuclei for the Stirling squadrons in 38 Group, many more aircrews were needed to bring these units up to full operational strength. No. 81 OTU at Tilstock, in Shropshire, was one of the few bomber OTUs still using Armstrong Whitworth Whitleys in 1943 (by then the majority were equipped with Vickers Wellingtons). On 1 January 1944, Tilstock and its satellite airfield at Sleap were transferred from 92 Group to 38 Group, within which they would provide a dedicated source of air support crews. No. 1665 HCU, based at Woolfox Lodge, was also taken into 38 Group, and moved its Stirling I and III aircraft to Tilstock on 22 January. In order to accommodate the Stirlings at Tilstock, it was then necessary to transfer the 81 OTU Whitleys to Sleap. This arrangement led to a scheme whereby the various aircrew categories would arrive at Sleap to form five-man crews and complete the OTU course on the Whitley, before progressing to the HCU at Tilstock, where they would convert to the Stirling, after being joined by their flight engineers.

Having qualified as a Wireless Operator/Air Gunner in Canada, Sergeant Noel Chaffey of the Royal Australian Air Force (RAAF) sailed to the United Kingdom in the late summer of 1943. After a short but fairly leisurely stay at No. 11 Personnel Dispatch and Reception Centre in Brighton, Chaffey was ready to get back to the business of flying. He arrived at 81 OTU in November 1943, while the unit was still at Tilstock, training crews for the strategic bombing role:

The day before my 21st Birthday we got a posting to No. 27 Operational Training Unit at Lichfield. Within two days they realised they'd made an error, so we had to pack up, and make our way across country

Sergeant Noel Chaffey trained at Sleap and Tilstock before serving with 620 Squadron from April 1944 to July 1945. This photograph was taken at the time of his commissioning in 1945. (*N.R. Chaffey*)

by train to Tilstock in Shropshire. The journey was pure murder. We went from one little station to another and it took us all day and half the night. There were no connections, you never knew where you were, there were no signs on stations – not even my worst enemy would I send on such a 'mission'.

However, it didn't take me long to love RAF Tilstock (though we called it 'Frog Hollow' because of the mud and puddles of water everywhere). The atmosphere was great and we were to fly Whitleys – anyone who flew in them felt 'safe'. Having joined No. 24 Course at No. 81 OTU, we were to 'crew up' and were told that if we were not chosen by the weekend, allocations would be made. All the pilots, navigators, bomb aimers, wireless operators and rear gunners had arrived from their different training schools, but we didn't get our flight engineers until our next move.

A Royal Australian Air Force pilot (who turned out to be English-born) approached me and asked if I'd crewed up yet, and if not, whether I would like to join him. He told me his name was Derek de Rome and with a grin I agreed to join his lot. My new pilot had already got an RAF navigator, Ben, and it didn't take us long to pick up our RAF bomb aimer, Bryan, but by the end of the week we were the only crew still without a gunner. An officer said that there was one on compassionate leave, his father having just died, and he'd be back the following Monday, so he was ours. His name was Pete, another RAF man, and we all fitted in with him perfectly – he was quiet lad, who loved playing patience during breaks, and was a very good gunner. So now it was the 'de Rome crew', and we remained so from November 1943 until July 1945, the only

An Armstrong Whitworth Whitley, parked among the puddles at Tilstock. (*N. R. Chaffey*)

change being the addition of Frank, our RAF flight engineer, when we converted to Stirlings. Now our war could begin.

The bomber OTU course at Tilstock included exercises in high-level bombing, cross-countries and air gunnery. The members of the 'de Rome crew' successfully completed this course in December 1943, but then found themselves being held at Tilstock, as the station was transferred to 38 Group. For the time being, they continued to fly in the Whitleys, but were now on No. 3 Airborne Course, following a new syllabus that was devised to train them for the air support role. At that time both Tilstock and its satellite at Sleap were used for the flying programme, which introduced the crews to low-level cross-country work, glider towing and supply drops. It took Flt Sgt de Rome and his crew just under twenty flying hours to complete successfully this course, over a period of about four weeks. They were then ready for conversion to the Stirling. Noel Chaffey was suitably impressed by his first encounter with this aircraft:

One of my greatest occasions of my RAAF life came at Tilstock when we heard, and then had our first close-up view of, a Stirling aircraft, actually landing on our aerodrome. Then the word buzzed round the station and everyone was over at the hangar trying to learn more of this enormous plane, having been told that the Whitley was out, the Stirling was in. We now had the chance to fly in the 'Queen of the Sky', as the Stirling was called. I had a feeling right from the start that we'd do well in this 'kite'.

So, early in 1944 we got ready to fly in the Stirling. We were each kitted out with a one-piece flying suit, fur-lined, with two pairs of socks, of which one pair was uniform dress blue and the other almost full-length grey and pure wool, and flying boots rather like fur-lined Wellies. If flying over water a bright yellow 'Mae West' lifejacket was essential. A parachute harness was worn, but one's chest-type parachute pack was stowed separately, and not clipped on unless an emergency arose. On each end of the pack was a carrying handle, and on the front a flap covered the release pins that were connected to the silver ripcord handle on the top front of the pack.

Only once did I open my parachute – but I hasten to add it was later, while on operations with the squadron. We had landed, and taxied around the perimeter track to our dispersal pad, there to await the crew transport truck. As the transport arrived, already loaded with other crews, we were leaving the Stirling, when lo and behold, yards and yards of silk billowed out before me. I was caught by the wind and pulled to the ground amidst hoots of laughter. It was only rookies who did stuff like that! Of course I'd grabbed the wrong handle, and to add insult to injury I had to pay the WAAFs 2/6d to repack the parachute for me.

Entering the Stirling's fuselage, through the door down by the tailplane, one's first impression was of a huge free space like a cricket pitch. Looking aft, there was the rear gunner's turret, entered by two little doors. After the gunner had got in, and hooked up the electrics, he would close his doors and we'd not see him again until we landed. Advancing forward was a bit of an uphill climb, for the front of the Stirling was very high off the ground. Strips of timber covered the floor, and when paratroops were carried they sat on this, backs to the outer skin, facing inward.

Further forward, on the port side, was the wireless operator's position, with a table, above which the transmitter and receiver were racked. There were a

A Stirling bomber fitted with a mid-upper gun turret: (left) fuselage, looking forward, and (right) fuselage, looking aft. (*W.D. Ely*)

number of switches for internal communication, together with 'Identification Friend or Foe' to let listening-out posts know who we were. The Morse key was on the right front of the table and there was space by my right foot for the spare radio coils, needed to cover the range of frequencies used on operations. Nearby was a container for parachute storage. My seat was a grand affair that towered almost from 'floor to ceiling'. It was leather covered and padded, with armour plate covering the back, thus offering some protection from fighters that might get past our guns and rake us with fire from behind. To the right of my wireless table was the 'Perspex' astrodome and on top of the fuselage, a little further forward, the Direction Finding aerial in its housing. Other aerials were also outside but controlled from my station. At the back of my equipment was a bulkhead with a doorway leading to the flight-deck proper.

The flight engineer's panel of gauges and dials covered the right-hand wall of the fuselage at this point. The little spare space available was also used as a walkway by any forward crew member wanting to use the 'Elsan' toilet near the back door. Frank, our engineer, had to sit out all his flying missions perched on a bar of about four inches width, in an open doorway. I'm sure if an inspection of all bums were carried out today, you could still tell the Stirling flight engineers by the indent of their sitting position!

Immediately through the doorway, on the left, was the navigator's position. A big table enabled maps to be unfolded, and attached to the inner wall of the

The Stirling wireless operator's position.
(*Bombardier Aerospace*)

aircraft were the radio aids to navigation, including 'Gee'. The nav. would sit facing sideways, and it was easy for him to change positions if he needed to take star fixes from the astrodome. He could be shielded from light by drawing a black curtain around his position.

A step or two further forward, were the seats for the pilot, and the co-pilot, if the latter was carried. The cockpit, being surrounded by 'Perspex' windows, was either a hot or cold spot, depending on whether we were flying by day or by night.

The last position, right up forward, was for the bomb aimer, and was entered by a step down past the co-pilot's seat. There was a simple bomb-sight mounted just forward of a hatch set in the floor as an emergency exit. To use the sight the bomb aimer lay full length on a lightly padded leather-covered mat, with the bomb or container release

The Stirling flight engineer's position. The flight engineer's seat (seen here) was usually removed from Stirling IV aircraft, since it impeded access to the rear fuselage via the gap in the centre-section frame. (*Bombardier Aerospace*)

The Stirling navigator's position. The 'Gee' set and other instruments have not yet been fitted to this aircraft. (*W.D. Ely*)

The cockpit of a Stirling IV. The long lever to the right of the throttle control box operated the glider tow-rope release mechanism. (*Bombardier Aerospace*)

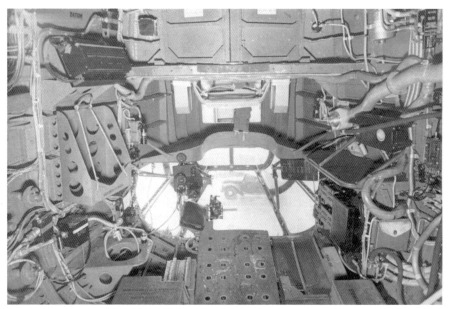

The Stirling bomb aimer's position. (*W.D. Ely*)

panels to his side. When the release button was pressed, electrical contacts on a 24-point clock face would be activated in sequence. These operated the latches in the bomb-bay, releasing the bombs or containers. If the latter were being dropped, static lines then opened their parachutes as they fell away.

When we had to fly at heights where oxygen was needed, it was supplied through our masks, which also carried microphones. Heating air came through the aircraft from front to back, via insulated pipes at floor level, with outlets at intervals. We also had a de-icing system installed on sections of the leading edge of the wings. This comprised rubber coverings fed by pipes from the engines. It made a hell of a racket when used (mostly on our later operations to Norway in winter), since the ice broke away and sounded like enemy fire as it hit the skin of the aircraft. When this happened we always had to alert Pete in the rear gun-turret or he'd get trigger-happy and shoot to kill whatever was about out there. His isolated position was a freezing one, because a complete 'Perspex' panel between the four guns had been removed for better vision and he

Sergeant Peter Griffin, air gunner in the 'de Rome crew', wearing flying clothing, and carrying his chest-type parachute. This photograph was taken next to one of 81 OTU Whitleys, fitted with a glider towing yoke. (*N.R. Chaffey*)

One of the first Stirlings to arrive at 1665 HCU, Tilstock. (*R. Glass via 190 & 620 Sqns Archive*)

had to wear a full-length inner suit heated by electrical wiring. Many times I've heard of gunners almost frozen upon landing because their electrics did not work properly.

To help keep out the cold we carried 'Thermos' flasks of tea or coffee on every operation, supplied by the cookhouse. The trouble was that on our long flights one then needed the loo. To unhook everything and go to the Elsan chemical toilet was often not worth the effort, so one 'hung-on'. Before boarding the aircraft, the last thing our skipper would do was to go behind the

No. 1665 HCU instructors with a Horsa glider at Tilstock. (*R. Glass via 190 & 620 Sqns Archive*)

A quiet moment: members of Flight Sergeant Derek de Rome's crew relax at Hawkstone Park, Shropshire, shortly before their posting from 1665 HCU to 620 Squadron. (*N.R. Chaffey*)

plane and 'water the horses'. Then if need be while flying, he'd use a beer or milk bottle, then open the window just on his left and throw it out. It used to drop with a scream like a bomb and probably scared the hell out of the cows below!

For a pilot, the Stirling was a big step up from the Whitley and other twin-engined types. At least half the flying time on the Heavy Conversion Unit (HCU) course was therefore devoted to circuits and landings, first by day and then at night, as he became used to handling the aircraft. Tilstock's 1665 HCU had its fair share of training accidents, although the incidence of these was probably no worse than for the Stirling HCUs in Bomber Command. Most mishaps occurred on take-off or landing, often because of the Stirling's marked tendency to swing. Unless corrected promptly, this could lead to an embarrassing ground loop, or even a collapsed undercarriage. The Stirling squadrons in 38 Group seemed to enjoy a remarkably good safety record, possibly because quite a few of their pilots had already learned the hard way on their HCU courses. The second, more applied, part of the HCU course at Tilstock concentrated on day and night cross-country flying, so there was very little time left for exercises such as air gunnery or parachute dropping. With seldom more than forty flying hours on the Stirling by the time they were posted from Tilstock to an operational squadron, crews would then need several further hours of practice in navigation, parachute dropping and glider towing, by day and night, before they could be declared operationally proficient in the air support role.

Back at Leicester East, the situation at the beginning of February 1944 was that 190 Squadron had its new Stirling IVs, but not enough personnel to maintain and fly them. On the other hand, 620 Squadron was still using its old Stirling IIIs, but did have experienced crews who were ready to resume operations. Although the latter aircraft were unsuitable for dropping personnel by parachute, they could carry supply containers in their bomb-bays, which were on the undersides of the fuselage and inner wings. Two sizes of container were used. The smaller type weighed up to 150 lb when loaded and was in the form of a steel cylinder. One end of this incorporated a perforated cone, designed to absorb the shock of landing. The stores were loaded through the other end, and this was closed by attaching a bucket-shaped receptacle, into which the parachute was packed. When the container was dropped from the aircraft, a static line withdrew the pin that kept the flaps of the parachute pack closed, then extracted the parachute canopy, the apex of which was connected to the static line by a weak tie. As the canopy and rigging lines extended fully, the tie broke, separating the parachute from the static line.

The 'CLE' container weighed up to 350 lb when loaded, and was named after the Central Landing Establishment, where parachuting of supplies was evaluated. For ease of loading, this steel cylinder was made up of two longitudinal halves, hinged together on one side and closed by locking pins on the other. As with the 150 lb container, one end was fitted with a shock-absorbing cone, while the other enclosed the parachute pack, which was opened by a static line withdrawing a pin. However, the CLE container had a different method of parachute deployment, since a spring-ejected auxiliary parachute was used to pull out the main one.

The most noticeable external differences between the Stirlings III and IV were that the latter mark had no dorsal gun turret, and in place of the front gun turret, its nose was fitted with a transparent dome. This provided the bomb aimer with much better forward visibility. A glider-towing yoke, similar to that embodied as a modification on 620 Squadron's Stirling III aircraft, was a standard fit on the Stirling IV.

CLE containers were used for the airborne delivery of a wide range of items, including arms, ammunition, food, clothing and petrol. One of the more unusual loads was the 'Corgi' folding motorcycle. (190 & 620 Sqns Archive)

A line-up of brand new Stirling IV aircraft. (*Bombardier Aerospace*)

The Stirling IV retained the same configuration of bomb-bays as the Stirling III and could carry either bombs or supply containers in these. The Stirling IV also incorporated a large aperture in the underside of the rear fuselage, through which parachutists and internally carried supplies could be dropped. This was normally kept closed by trapdoors in both the internal floor and the external skin. Inside the fuselage, there were two long rails, port and starboard, onto which static lines were clipped. Parachutists sat on the floor, either side of the fuselage, beneath these rails. After they had jumped, their static lines, with the inner bags of their 'X' type parachute packs still attached, had to be laboriously hauled back into the aircraft by the crew. The lines often tangled in the slipstream, making their retrieval even more difficult. While they were trailing through the fuselage hatch, the lines were prevented from tangling around the tailplane by a tubular guard, which was lowered into position before a drop took place, and retracted once the lines were back in the aircraft.

Stores dropped through the fuselage hatch were usually packed in rectangular wicker panniers that were made in two halves. The lower half telescoped into the upper one, and these were then secured by leather straps. Attached to one end of the pannier was a parachute, which was opened by a static line and an auxiliary parachute, similar to the arrangement used for the 350 lb CLE containers. Lightweight and unbreakable stores, such as clothing, were sometimes dropped in packages cushioned with kapok, without parachutes.

When the call came for 620 Squadron to go back into action, five of its Stirling III aircraft were sent to Hurn airfield (now Bournemouth Airport), on 3 February 1944. From there they were to fly to France on SOE operations, along with Stirlings and Albemarles from other squadrons in 38 Group. This detachment was to last nearly a fortnight, corresponding to a period of bright moonlight. During that time, the 620 Squadron aircraft were supported by their own ground crews, who they had towed to Hurn in Horsa gliders. One of the Stirlings returned to Leicester East, leaving four aircraft to take part in the operations.

A Stirling IV dropping supply containers from the fuselage bomb-bay. Note that the third container in the stick shows no sign of parachute deployment. (*190 & 620 Sqns Archive*)

When a drop of agents or supplies was being organised by SOE, the usual procedure was for the *Maquis* to be notified by means of a coded wireless message. At the DZ, lamps or torches were positioned in an 'L'-shaped pattern, to indicate the direction for the aircraft to fly into wind, thus minimising its ground speed and reducing the scatter of the drop. In more remote places, where there was less chance of detection by the enemy, fires were sometimes lit as markers on the DZs. There would also be a recognition light, flashing a Morse code letter at the aircraft, in order to give a positive identification of the DZ. There were many occasions when enemy activity on the ground prevented the members of a reception party from either reaching the DZ, or displaying lights if they did get there. Quite understandably, this was frustrating for aircrews, if they arrived at the right place and time but were then unable to drop because no lights were observed. However, even when a drop was successfully carried out, the recipients on the ground still faced considerable risks as they moved agents or supplies from the DZ, since their lights, together with the sound of the aircraft, could very easily give the game away.

Fg Off Ken Back navigated his crew, captained by Fg Off Geoff Murray, on three of the four nights that 620 Squadron aircraft operated out of Hurn in February 1944. The DZs were at widespread locations in France, including some places where high ground presented a serious hazard, as Ken Back recalled:

All three operations we did from Hurn were successful. One of these SOE trips was to the Haute-Savoie district of France. We were told where we had to go and we basically picked our own route. It was bright moonlight. We pinpointed a small lake near the DZ, and then had a short run from the lake up the valley. The altimeter reading was about 5,000 feet above sea level, with the mountains towering up on either side. The floor of the plateau was just below us, a matter of 200 feet. It was a most peculiar feeling. The DZ was in a lonely and inaccessible spot somewhere south of Lake Geneva, which was just over the Swiss border. The reception party lit bonfires as we circled, to give us our approach direction, and flashed the code 'K-King' on a torch or hand-lamp of some sort. We dropped our containers, and never met any opposition on those runs – it was the terrain that was the frightener.

During the evening of 4 February, the 620 Squadron Stirlings, captained by Sqn Ldr Fyson, Fg Off Murray, Plt Off Bunce and Plt Off Kay, took off from Hurn for DZs in south-east France. Each of these aircraft carried seventeen containers and one package. Stirlings from 196 Squadron and Albemarles from 295, 296, 297 and 570 Squadrons were also operating out of Hurn that night. The weather over France was good initially, but deteriorated as low cloud moved in. Several aircraft were unable to drop their supplies, because of these conditions. Although Fg Off Murray and his crew did not encounter any opposition on their operations from Hurn, others were less fortunate. Stirlings EJ110 of 196 Squadron, and LK395 'B', captained by 620 Squadron's 'A' Flight Commander, Sqn Ldr 'Teddy' Fyson, were both lost on the night of 4/5 February. Fyson's aircraft appeared to have been hit by light anti-aircraft fire shortly before it crashed near Bourges, killing all members of the crew. The other 620 Squadron aircraft were successful in dropping, but EF121, captained by Plt Off Kay, sustained flak damage to its tailplane.

On the night of 5/6 February, the three remaining 620 Squadron aircraft went to DZs in northern and central France. Their crews saw intense flak in the area where Sqn Ldr Fyson's aircraft had been shot down the previous night, but they all carried out their drops successfully.

Two more crews, captained by Flt Lt Hannah and Flt Sgt McNamara, were then sent to join the detachment at Hurn, so 620 Squadron was able to provide four aircraft for operations on the night of 8/9 February. McNamara and his crew were on their first SOE operation that night, and a lively one it was. Flying Stirling EF203 'Q', they broke cloud over an airfield situated to the west of Tours, and just north of the River Loire. Their flight engineer, Sgt Peter Graham, remembered what happened next:

McNamara went down to ground level to avoid a searchlight being directed at the aircraft, but then, just as the light was being shot out by the rear gunner, Billy Hughes, the starboard inner engine was hit. Oil was lost rapidly from the engine, preventing its propeller from being feathered, and as the Stirling climbed away, still loaded, the prop was windmilling. There were intermittent fires in the engine bay and the vibration became so severe that we prepared to abandon the aircraft. Things went from bad to worse as the damaged engine seized and the whole propeller and reduction gear assembly sheared off, flying into the forward lower fuselage and making a gaping hole which left the cabin floor sagging. Despite the extent of the damage, McNamara continued to climb the aircraft as he headed for home. Over the Channel, two containers hung up as the stores were jettisoned, and with fuel becoming low a ditching was discussed, but we decided to press on for Hurn. Reaching the airfield the fuel situation was now critical, but then we were unable to lower the undercarriage owing to damage to cables on the fuselage wall hit by the propeller. Therefore, a belly landing was made on the grass alongside the runway, and it was to the

Stirling EF203 'Q-Queenie' after her belly-landing on the grass at Hurn. (*190 & 620 Sqns Archive*)

great relief of all on board that the munitions in the remaining containers did not detonate.

It is evident from the photographs of Stirling EF203 that the crew members in the forward fuselage were very lucky to escape death or serious injury that night. It was also remarkable that this aircraft eventually flew again, after a rebuild at SEBRO (the Short Brothers Repair Organisation, near Cambridge).

During the final night, 11/12 February, they flew on SOE operations from Hurn. No enemy opposition was encountered by any of the four 620 Squadron crews taking part, but Plt Off Murray and his crew had to jettison their supplies and return

The large hole made by the flailing propeller is clearly visible in this later photograph of 'Q-Queenie', lifted on air bags and minus her engines. (*190 & 620 Sqns Archive*)

early after their starboard outer engine failed. The 620 Squadron detachment remained at Hurn until 16 February, when the Stirlings returned to Leicester East, towing the Horsas carrying the ground crews and their equipment.

While the detachment was at Hurn, the 620 Squadron crews left behind at Leicester East practised DZ runs and cross-countries with gliders in tow. They also started converting to the Stirling IV, following the delivery of the first one for the squadron on 4 February. As more of these new aircraft arrived, 620 Squadron phased out its Stirling III aircraft, many of which were transferred to the Stirling HCU at Tilstock. Because the Stirling IV had only a rear gun turret, the 620 Squadron mid-upper gunners were posted to other units, leaving six men in each crew.

Meanwhile, personnel continued to be posted to 190 Squadron, which commenced flying on 1 March, when Wg Cdr Harrison took a Stirling on an air test. Over the next few days, the squadron made up for lost time, by flying whenever the weather permitted. Twenty-two crews of the Glider Pilot Regiment were soon attached to 190 Squadron, and by the second week of March their glider-towing programme was well under way.

On 3 March, Stirling EF456 of 620 Squadron was involved in an accident at Welford airfield in Berkshire. This aircraft swung while landing in a strong cross-wind and collided with a stationary Horsa glider, but no one was hurt. Leicester East's first massed cross-country with gliders was flown by fourteen aircraft of 620 Squadron on 6 March. This exercise culminated in a simultaneous cast-off of the gliders when they returned to base. Everything went as planned, except for one glider, which landed outside the airfield and struck a tree, fortunately without harming its occupants. No. 190 Squadron was now catching up fast, and completed its first massed glider take-off and landing exercise on 15 March.

Three Horsas and two Waco Hadrians, belonging to the USAAF, were delivered to Leicester East during March 1944. These gliders were made available to American troops of the 82nd Airborne Division, who were stationed nearby, so that they could practise loading and unloading them. At that time, there were quite a few American aircraft movements at Leicester East, including C-47 transports, based at Greenham Common in Berkshire, which provided a shuttle service in support of the 82nd Airborne. There were also a number of more mysterious visits by B-24 Liberators, collecting 'special stores' for delivery to the Middle East.

In December 1943, various airfields in the south of England had been inspected, in order to assess their suitability for use by 38 Group. HQ AEAF then decided on the allocation of squadrons to the airfields that had been selected. Aldermaston and Greenham Common, both in Berkshire, would have two Albemarle squadrons each; Tarrant Rushton in Dorset, one Halifax squadron; and Fairford in Gloucestershire, and Keevil in Wiltshire, two Stirling squadrons each. This plan was later amended, so that Brize Norton and Harwell, both in Oxfordshire, took the Albemarle squadrons, and Tarrant Rushton an additional Halifax squadron. Three other airfields (Blakehill Farm and Down Ampney, in Gloucestershire, and Broadwell in Oxfordshire) were earmarked for use by Dakotas of 46 Group, Transport Command, but would be placed under the operational control of 38 Group.

By the middle of March 1944, the newly constructed airfield at Fairford was ready to receive 190 and 620 Squadrons. Right up to the time of the move to Fairford, aircrews continued to arrive at Leicester East, some fresh from the Stirling HCU at Tilstock, others from part-completed tours on Stirling bomber squadrons. The latter

Leicester Airport, looking northwards. Formerly RAF Leicester East, this is the home of the Leicestershire Aero Club, which uses three sections of the wartime runways. The dispersal points and bomb stores, previously seen in the vertical photograph from December 1943, are on the right-hand side of this oblique one. (*Leicestershire Aero Club, via S. Brice*)

crews included a number posted to 620 Squadron from 75 Squadron, which was in the process of replacing its Stirlings with Lancasters, at Mepal in Cambridgeshire.

Some Americans were still flying with RAF squadrons in 1944, as members of the Royal Canadian Air Force, which they had joined before the United States entered the war. There were also others, serving in the USAAF, who were seconded to the RAF; in this category was Flight Officer Thomas J. Higgins, a Stirling bomb aimer ('bombardier' in the USAAF) with 199 Squadron at Lakenheath in Suffolk. He noted in his diary that he was not very pleased with the prospect of his crew, captained by Fg Off Bill Chappell, being posted to 190 Squadron:

March 1944 (undated)
Well I'll be damned. Our crew is posted. We are to go to some 'drome just outside Leicester; one nine zero Squadron, with Stirlings IVs. The rumour is that we are to become glider tugs. Of all the things to happen that is about the worst. We would have finished our tour some time next month but now, well, it may be months yet. It's a cinch we shall be towing the boys over on the second front effort.

March 1944 (undated)
... we've just arrived on the Squadron. Some place! It's even more dispersed than Lakenheath, and muddier than hell. We seem to be vets among sprogs. Most of the crews are OTU types or 'con-unit' types with no 'ops'. It looks as though we won't operate for quite a few months, so I'm going to relax.

33

The Squadron is moving in about two weeks. Swinson or some such place. It's near London – bang on!!! Oh yes, I've almost forgotten. We're going on leave tomorrow, so I guess London will be the place for me. The Squadron is just outside Leicester, easy hitchhiking distance for an old champ like me.

17 March
The Squadron is moving to Fairford, the 25th, what a lousy break.

23 March
We're hitching up to a glider tomorrow or the next day, and off to Fairford we go. There was an invasion exercise the other day and over 500 aircraft with gliders and paratroops participated. What a load! I'll bet the second front is going to be a terrific show. Make mine a Coke, hi!

# CHAPTER 3

# Preparing for the
# Second Front

## March to May 1944

W hen the 'Opening-up' Party entered the new RAF station at Fairford, on 17 January 1944, the site was far from complete. Mud was everywhere and there were many 'works and bricks' problems waiting to be solved, including a shortage of drinking water. Boreholes had been drilled, but could not keep up with demand, so water had to be delivered in bowsers until a reliable mains supply was laid on. Most of the buildings were 'temporary' Nissen huts, a few of which are still used by the United States Air Force, over sixty years later. During the war, Fairford had only two prefabricated 'T2' hangars, and an airfield layout that was never entirely satisfactory. The main runway, 6,000 feet long, was aligned approximately NE-SW, whereas the prevailing wind often made it necessary to use the E–W runway. The latter was only 4,200 feet long when originally laid down, and not considered safe for Stirlings to take off with gliders in tow (it was eventually superseded by the present single runway, which is just under 10,000 feet long).

On 24 February, RAF Fairford's first Station Commander, Gp Capt A.H. Wheeler, arrived from the Royal Aircraft Establishment at Farnborough, where he had commanded the Experimental Flying Department. Allen Wheeler flew as a pilot for well over fifty years, and retired from the RAF with the rank of Air Commodore. After the war he was to become well known as a Spitfire owner and also for his involvement with the historic aircraft collection of the Shuttleworth Trust at Old Warden in Bedfordshire.

620 Squadron moved from Leicester East to Fairford on 18 March. Twenty-one Stirlings and twenty gliders transported all the aircrews and some of the servicing personnel, while most of the others travelled by rail. No. 190 Squadron was to stay at Leicester for a few more days, which were mainly spent flying on cross-country exercises, including one at night. As 620 Squadron's aircraft landed at Fairford, they were greeted by local people gathered at the end of the runway, a sight that was to become commonplace over the next few months. Among them was a schoolboy called Jim Jefferies, who remembered the impact the new airfield made on this rural part of Gloucestershire:

> In my earliest memories, the area now occupied by the airfield contained a large tract of woodland, known as Cat's Lodge forest. In the autumn it was rich with hazelnuts, which we gathered to salt down for Christmas. Where the fuel dump is now situated, there was a pond that was alive with newts and so was very popular with most local children.

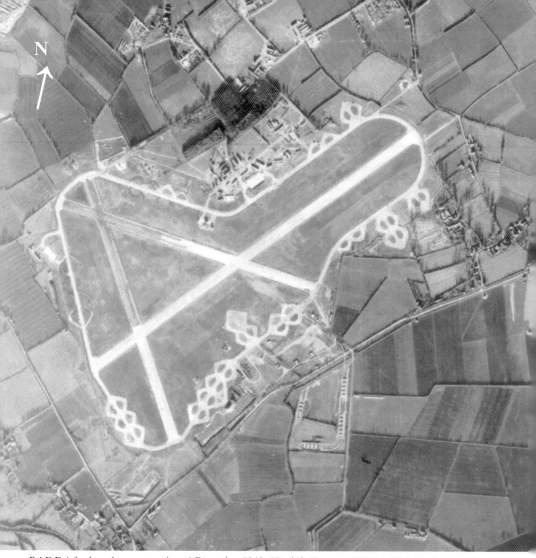

RAF Fairford, under construction, 4 December 1943. (*English Heritage (NMR) USAAF Photography*)

Late one afternoon, an elderly Bristol Bombay flew low and slowly over Whelford village. Two men could be clearly seen looking down from the open doorway onto the fields over which they flew. The search for suitable sites on which to build airfields was going on, but such was the secrecy of the time that no one could have imagined the true purpose of that flight.

Several weeks later a number of huts sprang up along the Whelford to Horcott road but were well camouflaged by the high hedgerows. During the daytime the occupants of these huts would disappear into the surrounding area. Then, one day, we were taken on a surprise picnic into the woodland. There, our teacher told us that the picnic was a significant event in itself. 'Look around the trees and remember them,' she urged us, 'for from now on this woodland will live on only in your memories. This is the last time you will see it. It's going to be turned into a bomber field as a part of the war effort.'

Within a short space of time, Sir Robert McAlpine's firm had moved in and a whole army of caterpillar tractors and huge scrapers were ripping up trees and tearing swathes of soil from the woodland floor. The mainly Irish workforce laboured hard, and often in conditions that could only be described as shocking. Generally, they were a genial, but often bewildering body of men. Many times we were invited into their huts to watch films put on to entertain them. Although many were notorious for singing anti-British songs, they proved to be extremely hospitable and kindly people. At this stage the airfield sustained its first fatality. Alfred McKearney, from County Sligo, died in a tragic accident and was buried at Fairford's Catholic Church. He was well liked by both local people and his own countrymen.

At Christmas 1943, McAlpines threw a farewell party for all the children of the immediate neighbourhood. With the airfield's completion growing near, local speculation intensified, and many considered that the airfield was going to be taken over by the Americans. However, when I got home from school one day, a Stirling was parked near the bottom of our garden. It was enormous. Its nose stood some 20 feet above the ground, dwarfing the handful of curious onlookers that gathered about it, and I found that even its wheels were larger than I was tall. This aeroplane was the first of its kind to land on the newly-built airfield, but just before dark the crew returned and it took off.

By this time, RAF personnel were taking up residence on the airfield, and then on a grey March morning the airfield became alive, as fire engines stationed themselves close to the control tower and the controller's chequered caravan was placed by the runway threshold. In the early afternoon, the Stirlings came, and emerging from the murk, they swept in to touch down in quick succession.

On 19 March, the day after their arrival at Fairford, the 620 Squadron Stirlings were unable to fly because of bad weather. The next day, conditions had improved and they took part in Exercise 'Bizz I', along with other 38 Group squadrons and C-47 aircraft belonging to the 53rd Troop Carrier Wing of the USAAF. The task was to drop 'Pathfinders' of the 21st Independent Parachute Company, followed by troops from 5 Parachute Brigade, and then to 'resupply' them with stores dropped by parachute. Other troops were to be carried in Horsa gliders and landed at Brize Norton and Southrop (the latter was a small grass airfield, about four miles northeast of Fairford).

High winds prevented the paratroops from being dropped during the initial stage of 'Bizz I', but two glider lifts did go ahead as planned and excellent results were achieved by the first of these. As part of the second lift, twelve of the 620 Squadron aircraft released gliders over Brize Norton, after towing them on a cross-country flight that took them as far afield as Hampshire and Dorset. This lift was carried out under conditions of deteriorating visibility, which made it difficult to deliver the gliders at exactly the right time and position over the Landing Zone (LZ) at Brize Norton. However, one of the main reasons for carrying out large-scale exercises was to identify and solve operational problems of this sort. With the Allied invasion of Normandy only a matter of weeks away, now was the time to address them, for when D-Day arrived there would be unforeseen difficulties enough.

190 Squadron flew an advance party from Leicester East to Fairford on 22 March, and some more personnel travelled to Fairford by train the next day. On 25 March, the last of 620 Squadron's old Stirling III aircraft, which had been left behind at Leicester East, were ferried to 1665 HCU at Tilstock. The same day, twenty Stirlings of 190 Squadron and nineteen Horsas were flown to Fairford, while most of 190

Squadron's ground crews made the journey by train. One of the airmen arriving at Fairford railway station that fine evening was John Smith:

> At the station, those who had bicycles were ordered to find them in the wagons attached to the train and ride them to the new camp. On the way, riding with my pal, Pete, we came to the first pub in the town, The Railway Inn, deciding as we passed to return and pay it a visit. This we did, entering the only bar open and finding it packed. We had only 2/8d between us (still awaiting pay day!), so armed with all our fortune in the world I fought my way to the bar and ordered two pints of beer from the landlady, who informed me that the beer was 1/- a pint plus a deposit of 1/- on each glass. I returned to Pete who was by the door and told him the terrible news. We were deciding what to do, when we were addressed by a tall, well-built man of mature age 'Not enough money?', he asked, 'No' I said. He then asked 'How much have you got?'

The steep approach that could be achieved by a Horsa with its flaps fully lowered is evident in this photograph, taken from a position close to the chequered caravan of the Aerodrome Control Post. (*190 & 620 Sqns Archive*)

> and I replied, '2/8d'. 'Give me two bob, I'll get your beer, but you'd better let me have the glasses back and I'll be watching you.' He did not look the sort of person you would want to cross. Needless to say, we accepted his offer, enjoyed our beer and returned the glasses.
>
> That man later became my father-in-law. When I asked him why he had made that offer to us that night, he said that he did not know, not having done it before or since!

While 190 Squadron's main move to Fairford was in progress on 25 March, 620 Squadron was involved in Exercise 'Bizz II'. As with 'Bizz I', this was organised jointly by 38 Group and the American forces. On this occasion, paratroops of 3 Parachute Brigade were dropped, and as before, gliders were released over Brize Norton and Southrop. These landings were followed by resupply drops, one of them at night. Ten aircraft from 620 Squadron took part in the second of the two glider lifts, which ended with a mass landing of fifty-four gliders at Brize Norton.

George Chesterton of 190 Squadron recalled:

> The normal procedure at the start of these exercises was for the gliders to be packed in nose to tail on one side of the runway, while the tugs taxied on one after another. We had so much practice at this that it became a smooth and slick operation. A tug lined up and immediately its Horsa was towed in behind, the rope was attached and airmen signalled the tug slowly forward. The rear gunner in a Stirling was able to keep his pilot informed, and ahead there were

traffic lights, which flashed to green as soon as the rope was taut. Take-off was nearly always uneventful; the glider would be airborne in about two hundred yards and helped to lift the tail of the tug, which made it possible to open the throttles fully rather earlier than normal. The take-off appeared long and cumbersome and a slow climb away accentuated this sensation. Usually the Horsa dropped into the 'low-tow' position at about a thousand feet. This position, below the tail of the tug, gave the glider pilot the best possible visibility. There was a primitive intercommunication system between the two pilots, but it was seldom possible to exchange anything more than monosyllabic messages.

Over the next few days, 190 and 620 Squadrons were kept fully occupied, as they practised glider formation and cross-country flights, some at heights as low as 500 feet. There were also parachute-dropping runs over the 'Local DZ' at Kelmscott, which was another small grass airfield, five miles east of Fairford.

Nos 3 and 4 Glider Servicing Echelons had been set up at Fairford on 15 March, to provide engineering support for the Horsas flown by 'G' Squadron of the Glider Pilot Regiment. By April 1944, there were 100 gliders in the charge of 'G' Squadron, which was organised into four flights, staffed by approximately eighty two-man crews in all. One of the glider pilots was Lieutenant Mike Dauncey, who went on to pursue a distinguished career in army aviation. He had been posted to fly Horsas at Leicester East, and then made the move to Fairford:

> I qualified as a Second Pilot in January 1944, with thirty flying hours in my Log Book. I had been trained to fly Tiger Moth aircraft and Hotspur gliders at RAF Booker and RAF Shobdon respectively.
>
> I had been commissioned into the 22nd (Cheshire) Regiment in 1941, but I was seconded to the Glider Pilot Regiment and joined 'D' Squadron at Leicester East. In March 1944, I was posted to 'G' Squadron at Fairford. Here Staff Sergeant Alan Murdoch became my First Pilot and we flew together until September 1944, when we took part in the Arnhem operation; he taught me to fly the Horsa glider, during flying training on the Squadron.
>
> There was a great bond between the glider pilots and the RAF aircrews who towed us. This had been fostered by AVM Hollinghurst, AOC 38 Group, who had ruled that the glider pilots should live on the same airfields as their tug pilots, many of whom had completed one or two operational tours.
>
> Living together in the same messes, we soon became good friends and when practicable, flew together as a glider-tug combination. When we got to know each other well, the custom started of exchanging the top buttons of our Service Dress tunics. My own tunic, with its RAF top button, is now in the Museum of Army Flying at Middle Wallop, in Hampshire.
>
> There was a wonderful air of expectancy throughout the country in 1944, which gave us a real sense of purpose. Our squadron flying training started with simple 'circuits and bumps', but soon progressed to increasing numbers of glider-tug combinations, flying on timed cross-country exercises. The navigation and exact timings of the RAF aircrews were excellent and stood us in good stead by the time of the mass flying exercises and, of course, the Airborne Operations to Europe.

At Fairford, the Horsa pilots were able to develop their tactical flying skills. On the airfield, white tape marked out a grass area on which the gliders landed, instead of using the hard runways. At times, this LZ became very congested. The judgment of the pilots was then put to the test, as they had carefully to select their touchdown points, in order to avoid collisions with those already on the ground.

After a few days of settling in at Fairford, 190 and 620 Squadrons were ready for SOE operations to France. However, for the time being these would be conducted from Tarrant Rushton, since some of the facilities at Fairford, including the Operations Room, were not yet ready. When operations were to take place, the usual procedure was for 38 Group to send a signal during the morning, specifying the number of aircraft required of Fairford. In the afternoon, the aircraft would be flown down to Tarrant Rushton, where they would be fuelled and loaded for the night's operations. Crews would not be given details of their routes and DZs until they were issued with maps at briefing time. All the maps had to be handed in when the crews were debriefed on their return from France. As a further security precaution, they were forbidden to make detailed entries in their flying log books after these flights, which had to be recorded using the standard phrase 'Ops as ordered'. Ken Back recalled the methods that were used when flying across France at low level and at night in lone aircraft:

> The members of each crew tended to develop their own technique. In our particular case, we interchanged and shared tasks as far as possible. The bomb aimer and rear gunner were equipped with quarter-inch to one mile maps, and often all three of us were map reading. The bomb aimer was in effect a 2nd Nav and 2nd Pilot. It was very much a team effort. The pilot exercised a light control over the crew, but in fact discipline was strong. Everybody knew his task and did it with a minimum of fuss. Most conversation in the air was informal and on Christian name terms but there was absolutely no backchat, no superfluous talk. I think we enjoyed our flying but we were deadly serious. On SOE or SAS drops we would use astronavigation as a check but I found it unreliable under the conditions in which we flew. Of course, it could prevent one from doing something ridiculous like relying on a duff compass. Occasionally, when in trouble, we tried MF/DF [medium frequency/direction finding] fixes on the way home, and also loop bearings, but found the latter variable in reliability and accuracy. We preferred to maintain radio silence as far as possible. On the later airborne support operations the Rebecca-Eureka combination was a boon for homing onto a DZ but these missions were of course mostly in daylight anyway and navigationally a piece of cake.
>
> We first received a Stirling IV in March 1944. This was 'W-Willie', EF237. We did most of our ops on this aircraft. The aircraft had a distant reading gyro compass located in the tail, with repeaters for the Nav and Pilot, as well as the usual magnetic compass. There was an astrograph above the navigation table that simplified the plotting of such astro shots as we obtained. The bubble-type sextant was an improved version with a clockwork motor that enabled one to take twelve shots quickly and then obtain the average reading. Group Exercises were practised frequently, both for paratrooping and for glider towing. Large numbers of aircraft would rendezvous, form into streams and converge in proper order on a DZ, in the shortest possible time without collision. I suppose this technique reached its epitome on the first main drop to Arnhem in September 1944, when the stream of aircraft and gliders reached ahead and behind in parallel lines as far as the eye could see.

Flying Officer Murray's 620 Squadron crew, beneath their Stirling EF237 'W-Willie'. Unofficially named 'Ubique', it bore an emblem of the globe, with the Dominions of the Commonwealth painted in red. Left to right: Flight Sergeant Allen Gould (flight engineer), Flight Sergeant Reg Greenslade (wireless operator), Flying Officer Geoff Murray (pilot), Flying Officer Ken Back (navigator), Warrant Officer Henry Hooper (bomb aimer) and Flight Lieutenant John Dawson (air gunner). (*190 & 620 Sqns Archive*)

41

If SOE agents were being parachuted to France, their Stirling crew usually met them for the first time at the door of the aircraft, just before taxiing out for take-off. Few words were spoken to these passengers. In fact, there was often only a shout of 'good luck', above the roar of the engines, as they were about to disappear through the gaping hole in the floor, out into the darkness and the cold night air. If they were to stand a reasonable chance of survival, these brave people needed an element of cover that would make their presence in enemy-occupied territory seem plausible, as Ken Back observed:

> I recollect one occasion when we took a man to somewhere on the border of Alsace-Lorraine and Germany. Under his jump-suit he was dressed in a dark business suit. He was wearing horn-rimmed spectacles, carrying a briefcase and appeared a typical 'absent-minded professor type' in his late middle years. I had the impression he was going back to his old stamping ground – a man of considerable courage, alone.

The first SOE operation flown by a 620 Squadron crew after the move to Fairford took place on the night of 30/31 March. Stirling LJ875, captained by Flt Sgt Clement, took off from Tarrant Rushton with the intention of dropping eighteen containers and two packages at a location in south-east France. Although no enemy opposition was encountered during this flight of six and a half hours, extensive cloud cover made navigation very difficult and the DZ could not be positively identified. Clement and his crew therefore had to return with their load, in accordance with instructions. Eighteen aircraft from 38 Group operated out of Tarrant Rushton that night, but only three carried out their drops, owing to the poor weather across France.

The first 620 Squadron crew to carry out an SOE operation after the move to Fairford: back, left to right, Flight Sergeant Joe Martin (wireless operator), Flying Officer Jack Hilton (navigator) and Sergeant Al Schofield (flight engineer); front, left to right, Sergeant Jack Bryce (bomb aimer), Flight Sergeant Ron Clement (pilot) and Sergeant Percy Hamley (air gunner). Flight Sergeant Martin wore a combined USA–Canada shoulder flash, as he was an American who had enlisted in the Royal Canadian Air Force. (*190 & 620 Sqns Archive*)

The next night, 31 March/1 April, 190 Squadron took part in an SOE operation for the first time. Flt Lt Gardiner and his crew took off from Tarrant Rushton, crossed the English coast at St Catherine's Point, and then climbed to a relatively safe height of 8,000 feet before making their landfall at Cabourg. Hindered by low cloud, they could not identify their DZ, 'Trainer 153', which was situated in the Dordogne. They found an alternative DZ, 'Trainer 151', but were still unable to drop, since no lights were observed there, possibly because of ground haze.

The first Stirling accident at Fairford occurred on 3 April, fortunately without any injury to the crew. There was a crosswind and visibility was poor, under very low cloud, when Plt Off Farren of 190 Squadron brought EF298 'Z' back to the airfield at the end of an air test to check the operation of its autopilot. On the approach to land, Farren saw some civilian workmen near the runway, but as he manoeuvred to avoid them the Stirling's port undercarriage struck a gun post. Although he opened the throttles and went round again, the undercarriage was seriously damaged, so it was decided that the safest course of action would be to make a wheels-up landing. After repairs, EF298 returned to service with 570 Squadron, but was shot down near Arnhem in September 1944.

On 1 April, Fairford had been ordered to prepare as many of its aircraft as possible for Exercise 'Dreme', which involved all the 38 Group squadrons. The plan was to use gliders to transport troops of 1 Air Landing Brigade to two LZs, in order to simulate the glider operation that would actually take place just before dusk on D-Day. The exercise was also intended to give Pathfinder paratroops practice in setting up Eureka radio beacons and laying out marker strips on the LZs. 'Dreme' went ahead during the evening of 4 April. The first wave comprised Albemarles from Brize Norton and Halifaxes from Tarrant Rushton, which released a total of thirty-five Horsa gliders over Brize Norton, at the end of long cross-country flights. The routes used by each of the 38 Group stations should have gone out over the English

A Horsa in the 'high tow' position behind a Stirling, photographed from 'D-Dog' of 620 Squadron. (*190 & 620 Sqns Archive*)

Channel, but this part of the plan had to be abandoned because naval operations were in progress there.

The Stirlings from Fairford and Keevil were towing Horsas in the second wave. Soldiers of the King's Own Scottish Borderers were carried as passengers in the Fairford gliders. Following a route over south-west England, they took about two and a half hours to reach their LZ at Brize Norton. Twenty-six of the Fairford gliders were released there, with two others having made forced landings after they cast off *en route*. The crews of 196 and 299 Squadrons from Keevil were less fortunate, since they encountered some bad weather on their cross-country. Faced with dense cloud, four gliders cast off from their 196 Squadron tugs near Petersfield and landed safely. But in the same area, another 196 Squadron Stirling and its Horsa were seriously damaged when they struck trees on high ground. The Horsa released from the tow, but stalled and crashed near Warnford, killing both pilots and all twenty-six passengers. The tug pilot fought to keep his Stirling airborne, but his brave efforts were in vain, for it crashed 15 miles further on, killing everyone on board.

In the third and final wave of 'Dreme', there were Halifaxes from Tarrant Rushton, and Albemarles from Harwell, all of which released their gliders over the latter airfield. In spite of the glider cast-offs and the two fatal crashes, 'Dreme' was judged by HQ 38 Group to have been successful from a military standpoint, since most of the gliders did in fact reach their LZs at the correct times.

While the glider towing and parachute dropping exercises were being built up in both scale and complexity, the arming of the *Maquis* was proceeding apace. On the night of 5/6 April, as the moon was waxing, 190 and 620 Squadrons each had three aircraft operating out of Tarrant Rushton on SOE operations. They were among forty-two aircraft, drawn from all ten squadrons in 38 Group, active over France that night. The three crews from 190 Squadron failed to observe any reception signals at their DZs and had to return with their loads. Although they encountered light flak, none of their aircraft was damaged. As for many of these special operations, the night's records are scant and do not state whether the 620 Squadron crews were successful. However, it is known that two of the 190 Squadron aircraft, and one of those from 620 Squadron, were diverted to Boscombe Down in Wiltshire, on their return.

On 6 April, one aircraft from 190 Squadron, and two from 620 Squadron, flew to Tarrant Rushton to prepare for SOE operations. These were later cancelled, so the Fairford aircraft returned to base, where it was a fine day, with glider towing, practice DZ runs and paratroop dropping on the flying programme. There was no flying on 7 April, owing to poor weather, which persisted into the next day and caused a paratroop dropping exercise, 'Hog I', to be cancelled. On 9 April, Fairford Stirlings took part in a container drop on the airfield at Netheravon. This was designated as the 'Divisional DZ', and was near HQ 38 Group. It was very surprising that there were no accidents on this exercise, as aircraft approached the airfield from various directions, rather than on an east-to-west run, as briefed. Following this episode, 38 Group firmly reminded its squadrons of the need to stick to the dropping procedures, precisely as laid down.

During the evening of 9 April, twenty of the Fairford Stirlings took part in 'Tour'. This was a navigational exercise over southern England and involved 188 aircraft from 38 and 46 Groups. No paratroops were transported or gliders towed, but ground observers were in place at rendezvous points and at a simulated DZ, in order to assess the positioning and timing of the aircraft. On the morning of 9 April, each

The first stick of 'paras' to be dropped by Flight Sergeant de Rome's 620 Squadron crew, photographed by Flight Sergeant Noel Chaffey at Fairford in the spring of 1944. (*N.R. Chaffey*)

of the Fairford squadrons sent two aircraft to Tarrant Rushton, to take part in SOE operations. Fg Off George Chesterton and his 190 Squadron crew were detailed to drop twenty-four containers and three packages to DZ 'Harry 24', midway between Argentan and Alençon. It was nearly one o'clock in the morning of 10 April when they took off in Stirling LK431 'F' and headed out over the English Channel at 6,000 feet. There was not much cloud cover to obscure the moon, and navigation over France was done by map reading, with assistance from Gee fixes. In the DZ area, three red lights became visible in a gap in some woods, although this was not at the exact position given to the crew at their briefing. Nevertheless, a flashing white letter 'P' soon confirmed it was the correct place. Chesterton reduced speed to 145 mph and turned onto a due easterly heading, to line up with the red lights, while aiming to be at a height of 500 feet over the DZ. Passing the first light, packages were dropped through the floor hatch and the containers were released, except for one that hung up. This container then fell from the aircraft about two miles beyond the DZ.

Having successfully completed 190 Squadron's first SOE drop on their maiden operational flight, Chesterton and his crew found there was 10/10ths cloud cover extending all the way from the French coast to beyond Tarrant Rushton. Of the eighteen aircraft flying on operations from Tarrant Rushton that night, fourteen were unable to return there because of the weather. Further north and east, conditions were clearer, with Boscombe Down, Hurn, Keevil and Middle Wallop all available as diversions. Chesterton landed at Boscombe Down, where his Stirling's bomb bays were inspected for any remaining hang-ups. He requested that a message be sent to Tarrant Rushton, stating only that a successful sortie had been carried out. SOE's work was surrounded by such tight security that 38 Group crews had strict orders not to discuss any details of their operations with personnel at diversion airfields.

The other 190 Squadron crew operating on the night of 9/10 April was captained by Fg Off John le Bouvier. Flying in Stirling LJ832 'U', they went to DZ 'Dick 84',

Flying Officer George Chesterton (fourth from left), with the members of his 190 Squadron crew.
(*G.H. Chesterton*)

near Nogent-le-Rotrou. Although the DZ area was found easily, no lights were displayed, so le Bouvier and his crew were unable to drop. They also diverted to Boscombe Down. The two 620 Squadron aircraft on operations that night were 'C' and 'X', captained by Flt Sgt Keogh and Flt Lt Francis, respectively. The names and locations of their DZs are not recorded. Keogh and his crew were unable to drop and diverted to Middle Wallop on their return. Francis and his crew diverted to Boscombe Down, but it is not known if their operation was successful.

During April 1944, more Stirling crews arrived at Fairford, most of them straight from training. Among those posted to 190 Squadron were Flt Sgt Ray Isaacson and his crew; their flight engineer, Sgt Malcolm Mitchell, remembered their first operation to France:

> We flew to Tarrant Rushton, to be briefed for a flight deep into France, near the Swiss border, where we were to deliver arms, explosives and other equipment to the *Maquis*. We took off in the dark, as was normal for this type of operation, and before long we were flying over the Channel, with the French coast ahead. There, our gunner, Arthur, called from the rear, for permission to test fire his four Browning machine guns. As we crossed the coast, we ran into the belt of German coastal flak. Our pilot, 'Ikey', put the aircraft into a series of evasive turns and kept changing height, to prevent a fix being made on us.
>
> Although I had experienced being bombed during the Blitz, this was my first taste of enemy fire; my feelings were mixed, partly interest in the show and partly fear that we would be hit. But the danger was soon past, and we emerged over the quiet French countryside. From there to the DZ was peaceful flying. I

Flight Sergeant Isaacson's 190 Squadron crew: back, left to right, Sergeant Ron Bradbury (wireless operator), Sergeant Arthur Batten (air gunner), Flight Sergeant Ray 'Ikey' Isaacson RAAF (pilot); front, left to right, Sergeant Malcolm Mitchell (flight engineer), Flying Officer Ross Vincent RAAF (navigator), Sergeant Bob Sutton (bomb aimer). (*190 & 620 Sqns Archive*)

was always surprised at how clear the view of the ground seemed, even on nights when there was not much moon.

Arriving at the DZ, we descended to 500 feet and circled, our aircraft flashing its light, using the pre-arranged identification code. On the ground, the correct reply was then flashed to us, and fires were lit in the field. At this, we circled again, made our run in, and the bomb aimer, Bob, lying in his compartment in the nose of the aircraft, dropped the long, cylindrical containers on their parachutes, to the brave people waiting below. For safety, I had put the engines onto the main fuel tanks for these manoeuvres, returning to the recommended order for using fuel from the various tanks once the drop was finished.

Then we went up and away from the danger area, for the long return journey, and eventually back to England, safety and daylight, to land at Tarrant Rushton. We were debriefed, and our aircraft was checked and refuelled, whilst we ate our breakfast in the mess there. We were then free to fly back to our own base at Fairford. Having learned the ropes in this way, we settled into a pattern of night operations, and daylight glider-towing exercises with the airborne troops, in preparation for D-Day.

On 11 April, a 190 Squadron aircraft was involved in a fatal accident at the Kelmscott Local DZ, when a paratrooper, fifth in a stick of thirteen, fell to his death after his parachute failed to open (unlike their American counterparts, British paratroops were not equipped with reserve parachutes at that time). The unfortunate man had not clipped his static line properly into place in the Stirling. This error went unnoticed by the paratrooper following him, and by the stick commander, both of whom should have checked the attachment. The subsequent Court of Inquiry recommended a change to the design of the 'D' ring at the end of the static line, to make it difficult to clip onto the anchor hook in the aircraft, other than in the correct manner.

On the night of 11/12 April, 38 Group launched its largest effort so far, as fifty-five aircraft, drawn from all its squadrons, took part in SOE operations from Tarrant Rushton. Thirty-eight of these aircraft successfully completed their tasks, but two others were lost, both Fairford Stirlings. The 190 Squadron crew captained by Flt Sgt Peter Croudis, a New Zealander, took off in LJ822 'D' at 2343 hrs, but only six minutes later the aircraft hit the ground and exploded at Knighton Farm, Hampreston. All six members of the crew were killed. The Court of Inquiry suggested that the heavily loaded aircraft had started a turn at too low a speed, stalled, and entered a spin from which it failed to recover. However, the AOC 38 Group noted that the cause of the accident was 'doubtful'. Although air accident investigation was still in its infancy during the Second World War, it is unfortunate that Courts of Inquiry seem to have frequently resorted to attributing crashes to aircrew error, if no other factors were apparent.

The 620 Squadron crew captained by Flt Sgt Leslie Brown, also a New Zealander, failed to return from their operation that night, in LJ867 'U' (the 620 Squadron Operations Record Book incorrectly states that this Stirling went missing the previous night, 10/11 April, when Tarrant Rushton was stood down). LJ867 was damaged by anti-aircraft fire, and crash-landed to the south-east of Bordeaux, killing the navigator, Plt Off Barnett. The aircraft caught fire, but the other members of the crew managed to excape. Flt Sgt Hargreaves (bomb aimer), Sgt Shaw (wireless operator) and Sgt Norman (flight engineer) were soon captured by the Germans, and after being given medical treatment, were transported to a POW camp. Flt Sgt Brown and his gunner, Plt Off Griffin, evaded capture and were concealed by the *Maquis.* Griffin had the misfortune to be captured on 6 June (D-Day) when he was with some Resistance men who were stopped at a roadblock. This was manned by the *Milice*, a paramilitary force set up by the Vichy government, and known unofficially as the 'French Gestapo'. After long interrogation Griffin was handed over to the German forces, to be detained as a POW. Brown was eventually repatriated, and summarised his experiences in France, in the following report:

> I took off from Tarrant Rushton at 2200 hrs on 11 April 1944. The aircraft was hit by heavy machine gun fire at about 0120 hrs on 12 April, and we made a forced landing in the vicinity of Anzex. Plt Off Griffin and myself set off together, while the other members of the crew, with the exception of the navigator, who was killed on landing, separated from us and were reported to have been captured on the following day. On 13 April we went to a farm at Fargues where we remained for two weeks, sleeping in the woods. At the end of this period a man in the Resistance who had been helping us was arrested, and we were moved on 26 April to some woods between Lavadac and Durance, where we hid for three weeks. On 14 May we moved to Larroque, near Condom, and from here onwards my journey was arranged.

In fact, Brown was on the run for several more weeks, during which he saw action with the *Maquis*. He was then taken by road to the Pyrénées, where he was joined by five escaped POWs, and Anne-Marie Walters, an SOE agent, who had been working with the 'Wheelwright' circuit (her story was later told in the book *Moonlight to Gascony*, published by Macmillan in 1946). Continuing on foot, the members of this

When he returned to the UK, Flight Sergeant Les Brown formed a new crew at 81 OTU, Sleap, before being posted to 190 Squadron. The members of this crew are seen here on a visit to RAF Riccall, in June 1945. Left to right: Sergeant P.J. Coles (air gunner), Flying Officer F.J. Moss (bomb aimer), Warrant Officer L.J.S. Brown (pilot), Sergeant J.C.J. Sims (wireless operator) and Sergeant G.J. Jack (flight engineer). Missing from the line-up is their navigator, Flying Officer Bob Powell, who took the photograph. (*190 & 620 Sqns Archive*)

party were guided over the 8,000 feet high mountains into neutral Spain. From there, via Gibraltar, Brown returned to the UK. In recognition of his exploits on the ground with the *Maquis*, he was awarded the Military Medal, a decoration rarely bestowed on Air Force personnel.

After the widespread activity during the night of 11/12 April, there was a lull in operations by 38 Group as the moon waned. In the meantime, the intensive training programme continued at Fairford. In the early hours of 13 April, Stirling LJ475 'V' of 620 Squadron crashed at Blackford Farm, Kempsford, just to the south of the airfield. It was captained by Flt Sgt Nelson Burns, a New Zealander serving in the RAAF. The aircraft had been engaged in a glider-towing exercise, but after releasing the glider late in the circuit, it made a steep descent to achieve the correct height over the rope-dropping area. It appeared that power was applied too late to check the high rate of sink, and as a result the aircraft struck the ground. The only survivor out of the crew of six was the gunner, Plt Off Leonard Halliday, who was seriously burned.

A Group Exercise, 'Posh', took place on the afternoon of 16 April, having been postponed from the previous day because of bad weather. Conditions were still far from ideal when 'Posh' went ahead, so the cross-country that formed part of the exercise had to be curtailed. Pathfinder aircraft dropped troops of the 22nd Independent Parachute Company onto two DZs on Salisbury Plain, where they set up

Eureka radio beacons to guide in the rest of the aircraft. Nos 190 and 620 Squadrons each had nine aircraft taking part in the main drop on DZ 'A', on Parsonage Down. They dropped troops of the 1st Polish Paratroop Battalion, followed by supply containers.

'Posh' was carefully analysed, as were all the big airborne exercises. Observers on the ground commented that many of the paratroops were dispatched too soon, with the result that approximately half of them landed outside their designated areas. This problem needed to be rectified before D-Day, when positioning and timing would be of the utmost importance. During 'Posh', one paratrooper was killed when his parachute failed to open. As a consequence of this accident, 'live dropping' from Stirlings was stopped after the exercise, but this ban was lifted the following day.

There was another fatal accident at 2255 hrs on 18 April, when Horsa LG263 crashed into the Fairford control tower. This glider was being towed aloft by Stirling 'G' of 620 Squadron when the tug-to-glider intercom failed (this used an electrical cable woven into the tow-rope, and was notoriously unreliable). However, thinking the tug was in distress, the glider pilots released the tow-rope and then turned to set up their approach to land on the airfield. In the darkness, and with visibility further reduced by hazy conditions, the glider drifted to one side of the flarepath and struck the unlit control tower. The 1st pilot, SSgt William Clark, later died from his injuries. The 2nd pilot, Sgt Morgan, was seriously injured, as was a passenger, LAC McDougall of 2706 Squadron, RAF Regiment. Several personnel on the ground sustained minor injuries in this accident.

On 21 April, the Fairford Stirlings took part in 'Mush', an Anglo-American exercise, in which some troops of the 1st Airborne Division were dropped by parachute and some landed by glider. The 38 Group squadrons towed gliders to Brize Norton and Harwell airfields, where paratroops of 1 and 4 Parachute Brigades had been dropped just after first light by American C-47 aircraft of the IXth Troop Carrier Command (TCC). Later on, resupply drops were flown by the IXth TCC and RAF Dakotas from 46 Group. Thirty Stirlings from 190 and 620 Squadrons towed Horsas on a cross-country flight, which lasted three hours and went as far as Cambridgeshire, before returning to release them over Brize Norton. These gliders carried soldiers of 1 Air Landing Brigade, who were equipped with jeeps, trailers, motorcycles and six-pounder guns. Broken tow-ropes and Stirlings with engine problems caused six of the Fairford Horsas to cast off *en route*. When the results of 'Mush' were assessed, HQ 38 Group expressed concern at the number of gliders that had failed to reach the LZs, but otherwise the exercise was regarded as having been a great success.

After the Fairford Stirling crews had landed at the end of 'Mush', they learned of the award of the Distinguished Flying Cross to 190 Squadron's respected and well-liked 'Boss', Wg Cdr Harrison. This was gazetted in recognition of the 'high skill, fortitude and gallantry' he had demonstrated in a previous posting, flying Stirling bombers with 149 Squadron at Lakenheath.

Several Station exercises were devised for the Fairford Stirlings during April 1944. These included air-to-sea firing (sometimes with gliders in tow) at the Stert Flats range, which was situated in the Bristol Channel, to the west of Burnham-on-Sea. There was also fighter affiliation, carried out in co-operation with the nearby stations of Aston Down and Colerne. April brought its traditional rain showers, but local flying took place almost every day at Fairford, with practice DZ runs, live parachute drops, and glider 'circuits and bumps' accounting for many of the hours flown that month.

Everyone at Fairford worked hard to keep the Stirlings in the air, but they also played hard, often making their own entertainment, both on and off the camp. All the local pubs were soon discovered, though wartime beer shortages did present a few problems.

Ron Remfry, 6620 Servicing Echelon, recalled:

At Fairford the corporals obtained permission to form their own club in part of the NAAFI building. This was in effect our mess, like those of the officers and sergeants, except we still had to take our meals in the cookhouse with all the other airmen. We were very jealous of this privilege and had to make sure that no other ranks squeezed in. We used to go cycling around visiting the pubs in the evenings. The problem was to find the pubs which had any beer. Quite often we had to make do with cider. It was quite fun cycling back to camp, singing away at the tops of our voices. That we were not in tune did not matter at all!

Pubs by the River Thames, such as the Trout Inn at Lechlade, the Axe and Compass at Kempsford, and the Anchor Inn at Eaton Hastings, were always popular with the service personnel from Fairford. Eric Titterton's favourite was the Anchor, which is sadly no more, having been destroyed by a fire in 1980:

The landlady, Bessie Avison, was a wonderful host to us all. She originated from Portsmouth and was, I think, used to sailors, for she would play the piano for our naughty songs, but was always respected by all. We did on one occasion buy the only barrel of beer she had, so she put a 'sold out' notice on the door, and we drank our purchase at leisure, admitting only one American officer who came to the pub. As we had bought the beer he drank as our guest, and he was delighted with our hospitality, saying he would provide the beer the following week. Bess sadly informed him that she was not due for another delivery, as transport was the problem. 'Don't worry' said the gallant Major, 'I will lay on transport.'

This he did, providing us with a barrel and turning up with one or two fellow officers, a riotous time being had by all. In fact, we finished up diving fully clothed into the Thames to rescue a supposedly drowning airman, who had been seen to fall into the river. We only stopped giving artificial respiration to him when one of our more observant fellows pointed out that the victim was humming Glenn Miller's 'In the Mood' in time with our efforts. These occasions were quite infrequent, and of course as such are well remembered, for we were sober most of the time but did now and then have a real beano.

While no one could ignore the deadly importance of the flying carried out by 190 and 620 Squadrons, there were also, from time to time, some carefree moments in the air.

Noel Chaffey, 620 Squadron, recalled:

Formation flying was in our training schedule, but this had not been planned, however, one day when a US Flying Fortress came alongside in smooth and level flight, its pilot wiggling his wings to indicate that he wanted to fly with us. We acknowledged by gesture and hence began half an hour of pure excitement and determination.

As big and bold as the Fortress was, the Stirling was bigger and, we hoped to show, bolder. The 'Yank' almost tucked the tip of his port wing into our fuselage behind the trailing edge of our starboard wing, flew for a time thus and then withdrew, giving us the 'thumbs up', with all windows and turrets showing smiling grins from crew members.

As we were still in formation our pilot, Derek, cut the starboard outer motor but then drew ahead of the Fort (now our windows were full of smiling faces). The Yank then cut his port and starboard outer engines and gradually flew on a few yards ahead (thumbs up again!).

However, our Stirling had an ace up its sleeve – we shut down both outer and inner engines on the starboard wing and giving full power to the remaining two engines shot on ahead of the Fortress. We got quite a reaction, thumbs up and claps from the Fort's crew, who 'wiggled' their wings again, as if to say 'You guys win, we can't do that with this kite'. Using their Aldis lamp, 'Good luck' was flashed to us; I replied from the astrodome 'And you!' with our lamp.

Flight Officer Thomas Higgins, the American bombardier in 190 Squadron, continued to make his diary entries at Fairford, describing the place 'warts and all':

16 April
Fairford is a hole first class, with nothing to do and nowhere to go. Enough said. We've been flying like hell the past week, dropping paratroops and towing gliders. I work like hell. It's mostly up to the bombardier to map-read the entire trip and to give the jumpers the various signals. Quite a work out.

One fellow's chute didn't open the other day. Wham – into the deck he went. It's a bigger thrill to watch troops drop than bombs. And also a great deal more work for me. I wouldn't mind jumping with the boys, and will, if ever given the opportunity. Sometimes the troops refuse to jump. They are court-martialled and given about three months in the 'glasshouse'.

We were on a mass exercise this afternoon, dropping Poles. Those boys are good jumpers all right; always singing. Personally I don't see anything to sing about. Plenty of guts, though. Must have been a thousand dropped in one field. Hell! They were coming down all over. Like rain on a tin roof in spring.

Had my first ride in a glider yesterday. Some fun. No engines to worry about.

25 April
We were on an exercise last night, glider towing and container dropping. It won't be long now. The old invasion is only a few weeks away and if you ask me its first blow will be an airborne effort. Every day streams of gliders and troop carriers pass by. Yes – the big day isn't far off.

From the number of light cannon that are mounted around this drome I think something is expected. Light machine guns are scattered all over the fields, small cannon on every vantage point. More fun!

28 April
Some of our kites are on 'ops' tonight but not us. Les was homing with a new gadget today and, from 20 miles distant, he was bang over the spot. It's what we are going to use when the dear old Second Front starts. It certainly is a 'gen' instrument; something like Gee, only better.

If we win the war it's certainly going to be due to the back room boys and all of their inventions. I think I'll invent something. What could it be? Maybe I'll have it in my next instalment.

The guns in the fields, mentioned by Thomas Higgins, were those of 2706 and 2886 Squadrons, RAF Regiment, which were responsible for airfield defence at Fairford.

During April, a gun control room was set up, in order to command and coordinate their actions.

In the air, accurate navigation was essential to the success of all the tasks carried out by the Fairford Stirling crews. To begin with, new crews concentrated on map reading by moonlight when flying at night, but they were soon expected to become proficient in the use of the 'Rebecca' sets that were being fitted to their aircraft. Rebecca was the 'new gadget' Thomas Higgins wrote about; it transmitted a pulse to a Eureka beacon on the ground, which responded by transmitting a coded signal on a different frequency. When this signal was picked up by the Rebecca set, a pulse was displayed on a cathode-ray tube. This represented the time elapsed since the last Rebecca transmission, and when calibrated appropriately, provided the navigator with an indication of the aircraft's distance from the Eureka beacon. By using a double aerial arrangement to receive the coded Eureka signals, it was possible to derive and display information on the direction to fly towards the beacon. To give the 38 Group crews practice in this type of homing, a Eureka beacon was set up at the Netheravon Divisional DZ, which also displayed lights at night, laid out in the form of a 'T'.

While technological advances were being exploited in the air, there were still plenty of mundane jobs to be done on the ground. As with the rest of the population, the Air Force was encouraged to 'Dig for Victory'. At Fairford this took the form of the Station Gardening Scheme. By the end of April, ploughing was well under way, in readiness for the planting of 17 tons of potatoes. This market gardening project eventually extended to 23 acres under cultivation, and supplied many of the vegetables needed by the messes on the station.

Every day from 27 to 30 April, Fairford Stirlings flew to Tarrant Rushton, to take part in SOE operations, albeit with limited success. During the night of 27/28 April, a 620 Squadron aircraft, captained by Flt Sgt Robinson, was the only one from Fairford to fly operationally, though it is not recorded whether a drop was made. The next night, 28/29 April, the weather was bad and the moonlight dull. Nos 190 and 620 Squadrons each had three aircraft that were unable to drop, but Flt Sgt Isaacson and his 190 Squadron crew were successful. On the night of 29/30 April, Flt Sgt McMillan's 190 Squadron crew dropped, but two other aircraft from 190 Squadron, and two from 620, returned with their loads. On 30 April/1 May, three aircraft from 190 Squadron and two from 620 Squadron operated. Two of the 190 Squadron aircraft, captained by Fg Off Kilgour and Flt Sgt Porter, were successful.

At dusk on 28 April, there had been another serious accident, when the tail of Horsa LH438 broke off as it was being towed on a cross-country flight from Fairford. The glider spiralled into the ground at Combe Hill in Berkshire, killing the pilots, SSgt Needleman and Sgt Brown. While LH438's crash was still under investigation, Lieutenant Mike Dauncey took part in a flight trial, in order to demonstrate to the other Horsa pilots that the type was safe to fly:

In April, the tail-fin came off a glider, while it was being towed. At the time, it was thought that this could have been caused by the slipstream of the towing bomber. It resulted in several glider pilots casting-off their gliders, after they had flown in the slipstream. To help regain confidence in the Horsa glider's airworthiness, our Squadron Commander, Major R.C. Croot, took a Horsa up to 4,000 feet, to check the effect of the continued slipstream caused by the Stirling tug aircraft. By then, I was the Squadron Adjutant and accompanied him as a timekeeper. We stayed in the slipstream for a long 30 minutes, by which time a banding strip had been ripped off the port wing. I was glad to get down again. However, Bob Croot's action put back the glider pilots' confidence in the Horsa.

The accident to Horsa LH438 was found to have been caused by a failure of the structure in the front of its fin. Subsequent inspections revealed that quite a number of gliders in the Horsa fleet were suffering from glue deterioration in this area, brought about by much longer exposure to the weather than had ever been intended. A repair scheme was devised, and implemented without delay, by working parties from the RAF and the manufacturers, Airspeed Ltd. Production of Oxford aircraft had to be suspended for a time, in order to release sufficient factory personnel for this task, which was completed by 11 May, with 470 Horsas pronounced serviceable.

May 1944 proved a good month for Fairford, in terms of overall hours flown. However, the Stirling crews were understandably 'browned off' if they were sent to Tarrant Rushton, only to find that SOE operations were then cancelled. This happened on several occasions during the early part of the month. Four crews from 190 Squadron went to Tarrant Rushton on 1 May, but operations were called off late in the day, after their aircraft had been loaded with containers. These were unloaded and the aircraft flew back to Fairford. On 2 May, three crews from 190 Squadron flew to Tarrant Rushton, along with four from 620 Squadron. This time they stayed at Tarrant Rushton overnight, after their operations were cancelled. The next night, 3/4 May, four crews from 190 Squadron, and three from 620 Squadron, did fly to France, but only Fg Off Siegert and his 190 Squadron crew were successful in dropping. Two aircraft from each of the Fairford squadrons sustained flak damage.

Thomas Higgins' diary:

1 May

Well, we're on again tonight. Not the entire crew but just Alan and me. We volunteered to go with F/Sgt Derbyshire, for two of his crew are U/S. The WOp/AG has ear trouble and Brown, his bombardier, fractured his skull and broke his nose when on leave in London. He fell in an air raid shelter.

We are going over to Tarrant Rushton to do the 'op'. It's a special low level effort dropping supplies to the French. I guess it's going to be one of those long efforts.

We flew down this afternoon, stayed around for a while and then were told that the operation was scrubbed. Some luck, dammit. The trip was to have been a long one, about six and a half hours or so – the south-west part of France.

2 May

We're on again tonight; anyway I am. This time I'm going with F/O Robertson. He needed a bombardier so I volunteered to go with him. It's to be one of those special low level efforts over France. We're leaving for Tarrant Rushton about 2.30 or so. See you soon.

4 May

What a time. We were briefed on the 2nd for a nice short trip SW of Paris but at the last minute it was scrubbed so we stayed for the next night. Was it short? No, no, no, no! Seven and a half hours of flight. Our dropping point was just a few miles from the Pyrénées, but we were unable to locate it because of the weather; low cloud most of the way which made pinpointing almost impossible.

We didn't see much in the way of opposition; a bit of flak going up near Bordeaux and a single engine job crossed in front of us but I guess we went unnoticed. Well! It's another one, anyway.

Group Exercise 'Confirmation' took place during the night of 4/5 May. An individual DZ was allocated to each of the five 38 Group stations participating in this navigational exercise, which involved 150 aircraft and was one of the most difficult yet attempted. The DZs had to be found visually by moonlight, without the use of ground aids, and each crew dropped a single, marked container, so that their accuracy could be assessed. Sixteen aircraft from 190 Squadron, and fourteen from 620 Squadron, followed a long route that stretched from Kent to Devon, then over the Bristol Channel to Pembrokeshire. From there, they made their run-in to DZ 'D', which was situated in a remote spot to the north-west of Brecon. When all the drops by the Fairford aircraft were analysed, the results were less than satisfactory, since only one-third of the containers actually landed on the DZ. One-third were dropped more than two miles away from the DZ, and problems with hang-ups accounted for about one-fifth of the containers being brought back to base. The remainder of the containers had landed up to two miles from the DZ. Needless to say, some valuable lessons were learned from 'Confirmation' and much effort was put into organising further practice drops, in order to get things right in time for D-Day.

On the night of 5/6 May, there were two aircraft from 190 Squadron, and one from 620 Squadron, taking part in operations from Tarrant Rushton. Only one of these aircraft was successful in dropping. The next night, 6/7 May, ninety-three aircraft, including nine from 190 Squadron and thirteen from 620, took part in Group Exercise 'Dingo'. The 38 Group orders for this exercise stated that it was sufficiently important to be given priority over SOE operations, so there were no Fairford aircraft sent to Tarrant Rushton that night. During 'Dingo', gliders were towed on a moonlit cross-country over southern England and the Midlands, *en route* to two LZs at Netheravon. Within 15 miles of the LZs, the tug crews were guided towards their release points by Eureka beacons. These had been set up, along with green 'Halophane' lights, by Pathfinder paratroops. The AOC in C of the Allied Expeditionary Air Force, Air Chief Marshal Sir Trafford Leigh-Mallory, watched as ninety gliders landed. After releasing their gliders, each of the tugs dropped a supply container before returning to its base. During the afternoon of 7 May, the Fairford Horsas that had landed at Netheravon during the night were brought back to base by Albemarle tugs.

On the night of 7/8 May, 190 and 620 Squadrons each had five aircraft taking part in SOE operations from Tarrant Rushton. Three aircraft from each Fairford squadron were successful in dropping, but 620 Squadron's LJ866 'U', captained by Fg Off Archie Swan RAAF, failed to return. This aircraft crashed at Poisson, approximately 80 kilometres north-west of Lyon, killing all six members of the crew. The DZs were widely scattered that night. One of the 190 Squadron aircraft, captained by Flt Sgt Sutherland, went to 'Mongrel 42', in the northern part of the Dordogne, but its containers and packages were not dropped, since no reception signals were observed. This aircraft escaped undamaged when it was fired on by light flak, believed to have come from a train to the east of the DZ. Two other aircraft from 190 Squadron are known to have gone far south-west, to the foothills of the Pyrénées. Flt Sgt Herger and his 190 Squadron crew went to DZ 'Trainer 222', near Montaner, but no reception signals were observed there. They then flew over a

Sergeant Bryan Garwood of 620 Squadron, map reading in the bomb aimer's position. Supply dropping from a Stirling IV was done with the aid of a Mk IXA course-setting bomb-sight. This was a much simpler device than the Stirling III's Mk XIV bomb-sight, which was linked to a large electro-pneumatic computer. (*N.R. Chaffey*)

When he was not map reading or directing the run-in to a DZ, the bomb aimer in a Stirling IV was expected to act as pilot's assistant. This photograph shows Warrant Officer Jack Riddell RNZAF, occupying the 'right-hand seat' in the 620 Squadron aircraft captained by Warrant Officer Norman Marriott, who was also a New Zealander. (*190 & 620 Sqns Archive*)

secondary DZ, 'Wheelwright 105', but with the same negative result, so they had to bring their load back. The other 190 Squadron aircraft flying to that area was captained by Flt Sgt Derbyshire. He and his crew were on their first operation, which took them to 'Paul 3', near Marciac. Their intelligence report, submitted after a flight of seven and a half hours, described the site of this DZ as 'rather difficult'. In order to line up with the white lights that indicated the wind direction, Derbyshire had to fly through a valley at less than 500 feet above ground level. However, visibility was good, the DZ was positively identified by a flashing letter 'A', and fifteen containers and three packages were successfully delivered.

Flt Sgt Derek de Rome and his 620 Squadron crew were also on their first operation to France on the night of 7/8 May. Noel Chaffey remembered this flight clearly:

Our first operational flight was in Stirling 'V for Victor', to Marçon, approximately midway between Le Mans and Tours. Climbing to a reasonable height from Tarrant Rushton, we crossed the coast with our IFF (Identification Friend or Foe) signal transmitting, and avoided wires from barrage balloons, before descending to fly at low level over the English Channel. We then had to gain height to cross the enemy coast, keeping away from their ack-ack batteries. These ops were usually done from about midnight onward, returning before daybreak, but with Ben's navigation and Bryan's map reading by moonlight up front, there were enough clues to keep us on track. Radio was never used except for emergencies, so I used to help observe from the astrodome, until the time came to run in, then I'd go aft to discharge any panniers with Frank's help.

As we were flying across France on our first operation, we saw a wonderful display by Bomber Command on a raid, the coloured chandelier flares of green dropped by Mosquito bombers of the Pathfinder Force marking out grids for Lancaster and Halifax aircraft following them to bomb – this together with searchlights actively sweeping the skies, bombs exploding, starting fires – all quite a way away but apparently so close. It seemed we were of no interest, for we saw no enemy aircraft about us.

Our valley was located and we saw three small fires lit by the Resistance, letting us know they were there. I then flashed a code letter on the Aldis lamp and got the correct letter in reply from a spotlight on the ground, so we opened the bomb-bay doors and proceeded to drop the containers. The fires were then extinguished and it was as if nothing had happened, as we climbed out over the mountains to make our way back home. No contacts were made with the

The members of the 'de Rome' crew, shortly after their posting to 620 Squadron at Fairford: sitting, left to right Flight Sergeant Noel Chaffey (wireless operator), Flying Officer Basil 'Ben' Crocker (navigator) and Fligh Sergeant Derek de Rome (pilot); standing, left to right, Sergeant Peter Griffin (air gunner), Sergeant Fran▶ Pearman (flight engineer) and Sergeant Bryan Garwood (bomb aimer). (*N. R. Chaffey*)

enemy and during a quick trip back over the Channel, IFF was switched on again before crossing the South Coast and we were almost home.

Back at Tarrant Rushton we were debriefed – asked what did you see, where, how many, what type, was there much water in the rivers? – so many seemingly silly questions, especially as one was longing for a fresh egg and a sleep. One of the perks of operational flying was the fresh egg for breakfast, instead of the powdered stuff. However, I never minded powdered egg or 'Pom' (powdered potato), and I loved the hard tack biscuits that used to be served with late tea or coffee. Usually it was only me who ate the biscuits, and I was known by our WAAFs at the cookhouse as the garbage bin, since I always piled my plate on with whatever was going. They were a great lot of girls, who did a fantastic job with the little they had to work with. However, the civilian population often did with much less.

In the late evening of 8 May, all the 38 Group crews who had not towed gliders on 'Dingo I' took part in 'Dingo II'. Thirteen aircraft from 190 Squadron, and twelve from 620 Squadron, made up Fairford's contribution to this exercise, which followed the same route as the earlier one. Five gliders towed by Fairford Stirlings cast off *en route*, two of them because of misinterpreted Aldis lamp signals from the tugs. Otherwise, the exercise went well – at least, up to the point where the gliders were released over Netheravon. Seventy-four gliders landed there, but with near-disastrous results, as approaches were made to the airfield in opposite directions. Many of the gliders were damaged through collisions on the ground, fortunately without any serious casualties. This lack of co-ordination gave rise to such grave concern that the AOC 38 Group, AVM Hollinghurst, immediately ordered a Court of Inquiry to be convened. Mike Dauncey was one of the glider pilots who flew from Fairford on 'Dingo II':

> By May 1944, we were taking part in large cross-country exercises by day and also by night. One mass night landing took place at Netheravon, the gliders landing at 10-second intervals. The gliders had been briefed to land from the south-east, only to find on arrival at the landing zone that the illuminated landing 'T' was at 180 degrees from that described in the briefing. Half the gliders stuck to their briefing, while the other half followed the direction of the 'T'. No one was injured, but the noise of the gliders crashing into each other on the ground was unnerving!

Thomas Higgins continued to note the various exercises in his diary:

> 9 May
> Was in an exercise, dropping gliders and containers. We're fully trained for gliders, paratroops and container dropping now, so I guess the Second Front will start soon. What a show that's going to be! On another exercise tonight, dropping 20 paratroops in moonlight.

> 10 May
> Just returned from exercise. What a show! Three thousand troops were dropped in our area, about 1,000 yards by 1,000 yards. There were paratroops all over. Hell! Boy! The invasion is going to be one sight to see!

The exercise on 10 May was code-named 'Drongo', and took place in the early hours of the morning. Between them, 190 and 620 Squadrons provided thirty-two aircraft to drop troops of 3 and 5 Para Brigades on a DZ at Winterbourne in Wiltshire. They were guided to the DZ by Eureka beacons and lights, set up by Pathfinder troops dropped from Albemarles. 38 Group observers commented that the dropping from the Stirlings was horizontally accurate in most cases, but they criticised the timing and height of these aircraft as they arrived over the DZ. The importance of these parameters became all too clear when it was learned that two paratroopers had been killed during 'Drongo'. Driver Herbert Holder, of 591 Parachute Squadron, Royal Engineers, had jumped from EF270 'K' of 190 Squadron, and Private John Wills, of the 13th Battalion, Parachute Regiment, from LJ872 'V' of 620 Squadron; each of these soldiers was descending under an open canopy when he was hit by a following aircraft. However, this type of drop was never going to be easy, since large aircraft flying close together in a stream were bound to encounter serious wake turbulence from those in front of them.

At the end of 'Drongo', there was a Stirling accident at Fairford. 190 Squadron's LJ826, captained by WO Ellis, burst a tyre on landing, as a result of which the port undercarriage leg collapsed, fortunately without causing any injuries. But there was to be another tragedy before the day was ended, as a motor vehicle from Fairford collided with an American army lorry, killing Air Fitter (E) Francis Dolan. He was one of a number of Fleet Air Arm ratings who had been seconded to Fairford to work with the RAF ground crews.

On the night of 10/11 May, 190 and 620 Squadrons each sent five aircraft to Tarrant Rushton to take part in SOE operations, the last before the end of the bright moonlight that month. Over France, the weather deteriorated during the night and of the Fairford aircraft, only two were successful in dropping. Three of the 190 Squadron aircraft diverted to Hurn on their return, while two from 620 Squadron went to Boscombe Down. On board Stirling 'O', which landed at Boscombe Down, were Flt Sgt Derek de Rome and his crew, who had just had their first close encounter with the enemy.

Noel Chaffey recalled:

> Our second operational trip took us a long way south to Moissac. Over Tours, we were coned by searchlights, but Derek knew the drill and threw the Stirling into a dive to port. Soon we lost them and carried on with our mission, a little scared but with our minds at rest – if we got out of that one we could do it with everything they could throw at us. That operation was eight and a quarter hours, the longest 620 Squadron had done to date.

Over the next few days, 190 and 620 Squadrons carried out a number of fighter affiliation exercises with Spitfires from Aston Down. On 19 May, twenty-four Fairford crews took part in Group Exercise 'Exeter'. This was a daylight exercise, in which they towed loaded Horsas along a route that took them over Buckinghamshire and Oxfordshire before they reached the Group Rendezvous point at Chipping Norton. They then headed to the LZ at Netheravon, where the King and Queen, accompanied by Princess Elizabeth, watched a drop of 300 Canadian paratroops, as well as the glider landings. Having released their gliders, the Fairford Stirlings flew back to base via turning points at Salisbury and Tetbury, with tow-ropes still attached. As they approached the rope dropping area to the south-west of the airfield, at a height of about 400 feet, there was a collision between two of the 620 Squadron aircraft, LJ880 'R' and EF244 'L', which both caught fire and crashed. Their respective captains were Flt Lt Richard Francis RCAF, and Flt Sgt Arthur Haynes RAAF. There was very little chance of any of the dozen crew members surviving the accident. When the Station Medical Officer and his orderlies arrived at the crash scene by ambulance, one man was still alive, but he died soon afterwards. Sgt Ken Hillier, an air gunner on board one of the other 620 Squadron aircraft, witnessed this horrific accident, which claimed the lives of several of his friends:

> Our Nissen hut billets each housed two crews, and we shared ours with Flight Sergeant A.B. Haynes RAAF, and his crew. 'Snowy' Haynes and our pilot, 'Tom' Herbert, had come from Australia together. Whilst in the main we tended to socialise within our own crews, our two crews often visited the local hostelries, and, of course mixed in the Sergeants' Mess.
>
> On 19 May 1944, we were briefed for Group Exercise 'Exeter'. I seem to remember that we were told that the King and Queen would see the drop at Netheravon. We were scheduled to take a Horsa glider, and Snowy Haynes was to formate on our port quarter, also towing a Horsa.
>
> On completion of the exercise, we continued in the same formation, returning to Fairford, where we were to drop our tow ropes. As we came into the rope dropping area, Snowy dropped back and followed us in, and of course, being in the tail gun turret, I was ideally placed to see what followed.
>
> At this time, I suppose our height was no more than a few hundred feet. The line of aircraft coming into the dropping zone stretched back for several miles,

Sergeant Ken Hillier of 620 Squadron. (*190 & 620 Sqns Archive*)

one behind the other, except for one which appeared to be attempting to break into the line, approaching from our starboard quarter at the same height. To my horror, I realised that he was on a collision course with Haynes' aircraft and it was apparent that neither had seen the other. He flew right into the starboard wing root of Snowy's Stirling, and they both crashed in flames. No one got out.

Sgt Ron Bedford, also a 620 Squadron air gunner, had a particularly narrow escape that day:

> We had taken part in 'Exeter' and were returning to drop our tow ropes in a field near Kempsford before entering the circuit for landing. The aircraft were approaching the field to drop in a loose gaggle, when one started to cut in. I warned my skipper, and then, realising the aircraft would hit us if he kept on his course, I told the skipper to climb like hell. He did. The other aircraft passed underneath us, but I shall never know how his tail fin missed my turret. Unfortunately, he then struck another aircraft on our port side and I saw them both fall away and hit the ground. I was told afterwards that one of the gunners was found in his turret in a hedge, but though he bore no signs of any injury, he died as he was lifted out.

Sergeant Ron Bedford of 620 Squadron. (*190 & 620 Sqns Archive*)

Jim Jefferies was one of the many local people who were left with vivid memories of this accident:

> That afternoon I was released from school early, and outside I found Charles Zimmerself, an American army sergeant, whose unit was responsible for assembling armoured vehicles in readiness for

the D-Day landings. We had struck up a friendship some weeks earlier. Not only did this kindly sergeant give me fruit and other items which were extremely scarce, but I was also writing to his niece, Sylvia, in Chicago.

On leaving the sergeant I wound my way towards home. In the distance, a number of Stirlings high-tailed over the tree-tops. Suddenly, the flight seemed to go higgledy-piggledy. I saw something pitch into the ground. When I looked again, a plume of black smoke was filling the sunlight.

I ran home and told my mother. I can't remember what she said, but we went out into the back yard. By this time the pillar of smoke and flames had reached awesome proportions. Four or five of us village boys raced to the crash site via the old washpool lane. The two aeroplanes had fallen onto a hedgerow, still locked together and were burning fiercely. Filled with the stench of burning oil and melting metal, the heat was intense. Beyond, the tail section of one Stirling still stood upright. It was from this section that the rescue services were working to extricate one man, but he died while he was being treated on site.

I was one of the last to leave the scene. The flames had gone out, the birds were singing again and grazing cattle moved towards the centre of the field. But as I walked away, I was swept by a feeling of intense sadness. I remember my mother saying to one pilot, 'Tell them on the airfield that we're all dreadfully

Flight Sergeant A.B. Haynes RAAF (pilot), Sergeant G. Powell (navigator), Sergeant A.T. Franks (wireless operator), Sergeant J.W. Taylor (flight engineer), Sergeant R.M. Cotterell (bomb aimer) and Sergeant G.P. Jones (air gunner), killed near Fairford, 19 May 1944. (*190 & 620 Sqns Archive*)

sorry about the awful accident.' I know this was said with every vestige of sincerity, and I can remember how she waited in worried silence, dreading that some of the boys for whom she did laundry had been involved.

Thomas Higgins' diary:

19 May

There was a cross-country this afternoon. Two aircraft pranged. Christ, what a mess. Fourteen [sic] guys went for the proverbial. Tough break for 620 Squadron for they have lost a few crews recently.

I damn near landed the kite this afternoon. I came close but not quite. Had to overshoot, dammit. Ah well, I'll get a landing in.

We did a bit of 'fighter affiliation' with a Mosquito and gave him a bad time. After his initial attack we had him coming and going – stuck on his tail, and had there been a front turret (and he a Jerry) he would have had it. Every time he would turn to get behind us we'd anticipate his turn and beat him to it, therefore he would be square in our line of sight. We had 90° of bank, and 4 plus on the turn indicator – which is some going in a Stirling.

According to the newspapers 'Der Tag' should be coming off pretty soon. They can't put the damn thing off for ever. The airborne units are fully trained now, or nearly so. I think – mind you I only think – that the airborne boys are going to take it on the chin when this effort starts. Jerry is keeping too many aircraft in reserve for this 'do' and should it come off on a moonlight night, well – make mine a coke.

During the night of 20/21 May, a signals exercise, 'Flint', was conducted by 38 Group. All five operational stations in the Group, including Fairford, took part in this exercise, which was intended to ensure that each could cope with its share of the huge volume of radio traffic expected to be generated during the forthcoming invasion.

'Flint' was followed on 22 May by 'Trap', which ran until early in the morning of 24 May. The latter was mainly a 'paper' exercise, for the benefit of the Operations Staffs of 38 and 46 Groups. They evaluated procedures for resupplying airborne forces, including Special Air Service troops, who had 'landed in Northern Ireland'. The various stages of this simulated assault were similar to those planned for the invasion. No flying was carried out as a part of 'Trap', but lorries did deliver supplies to the aircraft dispersals at Fairford, where one of the Stirlings was made available for loading practice.

As 'Trap' was starting on 22 May, most of the Fairford Stirlings were flying on a Station Exercise, 'Turnround'. Twenty-one aircraft from 190 Squadron, and twenty-two from 620 Squadron, took part in this exercise, the first phase of which culminated in a paratroop drop. There was then a refuelling stop, before the aircraft set off again, this time with gliders in tow. 'Turnround' therefore provided the aircrews, ground crews and army personnel with a realistic rehearsal for the sequence of events they would follow on D-Day.

Noel Chaffey recalled:

Exercise 'Turnround' was performed under the watchful eyes of AVM Hollinghurst and a number of high-ranking officers from Group Headquarters. Our Stirling aircraft were all assembled on the airfield, awaiting passengers from the airborne forces who were now living under canvas at Fairford. The gliders were filled with troops, jeeps and field guns as they would be on D-Day.

Airborne troops unload a trailer from a Horsa glider during Exercise 'Turnround'. (*190 & 620 Sqns Archive*)

Our Church of England Padre, Squadron Leader Chrissop, went by, astride one of the paras' little motorbikes, black cassock in full flow, stopping to beg from the tankers some petrol for his bike and a drop or two more for his lighter. He was a great guy, and used to distribute our Australian Comforts Fund parcels, containing knitted socks, balaclavas, gloves, scarves, razor blades and soap, each with a little note wishing us good luck and sometimes including an address. There were also some lovely sheepskin jackets – I never did get one of these and I quizzed the Padre about this at a squadron reunion after the war. He laughed and told me that he used to 'flog' them in the village and the 'funds' he got enabled him to throw great parties for the children in Fairford Village Hall from time to time during our stay there.

Whilst on the subject of the village, I must record the love and devotion that was felt for us in Fairford, especially for the overseas forces stationed there. A wonderful family befriended me and demanded I bring my washing to Mum, and each time I called to collect and pay for the service it would be neatly folded on the corner of the table in the front room. One just walked in and sat down for a chat on any visit and there was always a cuppa going. Their eldest son was in the army in North Africa and we used to discuss the war out there. I do hope he got home safely. They were a real down-to-earth, loving family and I wonder if some family elsewhere would have supplied such comfort to their son. I found this attitude everywhere I went in Britain, during my stay, more 'refined' than in Aussie, but nevertheless the same, loving and caring for family and friends. Can't say it's the same in the world today, more's the pity.

Two hundred paratroops, who would soon be flying across the English Channel to Normandy, used ten of the Fairford Stirlings to practise ditching drills on the

Members of Warrant Officer Herbert's 620 Squadron crew: left to right, Sergeant Ernie Fletcher (flight engineer), Sergeant 'Jock' Johnson (bomb aimer), Sergeant Ken Hillier (air gunner – in his turret), Warrant Officer 'Tom' Herbert (pilot) and Sergeant Eddie French (wireless operator). (*190 & 620 Sqns Archive*)

morning of 27 May. The next day, aircrews from 620 Squadron took part in Exercise 'Kingo'. This was carried out in the local area to give them some practice in evasion tactics. The pursuers, from the Gloucestershire Constabulary and the Home Guard, were given the slip by thirty-four of the seventy-two 'fugitives'.

SOE operations were flown from Tarrant Rushton on the nights of 28/29 and 29/30 May. On both these occasions, 190 and 620 Squadrons each sent a single aircraft to France, but none of these sorties was successful. For the final SOE operations of the month, on the night of 30/31 May, three aircraft from 190 Squadron, and two from 620, flew out of Tarrant Rushton. A 190 Squadron aircraft, captained by Fg Off Kilgour, was the only successful one. WO Herbert and his 620 Squadron crew experienced particular difficulties when they ran into an electrical storm and had to turn back.

There was a short break from SOE operations and all the usual training flights, when a Station Sports Day was staged at Fairford on the last day of May 1944. During the month, several film shows had been laid on, the Padre had started a recreational library, and the Station Gardening Scheme had been busy with further sowings. However, in contrast to these peaceful, everyday distractions, there were suddenly signs of much tighter security around the station. Operation 'Overlord', the long-awaited invasion of Normandy, was very close at hand.

# CHAPTER 4

# D-Day

## 6 June 1944

In the spring of 1944, the huge military build-up throughout the south of England could hardly go unnoticed, even by the most casual of observers. Nevertheless, the plans and preparations for Operation 'Overlord' needed to remain closely protected, as personnel at RAF Fairford were firmly reminded, shortly before D-Day.

John Smith, 6190 Servicing Echelon, recalled:

> Those not on essential duties were detailed to attend a lecture for all ranks. It was given by a Squadron Leader from Intelligence. He said he had been in the area for two weeks, going into shops and pubs. Then he proceeded to call out people's names, telling them who their families were, where they came from, etc. This information was gathered, he said, merely by listening to conversations. Unfortunately, details of an operational nature were also gleaned, and if he had been an enemy agent, things could have gone badly wrong. He concluded by saying 'Careless talk costs lives!'

Low clouds and strong winds swept across southern England on the first day of June 1944. Special operations from Tarrant Rushton were cancelled, as were paratroop drops by the Fairford Stirlings. On 2 June, air tests accounted for most of the flying at Fairford, since aircraft serviceability was now the priority. During the afternoon came the order that all personnel were confined to camp. For the next four days, contact with the outside world was severely restricted, but an open-air 'Gang Show' did go ahead as planned, and special dispensation was given for a delivery of beer to be made to the station.

Don Mason, 620 Squadron, recalled:

> For some weeks before D-Day, we had been aware that something was afoot. The perimeter fences around our base at Fairford were repaired and strengthened and patrols with dogs were initiated. During the middle of May, we had begun to receive more army personnel, including paratroops of the 6th Airborne Division, who camped near the airfield. Eventually the station was closed and no one was allowed to enter or leave. A ban on telegrams and phone calls in and out was imposed, and commissioned officers were given the job of censoring mail. Some of the letters were nostalgic, some sad, some downright smutty. It was a chore that we all took in good part but it signified even further that an event of a most serious nature was impending.

George Neale, 620 Squadron, recalled:

> I was the Duty Officer on the night they closed the station and a lady came up to me, asking if I could help her get out, because she was one of the cleaners,

'A' FLIGHT 190 SQUADRON
June 1944

'B' FLIGHT 190 SQUADRON
June 1944

The aircrews of 'A' and 'B' Flights, 190 Squadron, in June 1944. (*190 & 620 Sqns Archive*)

The aircrews of 620 Squadron, shortly before D-Day. (*190 & 620 Sqns Archive*)

This photograph of the Commanding Officer of 620 Squadron, with his two Flight Commanders, was taken outside a public house on their way back to Fairford after the D-Day briefings at Netheravon. Left to right: Squadron Leader 'Bertie' Wallace DFC ('B' Flight), Wing Commander Donald Lee DFC (CO) and Squadron Leader 'Bill' Pettit OBE DFC RCAF ('A' Flight). (*Mrs R. Lee via 190 & 620 Sqns Archive*)

and they had locked her in. She said her husband was waiting for her to get him his tea, so I said I was awfully sorry and would try to get a message to him. They only lived just the other side of the airfield, but the camp was so secure that she had to stay and we put her up for the night.

On 2 June all the Squadron and Flight Commanders in 38 Group went to Netheravon for a conference, at which they were briefed on the air routes to be used on D-Day, and shown detailed models of the DZs and LZs. The few suitable dates for the start of the invasion were determined by the need for low spring tides to expose firm sand at daybreak, as the first of the seaborne troops arrived on the beaches. The plan also required reasonable weather, without excessive cloud cover, so that the full moon associated with the spring tides could provide illumination for the initial airborne assault in the early hours of D-Day. Considering these factors, it probably came as no great surprise to the senior officers when they learned that D-Day was scheduled for Tuesday 5 June.

The first specific D-Day briefings at Fairford were for the pilots and bomb aimers, on 3 June. Thomas Higgins of 190 Squadron included a cautious reference to the 'plans', as he continued to record events in his diary:

2 June
Just returned from leave this morning and just about in time for the second front. No sooner had I set foot on the station than I found that we are all confined to camp. No more leave, days off, or outgoing and incoming mail. The Squadron is sealed as tight as a drum in spring. The aircraft were all flight-tested today and haven't otherwise been flown for almost a week.

The glider pilots' rings are twitching these days. Ha! Ha! They've got one tough job. Only one trip to do but what a trip!

3 June
It won't be long now. I know all the plans already. They're too important to put in the book just yet, though.

We met troops we are to take over, shined up the aircraft nose, and all is ready for 'Der Tag', which will be very soon.

Our mess was an interesting sight today for assembled there were Special Airborne, Paratroop Officers, and war correspondents, who are to go in with the first wave of paratroops, all discussing the invasion, which is quite natural. Very calm at that.

The paratroops, members of the 6th Division, are *very* calm and happy. They all know what they are to do and how to do it. Personally, I think they don't realise what they're getting into, though, for they have one tough job in front of them.

The equipment they carry is amazing; everything from Tommy guns to plastic explosives, which is something new to me. All they have to do is take a chunk out and put a fuse in – wham!

This is going to be the biggest attack ever launched by anyone at any time. All our aircraft and gliders have had these huge white bands painted around the body and wings. This is so the Navy can recognise us. Christ, I hope it helps for those guys don't know the difference between an Me 109 and a Stirling. It will probably end up with the bastards shooting down half the airborne divisions.

One job, hastily completed by the ground crews, and to which Thomas Higgins referred in his diary entry of 3 June, was the application of 'invasion stripes' to the aircraft. Even in this time of great urgency, the materials required to complete the

A Stirling takes off with a Horsa in tow, both emblazoned with invasion stripes. This position on Fairford airfield next to an active runway, was normally out of bounds. On this occasion, Flight Sergeant Derek de Rome of 620 Squadron had been authorised to taxi his Stirling there, to carry out a compass swing. Never one to miss a good photo opportunity, Flight Sergeant Noel Chaffey captured this scene, which epitomises RAF Fairford in 1944 (*N.R. Chaffey*)

job were carefully measured out – each Stirling was allowed 6½ gallons of black distemper, and 9¼ gallons of white, plus four brushes to paint these markings on the wings and rear fuselage. Smaller quantities of paint and only two brushes were issued for each of the Horsa gliders.

For well over a year before D-Day, an extensive deception operation, code-named 'Fortitude', had been providing the Germans with misleading information, from which it was hoped they would draw the wrong conclusions about the time and place of the invasion. The information was divulged using a variety of methods, which included generating wireless traffic to indicate a build-up of imaginary ground forces in certain parts of the UK. Because there were relatively few flights out of Fairford and the other 38 Group stations during the week running up to D-Day, another important part of the signals trickery was to give enemy eavesdroppers the impression that a normal flying programme was going on. At Fairford, this was achieved by the Stirling wireless operators keeping their airborne radio frequencies alive with apparently routine transmissions.

Noel Chaffey, 620 Squadron, recalled:

> Shortly before D-Day, the wireless operators from both 190 and 620 Squadrons were ordered to go to the radio section and complete exercises on the ground transmitters. This was undertaken as though we were flying, so that the airwaves would be full of signals, though no aircraft were actually airborne. This we did for three consecutive days, with the intention of confusing enemy listening stations across the Channel.

Air tests continued at Fairford until 4 June, when all the Stirlings were grounded for final checks. While these were being carried out, the station was visited by the

Wireless Operators of 620 Squadron at Fairford; Flight Sergeant Noel Chaffey RAAF is seen standing, far left. *(190 & 620 Sqns Archive)*

C-in-C Allied Expeditionary Air Force, Air Chief Marshal Sir Trafford Leigh-Mallory. He addressed all the RAF aircrews and Army glider pilots, though not everyone was too impressed, as one officer noted.

Thomas Higgins' diary:

June

The C-in-C of our Force paid us a visit today. Air Vice-Marshal [*sic*] Mallory by name. Everyone thought he was a pain in the ass, and after he finished his speech someone murmured 'Thank Christ for the Americans'. He said the same thing over three times, only with different words on each occasion. 'Tough job, blah, blah; You're tough, blah, blah, you can do it, blah, blah; without the Air Force the entire operation would not take place, blah, blah! The success of the invasion depends on the Air Force, blah, blah, blah!'

The navigators and bombardiers were briefed today; the entire route, etc. Still too damn important to go in here. The weather has taken a turn for the worse but the met man assured me tonight that all will clear for 'Der Tag'. I hope the hell it does. Anyway, it's raining right now.

Some 'erk' (ground crew) type from a nearby airborne drome left camp, was caught, and got four years in the clink. Which goes to show that they are not fooling around.

There is quite a lot of drinking going on in the mess, crap shooting, etc. But old Higgins Junior is just taking this thing in an easy style, which is typical of a Higgins at any time, invasion or just a pub crawl.

On 4 June, paratroops at transit camps in Oxfordshire and Wiltshire boarded lorries that were to take them to Fairford, to join the members of the airborne forces who were already at the airfield. Late in the afternoon, a lone Airspeed Oxford landed at Fairford, bringing Top Secret instructions and maps from 38 Group, but it now seemed unlikely that the weather would be good enough for the initial landings in Normandy to go ahead early the next morning. By the time the paratroops arrived at Fairford, it had been decided to postpone the start of the invasion for 24 hours, so they were sent back to their camps. While understandably frustrated by this delay, these soldiers were, at this stage, perhaps more fortunate than the many who had set sail for rendezvous points in the Channel, only to find themselves facing miserable sea sickness after their progress had been halted.

For the Stirling crews, Horsa pilots, and the airborne troops remaining at Fairford, the tension was also beginning to tell. The extra day of waiting provided some with an excuse to have quite a few more drinks, the result of which was some boisterous behaviour.

George Neale recalled:

We'd been locked in for three days, doing nothing, and we were just waiting for the word to go. One big party was going on in the Officers' Mess, with some high ranking officers in with us. There was a group of four, including a General and a naval Captain, sitting playing bridge at a table, when all of a sudden there was a terrific roar. Army officers (and some officers from the RAF) gave the shout 'Charge!', and they went down through the Mess, ploughing everybody out of the way. Up went the table, the cards and in fact the officers around it. Those responsible had been drinking rather more than they should have done, but one of the senior officers said, 'Gentlemen, I think we should retire at this stage', and they simply walked out of the Mess and went to their billets.

Things were not much better in the Sergeants' Mess, as Malcolm Mitchell of 190 Squadron observed:

> The atmosphere in the Mess became electric. After the evening meal, 6th Airborne Division lads, glider pilots and others began drinking and letting off steam, a process which ended with them stacking up all the furniture in the mess at one end of the building. They then proceeded to climb this piled-up jumble to reach the metal struts holding up the roof – from which they then attempted to swing. We staid RAF men could only watch in amazement.

Early in the morning of Monday 5 June, the Supreme Allied Commander, General Eisenhower, took the decision to proceed with the invasion. The weather was still very unsettled, but there was a prospect of some improvement by the morning of 6 June. Throughout 5 June, further instructions were received at Fairford. These included details of diversion airfields allocated to 190 and 620 Squadrons. Hampstead Norris in Berkshire was the first choice, and Long Marston in Warwickshire the second, if bad weather made recovery to base difficult after the initial airborne assault, code-named 'Tonga'. This operation would be carried out during the early hours of 6 June, in order to secure the key points along the eastern flank of the Normandy beachhead.

Thomas Higgins' diary:

5 June
Well, we're on again tonight!

At 1645 hrs on 5 June, the 190 Squadron crews attended their briefings, which were followed by those for the 620 Squadron crews at 1730 hrs. They all learned that they would be taking part in Phase II of Operation 'Tonga'. In Phase I, six Horsas would be towed by Halifax aircraft from Tarrant Rushton and landed at 0020 hrs on 6 June, close to the bridges over the Caen Canal and the River Orne, east of Bénouville. These gliders carried a small *coup de main* force, charged with capturing the bridges, which needed to be kept intact at all costs. This action would preserve a vital route from the beaches to the DZs and LZs east of the canal and river. At about the same time as these glider landings, Pathfinder troops of the 22nd Independent Parachute Company would be dropped in the area between the Orne and Dives rivers, by Albemarles based at Harwell. These troops had the task of taking control of three zones, designated 'N' (on the north-east side of Ranville), 'K' (west of Touffréville) and 'V' (west of Varaville). They needed to set up lights and Eureka radio beacons on each of these zones, to guide in further Albemarles from Brize Norton and Harwell. These aircraft would be bringing advance parties, of 5 Para Brigade to DZ/LZ 'N', and of 3 Para Brigade to DZs 'K' and 'V'.

During Phase II of 'Tonga', Stirlings from Fairford and Keevil, and Dakotas of 46 Group, would carry out the main drops of 3 and 5 Para Brigades. As part of the 5 Para Brigade assault, the Stirlings of 190 and 620 Squadrons had the job of dropping paratroops of the 7th Parachute Battalion on DZ/LZ 'N', half an hour after the glider landings next to the canal and river bridges. The 7th Battalion troops were required to hold DZ/LZ 'N' and make contact with the *coup de main* troops at the bridges. The Fairford Stirlings were also transporting support troops, including sappers of the Royal Engineers, who had been given the task of clearing obstructions from DZ/LZ 'N' in readiness for Phase III of 'Tonga'. This final stage of the initial airborne assault would comprise glider landings on DZ/LZ 'N' and at the Merville coastal gun battery. Throughout 'Tonga', Mosquito night-fighters would be providing cover for the troop-carrying aircraft and gliders, as well as carrying out intruder sorties over enemy airfields.

The evening of 5 June saw the return to Fairford of the paratroops who had made a wasted journey the previous day. They were given a meal, before attending a service conducted by the 7th Battalion's Padre, Captain Parry, who was to go with them when they parachuted into Normandy. After the service, the paratroops boarded lorries for the short journey onto the airfield, where the Stirlings of 190 and 620 Squadrons were marshalled according to their order of departure.

Each vehicle stopped at its allotted aircraft, identified by a number chalked on the fuselage, and the passengers stepped down, heavily laden with parachutes, weapons and equipment. Although it was nearly 2300 hrs, darkness was only just falling, since Double Summer Time was in operation. While waiting to board the aircraft, the paratroops gathered around their platoon commanders to take a last look at maps of the DZ area. They were doing their best to concentrate on the task that lay ahead, but some had obviously adopted a fatalistic attitude, as they were offering prized possessions, such as watches and pens, to those staying behind at Fairford – remarking that they, the paratroops, might not be needing them much longer.

Don Mason recalled:

On 4 June we had been called to briefing and the plan was revealed. We were to fly 22 paratroops with their equipment and drop them at Ranville, on the east bank of the River Orne. There they were to assist in holding the bridge over the Orne, in order to protect the left flank of the beachhead when the invasion came onto the beaches early on the morning of D-Day.

We were to take off just before midnight on 5 June to drop the paratroops at about 0110 hours, 6 June. In our aircraft, LJ865, 'D-Dog', we carried a BBC War Correspondent, Guy Byam, who jumped with the paratroops. He was subsequently lost in February 1945, on a mission to Berlin with an American Fortress Group. The paratroops were all quite small men, armed to the teeth and jumping with kit bags full of gear strapped to their legs. These were good-humoured, brave men, but I would have pitied anyone who came up against them. We were issued with tin crickets, those toys that make a click-click sound when squeezed, being told that all Allied forces would have them and that in the event of being forced down they would be a means of identifying ourselves to our own troops as being friendly.

Shortly before 'Tonga' commenced, each Stirling's engines were run for a short time to warm them, but then shut down to allow the paratroops to climb on board. Everything appeared strangely quiet, as the signal to go was awaited. When it came, engines were restarted without delay and the Stirlings began to taxi towards the runway holding point.

Twenty-three Stirlings from each of the two Fairford squadrons took part in 'Tonga', carrying a total of 887 paratroops. At 2315 hrs the first of the 190 Squadron aircraft, captained by Wg Cdr Harrison, lifted off from the runway and climbed into the rapidly darkening sky, with the others following at 10-second intervals. The 620 Squadron aircraft took off from 2330 hrs onwards, led by Wg Cdr Lee, with Gp Capt Wheeler acting as his co-pilot.

Ron Remfry, 6620 Servicing Echelon:

Plane after plane were soon roaring down the runway. The sky was alive with the sound of aircraft circling until it was time to head away to the south. Then the silence descended. That silence stood out in my memory as we knew that the invasion was on, but we had no idea where, nor how effective it was. All we knew was that we were on 24-hour standby, and that if and when the aircraft came back, they had to be serviced and readied for immediate action.

The Fairford Stirlings climbed initially to 2,500 feet, before turning back to fly overhead their base, where they set course for their first waypoint at Netheravon. The next heading took them towards their Group Rendezvous (RV) at Bognor Regis. This point was marked by a Eureka beacon, plus a light flashing the Morse letter 'N', to denote the route being used by aircraft destined for DZ/LZ 'N' (the other Group RVs were at Littlehampton and Worthing for aircraft going to DZs 'K' and 'V', respectively). Using the Southern Gee Chain as their main navigation aid, the Fairford aircraft descended to 1,000 feet, while cruising at 165 mph, on their way to 'Turning Point A', NNW of Le Havre. There they altered course slightly to starboard, but maintained 1,000 feet as they headed for the Target RV, located on the French coast between Cabourg and the mouth of the River Orne.

At this stage, there was little conversation on board the aircraft and lighting was kept to a minimum, as the crews sought to identify their landfalls visually. Under a bright moon, visibility was initially good, but conditions became less favourable as the French coast drew near, with cloud cover reported as 7–10/10ths at 2,000–4,000 feet. However, most of the crews were successful in monitoring their positions using Gee, in spite of a weak signal from one of the transmitters. There were some reports of enemy jamming of the Gee chain, but this proved to be ineffective for the most part.

As they crossed the French coast, many of the Fairford Stirlings ran into anti-aircraft fire, and paratroops in several aircraft received shrapnel wounds. To make matters worse, some pilots were forced to take evasive action just as their troops, weighed down with parachutes, weapons and equipment, struggled to stand up in anticipation of the signal to jump. The large aircraft became even more vulnerable as they reduced speed and height, aiming to be at 135 mph and 600 feet on the run-in to DZ/LZ 'N'. Unfortunately, some of the Pathfinders of the 22nd Independent Parachute Company had landed to the east of their DZs, and many of the Eureka beacons and coloured 'Halophane' lamps had been either lost or damaged during their container drops. Furthermore, the effectiveness of the surviving Eureka beacons at the DZs seemed to be very limited. Less than a quarter of the 38 Group crews were able to detect them, and then only out to a range of about five miles at the dropping height.

The Fairford crews pressed on as best they could. As each Stirling arrived over DZ/LZ 'N', its navigator gave a green light to his paratroops, commanding them to jump. Once the stick had cleared the aircraft they were followed by supply containers from the bomb-bays. The parachute static lines were hauled in and the aircraft turned sharply to port, to head eastwards. This was soon followed by a turn onto a northerly heading, which was maintained until a position abeam Le Havre.

The Fairford Stirlings then altered course to the north-east, and climbed to 5,000 feet, to ensure they were well above a force of Bomber Command Stirlings and Halifaxes operating at 1,000 feet. These bombers were taking part in Operation 'Titanic', which involved the dropping of 'Window' strips over the sea, in order to produce large and confusing returns on the German radar screens. The 'Titanic' force also dropped dummy paratroops and a 'live' patrol from the 1st Special Air Service Regiment, near Yvetot. Both dummy and real troops were equipped with pyrotechnics to simulate gunfire, the intention being to fool the enemy into believing a large-scale parachute drop was taking place a considerable distance from the true area of the landings.

Overhead Ypreville-Biville, a small village inland from Fecamp, the Fairford Stirlings turned onto a north-westerly heading, to take them towards Bognor. They carried out a cruising descent over the Channel and levelled out at 2,500 feet, which was maintained until they reached Fairford. To reduce the risk of collision in the crowded airspace that night, navigation lights were switched on within 15 miles of the English coast.

Don Mason recalled:

So eventually, all loaded, we took off at 2340 hours on 5 June, with everyone excited, somewhat fearful, but glad to get on with it. There were no incidents on our outward flight to the DZ, but the sea between the Isle of Wight and the turning point over the Channel (called if I remember rightly 'Piccadilly Circus'), was alive with boats and ships of all types and sizes.

The night was fairly clear and we came up to the Normandy coast on track, but we had previously needed to orbit mid-channel, otherwise we would have been slightly early for our ETA; at briefing it had been impressed on us that we were to drop our troops on an exact location at a precise time, hence our manoeuvre. The DZ was approached at the 600-feet drop height, which was critical if we were not to fly into other paratroops dropping ahead of and around us. It was part of my job to go to the rear of the fuselage to lower the guard which prevented the troops' parachute strops from wrapping around the tailplane and elevators in the slipstream, and to open the door in the floor of the fuselage for the troops to go, and to see that they went. Then I had to help wind in the strops by winch on either side of the fuselage, before closing the door and retracting the guard. As I returned to my position I had been exhilarated by this action but was exhausted by the effort. While this was going on there was no sign of activity on the ground, with no flak, so obviously we were not expected!

Our flight plan for Operation 'Tonga' then required us to fly in a north-easterly direction as if we might be making for the Pas de Calais, but apart from a few bursts of light flak and tracer in the Le Havre area there was little opposition at this stage and we returned to base unharmed.

By the time the Fairford Stirlings dropped their paratroops, the canal bridge near Bénouville had been successfully attacked by the glider-borne troops of the Oxfordshire and Buckinghamshire Light Infantry. Their arrival in Normandy must rank as one of the most remarkable feats of airmanship during the Second World War, as the glider pilots landed in a confined and marshy space next to the canal, with no illumination other than moonlight. To the east of this, the river bridge was also quickly taken, even though the attacking force was depleted after one of the three gliders assigned to this objective landed a long way from its intended touch-down point.

The troops of the 7th Parachute Battalion, dropped by the Fairford Stirlings, had the task of forming a defensive perimeter around the bridges, as well as protecting DZ/LZ 'N'. However, they were scattered over a wide area when they landed, and this caused serious delays in their regrouping. As D-Day dawned, the sound of naval guns announced the start of the beach landings, but by then the Germans were counterattacking and the 7th Batallion faced a very difficult situation. 'A' Company was cut off in Bénouville and sustained heavy casualties, among them the Battalion's chaplain, George Parry, who was killed. 'B' Company, at Le Port, and 'C' Company, surrounding a nearby *château*, were also engaged in fierce fighting as D-Day wore on. The paratroops did hold the bridges, until they were relieved later in the day by troops from the beaches, but it was a close run thing.

Between 0048 and 0112 hrs on D-Day, the 38 Group squadrons dropped 2,026 troops and 702 containers over Normandy, but one Halifax and five Stirlings failed to return. Three of the missing Stirlings belonged to 620 Squadron, and were shot down by flak before they could reach DZ/LZ 'N'. Stirling EF295 'J' was captained by the 'A' Flight Commander, Sqn Ldr W.R. Pettit, and EJ116 'U' by Flt Sgt A.H. Barton. These two aircraft crashed close to each other, some 13 kilometres east of DZ/LZ 'N', while Stirling EF268 'R', captained by Fg Off I.N. Caskey, crashed just to the east of Dives-sur-Mer, near the Houlgate coastal battery. All the crew members and paratroops on board EJ116 and EF268 were killed.

A number of the Fairford Stirlings, including the three lost by 620 Squadron, ran into an area of concentrated anti-aircraft fire, which aircraft flying further to the west seemed to have avoided. Viewed from the air, the River Dives bears a resemblance to the River Orne, so it is possible that some crews wrongly pinpointed their positions as they reached the French coast. The extensive cloud cover over France, a westerly wind that was stronger than had been forecast, and the problems with Gee may also have been factors contributing to a situation in which some aircraft flew east of their intended track.

Two members of Stirling EF295's crew survived their crash, one of whom was Sgt Bert Pryce, the air gunner. The author is indebted to Bert's son, Philip, for providing

Flying Officer Irvine Caskey RCAF (kneeling, left), with the members of his 620 Squadron crew and their ground crew, in front of Stirling EF268 'R', lost on Operation 'Tonga'. (*190 & 620 Sqns Archive*)

the following detailed account of the harrowing events surrounding the crash of EF295:

My father, Bert, joined the Royal Air Force in April 1942 as an air gunner and signed on as a Regular for twenty-one years. After completing training in early November 1943, he and his crew initially joined 513 Squadron, flying Stirlings at Witchford, but within a couple of weeks the squadron disbanded and they went to 620 Squadron at Leicester East. At that time, the crew comprised: WO Andy Arnesen RNZAF (pilot), Fg Off George Watkins (navigator), FS Ted Atkinson RNZAF (bomb aimer), FS Bob Kebbell (wireless operator), Sgt Geoff Maund (flight engineer) and Sgt Bert Pryce (air gunner). Shortly after this posting, Andy Arnesen left the crew owing to illness, and Sqn Ldr Bill Pettit took over as captain.

On the night of the 5/6th June 1944, they were tasked to fly Stirling EF295, carrying fifteen paratroops from 591 Parachute Squadron, Royal Engineers, and two (the Intelligence Officer, Lt John Shinner, and his assistant) from HQ Royal Engineers. 591 Para Squadron's task was to clear a LZ for the gliders, and the sappers carried 5 lb sausages of plastic explosive around their chests, to be used in blowing up obstructions.

The flight over the Channel was uneventful, but as the aircraft crossed the coast of France, Bert saw tracer rounds coming from the starboard quarter and he rotated his turret to engage. Seeing a Ju 88 night-fighter approaching, he fired over open sights towards it, attempting to put it off, but the top of his turret shattered and showered him with shards of Perspex and metal. The fuselage and wings were also hit. This attack did not continue, but then EF295 was coned by searchlights and fired on by the coastal defences. At a few hundred feet there was little that Bill Pettit could do to avoid them.

The green jump light went on and four of the paratroops were able to escape before the red light came on again; the Stirling had now lost too much height for safe jumping. Of the four paras who jumped, three were captured, while the fourth, Driver Jacklin, escaped by swimming around to the beachhead. Meanwhile, in the rear of the fuselage, Bob Kebbell was fighting a fire with extinguishers passed to him by Bert, who had vacated his damaged turret. Bob Kebbell heard over the intercom that Bill Pettit was wounded in the neck, and Ted Atkinson was trying to help Bill fly. EF295 was heading westward towards a ridge of high ground just inland from Dives-sur-Mer. By now both starboard engines were on fire and though the fuselage fire was out, the aircraft was too badly damaged to fly much further.

Sergeant Bert Pryce.
(*A. Pryce via 190 & 620 Sqns Archive*)

A farmer in the area saw the Stirling flying in a shallow dive, possibly trying to crash-land. But, approaching the ground, the starboard wing hit a large tree on the edge of a field and the aeroplane crashed in a flash of fire. Both wings of the Stirling disintegrated, and the fuselage broke just aft of the wings. The cockpit area was in flames and Bill Pettit, George Watkins, Ted Atkinson and Geoff Maund were killed outright in the crash, along with three of the paratroops. Ten of the paratroops survived the crash, although two were badly injured, one of whom died next day in a German Field Hospital.

A fire was burning in a nearby field, and the survivors heard a lot of shooting and could see tracer flying around. The fire was the blazing wreckage of Stirling EJ116, also from 620 Squadron, which had come down with the loss of all on board, the 'gunfire' being its ammunition exploding in the flames. Both EF295 and EJ116 had crashed in the grounds of the Château de Grangues, about 20 kilometres east of Caen. Later in the night, at least four Horsa gliders also came down in the same area, two of them crashing in the grounds of the Château. One of these, carrying Divisional HQ personnel, hit trees, from which its wreckage was left hanging. Another landed just outside the grounds and a fourth about 1.5 kilometres away.

The Château was owned by the de Noblet family, but had been taken over by the German 711th Coastal Defence Division, possibly as a company headquarters. The 711th was a poorly trained, second-rate static unit, manned by a variety of nationalities and unfit troops. The officers occupied the Château, though the de Noblet family and their servants were allowed the use of some of the rooms, while the other ranks camped in the grounds of the house.

On the night of the 5/6th June, the de Noblets (including the present owner Jocelyn and his younger sister) and their staff were in the cellar of the house

Château de Grangues. (*190 & 620 Sqns Archive*)

During the summer of 1944, the AOC 38 Group, Air Vice-Marshal Hollinghurst, visited Stirling EF295's crash site. No. 38 Group records state that 'It had piled up at high speed, and it is miraculous that any of the crew survived'. This photograph shows the section of fuselage that contained the army survivors. (*190 & 620 Sqns Archive*)

along with a young Red Cross worker, Therese Ann. They could hear all the noise but at the time could do nothing to help.

Although some of the less badly injured paratroops from EF295 attempted to evade capture, all were soon rounded up by the Germans and taken to the Château. The two RAF survivors were seriously injured. Bob Kebbell awoke lying in the field away from the main wreckage. He had shrapnel wounds to his legs and burns to his face and hands. He tried calling for Bert but got no answer, so he crawled across the field to a lane and continued until he reached a small farmhouse across the road from the field. The farmer and his wife made Bob as comfortable as possible but could do nothing to help him escape as his injuries needed treatment. Later he was collected by the Germans and taken to the Château.

Bert also lay in the field, but he was too badly injured to move. He had sustained severe concussion, his right arm, left wrist and left leg were broken,

The extent of EF295's disintegration is evident from this photograph, which shows an engine cowling, with one of the Bristol Hercules engines behind it. The wreckage remained at the crash site for a long time – this photograph and the previous one were taken in January 1946. (*190 & 620 Sqns Archive*)

and he had a bullet wound in his right thigh and shrapnel wounds. He drifted in and out of consciousness, but eventually heard voices and called out for help. A German ordered him to put his hands up, but as his right arm was broken he could only raise his left arm, and was then shot through the wrist by one of the nervous enemy soldiers. With that he lost consciousness again. The next thing he remembered was being carried along a road on some sort of stretcher. It was a rough journey and when his broken leg slipped and swung over the side of the stretcher he fainted again from the pain.

All the prisoners, apart from Lt John Shinner, who had been taken away by car to another German HQ, were kept in a group on a large patch of grass

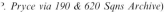

his reconnaissance photograph was taken shortly after D-Day, and shows Stirling EF295's crash site (towards he top left). To the south of this is EJ116's crash site, plus a number of bomb craters. *?. Pryce via 190 & 620 Sqns Archive*)

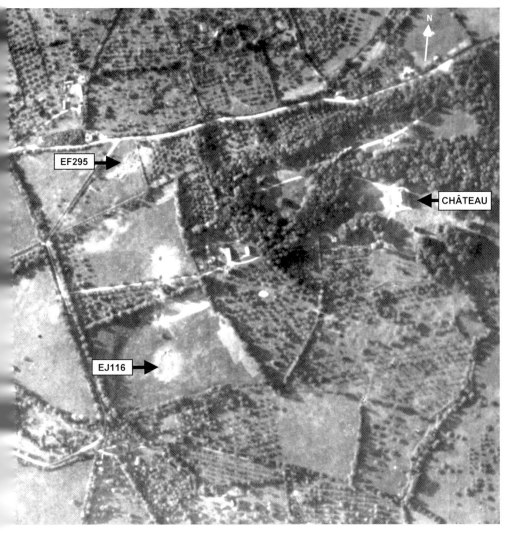

outside the servants' quarters at the Château. Bert was left to one side of the group, still on the makeshift stretcher, and covered from head to foot, probably because the Germans thought he was dead or soon likely to be.

Throughout the rest of the night and the following morning the group of prisoners grew as more paratroopers were brought in. One of these was Alan Slater, a medic with 225 Parachute Field Ambulance. He had been dropped in the wrong area and was captured near the Château around mid-morning. He was taken to the Château to treat the wounded, though Therese Ann and an older Frenchman were already trying to help as best they could.

One of the first casualties Alan Slater checked was a young RAF sergeant lying on a stretcher and covered over with a coat or blanket. He was surprised to find him still alive and he tried to treat the airman's many injuries with his limited medical supplies. Eventually, a German Army ambulance arrived, driven by an Italian Army sergeant, and Alan ensured that the airman was the first to go off to a German Field Hospital.

Later in the afternoon, the German Military Police arrived to take away the rest of the uninjured prisoners. However, the seven paratroopers from EF295, and a glider pilot, had tried to escape and had wounded a German guard. The eight men were locked in a storeroom at the corner of the servants' quarters and later taken away and shot.

The story of Lt John Shinner's survival was remarkable, not only insofar as he escaped from the crash of Stirling EF295, but also because he was extremely fortunate to be away from the rest of the prisoners at the time of the atrocity that followed. He later recorded what happened, as part of a diary written during his time spent as a POW:

D-1, the 5th June 1944, dawned fine but windy at our transit camp at Harwell. We looked out of our tents as we woke up, to see that all the aircraft and gliders had overnight become zebra-like in black and white identification stripes. I made quite certain that my kit was all correct, and stowed away my camp bed and stuff to be left behind, and put it all in charge of Driver Dunstan.

Towards the end of the morning we got our small team (an advance parachute party) together, and with the latest and largest photos of the DZ, we went through final details of our plan. In the afternoon I slept for an hour, sunbathed a little and ate a large meal at 7.00 pm. We left for Fairford, our take-off airfield, at 7.30 pm. We had a pleasant drive of 30 miles or so, through the English countryside – I think we all wondered a little how long it would be before we saw it again – I know I did.

We were to fly in a Stirling of 620 Squadron, the skipper being Sqn Ldr Pettit of the RCAF. Most of our people had been up a couple of days previously for a flight to familiarise themselves with the aircraft and crew – I had missed this because I was away at Tarrant Rushton. Once on the airfield I felt no nervousness – just a slight feeling of expectation and excitement. The wind was still strong but was forecast to drop at about 10 pm; sure enough, it did.

The trip across could not have been more uneventful. Until 20 minutes before jumping time we had the lights on, then the rear gunner went to his turret, the lights went off, and for a moment all we could see was the big luminous 'D' above the dinghy toggle. Then one's eyes adjusted to the moonlight coming through the portholes, and it was possible to see the ripples in the sea below. We were to jump at 1.00 am, and our last two minutes flight was overland.

Three minutes to go and leaning over to a porthole I could see the surf and a strip of sand. Red light on.

Then, someone on the beach picked up a handful of pebbles and threw them against the fuselage. Then another, and another – only they were not pebbles, they were flak. One bit nicked my right arm – it didn't hurt, but felt a bit numb. The sky seemed to be full of vivid flashes and orange streaks. Suddenly there was a flash and a burst of flame inside the aircraft – astern of where I stood. In a matter of seconds the whole of the inside of the aircraft was blazing. Each of the sappers had been carrying plastic explosive in the form of 'sausages' (for the demolition of obstruction poles on the LZs) and one poor chap had his hit, and it burned fiercely. Five or six of us at the forward end of the fire were forced forward towards the main spar by the flames. I felt the flames singeing my face and yelled to someone to get the escape hatch off to let out the suffocating smoke. I told one of the sappers (Reardon-Parker) to go forward to the radio cabin to find out what the situation was. He contacted one of the crew, but obviously things were badly wrong up there, because they passed the order to jump and then immediately cancelled it. In any case we could not have got out past the blaze between us and the hole.

Almost immediately after this the nose dipped, there was an horrendous rending and crashing, and I had the sensation that we were being rolled over and over. It seemed to go on for an awfully long time. When all the movement stopped I became aware of something (fuel?) swilling over my face and that there was a fierce fire burning in the forward part of the aircraft, a few feet away. I also realised that I couldn't move of my own accord because I was hanging upside down, by one leg, on my static line, which had become entangled with the roof of the aircraft.

If I didn't do something I was going to cook in the very near future. Again my luck was in, and the urgent action required was taken by another survivor who came staggering my way. I yelled to him to cut me loose and in two seconds his fighting knife had done the job and we were both on our feet. We only had a few feet to walk, because just behind where I had been hung up, the fuselage was broken off and there was a pile of wreckage and dead and injured men. We couldn't see any sign of the tail!

We two set about getting some of the injured out. As far as I could tell – I was pretty dazed and shaken – there were few of us on our feet, three or four men alive but badly injured, and the others dead. The front part of the plane was a raging furnace and there was obviously nothing to be done for the aircrew. We pulled out two of the injured sappers but couldn't shift the third man who was very firmly trapped in the wreckage. There was a good deal of tracer flying about – I don't know where it came from or who it was aimed at – and a fair amount of banging.

We thought that we had crashed a little way south of our DZ and that we might be able to make friendly contact, so I left two men at the crash site and Corporal Kelly and I went to a lane at the side of the field to see if we could locate ourselves. Another fire was burning in the next field and I thought it was another unlucky one (later we heard it was the tail of our aircraft). I got out my compass and map and we started off – with difficulty because we were both injured – northwards, towards where we thought the DZ was. We couldn't make anything of the country – it was not nearly as open as we had expected – and after a while we started back the way we had come. We had not gone far before I spotted two German helmets bobbing up and down in the field on the left of the lane. At the same time they saw us and started to climb through the hedge. I let off at them with my Colt but because my arm was nearly useless it went way over their heads. At the same moment another half dozen appeared in the lane behind us, and it was a case of 'Put your hands up' or be bayoneted. We put our hands up.

The patrol which had captured us was led by an *Unteroffizier*. As we passed the wreckage of the aircraft two men were detached, went back to the wreckage and shot at something on the ground (unlike what happened later I think that this was done with humanitarian motives).

We were marched maybe a quarter of a mile and down a drive through some trees to a fair sized house, evidently a company HQ. Here we had our equipment removed and one of our chaps was allowed to put a shell dressing on my arm, after which I was tied up with a piece of rope. There was a good deal of banging and crashing going on, and the Germans were in a state of some agitation.

After what I judged to be about half an hour an officer arrived in a car. He immediately ordered me to be untied and I was separated from the others, put into the car back seat alongside him and we drove away. We travelled about four miles, twice running through road blocks and once narrowly avoiding a dead German lying in the road. Our destination was a fairly big (Battalion or Brigade, or even Division) headquarters. I was taken into a small room where a senior staff officer, in mess kit (red stripes on trousers etc.), was sitting with a phone in each hand. He was furious at the intrusion – I was filthy and dripping blood onto his carpet – and I was hastily removed and taken to an office where there was an Intelligence Officer. He was totally reasonable and correct. He first produced a British para medical orderly, who dressed my arm as best he could. The IO then gave me a superficial search (none of the searches I had revealed the set of British codes for the day, which I was carrying and managed to dispose of next day. Nor was my army issue wristwatch, which I wore under bandages, ever found, and I brought it back to England).

The IO asked my number, rank and name. He then asked for further details, with the suggestion that by giving them, news would get quickly to my family. When I refused, he made no attempt to press the matter. I was then taken away to a stable and locked in with about eight other people.

Lt Shinner was eventually moved to a POW camp, *Oflag* 79, where he was reunited with Major P.A. Wood, one of the few who managed to jump from EF295 before it crashed.

On D-Day, fifty-two Allied personnel died in the area immediately around the Château de Grangues, as a result of the aircraft crashes, executions and fighting. These casualties were buried in temporary mass graves in the grounds of the Château, then re-interred in the Commonwealth War Graves Commission Cemetery at Ranville after the war.

Bert Pryce said very little about his D-Day experiences until 1987, when his son Philip started to research what had happened on that fateful day. Bert knew that Bob Kebbell had survived, but they had lost touch after the war. However, Bert had not known that any of the paratroopers had survived until he received a letter from the Ministry of Defence, in answer to a query he made about Stirling EF295's crash. The Royal Engineers' Association helped Philip to get in contact with John Shinner, whose enthusiasm brought forth a mass of information and other contacts, including Alan Slater, the former medic who had given Bert first aid.

Bert Pryce was soon back in touch with Bob Kebbell, and also made contact with John Porter, whose brother, a Navy telegraphist, died in the glider that had crashed into the trees on the Grangues estate. From these three gentlemen came the proposal that the loss of so many on D-Day, at a place remote from the main actions of the Normandy campaign, should be commemorated by way of a special memorial. They were successful in receiving support from many individuals and a number of Service Associations, and raised sufficient money to pay for a plaque to be placed in the village churchyard at Grangues. This was unveiled during a ceremony on 7 June 1994, but since neither Bob nor Bert felt up to attending such an emotional occasion, Philip Pryce (then serving in the RAF himself) laid a wreath on behalf of the 620 Squadron veterans, ten of whose comrades had died at Grangues.

The first of the Fairford Stirlings to return from Operation 'Tonga' touched down at 0217 hrs on D-Day. Except in the case of one 190 Squadron aircraft, which came back with eighteen paratroops still on board, all their crews reported having reached the DZ. Twenty-seven of the Fairford Stirlings were found to be unserviceable after the operation, many of them as a result of damage by flak and small arms fire. The ground crews set to work immediately and it was thanks to their efforts that all but two of the aircraft were repaired in time to take part in Operation 'Mallard', the main glider lift during the evening of D-Day. Most of the aircrews who took part in 'Tonga' were also detailed to fly on 'Mallard', so after debriefing and breakfast they tried to get some sleep. During this interval between 'Tonga' and 'Mallard', Thomas Higgins found time to write a very colourful and topical account of the start of D-Day, in his diary:

6 June

Just returned. The greatest invasion in history is now on, and I do mean ON!!!!

There are quite a few things I would like to put in this morning but I'm too damn tired, so will only enter my experiences – will put the rest in later.

First of all, we've known our target for the past few days; Caen area. Our dropping zone was 4 miles this side of Caen and 1½ miles from the Orne river, an open field about 1½ miles by 2. We were to drop paratroops who were to take the bridge which crosses the Orne river and canal. They knew their jobs and we knew ours. So here goes.

We were off track on the way to the south coast and almost ran into the balloon barrage at Southampton. Christ! The squeakers were going like mad. Their sound is horrible – eek – eek – eek – enough to panic anyone. I picked up a pinpoint and map read us to our forming-up zone which was designated by a white light flashing 'N'. From there we dropped to 600 feet and crossed the Channel. By this time streams of aircraft were all around us, all carrying paratroops. The channel was filled with shipping but all I could see were a number of invasion barges in two long lines. The British Navy was to have stretched from Cherbourg to Le Havre, but not until later. As yet they were still forming up.

As the French coast came into view I could see sporadic machine-gun fire (at our aircraft). Then it grew in intensity and over the mouth of the Orne river one Stirling was absolutely coned in eight to ten streams of this light cannon or machine gun tracer. We were headed straight for it, which was off track. Using this as a pinpoint we altered course and crossed the coast dead on track. There were a few ack-ack guns on our port but they were busy with other kites which were near them.

From the coast to the DZ the time was 2¼ minutes. A minute passed and then we ran straight into the shit – light A/A guns. There was a fierce fire burning on the ground – one of our kites. Well these guys came damn close. We were coned in machine-gun fire.

Then we reached the DZ and thousands of paratroops were coming down. We damn near ran into a number. Machine-gun fire was coming up from the river bank and near the north-west corner of the DZ we were in the middle of it. The tracer seemed to come right into my compartment. Boy, it was a tense moment. I thought I could hear the stuff hit the kite. Finally we zig-zagged our way clear (I was looking for a place to hide but there isn't any).

The troops for the most part were in the DZ but a few of them were a bit outside. The machine gunners were also shooting at the paratroops as they were going earthwards. It was some sight.

We then dropped the supplies and made for home. Ran into a bit of A/A fire but it wasn't meant for us, crossed the coast in cloud and came back to base. Damn near crashed into another kite before landing.

The Lancs are just returning from a bombing trip now, and the Forts are on their way out. It's like a thunderstorm.

6 June (later)

The initial operations of the invasion are a terrific success. The troops we dropped have taken the bridges over the Orne river and canal, the entire coastal area (our sector) is in British hands. This includes the town where the light flak is situated – thank the Lord.

One of the big shots sent us a wire congratulating us on our accuracy and tremendous (ha! ha!) fortitude, etc. If only he could have seen me – ha! ha!

We're on again tonight, or should I say today, for it's a daylight operation with gliders. The LZ is on the right side of the Orne and two miles inland. We are No. 2 kite and are leading the Squadron Leader (Major). There is to be great fighter cover – we will need it. Half the kites are without guns. Take-off is 7.30. We reach the LZ at 9.15, I hope.

We are to cross the Channel at 800 feet, climb to 1,000 feet to release the gliders, dive to 200 feet, drop the containers and ropes and then whip out over the Channel at 200 feet. At the East Coast up to 2,000 feet back to base. Anyway that's the plan.

We have sixteen squadrons of British Mustangs and Spits as our personal escort and the entire US Eighth and Ninth Air Forces as indirect protection, for they are going to shoot up all the Jerry dromes for 200 miles around our area. Christ! This should be some show. The navy is said to be stretched right across from Cherbourg to Le Havre. We just can't miss this! Well, that's all for now, folks.

We lost three kites on the first op last night. Our old pal Sqn Ldr Bill Pettit, former Flight Commander at 199, is missing. He was one swell guy. He also had the DFC which he won over Berlin last summer. A swell guy and a great leader.

Oh, yes! Part of our job which our boys had last night was to capture a local Mayor who is a Quisling. Other than that no prisoners were to be taken. Every Jerry was to have been killed.

A Horsa lifts off the runway at Fairford. (*190 & 620 Sqns Archive*)

> One of our men shot himself before take-off last night. I guess it was an accident. I hope so, for his sake, anyway.

During the afternoon of D-Day, the crews of the Fairford Stirlings and Horsas attended the briefings for the main glider lift, Operation 'Mallard', which was to be completed in daylight. Between them, 190 and 620 Squadrons were to tow thirty-six gliders carrying thirty-three jeeps, twenty-nine trailers, eleven motorcycles, eight 75-mm guns, and 254 soldiers of 6 Air Landing Brigade. By the time the briefings were taking place at Fairford, the Horsas had been loaded with their cargoes and were positioned out on the runway. The troops boarded them half an hour before the start of the operation, scheduled for 1910 hrs at Fairford.

Right on time, a green light was flashed to Wg Cdr Lee, 620 Squadron's CO, who was piloting the first Stirling in the long line of tugs and gliders. As soon as his combination had taken off, it was followed by the others in a carefully planned sequence. With 190 and 620 Squadrons each contributing eighteen aircraft to 'Mallard', it took fifty minutes to get all the combinations airborne.

Ivan Fairfax, 6190 Servicing Echelon, recalled:

> During the evening the tug aircraft formed up on one side of the runway, with the gliders on the opposite side. Immediately prior to take off, aircraft and gliders were connected with the towing cables. With precision timing they took to the air, gradually to form a disciplined air armada which reached all horizons. It would have been a startling if not frightening sight to any foe, and I felt proud to have had a small part in its preparation.

Mike Dauncey, Glider Pilot Regiment, recalled:

> On D-Day, half of 'G' Squadron of the Glider Pilot Regiment flew to Normandy from Fairford. It was an incredible sight to see the take-off of the

Crews of the Glider Pilot Regiment at Fairford, June 1944. *(190 & 620 Sqns Archive)*

tug-glider combinations. There was a carnival mood and everyone not going (including me, worse luck) assembled on the runway – the Station Commander, aircrews, glider pilots, clerks, WAAF ground staff, drivers and even the cooks in their white hats. Every combination was waved off to great applause. Miraculously, there were not as many casualties as had been anticipated and our squadron's glider pilots were back at RAF Fairford a few days later.

The Fairford Stirlings and Horsas climbed to 2,500 feet, before turning back to set course overhead the airfield. Cruising at a speed of 145 mph, they passed over Middle Wallop, *en route* for their Group RV at Bognor, and then descended to 800 feet before reaching a turning point about 20 miles off the French coast.

Arthur Batten, 190 Squadron, recalled:

What a sight to remember, and to be part of. As we crossed the English coast the crew up front were remarking on the ships ahead and what they could see! I waited in the tail, still looking back and seeing aircraft above and below, and then having reached the Channel I saw this amazing sight, ships of all sizes and types, a naval and air show of an immense armada, heading for the French coast.

Ernest Fletcher, 620 Squadron, recalled:

Approaching the south coast, the sight was unbelievable. The sky appeared to be full of tugs and gliders and fighter escorts, all with their white stripes painted on the wings and fuselages, and below, the sea was full of ships of all shapes and sizes. A column of ships stretched from England to the French coast and it just looked as though you could have walked across the Channel on their decks.

Operation 'Mallard': Stirlings towing Horsas on the evening of D-Day. (*Imperial War Museum, CL 22*)

As the slow-moving tugs and gliders approached the French coast, fighter cover was provided by Spitfires and Mustangs weaving high above them. Ready to offer assistance, to those unfortunate enough to ditch, were forty Walrus and five Warwick air-sea rescue aircraft, together with 100 high-speed launches from the RAF Marine Craft Units. After a bright morning, cloud cover had increased during D-Day, bringing with it some light rain. Visibility was reasonably good in the evening, at 10 to 15 miles, but the glider pilots had to work hard to maintain station behind their tugs, as a gusting north-westerly wind swept across the Channel. These tricky conditions contributed to the loss of a Horsa towed by one of the 620 Squadron Stirlings.

Noel Chaffey recalled:

When it came to our turn to 'join the party', we had containers in the bomb-bay, a full load of fuel and were towing a Horsa, No.189, with two glider pilots, Staff Sergeant Turvey and Sergeant Stanley, and five soldiers of the 12th (Airborne) Battalion, The Devonshire Regiment, equipped with a jeep and trailer.

Safely airborne, we climbed to gain our position in the streams of similar aircraft and gliders from Fairford and neighbouring airfields. We crossed the coast and turned towards Normandy, with our glider pilots flying in the 'high tow' position. They were experiencing a roughish ride because of the turbulent air, not only from the weather but also from the many four-engined bombers in the stream ahead. These were at different heights and the mixing slipstreams caused considerable difficulties. We were flying over what can best be described as a carpet, a patterned carpet, of grey-blue with dark boats trailing white wakes. Air-sea rescue launches were making diagonal patterns across the convoys. We must have looked an impressive sight from sea level with the continuous flow of the huge Stirlings – all black on the underside, interrupted by the newly-painted triple white bands on the fuselage and wings, the invasion markings.

Coming up to the French coastline, word came from our glider, via the cable plaited into the tow-rope, requesting permission to descend into the 'low tow' position, in preparation for the release over the LZ. As we would soon be near the LZ our pilot, Derek, re-trimmed the Stirling and gave permission for the Horsa to change position. Just then a strong gust of air swung us aside and we heard a loud bang, and we shot forward and upwards with the engines screaming.

Our Horsa had snapped the rope when it came down through the turbulent air of our slipstream. Having broken loose its pilots were committed to heading for the

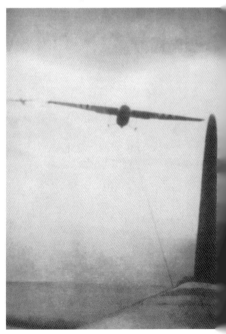

Flight Sergeant Noel Chaffey took this photograph of the doomed Horsa, moments before its tow-rope broke. (*N. R. Chaffey*)

Operation 'Mallard': Horsas and a Hamilcar on Landing Zone 'N'. (*Imperial War Museum, CL 59*)

sea, just off the French coast. Our navigator, Ben, quickly plotted our position and I broke radio silence to alert the air-sea rescue service. As we circled overhead we could observe soldiers on the wing of the Horsa, still floating on the rough sea. Our flight engineer, Frank, got the Stirling's rubber raft ready to throw out when we flew over the ditched glider, which then began to sink and quickly went under.

The Target RV for the Fairford Stirlings and their gliders was over the French coast, just west of the mouth of the River Orne. As they reached this position, about one and a half hours after take-off, the crews could see that the port of Ouistreham, to their left, was practically deserted, although there were signs of heavy fighting just north of Caen.

Henry Hooper, 620 Squadron, recalled:

On approaching the French coast we were presented with an impressive sight, with ships of every description, including the battle cruisers standing off, bombarding the enemy positions, and the aircraft and gliders going into the landing zones. The only opposition most of the aircraft experienced was from small arms fire, which appeared to be coming from a building on the coast as we came back, and some collected one or two bullet holes.

From the Target RV, the Fairford Stirlings climbed to take their gliders to their release height of 1,000 feet. They were aiming for a position north-west of LZ 'W', which was situated on the west side of the Caen Canal, between Bénouville and Ouistreham. LZ 'W' was marked out with two parallel landing strips, whereas LZ 'N', to the east of the Orne, had four strips, one of which was reserved for the large Hamilcar gliders. Aircraft destined for LZ 'N' had assembled into their stream over Littlehampton, and on the run-in to their Target RV on the French coast they were flying parallel to, and three miles east of, those going to LZ 'W'.

As they approached their glider release point, members of one of the 190 Squadron crews had problems when they experienced runny eyes, triggered by fumes from an overheating Gee set. Otherwise, everything was fairly straight-forward at this stage. The Eureka beacons were now working well, and ground markers and smoke identified the individual landing strips on LZ 'W'. Using the primitive tug-glider intercom system, the Fairford navigators passed information on wind speed and direction to the glider pilots, to assist them in planning their approaches. Each Stirling then held a steady course, leaving its Horsa pilots to decide the right moment to release from the tow-rope.

A total of 110 gliders were landed on LZ 'W' within a period of twenty-eight minutes, though there appeared to be some confusion as to the correct direction for landing. In any case, later arrivals were faced with limited choices as they selected their touchdown points in a field that was cluttered with gliders being unloaded. Inevitably, there were some collisions on the ground, but most of the damage to the gliders was confined to broken wingtips, and there were few serious injuries to their occupants. The enemy had placed obstruction poles across the area that included the LZ, but these proved fairly ineffective, since many of them were so short that the gliders' wings passed over the top of them.

During Operation 'Mallard', the aircraft of 38 and 46 Groups towed 257 gliders, all except ten of which arrived at the two LZs. Four Horsas, including the one towed by Flt Sgt de Rome's Stirling, broke away from their tugs *en route*, but no Hamilcars were lost. By the evening of D-Day, the troops holding the areas around the bridges and the DZ/LZs urgently needed larger-calibre weapons to repel German armoured vehicles. The massive fleet of gliders, bringing troops equipped with motor vehicles, howitzers, anti-aircraft and anti-tank guns, must have therefore presented a most welcome sight to those already on the ground.

Once its glider had released, each Fairford Stirling jettisoned its tow-rope and dropped nine supply containers, before turning to the right and heading for home. Since it was still light, the low-flying Stirlings were easy targets for light flak and small-arms fire, which hit seven aircraft from 190 Squadron, and six from 620 Squadron. Flying past the invasion beaches, they had to negotiate a further hazard in the form of Allied barrage balloons tethered across their track. Over the Channel, they took a route that was the reverse of the one followed on the way to France.

After providing assistance to their ditched glider, Flt Sgt de Rome and his crew had rejoined the stream of aircraft heading for the container DZ.

Noel Chaffey recalled:

We still had our supplies to drop, so we climbed back up into a lower position in the oncoming stream – this time mostly Dakotas towing Waco Hadrian gliders. We also observed increasing activity of enemy AA fire and could not help wondering why so many of the smaller aircraft were being hit and damaged whilst we, in a larger four-engined bomber, at a lower altitude, were just flying through the enemy fire.

The DZ was clearly visible and our bomb aimer, Bryan, gave us a slight alteration to course, bringing us straight in over the field. With a quick trip of the switch the containers were released, their parachutes opened and they descended into the designated area. With a lower weight the Stirling had an increased burst of speed and we quickly headed back to the coast. After returning over the Channel, Bognor Regis was our allotted landfall point and then we flew direct home to Fairford, with very mixed feelings because of the loss of the glider.

On landing we quickly inspected the Stirling for any damage – we had not sustained a single scratch! Then it was into the trucks back to Station HQ, from our dispersal, which was the furthest away from all the buildings. There was a special debriefing that night. We gave details of our glider's plunge and Derek went to the office to ascertain the fate of its crew. We eventually learnt with regret that both the pilot and co-pilot had been killed on impact with the water. Their bodies were never found. Privates Palmer and Nicholls also died, but were presumably washed ashore, as their graves are at Le Havre. However, the other three passengers managed to get in the dinghy dropped to them, only to drift into the harbour at Le Havre, where they were captured.

It was nearly midnight when the last Stirling landed at Fairford, at the end of 'Mallard'. Among the damaged aircraft was LJ818 'K,' captained by Sgt Coeshott of 190 Squadron. This aircraft's nose was perforated by bullet holes and a larger, jagged shrapnel hole. Sadly, it brought back the body of 190 Squadron's only fatality on D-Day, its bomb aimer Sgt Clifford Bevan, who had been killed by a machine-gun bullet.

One of 620 Squadron's aircraft failed to return from 'Mallard'. At debriefing, Sqn Ldr Dave Gibb and his 190 Squadron crew reported having seen this Stirling making a crash-landing on French soil:

Excellent shooting (tracer) from flak just inland on track coming out. Stirling Mk IV port outer on fire turned back inland from over sea and pranged at Plumetot (approx), believed to be a/c 'E' or 'L'.

Thomas Higgins had also observed the crash-landing of the 620 Squadron Stirling, as he noted in his final diary entry for D-Day:

6 June (later still)
Have just returned. Just had a first hand look at the Second Front. It's quite a sight but nevertheless a bit disappointing.

Our air cover was perfect. We were picked up at the English coast by Spits and Mustangs which patrolled up and down our streams like watch dogs.

Just off Selsey Bill, prominent landmark on the south coast, were over 100 small craft of various sizes, all getting ready to move across the Channel. Our air cover kept playing about at a safe distance and not a Jerry fighter was seen during the entire operation, which proves we have the air superiority they talk about.

About halfway across the Channel we converged with two other streams of airborne kites; Halifaxes with the huge tank-carrying Hamilcars; Albemarles with Horsas; and other Stirlings. One Hamilcar [sic] broke loose from its tug and crash-landed in the water. On the way out we passed over it and four men were standing on the wings. There were plenty of dinghies around so they were OK.

As we came into the Le Havre area we could see part of the Fleet parked just offshore. It looked as though there were three or four battleships in the lot, with landing craft preparing to go to the shore.

A Stirling was hit by machine gun fire from the beach; an isolated gun post. Port outer caught fire and it crashed into the water and blew up. Picked up a pinpoint on the coast, the glider released itself, we dropped the containers and rope and turned out.

The kite in front of us was hit by that same isolated machine gun. Its port outer went and it dove to the water but righted itself in time and crash-landed on the beach. It was one of our aircraft – 620 Sqdn. Some of our kites were hit by this gun and Coeshott's bombardier was killed.

We crossed the coast at 200 feet and sped back to the English coast. We could see the troops marching up the road to Caen, which was covered in dust and smoke. I waved to some fellows and they waved back. I guess they're in the middle of the fray now.

The glider op was highly successful. Personally I don't think any of them missed the LZ. So the ground force should be well supplied by now. A tank force was dropped on LZ 'N', our area last night. We were on LZ 'W' this evening. A few houses were burning near the zone and a Spit had crashed nearby, all adding to the picture. But I still think there should be more action for a second front!

The stricken 620 Squadron Stirling was in fact LJ849 'E', captained by Flt Lt Gordon Thring, a Canadian. Having released its glider and containers, this aircraft was hit by fire from guns concealed in a small wood. One of the fuel tanks in the port wing caught fire, but Thring succeeded in making a belly landing without injury to any of his crew, all of whom managed to scramble out of the aircraft just before it blew up. However, this turned out to be only the start of their adventures on French

Flight Lieutenant Gordon Thring's 620 Squadron crew, shot down on D-Day: left to right; Flying Officer M.E Price (navigator), Flying Officer H. Braathen (bomb aimer), Flight Lieutenant G.H. Thring (pilot), Flight Sergeant R.W.A. Burgess (wireless operator), Flying Officer G.F. McMahon (air gunner) and Sergeant W. Buchan (flight engineer). (*190 & 620 Sqns Archive*)

soil – Thomas Higgins' diary entry of 9 June includes an account of what happened subsequently to Thring and his crew:

Listen to this!

The crew which was shot down just in front of us the other day has returned to the Station. After crash landing they jumped out of their burning plane and went into hiding. When darkness fell they decided to find the British lines so off they went and after an hour or so of walking some troops came up to them, and one guy said 'Heil!' – which they mistook for a Yank 'Hi'. The rear gunner jumped up and shouted 'Hi Ya, Bud!', still thinking the party were Yanks. They soon found out otherwise and were promptly taken prisoner.

The Jerries took their guns and supplies and marched them along in the centre of the company, which was around fifty men. That night they spent with the Jerries and next morning resumed their marching. They were sniped at by British snipers; were under mortar fire, etc. By afternoon they were joined by more Jerries; at least twenty of the originals were killed during the first part of the day. This made the total over ninety or so. The sniping went on all day and naturally took its toll. By nightfall they reached a barn and the Jerry commander gave them the option of staying in the barn or going underground with them, which they decided to do. An hour later the barn was blown up by a direct hit.

Next day they were sniped at until the number was further cut down. Anyway, the Jerries got a bit fed up with the way the war was going and decided to let the aircrew boys take *them* prisoners – which they did. Two of the crew went out and found a British Tommy and, with the Tommy's guidance, they marched the Jerries down to the beach at the Orne's mouth – amid cheers and laughter from English Tommies. They then turned the body over to the beach party, and everywhere they went the foot-sloggers cheered like mad. It certainly must have been a funny sight; six aircrew types marching sixty-one Jerries down the road from the Caen area. They left the beach last night – arrived here today!

# CHAPTER 5

# Summer Nights

## June to August 1944

As the Allies fought hard to keep a foothold on the Normandy beachhead, the RAF carried out resupply drops. These were code-named 'Rob Roy', and started with one made to LZ 'N' by Dakotas of 46 Group, late in the evening of D-Day. These operations would continue until the 'Mulberry' harbours were assembled off the Normandy beaches, thus enabling more substantial deliveries to be made by sea.

Although 190 and 620 Squadrons took part in some of the 'Rob Roy' drops, they quickly reverted to their more specialised role of flying across occupied France at night on covert operations. From now on, these would include infiltration and re-supply drops (known at first by the code name 'Sunflower') for the Special Air Service (SAS), as well as the drops for SOE.

In the interests of maximising the enemy's surprise at the start of the invasion, no Allied special forces were deployed in France before D-Day. Delivery of airborne forces to the flanks of the invasion area had to take priority on D-Day itself, but an entry made in the RAF Fairford Watchkeeper's Log does reveal that at least one Stirling took off on a 'Sunflower' task (probably dropping an SAS advance party) at about the same time as the first of the 'Tonga' aircraft.

After training in Scotland, many of the SAS troops had moved to camps in the south of England during May 1944. They were to form a close working relationship with RAF Fairford, which was the main departure airfield for SAS troops and supplies going to France. The wartime SAS Brigade comprised two British Regiments (1 and 2 SAS), two French Battalions (3 and 4 SAS) and one Belgian Company (5 SAS), with a total strength of approximately 2,500 soldiers. Once the invasion was in progress, the SAS commenced five large-scale operations in France. These were: 'Bulbasket' (1 SAS in the Vienne); 'Dingson' and 'Samwest' (both 4 SAS, in Brittany); 'Gain' (1 SAS, near Fontainebleau) and 'Houndsworth' (1 SAS in the Morvan). Each of these operations was initiated by the dropping of an advance party, which included 'Phantom' signallers of GHQ Liaison Regiment. Before carrying out a reconnaissance of their operating area, the troops in this party would establish wireless contact with the 1st Airborne HQ in Hertfordshire, and also seek the co-operation of the *Maquis*, whose local knowledge would be invaluable when setting up bases and DZs.

In France, the SAS and the *Maquis* would work along similar lines, particularly in terms of disrupting the transport networks being used by enemy reinforcements moving towards Normandy. To carry out their tasks effectively, the SAS troops needed to be based deep inside enemy-occupied territory, rather than close to the main battle area, where their concealment would be much more difficult. Therefore, the only practicable way of sustaining these troops was by resupply drops, many of which were flown by the Fairford Stirlings during the summer of 1944.

While the aircrews at Fairford were waiting to resume their special operations after D-Day, Flight Officer Thomas Higgins of 190 Squadron took the opportunity to bring his diary up to date:

7 June
Nothing doing tonight. We are all on a stand-down, but as the camp is still well sealed it's not much use. Can catch up on my sleep though.

The entire invasion is going successfully, from Cherbourg to Le Havre, and Caen has been entered by British, American and Canadian troops. Our landings, which were at Ouistreham, were highly successful. Cherbourg should be taken before long. 13,000 air sorties made. It seems as though the Allies dropped some dummy paratroops which blew up when the Jerries touched them. Their purpose was to divert the Germans from the real paratroop landings. Some trick!

I see by the papers where Field Marshal Goering has ordered the *Luftwaffe* to either win or perish. I hope they perish. The Jerries are supposed to have at least 2,000 fighters and 500 bombers but I guess the Allied intruders are keeping them on the deck.

7 June (later)
Six kites are on tonight. I think it's a supply dropping trip but I'm not certain. Believe it or not, I feel bored. Lack of activity, I guess. It's funny how 'ops' get me keyed up and how an inactive day gives you that down and out feeling. I'd just as soon be on this effort tonight.

The beachhead resupply operation planned for the evening of 7 June, 'Rob Roy II', was postponed until the following day, but two 620 Squadron aircraft did go to France during the night of 7/8 June. They were carrying troops of B Squadron, 1 SAS, which was in the process of setting up the 'Bulbasket' base in the wooded hills of the Vienne. Flt Sgt Clement and his crew were unable to see any reception signals at the DZ, and therefore had to return to Fairford with their troops and containers still on board. The other crew, captained by a New Zealander, Fg Off Bell, reached the DZ late, but observed three white lights, plus a fourth flashing the recognition letter 'B'. As the Stirling flew over the DZ at 600 feet, an officer and eight men jumped with their kitbags, and were quickly followed by nine containers packed with supplies and equipment, including a Eureka homing beacon.

'Rob Roy II' went ahead in the early morning of 8 June. In spite of smoke haze and sea mist, which seriously impaired visibility, six Stirlings of 190 Squadron successfully dropped 142 containers, along with various panniers and packages. There was some enemy gunfire from the ground, but all the aircraft returned safely. 'Rob Roy III', which took place later the same day, and 'Rob Roy IV', early on 10 June, were carried out by Stirlings and Halifaxes, from Keevil and Tarrant Rushton, respectively.

Thomas Higgins recorded in his diary:

8 June
All our glider pilots are back on the station. It was a 100% show except for one kite which broke its rope and went into the Channel. Their Major had nothing but praise for our crews. As a matter of fact his speech this morning was the most sincere I've yet heard.

Flight Officer Thomas Higgins is seen here, standing, far left. Alongside him are the other members of his crew; left to right: Flight Sergeant D. Oxley (flight engineer), Pilot Officer A.G. Pool (wireless operator), Flying Officer W.H Chappell (pilot), Pilot Officer L.J. Crossman (navigator) and Flight Sergeant W.R. Dunkley (air gunner); kneeling members of their ground crew, including a Fleet Air Arm rating. (*190 & 620 Sqns Archive*)

Just after we left, eight Ju 88s screamed over the beachhead and inside five minutes the Spits had them all shot down. Some show! The boys say that the machine gun which caused us so much trouble was manned by a Jerry soldier and a Catholic priest. That is unconfirmed, though I will get details later.

One of the war correspondents on the Station dropped on the first night was 'on the air' tonight. He gave a vivid description of the entire paratroop operation. After he landed in a cornfield, which was just on the other side of the DZ (about that time the crew that dropped him slid out of the mess, amid roars of laughter), he made his way to the DZ where he rejoined the Division. He also told about the bridge over the Orne being taken. Good show! – for the Major in charge was dropped by our crew.

He said the boys had some rugged fighting at first but were able to hold their own until the seaborne division arrived some hours later. They also destroyed the remnants of the coastal battery which was in their sector. It was certainly a grand job.

The Lancs are going out now, even though the weather is duff as hell. We should be on again tomorrow!!

9 June

The weather has been duff all day and there is nothing on although only three crews are allowed off the station and the rest are standing by. Our crew is one of the three but the Sqn Ldr's bombardier wanted to see his wife so I am standing in for him, but I don't think there will be anything though.

Mike and Bill, two of our glider pilots, are back at the station. Mike has a Jerry 'Africa Star' – took it from a prisoner who said he was damn glad to be out of the entire mess. Mike had a few experiences. Said that the fellow who shot down all the kites was finally tagged, and that in a village a Jerry and a Catholic priest, the one I mentioned the other day, held up a number of troops before they were captured. He rode down a mined road three times before he found out that it had been mined. Also said that our paratroops took a terrific beating, not so much from the Jerries, but the Lancasters with their four and eight thousand pound bombs, of which some missed their targets and got our 6th Division paratroops. Twenty-four were completely blown to bits on one occasion.

Only one of our glider pilots was killed, out of seventy, which is really a good show. They expected to lose at least half of the Company. Therefore the boys are keen to go on another trip – which they will get before long.

Bill said the front is so fluid that 10 hours after we dropped the gliders on the LZ there was a terrific tank battle going on there, and that the Jerries are in complete possession of Caen. Landing zone 'N' was under mortar and machine gun fire all day. The bridge is still intact. One of the men won two decorations for bravery, the DCM and something else.

Jerries bombed the ships at night but didn't do much damage because of the terrific amount of flak thrown up by the beach and ship guns. Two raiders were shot down. Bill Gardiner, our Deputy Flight Commander, was talking to a Dakota crew last night in a pub. Their losses were terrific. Twenty-six kites in two nights. I think our Squadron has been the luckiest yet, without a loss, while 620 Sqn lost four with one crew saved – the one that went down in front of us the other day.

620 Sqn are taking some paratroops over tonight They're yelling and shouting like mad. You can hear them all the way across the drome. Boy! If only they knew what they are in for! There aren't many going so I guess it's a special job. Bill, our Skipper, knows where they're going and what they're going to do. This means some stupid type has been talking out of turn and should get one great extra-large kick in the rear end!

Our beachhead isn't as good as one would think by reading the papers. I hope the hell we have enough men and heavy guns, etc., ashore before the Jerry's heavy armour comes into play.

Early this morning the airborne troops of an anti-tank unit started to roll in, and now they are all set. The gliders are loaded and ready to go – maybe tomorrow. The anti-tank guns will certainly be needed when Jerry brings up his tanks and other heavy armour. There have been some tank clashes but only involving between them 150 tanks. These anti-tank guns look like they could stop just about anything, even a Tiger.

In fact, there were to be no more glider operations until the Arnhem landings at the end of the summer of 1944. Nevertheless, 190 and 620 Squadrons needed to maintain their proficiency in glider towing, so the flying programme after D-Day included many more practice flights with the Horsas, by both day and night.

There was a fatal accident at Fairford when glider towing was taking place late in the evening of 9 June. A 620 Squadron Stirling, LJ869, had been cleared by Flying Control to take off with a Horsa. As it accelerated along the runway, the Stirling crashed into another Horsa, LH562, which was being towed by a vehicle, after landing. This glider was not displaying any navigation lights. Its pilots, SSgt Fletcher and Sgt Hebberd, were killed in the collision with the Stirling, whose captain was Flt

Sgt Peter 'Lucky' Jordan. He and his crew had just been posted from 1665 HCU at Tilstock, to replace one of the three crews lost by 620 Squadron during the early hours of D-Day. Peter Jordan described the events surrounding this tragic accident:

After training we arrived at RAF Fairford on D-Day. We were airborne the next day to familiarise ourselves with the airfield and local terrain. Alas, disaster struck us on the night of 9 June. We were practising 'circuits and bumps' towing a glider. I was given the usual 'clear for take-off' by Flying Control and set off down the runway at full throttle. I was about to lift off when I saw an obstruction on the runway. I did not know what it was and in any case, it was too late to abort the lift-off. I stuck to procedure and lifted off extra carefully as I was not quite up to safety speed. We hit something but kept going. I tried to retract the undercarriage but, as I suspected, there was nothing there. I climbed to 1,000 feet, called Flying Control and reported briefly what had happened, asking to release the glider in the normal way. Permission was granted and the glider pilot landed safely. I was grateful to him for keeping his cool. On a previous occasion, a learner glider pilot had shot up into the air, pulling my tail up and sending us earthwards. Fortunately, we were high enough for me to pull out, snapping the tow-rope, leaving the glider pilot to

Flight Sergeant Jordan's 620 Squadron crew. Left to right: Sergeant Les Pountney (navigator), Sergeant 'Jock' McLeod (flight engineer), Flight Sergeant Peter 'Lucky' Jordan (pilot), Sergeant Jake Etkin (bomb aimer), Sergeant Bill Hall (air gunner) and Sergeant Ted Sykes (wireless operator). (*190 & 620 Sqns Archive*)

find his own landing spot from whence he was recovered later, unharmed but wiser. However, the night of 9 June was by no means over for us. Flying Control instructed me to fly at 2,000 feet whilst operational aircraft were sent on their way – I found out later that they had also to clear wreckage off the runway. It was nearly an hour before Flying Control tried to contact me again but the R/T had become faulty, probably because of the impact. I checked that the crew had recovered their stomachs and were in philosophical mood. I ordered our gunner, Bill Hall, out of his turret to assume the crash positions with the others. I figured that Flying Control could hear me, so I said I was coming in to do a belly landing providing they shone a green light from the control caravan at the start of the runway. As I turned onto the final approach I got the green light and instructed Bill to open the exit door and get out when I shouted 'Go' after landing, the others to then follow and clear the aircraft. I would count out the height of the aircraft as we descended. I got to 100 feet, then there was a deathly silence before the hull of the plane scraped along the runway. I cut all four sets of ignition and fuel switches and shouted 'Go!' as we came to a halt.

We finished up in the sick bay after being stuck in the arm with some concoction, which put us out cold for several hours. Next day we found out that the wreckage was that of another glider that had landed in the wrong place, without lights, unknown to Flying Control. Both the instructor and learner pilot in the glider were killed instantly – a shocking waste of life. It is a tribute to my crew that this experience was not allowed to affect their morale. We were airborne within 24 hours to make sure there were no after-effects and, within a further 24 hours, we were on night operations deep into Europe.

Sergeant David Evans was the flight engineer in one of the other two crews posted to 620 Squadron on D-Day:

Very early on D-Day we were awakened at Tilstock to be told that the invasion of Europe had started, and that we were posted to Fairford. We had only slept an hour or two, after landing from a long cross-country flight the night before. Although tired and bleary eyed, we had a terrific feeling of elation, for our chance had come at last to pit our wits against the enemy. We got our clearance from Tilstock arranged in double quick time, and were on our way south and nearer to where the action was taking place.

We had been allocated to 620 Squadron. We soon settled into our new quarters and met the crews with whom we were going to share some adventures in the skies of Europe. However, as a new crew we needed to demonstrate our flying abilities to our senior commanders, because they had to be satisfied that we were capable of all that was to be expected of us in the weeks ahead.

At first, we were a little frustrated at having to carry out the same old routine as at Tilstock, but after one or two cross-country flights, the opportunity came to cross the Channel for the first time. In my log book it just says 'SOE Operations'; so secret were the activities of the Special Operations Executive that we were not allowed to say where. I forget now where in France we were to take a load of supplies to the French underground fighters, but we tried to treat that first operational flight just like any other cross-country, none of us wanting to show any sign of apprehension to the others in the crew.

The worst period was the hour before take off. The procedure was to travel out in the crew-bus to the aircraft at the dispersal, near the perimeter track, about an hour before take-off. Briefing had taken place earlier in the day, and one of my jobs as flight engineer was to calculate the quantity of fuel required and the speed we would be using on the outward and return journey. On arrival at the aircraft, I inspected it to check that everything appeared normal, the most important job being to check that the cover over the pitot tube was removed, as forgetting to do this could result in an aborted take-off when the required air speed indication failed to appear. The pilot and I would then run all four engines and make various checks before shutting them down.

When all was ready, we would get out and sit around, some having a last smoke, some chatting incessantly about everything except flying, while others would be silent in thought. Suddenly the time would come to climb back into the huge aeroplane. All four powerful engines would burst into life, and we would move slowly to the end of the runway and stop to await a signal, then brakes were released and throttles opened. As the aircraft became airborne, within seconds the engines were throttled back slightly and the climb to operational height begun. Over the Channel, the gunner would ask permission to test his guns and we would hear them rattle as he aimed at imaginary targets. By now we would be looking towards the Channel Islands and waiting for the enemy to start throwing up some anti-aircraft fire. As soon as it appeared the pilot would start weaving about to foil the German AA gunners' aim.

In those summer nights of 1944 we would be presented with a wonderful display of pyrotechnics as we flew on our way south over Normandy. This was the only indication we had that the Allied armies were fighting to maintain the vital bridgehead that was needed to move on to victory over Nazi Germany. But we had a job to do further south.

'Sunflower III' operations for the SAS were carried out during the night of 9/10 June. Three aircraft from 620 Squadron dropped fifty paratroops, twenty-three containers, four panniers and a package for 'Samwest'. There were also three Keevil-based aircraft flying out of Fairford that night, to 'Dingson' DZs. The Secretary of State for Air, Sir Archibald Sinclair, visited Fairford on 10 June and talked with many of the officers who had taken part in the D-Day operations. In the afternoon, the RAF Regiment gunners who provided airfield defence were alerted to the presence of a German Fw 190 fighter in the Gloucester area, but this turned out to be a captured aircraft on an evaluation flight.

Thomas Higgins' diary:

10 June
We have three kites on tonight, the Wing Commander, Gardiner and Robertson. The W/C is getting to be a pain in the behind – always flying. Each time he goes it takes a trip from one of the other crews. He's sweating out the DSO if you should ask me.

Sir Archibald Sinclair, Britain's Minister of Air, was in our mess for tea this afternoon. Not a bad old guy.

The glider pilots who came back from France are holding a party in the mess – throwing knives in the big map of Europe, and hell in general.

The three 190 Squadron aircraft mentioned by Thomas Higgins on 10 June were taking part in 'Rob Roy V', a further beachhead resupply operation. These aircraft carried seventy-two containers, which they were intending to drop at dusk. However, this operation was beset by technical problems, including the failure of the bomb doors to open properly on Wg Cdr Harrison's aircraft, so in the event only forty-seven of the containers were dropped.

After nightfall on 10 June, eight aircraft from 620 Squadron took off on 'Sunflower IV' operations for the SAS. Two of them, captained by Fg Off Griffiths and Flt Sgt McNamara, were carrying the advance party for Operation 'Houndsworth', and dropped a total of twenty-two paratroops of A Squadron, 1 SAS, plus three panniers and a package. 'Houndsworth' became the largest SAS operation in France, and remained active until September 1944. Its troops hid amongst the hills and woods of the Morvan, around a main base that was close to important lines of communication extending north-west towards Paris. They caused substantial damage to the railways and also identified targets for bombing attacks.

In the early hours of D-Day, two officers of B Squadron, 1 SAS, and a 'Jedburgh' team, code-named 'Hugh', had been dropped into France. It had been decided that the Jedburgh troops, after making contact with the *Maquis*, would take on the task (designated Operation 'Lot 1') of putting the Limoges to Vierzon railway line out of action, while the troops of 1 SAS would deal with the Bordeaux to Tours line (Operation 'Lot 2'). The Jedburgh teams ('Jeds') were multi-national. Each team consisted of a three-man combination of British, American, French or Dutch service personnel, and included a native language speaker and a radio operator. The plan was for these teams to work behind enemy lines and liaise with the SAS and the *Maquis*, for whom they provided communications with SOE in London. During their brief period of existence, the Jedburgh teams were subject to various changes of command structure, but when they first went to France they came under the operational control of Special Forces HQ in London. This had been established jointly

Flying Officer Geoff Gawith with members of his 620 Squadron crew; left to right: Sergeant E. Edwards (air gunner), Flying Officer S.J. Payne (navigator), Flying Officer G.F. Gawith (pilot), Flying Officer I. Langdon (bomb aimer) and Flight Sergeant D.G. Jervis (wireless operator). Missing from this photograph is Sergeant K. Watson (flight engineer). (*190 & 620 Sqns Archive*)

Flight Lieutenant Alastair Jack (third from left), with the members of his 620 Squadron crew.
(*190 & 620 Sqns Archive*)

by SOE and the American OSS. Most of the Jedburgh operations were in France, with only six other teams being sent to Holland, when Operation 'Market Garden' was under way in September 1944.

On the night of 10/11 June, two 620 Squadron aircraft, captained by Fg Off Gawith and Flt Lt Jack, took off with the 1 SAS troops for 'Lot 2'. Each aircraft dropped two teams of four men. Three of the teams successfully reached their targets and completed their tasks, but the fourth landed close to German troops. One SAS trooper was captured and his comrades were forced to abandon their equipment. These operations were risky indeed, for any special forces soldier caught inside enemy-occupied territory was highly unlikely to survive as a POW.

The next 620 Squadron aircraft to take off on the night of 10/11 June was captained by Plt Off Carey. It carried two female SOE agents and some supply containers, as well as the main party for 'Bulbasket', which comprised twenty troops, including a 'Phantom' signals team. The SOE drop was carried out successfully, but the SAS troops were unable to jump because no reception lights were seen at the 'Bulbasket' DZ, situated between Limoges and Poitiers. The final three 620 Squadron aircraft to take off on operations for the SAS that night were captained by Fg Off Kay, Fg Off Maloney and Fg Off Murray. All were successful in dropping to a 'Samwest' DZ. Three Stirlings from 196 and 299 Squadrons at Keevil also flew out of Fairford that night, on an operation for 'Dingson'. One of these aircraft was successful in dropping SAS troops and containers.

Thomas Higgins' diary:

11 June

The three kites which went last night returned safely but were unable to release all their supplies because of electrical failures in their aircraft.

Just found out that we were hit by machine gun fire the other day. If we had 'Mugs' (the mid-upper gunner) with us he would have been close to getting it.

First of all today there was one kite 'on', then he was scrubbed and we were all to operate. Next our crew was taken off, then half an hour later, the W/C wanted to fly so we were put on again with him, then taken off again and finally the whole damn operation was scrubbed.

I'm telling you, boy! This is getting a bit 'cheesing' as these English types say. One minute you're on and get all keyed up, then you're off and you relax. Then you're on once again, get keyed up, and bang! The whole thing is off. It tends to get a guy down because we're not allowed off camp at all, only once a week.

Although the attempt to drop their main party on the the night of 10/11 June had failed, the 'Bulbasket' troops already in France were sending back valuable intelligence. They reported the presence of petrol wagons in railway sidings at

A group of 190 Squadron pilots, including Pilot Officer Reg Fogarty (standing, far left), and Flying Officer Jack Connell (kneeling, right), both of the Royal Australian Air Force. (*H.B. Allan*)

Châtellerault, which were then bombed by Mosquitoes in the evening of 11 June. During the night of 11/12 June, two Stirlings from 190 Squadron took part in 'Sunflower V'. This was a second attempt to drop the 'Bulbasket' main party. There was 10/10ths cloud cover, but good visibility below its 1,500-foot base, as Fg Off Connell's aircraft arrived at the DZ. This was manned by both SAS and *Maquis* personnel and displayed three lights in a row, with a fourth flashing a Morse letter 'B'. Six of the troops were dropped, and on a second pass, six more, plus thirteen containers. When the other aircraft, captained by Flt Sgt Fogarty, arrived just over an hour later, visibility had deteriorated. The DZ position was established using Gee, following which the crew were able to recognise a light flashing through the cloud. They then glimpsed the DZ itself, through a gap in the cloud, and succeeded in dropping their eleven paratroops, twelve containers and a package.

On the night of 12/13 June, 'Sunflower VI' was carried out by five Stirlings from 620 Squadron, and thirteen from Keevil, flying out of Fairford to drop SAS troops and containers for 'Dingson'. All these aircraft were successful. 'Sunflower VII' took place the next night, 13/14 June. This time, 190 and 620 Squadrons each sent five aircraft, and all but one were able to drop containers and packages, again for 'Dingson'.

On 14 June, there were further resupply flights to the Normandy beachhead. No. 620 Squadron sent five aircraft on 'Townhall IV', dropping containers on DZ/ LZ 'W', west of the Caen Canal. During the night of 14/15 June, two 190 Squadron aircraft took off on 'Sunflower VIII'. They had been given the task of dropping SAS troops and supplies to an SOE DZ, 'Historian 8', which was providing reception on behalf of the 'Houndsworth' operation. One of these aircraft, captained by Fg Off Connell, dropped fifteen troops and returned safely to base. The other was unable to drop because its crew failed to see any reception signals. Its starboard outer engine was later damaged by flak, forcing the pilot, Flt Sgt Sutherland, to make an emergency landing at Ford in Sussex.

Thomas Higgins' diary:

12 June
We were on and off an 'op' today; finally scrubbed the whole show.

14 June

We were on 'ops' tonight but the weather stepped in and everything was called off.

I'm getting fed up with this life. When this damn second front started I thought we would be operating day and night. But no such thing the damn things are rationed.

We still can't have our leaves. I wish to hell they would get off the dime and start them again. And our days off are worked in such a manner that it's almost impossible to go to London.

15 June

Nothing doing tonight for us but two crews are on from 'A' Flight.

Operations from Fairford planned for the night of 15/16 June were cancelled because of bad weather. During the night of 16/17 June, Flt Sgt Fogarty and his 190 Squadron crew took part in 'Sunflower IX' and were successful in dropping twelve troops of D Squadron, 1 SAS, plus fourteen containers. This was done in support of Operation 'Gain', which had the job of halting enemy transport through the 'Orléans gap'. Two other 190 Squadron aircraft should also have dropped to 'Gain' that night, but both became unserviceable and were unable to take off.

On the night of 17/18 June, three aircraft from 620 Squadron took off with the 'Houndsworth' main party. Between them, they were carrying forty-five troops and forty-two containers, to be dropped on DZ 'Houndsworth V'. The crews were briefed to the effect that if they found the DZ, but there were no reception signals, they were authorised to drop 'blind', up to five miles away. As things turned out, two of the Stirlings reached the DZ area, but precise navigation was impossible because of very bad weather, so they did not drop. The third aircraft, LJ850 'Y', captained by WO Robert Crane RAAF, failed to return from this operation and has never been found. Its last known position, from a radio fix plotted at 0050 hrs, was over the Channel, outbound for France. This Stirling almost certainly went down in the sea, with its crew of six, and one officer and fourteen men of 1 SAS.

Stirling LJ850 'Y' at Fairford, just before D-Day (chalk guidelines have been applied to the rear fuselage, preparation for the painting of 'invasion stripes'). The nose bears the name 'Yorkshire Rose', above a white ro motif. This aircraft had a short operational life. It was flown by Warrant Officer Crane and Flying Officer Murr: on Operations 'Tonga' and 'Mallard', respectively, before it was lost with Crane, his crew and passengers, on t night of 17/18 June 1944. (*190 & 620 Sqns Archive*)

arked next to Stirling LJ952 'Yorkshire II' of 620 Squadron, Flying Officer 'Ben' Crocker, navigator in the ...e Rome crew', relaxes in the spring sunshine. (*N.R. Chaffey*)

During the evening of 18 June, nine Stirlings from 190 Squadron, four from 196 Squadron and five from 299 Squadron took off from Fairford on a beachhead re-supply operation, 'Townhall VIII'. They arrived over the DZ on time and dropped 401 containers, sixty panniers and a quantity of spare tyres in only four minutes. The aircraft from 196 and 299 Squadrons then returned directly to their base at Keevil. Low cloud over northern France had been forecast for the night of 18/19 June, but the weather turned out to be excellent for 'Sunflower XII', as three aircraft from 620 Squadron dropped containers (and paratroops as well, from one of them), in support of 'Dingson'.

Thomas Higgins' diary:

18 June
We were on a 4½ hour 'cross-country' last day. Christ! This place is like an OTU.

620 have lost another kite. Nine of our kites went to France this evening and have just returned. They look damn nice in formation.

After D-Day, the fleet of Horsa gliders was seriously depleted, since very few had been brought back from France, in spite of efforts to salvage any that could be returned to service.

After the loss of Stirling LJ850 'Y' on the night of 17/18 June 1944, LJ952 became 620 Squadron's 'Y-Yorker'. The latter aircraft, bearing the title 'Yorkshire II', was flown regularly by Flight Sergeant Derek de Rome, seen here in the cockpit. (*N.R. Chaffey*)

Consideration was therefore given to equipping the Glider Pilot Regiment with additional types, such as the American-made Waco Hadrian, four of which were delivered to Fairford on 19 June. The Hadrian had been towed by RAF aircraft during the invasion of Sicily in July 1943, though it carried a much smaller load than the Horsa. Some flight trials were carried out at Fairford to assess the suitability of the Stirling for towing the Hadrian, but there is no record of this tug-glider combination ever being used operationally by 190 and 620 Squadrons.

Thomas Higgins' diary:

21 June

Well, we're on again tonight – special low-level priority job. We were especially put on by the Wing/Co and only the three most experienced crews are going. The job is to take sixteen paratroops, who have been especially trained to lead the French patriots; also a number of containers filled with special equipment for their use.

It's going to be damn hard to find the spot – cloud conditions and bad weather most of the way. Also high ground with hill fog near the DZ. The British Navy has been told that we are coming so I hope the dim bastards have enough brains not to belt at us.

We are to cross the French coast to the east of the River Orne. Jerries have moved a number of flak guns there, so we should have a bit of fun. We are taking a Canadian second pilot tonight, just over from Canada. But his job is purely 'passenger'. If anything goes wrong I take over. We are to be diverted to Chivenor, which is a few miles from the Bristol Channel.

After various changes of plan, a total of five aircraft from 190 Squadron went to DZs 'Houndsworth 9A' and 'Houndsworth 9B' during the night of 21/22 June. They were all successful, with a total of forty-seven SAS troops being dropped. It is thought that a number of Keevil Stirlings also flew out of Fairford that night. These operations had gone ahead in the knowledge that the early morning weather would be too bad for recovery to base, but the 190 Squadron aircraft were diverted to Tarrant Rushton on their return, instead of Chivenor, which had been the original intention.

Thomas Higgins' diary:

22 June

Just returned. It wasn't a bad trip. A bit of flak was put up; saw a large fire on the southward journey, and a twin-engined job kept playing games with us as we crossed the Channel on the return leg. It made two spoof attacks but never fired anything. We took evasive action and that's all there was to it.

We located the DZ OK. Les's navigation was 'bang on' for a change. Dropped the paratroops in two 'sticks'. After the first one (stick) went we turned around to come back for the second run-up and I accidentally kicked on the jumping light. So one guy 'hit the silk'. We were able to stop the rest, though. He dropped about a mile north of the DZ and should be able to find the remainder of his party. Their job is to lead the French 'underground' in a rebellion.

We damn near ran into a mountain after the final run-up. Well, that's all for now, bed calls.

22 June (later)

The odd 'bod' made it to the DZ OK so the mission was 100% success for a change. There certainly must be some organisation on the other side, for Group

HQ knew all about it within three hours, even before we returned to the station, most likely.

These special troops are the most decorated men I have ever seen, especially the officers – quite a number have the DSO and Bar. There is quite a collection of 'vets' in the mess these days, mostly with specialised jobs.

The next night, 22/23 June, was the first in a series of three in which SAS drops were made for Operation 'Grog'. Five of 190 Squadron's aircraft set out for DZs 'Grog A' and 'Grog B'. Three of them dropped containers and troops; one dropped troops, but did not drop its containers on a second run, because the DZ lights were then extinguished; and one had to return to base with its load, as no reception signals were observed. 'Grog' had been set up near Pontivy by French troops of 4 SAS, after the break-up of the 'Samwest' and 'Dingson' operations, both of which also involved 4 SAS in Brittany. The 'Samwest' base, near St-Brieuc, had been stormed by the Germans on 12 June, after being in place for only a few days. Some of the troops from this operation moved south and joined 'Dingson', near Vannes, but the Germans attacked the base there on 18 June. Despite this second setback, many of the 'Dingson' troops remained in the area and continued to receive supply drops during June, July and into August. They were able to carry out further successful attacks on enemy road and rail communications, in anticipation of the American advance through to Brest in August.

On the night of 23/24 June, ten aircraft from 620 Squadron took part in 'Sunflower XV' for the SAS. The DZs were 'Grog A', 'B' and 'C', and eight of the aircraft were successful in dropping containers and panniers. Another 620 Squadron aircraft, captained by Flt Lt Jack, went to a 'Bulbasket' DZ, but was unable to drop, since no reception signals were observed. 'Sunflower XVI' went ahead the next night, 24/25 June, as eight aircraft from 620 Squadron took supplies to the 'Grog A' and 'B' DZs. This time, seven were successful in dropping.

Several supply drops to 'Bulbasket' and 'Grog' DZs were planned for the night of 27/28 June, but all were then cancelled, leaving just one Fairford aircraft to fly on 'Sunflower XVIII' to DZ 'Gain 7'. Sqn Ldr Gilliard and his 190 Squadron crew made a successful drop of containers and panniers to this SAS DZ, in spite of their aircraft having sustained flak damage while crossing the French coast near Cabourg, on the outbound journey. The only other 38 Group aircraft operating that night was a Halifax from Tarrant Rushton, which dropped two paratroopers, a Jeep and supplies, also to 'Gain 7'.

The Fairford Stirlings took part in various exercises during the last few days of June. One of these was appropriately called 'Find-it', in which sixteen crews from 190 Squadron flew on a long cross-country to a remote location near Clun, in the Marches. A Eureka beacon had been set up there and was detected at a range of over 40 miles, as the aircraft ran in to 'bomb' a target with sandbags. Despite his grumbles about this type of exercise, Thomas Higgins admitted that his crew scored top marks on 'Find-it' – and, in doing so, won the squadron sweepstake!

26 June

Yesterday we were on our one long 4½ hour 'cross-country'. A pain in the neck, but we won 16 shillings anyway. We were the most accurate over the DZ which was in the mountains. Christ! They sent us over 200 miles of water and a 3¾ hour journey, when we could have done it with a 1½ hour cross-country. Nuts! This place is worse than an OTU.

27 June

We were to have been on ops tonight but they were scrubbed – good show!

The way our tour is worked in this Group is as follows: – 18 months on a 38 Group Sqdn or 600 flying hours in the Group. This means that operations mean no more than 'cross-countries' as far as the hours go. So I have 263 more hours to go, which means at least 30 more operations. Which is one poor show on the part of the RAF 38 Group. In the last three months our crew has only flown 90 hours. So by that you can see it's going to be quite a long time before the tour is complete.

28 June

We were on tonight, but scrubbed due to bad weather.

By the end of their first month in France, the SAS and Jedburgh troops had achieved many successes, most notably in sabotaging railway lines and attacking enemy road transport. These operations were highly dependent on the delivery of essential supplies by air, particularly when SAS patrols were equipped with light vehicles, which required tyres and other spares, as well as fuel. Most of the failed attempts by 38 Group aircraft to drop to SAS or SOE DZs were the result of either bad weather or an absence of reception signals. The latter problem was sometimes brought about by difficulties in establishing wireless contact between Special Forces HQ and personnel in the field, but there were also many occasions when a DZ was set up, but those present were forced to leave in a hurry because enemy troops were in the vicinity.

David Evans recalled:

Sometimes, although we knew we were in our target area, there was no response from the ground; no bonfire or flashing light. Our briefing for such an occurrence was not to linger, but to return for home, because the likelihood was that the enemy was active in the area.

On our second or third operation, this happened to us, but in our eagerness to supply our French allies, we kept circling hoping to see the fire lit, and time flew without our noticing. Suddenly, when we were at about 2,000 feet, all hell broke loose; we were enveloped in light and tracer bullets came up at us from all directions.

We had been caught by mobile searchlights and guns, which had been drawn to us by the noise we were making as we circled round and round. The Skipper reacted quickly and dived out of the searchlights' range, throttles were opened up and we sped away at nought feet until out of danger. This taught us a lesson, not to let our enthusiasm overcome our briefing orders.

The weather was quite changeable during July 1944, and this had a significant effect on both operational and training flights out of Fairford and the other 38 Group airfields. On several nights during the month, Stirlings returning to Fairford from France had to be diverted, or else Fairford received aircraft from other bases in the Group, according to local variations in the weather pattern. As with the previous month, there were a number of occasions in July when operations were planned, but then cancelled very late in the day, much to the annoyance of the aircrews.

Thomas Higgins's diary:

2 July

We've been on operations every day since the 27th and every night the damn things have been scrubbed.

3 July

We're on again tonight. Of all the lousy luck! A special effort, twenty-four kites of which twenty were going to Brest and the other four, of which we are one, to a more distant and important place. Well, all but our target has been scrubbed.

The weather is terrible; raining even now; low cloud all the way with a chance of clearing over the DZ. 'Met' said it would improve later, and base should be OK on return, they hope! We are carrying twenty-four containers and four extra parcels filled with guns, ammo, etc., for the French patriots, who need them at all costs.

What a ropey deal. The damn thing has been scrubbed. Christ! At this rate we'll never do an 'op'. I hope we get a day off tomorrow.

Although there was bad weather on the night of 3/4 July, two aircraft of 190 Squadron were successful in dropping supplies to the 'Bulbasket' troops. One landed back at base, while the other diverted to Harwell. There were seventeen sorties planned for 190 Squadron on the night of 6/7 July, but fourteen of these had to be cancelled. The remaining aircraft were all successful in delivering containers and panniers for 'Houndsworth', although there were some atrocious conditions over France that night.

Thomas Higgins's diary:

6 July

Well, we're on again tonight. The weather is foul and I guess the whole thing will be scrubbed later. See you soon.

7 July

What a trip!! The worst, roughest, and most exciting I've ever been on. In the first place the weather wasn't fit to take a car ride in, let alone do an operation. Even the birds were walking. But we flew! From take-off until landing we dodged terrific bolts of lightning, flew through rain, sleet and hail. We dropped out of the sky on one occasion, a thousand feet in half a second. It was the most horrible feeling I've had in all my days. Seventy tons of Stirling just quit going forward and dropped. All the way it was the same; lightning which must have been powerful as hell. I've never seen anything like it.

We found the DZ and I map-read quite a way back. Gee packed up after the terrific jolt. On the way back there was so much lightning about I just could not tell it from flak. Just this side of Paris we were nailed by a bolt of lightning – Christ! The damn thing hit the nose; blinded me and the skipper. How he kept the kite level neither one of us knows. It was just like being hit by a bomb. We flew through terrific rain all the way back to base.

When crossing the French coast a terrific tonnage of light and medium flak was being tossed up. We could also see the gun flashes of the armies in the Caen area. Coming out, we were nailed by flak. At the time we were in 10/10 cloud and Bill had to do his evasive action by instruments. We finally got clear, made our way back to base and, well, here we are. More by the grace of God than anything else.

The entire crew is shaky as hell just about now. Personally, I'm like a bowl of jelly in a spring breeze. I must admit we worked better as a crew last night than ever before. It would have been our royal asses if we did not. I found many more pinpoints than usual and the boys at the DZ were so happy to see us they kept flashing THANKS on their Aldis lamp. Bill did a great job of flying, by Christ! I think he should get the DFC for his work.

7 July (later)
Checking the aircraft this morning the armourer found one of the twenty-four containers had not dropped. It was not indicated on my after-bombing check so possibly the lightning storms had played tricks with the electrical system. Pity that. Our first 'hang-up' ever.

Over the next few nights, the Fairford Stirlings were kept busy as they attempted to carry out drops for the SAS whenever the weather permitted. On the night of 7/8 July, 190 Squadron sent three aircraft to drop further supplies for 'Houndsworth', but there was heavy rain and low cloud over the DZ, and only one of them was successful. The same night, 620 Squadron sent four aircraft to a 'Grog' DZ, but no reception signals were observed, so all their loads were brought back.

On the night of 8/9 July, Fairford aircraft went to DZs set up by 'Grog' and 'Wash'. The latter operation involved French troops of 4 SAS, based in the part of northern Brittany where 'Samwest' had previously been active. Six aircraft of 620 Squadron were operating that night, and it is believed they were all detailed to drop to 'Grog', though the surviving records are unclear on this. However, it is known

Warrant Officer Dave Dawe and his 620 Squadron crew. Standing, left to right; Warrant Officer L.H.F. Petersen (bomb aimer), Flight Sergeant A. France (wireless operator), Warrant Officer D.M. Dawe RNZAF (pilot), Sergeant D.J. Johnson (flight engineer); kneeling, left to right; Pilot Officer C.W. Walker (air gunner) and Pilot Officer W.J. Old (navigator).
(*190 & 620 Sqns Archive*)

that two of them were successful, while the other four were unable to drop because no reception signals were seen. The radio aerial on LJ566, captained by WO Dawe, was severed by flak, but the aircraft was brought safely back to base. Five aircraft of 190 Squadron took off later, in the early hours of 9 July, and all were successful in dropping to 'Wash'. The weather was reasonable over France, but closed in at Fairford during the night. One aircraft from 190 Squadron, and one from 620, diverted to Pershore in Worcestershire, where they remained until the evening of 9 July, as heavy rain put a stop to flying for most of the day.

On the night of 10/11 July, 190 Squadron sent seven aircraft to 'Grog' DZs. All except one were successful, as troops, containers and panniers were dropped. The next night, 11/12 July, six aircraft from 620 Squadron went to 'Grog', 'Houndsworth' and 'Haft' DZs, and all of these were successful in dropping troops and supplies. 'Haft' was an intelligence-gathering operation, carried out by a small party of 1 SAS troops in the Le Mans area. Three other aircraft from 620 Squadron were operating for SOE that night. They dropped to the Jedburgh team 'Ian', which was working with the 'Shipwright' SOE circuit in the Vienne and Charente *départements*.

On 13 July, drops to 'Grog' and 'Wash' DZs were planned, but later cancelled, leaving a single aircraft from 190 Squadron to go to a 'Bulbasket' DZ that night. No reception signals were observed, so this aircraft, captained by Fg Off Matheson, was unable to drop. Owing to poor weather at base, it diverted to Ford in Sussex, as did a number of other 38 Group aircraft that night.

There was cause for celebration at Fairford on 14 July, when the announcement was made of the award of the Distinguished Flying Cross to 620 Squadron's Flt Lt Gordon Thring, who had spent an eventful but thankfully short time as a POW, after he and his crew were shot down on D-Day.

Twenty-five Fairford Stirlings were requested for operations on the night of 14/15 July. The weather was favourable and there were only a couple of cancellations, though one sortie had to be abandoned later, when an aircraft punctured a tailwheel tyre. Ten aircraft of 190 Squadron went on SOE operations to six different DZs, 'Stationer' 110, 163, 168, 174, 175 and 181. These DZs all used the name of a circuit that had operated over an area extending from Châteauroux to beyond Limoges, but by this time its activities had been taken over by the 'Shipwright' and 'Wrestler' circuits. Each of the 190 Squadron aircraft was carrying twenty-four containers and two panniers, and eight of them were successful in dropping these. Meanwhile, 620 Squadron had thirteen aircraft operating that night, and all of them dropped successfully to SAS DZs.

ght Lieutenant Gordon Thring RCAF (left), h his air gunner, Flying Officer Gerry Mahon DFM. (*190 & 620 Sqns Archive*)

On the night of 15/16 July, 620 Squadron sent three aircraft on operations for the SAS, and a total of five to SOE DZs 'Stationer' 163, 166 and 181. Although the weather was good, the 620 Squadron Operations Record Book noted that the night's sorties 'were only partially successful, owing to confusion over ground signals and stiffened enemy opposition due to Bomber Command aircraft operating in the vicinity.'

SAS drops planned for the night of 16/17 July had to be cancelled on account of the weather, but the next night, 17/18 July, 190 Squadron sent fifteen aircraft to 'Dickens' and 'Grog' DZs. Between them, they were carrying 338 containers, thirty-two panniers and thirteen troops. Twelve of these aircraft were successful in dropping. 'Dickens' involved troops of 3 SAS, who carried out attacks on railway lines and roads, as well as intelligence gathering, in the western part of the Val de Loire.

In spite of a warning of low cloud and thunderstorms over France, operations went ahead on the night of 18/19 July. Five aircraft from 190 Squadron flew on SOE tasks to 'Percy' DZs, north-east of Brive, and three were able to drop their containers. It is thought that 620 Squadron sent four aircraft to SOE DZs, and six to SAS 'Grog' and 'Wash' DZs, that night. Seven of these aircraft were successful in dropping. Plt Off McNamara and his 620 Squadron crew had a special passenger, as the AOC 38 Group, AVM Hollinghurst, flew with them. Five instructors from 81 OTU at Sleap also flew in 620 Squadron aircraft that night, in order to gain some first-hand experience of the role for which they were training aircrews.

Thomas Higgins' diary:

18 July
Well; we're on again tonight. Another long, low-level trip. Only four crews from our Sqdn are on and, naturally, we're it.

19 July
Well! Some trip! The weather was duff but we made the DZ OK. Not much excitement – a few fighter flares, plus the fact that we were nobbled by seven searchlights, but soon got away. It was funny, searchlights, but no guns. I just don't understand it. Oh, well, what the hell. I'm tired, so to bed I go.

Eighteen aircraft from 190 Squadron went to SOE DZs on the night of 20/21 July, but there were severe thunderstorms over France and few of the aircraft were successful in dropping their supplies. Seven aircraft from 620 Squadron also operated for SOE that night. Their DZs included ones for 'Hamish' (a Jedburgh team working with a similar team, 'Hugh', in the Haute-Vienne), and 'Wheelwright' (a circuit that covered a wide area in south-west France). Two of the 620 Squadron aircraft are known to have been successful.

Thomas Higgins' diary:

20 July
On again tonight. It's a long, low-level one; just a bit longer than the one the other night. Weather is duff.

21 July
Quite a trip. The weather was hopeless; lightning, cloud and rain all the way. Near Le Havre the Jerry A/A guns started belting at us but they never got closer than 50 yards or so. The entire route lightning, clouds and rain predominated.

We were able to see the letter flashing at the DZ so we let the load go. We were almost nabbed by searchlights on the way out but again we managed to elude them, with evasive action. A few flares were also used in conjunction with the searchlights. Lit the place up like day. I'll bet it's going to be tough on a clear night. Jerry is putting more and more defences in the French coast area.

On the night of 22/23 July, 190 Squadron sent eleven aircraft on SOE operations for 'Felix' (Jedburgh team, working with the SAS in Côtes du Nord), 'Fireman' (SOE circuit, operating around Limoges), 'Francis' (Jedburgh team, working with the

SAS in Finistère), 'Frederick' (Jedburgh team, working with the SAS in Côtes du Nord), 'Glover' (SOE circuit, in the Chaumont area), 'Ventriloquist' (SOE circuit, south of Orléans) and 'Percy'. Nine of these aircraft were successful. There were also five aircraft from 190 Squadron flying to 'Gain', 'Wash' and 'Rupert' DZs for the SAS. Four out of the five were successful in dropping ninety-six containers, thirteen packages and two vehicle wheels. A message, to which the AOC 38 Group added his personal congratulations, was received from 'the other side' a couple of days later, reporting that the 190 Squadron crews captained by Plt Off Porter and Plt Off Brain had made 'impeccable' drops to a 'Wash' DZ that busy night.

The fifth 190 Squadron aircraft detailed for an SAS drop on the night of 22/23 July did not return. Captained by Fg Off 'Danny' Kilgour RNZAF, this was LJ882 'H', which had the 'Rupert' advance party on board. 'Rupert' was a 2 SAS operation, intended to disrupt rail transport in the area around Metz, in north-east France. Although the 190 Squadron Operations Record Book states that there were three paratroopers and one dispatcher on board LJ882, there were in fact ten personnel being carried in addition to the usual crew. Two officers and four men from 2 SAS, plus two 'Phantom' signallers, were to have been dropped, with Plt Off Copland of 190 Squadron and a trooper from 2 SAS acting as dispatchers. After its crew failed to observe any signals at the primary DZ, the aircraft was proceeding to another one when it struck high ground, killing thirteen, including the 'Rupert' commander, Major Symes. One SAS soldier, Private Boreham, survived, along with two members of the crew. Flt Sgt Paul Bell, the Canadian air gunner, escaped without serious injury. He managed to evade capture and returned to to the UK in September 1944. The other surviving crew member was the navigator, Fg Off Joe Vinet, also a Canadian:

> A stick of eight paras was to be dropped near Chaumont, but by deciding to nip in between the cloud base and the ground we clipped the forest and ploughed in. Our air gunner, Paul Bell, wasn't injured the French moved him into Paris and back to the squadron on its release. The one para and I were carried off and hidden, but were hospital cases, so the local doctor dictated, and we were sent via Chaumont military hospital to internment.

Ten of 620 Squadron's aircraft flew on SOE operations during the night of 22/23 July, but three returned without dropping, having encountered poor visibility in their DZ areas. Fg Off Harold 'Nipper' McLeod and his crew had a lucky escape when they were attacked by two Ju 88 night-fighters near Angers. Although their Stirling, LJ899 'O', was not damaged, they faced a further problem when an engine failed, forcing them to jettison their load over the Channel, before landing at Ford.

As the morning of 23 July dawned, one of the 620 Squadron aircraft was also posted as missing. This was LJ864 'A', captained by a Canadian, Fg Off Ernest Oke. It had been on its way to an SOE DZ, 'Stationer 117', when it crashed to the north-west of Limoges and caught fire. All members of the crew were killed.

On 25 June, the 1 SAS 'Bulbasket' base had moved to a new location in wooded country near Verrières, some 30 kilometres from where Stirling LJ864 crashed. The Germans soon learned of the whereabouts of this camp and attacked it in the early morning of 3 July. Caught unawares, most of the soldiers in the camp were captured. Shortly afterwards, they were executed by firing squad and buried in unmarked graves. This was usually the fate of SAS troops captured in France, but there was one particularly shameful aspect of the treatment meted out to the 'Bulbasket' prisoners; it was later discovered that three wounded men were sent to

Flying Officer 'Nipper' McLeod (third from left), with his 620 Squadron crew. (*190 & 620 Sqns Archive*)

hospital, only to be put to death when they arrived there. It is believed that the Germans killed thirty-five 'Bulbasket' prisoners in all.

A few of the troops at the 'Bulbasket' camp managed to escape when the enemy struck, and some others were away on patrol at the time. These survivors remained active in France for another month, receiving supply drops and carrying out more attacks on the railways. At the beginning of August 1944, they were flown out of an airstrip, after being relieved by French troops of 3 SAS, who had been deployed on Operation 'Moses' in the Poitiers area. While waiting to be repatriated, some of the 'Bulbasket' survivors were staying near to the site of Stirling LJ864's crash. They were able to obtain details of the aircraft's casualties, which they transmitted to the UK on 25 July. In spite of the obvious risk to themselves, an SAS officer and two of his men attended the burial of the six members of LJ864's crew at Brillac. It has been suggested that there were actually eight men on board LJ864, although there should have been no need for extra crew members, since the aircraft was only to have dropped supplies for SOE. Nevertheless, entries in the RAF Fairford Watchkeeper's Log do show that there was some confusion as to the exact number on board. The SAS and Glider Pilot Regiment were asked if any of their personnel might have gone along on an unauthorised trip, but these enquiries proved negative. The members of the ground crew who saw LJ864 depart from Fairford were also adamant that they observed only the usual six men boarding the aircraft.

It is not known whether Stirling LJ864's crash was an accident, or the result of enemy action. However, it was not surprising that some 38 Group aircraft failed to return from operations because of accidents, considering they flew at night and at low level, often in bad weather and near high ground. Flight engineer Malcolm Mitchell remembered one incident that could have very easily led to the loss of his 190 Squadron crew:

One operation to France proved very memorable, as it was very nearly our last. Setting off at night, as usual, we crossed the French coast, finding that the flak belt had more or less disappeared. So, on we flew inland, to our DZ. Reaching

116

it, we identified it and descended, to drop the supply canisters. Then up, to be away. Suddenly, the aircraft tilted nose down and on my instrument panel I saw four red lights appear – indicating that none of the engines were getting any petrol. I immediately jumped about four paces to the rear of the aircraft, where the two banks of fuel cocks were located, and threw every cock on. The aircraft then righted itself, to my relief, and the red lights disappeared.

As we then climbed away, we learned what the problem had been. Our pilot, Ikey, had a stomach upset, and, as we climbed away from the DZ he had fainted over the controls, sending the aircraft hurtling down from our already low altitude. By a stroke of extraordinary luck, that night an army glider pilot had asked to come on the operation with us, and he was sitting in the co-pilot's seat. He had reached across and pushed 'Ikey' away from the controls, and righted the aircraft. The four red lights I had seen were the result of a sudden change in 'g' [gravitational acceleration], which had starved all the engines of fuel. We had never been closer to a crash, which would have remained un-explained. As it was, we were able to make a safe journey home.

Thomas Higgins' diary entries mention the Stirling losses of the night of 22/23 July, and also describe how the presence of friendly but unidentified night-fighters could be almost as wearing on the nerves as enemy aircraft:

22 July
Well, we're on again tonight. It's truly unbelievable, 'on' three nights out of five. This Group is getting off the dime at last. It's another long, low-level job – we get all the long ones. Oh well! What the hell! Briefing is at 5.30, so I guess I'll get a few hours' sleep.

23 July
Just returned; and am I tired. The weather wasn't so bad, for a change, but it wasn't real good. Quite a bit of cloud, etc. We got the usual flak near Le Havre and a bit from the starboard as well. It was accurate for height but quite a distance away. After that it was very quiet.

I got a few pinpoints and was able to map-read – more or less – to the DZ. We let the stuff go and turned tail for home. As we crossed the French coast on the way out two kites came after us but never fired. We didn't know whether they were Ju 88s or Mosquitoes – put the wind up us anyway. Arrived back at base OK. A bit of haze but that didn't bother the skipper.

Before we took off the Wingco said our target was the toughest. Of the three long trips we were the only ones to drop. One of the three aircraft is missing. Also two of 620 Sqn aircraft are missing.

23 July (later)
As a result of last night's 'ops' two aircraft are missing and one was shot up by flak. Another kite had the same deal as we had crossing the French coast – dummy attacks by two unidentified aircraft, presumed Mosquitoes, but with a possibility of them being Ju 88s.

620 Sqn is operating tonight and tomorrow. We will only operate tomorrow if it is urgent. I don't understand it. This Group is certainly operating like mad these days. Must be a war on!

We've just had the latest news about finishing operations. The way it's worked out our crew finishes the end of August, whether we do another 'op' or not. But, the way things have been going lately, we will probably do quite a few.

Or at least be 'down' for quite a few. Personally I would like to do at least another 10 or 11 trips, but no more. Things are starting to get a bit too tough to do more than that.

The weather remained unpredictable towards the end of July, but the Fairford Stirlings flew on operations whenever possible. On the night of 23/24 July, 620 Squadron sent eight of its aircraft to 'Actor' (SOE circuit in the Bordeaux area), 'Digger' (SOE circuit, south of the River Dordogne), 'Fireman', 'Footman' (SOE circuit, Lot *département*), 'Hamish' and 'Historian' DZs. Five of the aircraft were successful, with each of them dropping twenty-four containers. The crews of the other three did not observe any reception signals.

620 Squadron was active again the next night, 24/25 July. This time six aircraft were sent to SOE DZs for 'Donkeyman' (SOE circuit, active in various parts of France, including the Yonne *département*), 'Ian', and (at unspecified locations) 'Donald' and 'Peter'. It was a clear night and all but one of the aircraft were successful in dropping their supplies. The three aircraft that went to 'Ian', 'Donald' and 'Peter' DZs also dropped propaganda leaflets, known as 'Nickels'. The 'Donald' DZ is not thought to have been connected with an operation that used the same code name, but commenced twelve nights later, when an American Operational Group (OG) went to Brittany. The OGs had been set up by the Office of Strategic Services, and were special forces units with tasks similar to those of the SAS Squadrons.

It was 190 Squadron's turn on the night of 25/26 July. Two aircraft dropped to 'Houndsworth 37' for the SAS, and three others to 'Ian 1B', 'Ventriloquist 42' and 'Ventriloquist 45' for SOE. Two aircraft that went to another SOE DZ, 'Luke 104', were unsuccessful. On 26 July, it was planned to send twenty of 190 Squadron's aircraft to SAS and SOE DZs in France. All of these sorties were later cancelled – some of them at the last minute.

Thomas Higgins' diary:

26th July

We're on again tonight!!! And it's the greatest occasion in the History of T.J. Higgins, Jr, for it's to be our last trip!!! Yep! Screened at last. It's an easy trip, too, and damn short. Brest area with containers. Happy day – see you soon.

26th July (later)

Too damn soon!! The damn operation has been scrubbed. We were taxiing down the runway, just about to take-off and it was scrubbed. It was to have been the shortest trip yet. Certainly a shame it was scrubbed – dammit.

So we still have one more 'op' to do before we're screened. Christ! I can't believe it. I think I'll volunteer to do a tour on 'Forts', with the Yanks. It should be interesting. Or would it? Anyway, I've still one more to do. Personally, I wish it was this time next week instead of now – if you know what I mean.

On the night of 27/28 July, four aircraft from 190 Squadron took containers to DZs set up by Jedburgh teams 'Francis' and 'Gilbert' in Finistère. All of them dropped successfully. No. 620 Squadron sent eighteen of its aircraft to 'Grog', 'Haft', 'Houndsworth' and 'Wash' DZs for the SAS the same night. Eight dropped, but the rest did not, since there were no reception signals at their DZs. Two Dakotas from the nearby airfield at Blakehill Farm operated out of Fairford in daylight on 28 July, taking twenty-two SAS troops, plus stores, to landing strip B14 at Amblie in Normandy.

Thomas Higgins' diary:

28 July
Our screening is still hanging on the hook. I wish the AOC would make up his mind, and quick.

The boys were 'on' last night and one of the long trips was damn tough. Fighter flares marked his track all the way. Boy! That must have had a terrific mental effect on the crew, even though they weren't attacked. These things are going to get tougher than hell before long. Mark my words!
There's a big mess dance and drink tonight – clear the deck.

29 July
Did I say clear the deck? Well! It's been cleared! And how! I've never been such a drunk in all my days. Pint after pint; quart after quart; all night long. I ended up about 4.30 (in the morning) throwing pints of beer on the mess floor. After that got too tame, bucketfuls were used. My shattered nerves – what a night!

Had a wrestling match with Bill Berry, one of the glider pilots. We had quite a tussle. After about 15 minutes I finally won.

On the night of 29/30 July, 620 Squadron took part in operations for both the SAS and SOE. Eight aircraft went to 'Grog' DZs for the SAS, and seven of these were successful in dropping containers and packages. The SOE operations were for Jedburgh teams. Two aircraft went to a DZ set up by 'Giles' (working with the *Maquis* in Finistère), and two to DZs 'Hamish 6' and 'Hamish 7'. Two out of these four aircraft were successful. The last five aircraft to return early in the morning of 30 July were unable to land at Fairford, where ground mist was drifting in, so they diverted to Harwell.

ne of the WAAF Intelligence Officers at Fairford was Section Officer Margaret Steven. She is seen left, about to y as a passenger with Flight Sergeant Derek de Rome's 620 Squadron crew, and right, observing the operation of e Gee receiver during the flight. (*N.R. Chaffey*)

The next night, 30/31 July, 190 Squadron sent thirteen aircraft to SOE and SAS DZs, the latter having been set up by 'Dingson' and 'Grog'. Eleven aircraft were successful, including two that dropped containers and panniers to 'Grog 37C', in conditions of excellent visibility and practically no cloud. According to the intelligence report submitted by Plt Off Walter Brain and his crew, this was 'A Bang On trip'.

On their return from an operation, aircrews could normally expect some special treatment, by way of food and drink, but this was not always the case, as Don Mason of 620 Squadron recalled:

> It was usual when arriving back from operations to be debriefed by Intelligence Officers and get a welcome cup of hot coffee with a tot of rum in it. Whether this was for medicinal purposes or merely to loosen our tongues one never found out. It was also the practice to be served with bacon and eggs for breakfast, a real treat as these were in extremely short supply. One morning the returning crews did not get bacon and eggs but a wishy-washy bubble and squeak. Incensed by this, they emptied the fire buckets in the Sergeants' Mess, filled them with further diluted bubble and squeak and proceeded to paint the inside walls of the mess with this pungent mixture. Needless to say, because no one culprit could be identified the Squadron was confined to camp for two weeks.

The Air Force recognised that the granting of leave at regular intervals was important if aircrew personnel were to remain efficient in their duties. Flt Sgt Noel Chaffey always looked forward to these breaks, and took full advantage of opportunities to visit new places:

> On the squadron we were given a week's leave every six weeks to allow the nerves to settle. If we had leave and wanted to go somewhere special we could call on the Lady Frances Ryder Scheme. It needed just a telegram or phone call to let them know of our leave dates and they would reply, telling us where we would be welcome. I had a most wonderful fortnight in the Lake District on

Sergeants Pete Griffin (left) and Frank Pearman, caught by the camera of Flight Sergeant Noel Chaffey as they concentrate on a game of patience in Hut 12A, the billet of the 'de Rome crew' at Fairford. (*N.R. Chaffey*)

one occasion – I was met by car at Keswick railway station, and driven home to an amazingly grand house, owned by an ex-timber merchant who had been in New Zealand before the war. The driver turned out to be the lady of the house.

This generous couple had arranged for service men and women to share their home in twos and threes, providing some very relaxing days on leave. Their beautiful house was fronted by a huge area of lawn sweeping down to the lake edge. The lounge had a great walk-in fireplace surrounded by amazing plaster work and the back wall, panelled, held a minstrels' gallery which turned out to be the lead into the sleeping quarters – also overlooking the lakes.

There were two daughters and their friends and six or seven cycles available for us all to spend days circling the lake with baskets of packed lunches. Our mixed group, of two Aussie airmen, a New Zealand soldier, three Canadian soldiers and one sailor made up a party, and we were shepherded along by the two daughters and some other girl friends. All on a jolly holiday cycle ride.

Back at the camp, entertainment was usually of the home-made variety, but there were sometimes occasions when things became quite rowdy.

Don Mason recalled:

Recreation usually consisted of a beer in the mess, a game of cards or snooker, or maybe writing letters home, reading or just having a yarn and a laugh. There were also various sorts of clubs, like one for music. However, sometimes there would be a party which got a little bit out of hand. There was a penchant for stacking furniture up like a tower, climbing up and implanting footprints up the wall, across the ceiling and down the other side, as if someone had walked

Flight Lieutenant Frank Cox RNZAF (pilot), on left, with members of his 620 Squadron crew, left to right: Warrant Officer Fred Waite (navigator), Warrant Officer Eric Winter (flight engineer) and Pilot Officer Don Mason (wireless operator). (*190 & 620 Sqns Archive*)

across, mostly upside down. As the Mess was a large Nissen hut, the ceiling was not flat so a continuous line of footprints went from the floor on one side to the floor on the other (bare feet were doused in beer to make the imprints). One could scarcely imagine a teetering tower and odd bits of furniture with a figure on top doing his best when one over the eight to place his feet in the correct position. This was very hilarious when under way but often resulted in bad sprains and on one occasion a broken arm and leg.

One event I remember was when an Officers' Mess Dinner was arranged for quite a number of 'Brown Jobs' (Army Officers) from the Airborne and Glider Pilot Regiments and some American Officers. I suppose it was an effort to foster good relations with the people we were transporting in 38 Group. Later in the evening, the high spirits turned to cutting off ties below the knot with a pair of large sharp scissors. Most of us, like it or not, were denuded in this way and there happened to be an American General in the assembly who also had his tie docked. Unfortunately my skipper, Frank Cox, was blamed for this although he was innocent. He was instructed by the Station Commander to get the General another tie, so off he went to his billet and brought back his spare black RAF tie and put it on the General who looked very silly in a black tie with a khaki colour uniform with lots of gongs.

At the end of July, Thomas Higgins was still eagerly awaiting news of the end of his crew's tour with 190 Squadron:

30 July
Well, we're on again tonight. By all rights it should be the last trip in our operational tour, but with this Wing Co you never know where in the hell you stand.

Oh well. It's the same short one as the other night, which is one good thing, for most of the squadron are on seven and eight hour trips.

31 July
Just returned. It was the easiest 'op' yet. Didn't see a thing, except the DZ lights. There was some bombing going on near Cherbourg. I don't know if it was our aircraft or Jerries.

31 July (later)
Still no word about our screening. I wish they would make up their minds, the dim buggers. This morning the mess smells like an Egyptian brothel on a hot summer day. Christ! Anyone who can sit in the mess must have a distorted sense of smell. We're still waiting for a letter from Group which will confirm our screening. I hope the damn thing comes through soon – two weeks' leave – oh, boy!

July 1944 had been a very busy month for the Fairford Stirlings. The total operational hours flown were 502 and 558 for 190 and 620 Squadrons, respectively, with 58 per cent of sorties deemed to have been successful. The relentless demand for special operations meant that they were routinely being carried out without the benefit of very bright moonlight, while the risks associated with 'blind drops', i.e. without reception signals or sight of the ground, were often regarded as acceptable when delivering SAS paratroops 'behind the lines'.

Although their special operations were always challenging, and on many occasions extremely hazardous, the 38 Group squadrons experienced much lower loss rates than their counterparts in Bomber Command. According to these statistics, aircrews flying Stirling or Halifax aircraft in the air support role stood a good chance of surviving long enough to be promoted by at least one rank during their operational tours. For NCOs, there could also be the prospect of a commission; shortly after D-Day, Warrant Officer Don Mason made the transition to Pilot Officer:

> Although all newly commissioned officers were supposed to have an Officer Training Course, it did not happen in my day. I was given a cheque for £75 and sent on 48 hours' leave to buy my uniform, and then came back to camp having changed from a Senior NCO to a sprog officer. This was not a nice feeling, especially as one had to get used to being saluted and called 'Sir' and also rather lost that matey feeling of belonging to the crowd, as well as having to get used to mixing in the Officers' Mess with many of those whom one had not dared to speak to previously.
>
> There was also a new protocol to learn, including Dining In Nights and the loyal toast, mess bills and the like. Rather like any other job, when new you drew the short straw. Shortly after being commissioned, I was appointed Duty Officer, a 24-hour stint, one of the chores being to accompany the Orderly Sergeant to the Airmen's Mess where he would blow a whistle rather like a referee at a football match and shout out, 'Orderly Officer, any complaints?'
>
> On this occasion, as soon as he had closed his mouth, pandemonium ensued with plates, dishes and irons being banged on the tables and everyone standing up by the refectory-like tables bawling their heads off. Eventually when the din had subsided enough for me to make myself heard, I found that the problem was caused by earwigs in the cabbage, which was still being dished out. I immediately stopped this of course and called for the cookhouse Senior NCO, a Warrant Officer regular who hated duration people anyway. He and I had a real set-to over this cabbage but eventually it was taken off and baked beans hurriedly substituted. Needless to say, I was never forgiven by that particular Warrant Officer, but was cheered to the echo by the erks.

There were no operations flown by 38 Group on the night of 31 July/1 August, but the next few nights were hectic ones. On the night of 1/2 August, 190 Squadron sent six aircraft on an SOE operation, dropping containers to a 'Donald' DZ, which was recorded as being south-east of Paris.

The same night, 1/2 August, 620 Squadron sent four aircraft to DZs set up for 'Ian' and 'Pimento' (the latter was an SOE circuit with widespread activity, including operations in the Rhône valley and the Tarn-et-Garonne *département*). Two of these aircraft were successful in dropping. There were also nine aircraft of 620 Squadron on operations in support of the SAS, dropping to 'Grog' and 'Wash' DZs. Five of these aircraft were successful.

Poor visibility caused problems at Fairford and other 38 Group airfields on several mornings in August, as aircraft were returning from DZs in France. Nevertheless, most of the supplies they dropped were getting through to their intended recipients, who sometimes managed to send grateful messages back to the squadrons. These included congratulations on 'a grand drop' by Flt Sgt Coeshott and his 190 Squadron crew to the SAS, during the night of 2/3 August. Various tasks had been planned, cancelled and then reinstated on 2 August, but both Fairford squadrons went ahead with operations, including drops for 'Dunhill', which 2 SAS commenced that night, in the eastern part of Brittany. 'Dunhill' turned out to be a short-lived operation, since it was soon overtaken by American ground forces. There were also drops to 'Dingson' and 'Gain' DZs that night. The gunners in two of the 190 Squadron aircraft opened fire on Ju 88 night-fighters, and Fg Off Murray of 620 Squadron brought his aircraft back with some flak damage. No. 620 Squadron had some important passengers that night, namely the AOC 38 Group, AVM Hollinghurst, and the General Officer Commanding Airborne Forces, Lieutenant General Browning, who flew with Plt Off McHugh and Fg Off Bunce, respectively.

David Evans recalled:

Some time in July 1944 our pilot was commissioned and left us for the Officers' Mess, where one evening at a social gathering he met Air Vice-Marshal Hollinghurst, who was in command of 38 Group. On this occasion, our skipper (now Pilot Officer Maurice McHugh) invited the AOC to fly with us when we were next operational, and it was with considerable surprise that we learnt one day that he was to be a passenger on our sortie that night.

Soon after we had completed our pre-flight checks, Air Vice-Marshal Hollinghurst arrived at the dispersal point, in a staff car, accompanied by the Station Commander. We formed a line and stood to attention and our pilot introduced each of us in turn. The AOC made it clear to us that once in the aircraft our pilot would be in command and that we were to take no notice of our VIP passenger. He sat in the second pilot's seat and it was a very uneventful but successful operation during which all of us behaved impeccably.

However, it was with some relief that we said goodbye to our passenger on landing back at base. He must also have been pleased with us as a crew, because he flew with us again in August. On this later occasion we were diverted to another airfield on our return and he joined us in the mess for our bacon and eggs, causing no end of a hullabaloo amongst the staff serving the meal.

The diversion, to which David Evans referred, was early in the morning of 3 August, as forty out of sixty-five aircraft from 38 Group landed away, mostly at airfields in West Wales. Out of twenty-two Fairford Stirlings returning from operations, sixteen went to either Brawdy in Pembrokeshire, or Fairwood Common (now Swansea Airport) on the Gower peninsula. All landed safely, though EF270 of 190 Squadron was subsequently damaged when it taxied onto rough ground at Fairwood Common.

Noel Chaffey recalled:

On the night of 2/3 August, we returned to the UK to find we were fog-bound at Fairford. We were advised over the radio to divert to Brawdy airfield. It was well after midnight when we bedded down and we were restless until dawn. However, after breakfast it was a lovely morning as a rain shower had cleared the air, so we took off from Brawdy and flew home to base – another operation successfully completed.

On 3 August, drops to SOE DZs by both 190 and 620 Squadrons were planned, but cancelled in the early evening, leaving 190 Squadron to provide all the aircraft for SAS drops that night. After further cancellations, and some late changes to the loads, 190 Squadron sent a total of ten aircraft to 'Dingson', 'Dunhill' and 'Gain' DZs. There was no reception for two of the aircraft that went to 'Dingson' DZs, but all the others were successful. The drops to 'Dunhill' DZs included troops, containers and two bicycles. On the way back, Fg Off Connell's aircraft was attacked by

Pilot Officer Robinson's 620 Squadron crew. Standing, left to right: Flight Sergeant Ken Johnson (wireless operator), Sergeant Graham Granville (flight engineer), Flight Sergeant Jim Lewis (navigator), Pilot Officer Edward Robinson RNZAF (pilot) holding 'Laddie' the mascot, Warrant Officer Peter Sturges RAAF (air gunner) and Warrant Officer 'Ike' Trainor RNZAF (bomb aimer); kneeling, the airmen of their ground crew, left to right: LAC Bill Longhurst, LAC Bert Hall, Corporal Lynch, LAC Robinson, AC1 Shields and LAC Brinson. *190 & 620 Sqns Archive*)

a Ju 88 near Deauville, but his Canadian gunner, Sgt Conley, returned fire with 1,000 rounds and the enemy aircraft broke away.

Thomas Higgins' diary:

3 August
We're on again tonight. And yet another 'op'. One of these days we'll be screened, but when, I don't know. It's a low-level trip to France; medium length, about 4.30 or 5.00 hours. The shorter, the better.

3 August (later)
Scrubbed! Boy! What a life.

4 August
We're on again tonight. Will we go? That's the big question. I hope so.

The Fairford Stirlings did indeed go, on the night of 4/5 August. Ten of 620 Squadron's aircraft were sent to 'Dingson', 'Grog', 'Houndsworth' and 'Wash' DZs for the SAS, but one of two aircraft detailed for 'Houndsworth 44' failed to return. This was LJ920 'A', captained by Plt Off Edward Robinson, a New Zealander. The seven crew members (a 2nd bomb aimer was on board) and two Royal Army Service Corps (RASC) dispatchers were killed when the aircraft was hit by flak and crashed at Notre-Dame-de-Livaye, near Lisieux. The same night, 190 Squadron was busy

125

dropping on seven DZs for SOE, and all except one of the sixteen aircraft sent were successful. Keevil Stirlings, four from each of 196 and 299 Squadrons, also operated out of Fairford that night, probably dropping to the SAS.

Thomas Higgins' diary:

5 August
It's another one in and over with. Wee! Not very exciting; a bit of heavy flak going up; also light cannon tracer near the DZ.
    Our trip was successful; the ninth in the squadron, a pretty good record.

During the afternoon of 5 August, three Stirlings from 620 Squadron's 'B' Flight flew to the USAAF base at Harrington in Northamptonshire, to take part in an Anglo-American operation. The aircraft were captained by Fg Off Bunce, Fg Off Murray and Flt Sgt de Rome, with their Flight Commander, Sqn Ldr Wallace, flying in Murray's Stirling. A number of armourers and an RAF dispatcher also went with them, to supervise the loading of the aircraft. The 801st Bomb Group had been flying 'Carpetbagger' missions from Harrington, dropping personnel and supplies to DZs in France, in a role similar to that of the 38 Group squadrons. The same day, 5 August, that the 620 Squadron detachment arrived, B-24 Liberators of the 492nd Bomb Group took up residence at Harrington, to replace those of the 801st Bomb Group, which was about to move to Cheddington in Buckinghamshire. The Stirling crews were to assist the Americans by flying to Brittany and dropping an Operational Group of four officers and twenty-nine men, at the start of Operation 'Donald'. The original plan had been for the 'Donald' troops to be dropped with their supplies from six B-24s, but then it was decided that the larger capacity of the Stirlings would enable the mission to be carried out using half the number of aircraft.

    The 'Donald' OG comprised two sections, 'Red' and 'Blue', and was commanded by Lieutenant Colonel Serge Obolensky (who was to be known by the code name 'Milton' on this operation). Aged fifty-three, he was a Russian Prince who had fought for the Czar against the Bolsheviks before fleeing to England. Obolensky became a US citizen in 1932, and, as an adviser to OSS on guerrilla warfare, had translated and adapted a Russian manual of tactics for Anglo-American use.

Lieutenant Colonel Serge Obolensky. *(801st/492nd Bombardment Group Assn, via 190 & 620 Sqns Archive)*

    By the beginning of August 1944, Brittany was almost cut off by American troops advancing westwards. In order to facilitate their further progress, there was to be a combined effort to protect roads, railways and bridges in the region. The SAS, OGs, 'Jeds' and *Maquis* were all involved in this. The 'Donald' troops would be dropped at night, about 40 kilometres east of Brest, where their reception was being organised by Jedburgh team 'Hilary', working in conjunction with the *Maquis*. The DZ location was chosen because of its proximity to a viaduct on the Landivisiau-Morlaix railway line, a key point that needed to be kept intact until the arrival of the American ground forces.

Noel Chaffey recalled:

July and August 1944 were busy months for us, during which our crew completed eleven operations. Included in these was a special one, for which the Bunce, Murray and de Rome crews were chosen. We were going to Harrington, the home of the 'Carpetbaggers', who were flying B-24 Liberators. It was a lovely afternoon on 5 August as we took off from Fairford at 1500 hrs, landing at Harrington forty-five minutes later. We were directed to a standby area where we seemed to be surrounded by half the station, for this was their first close-up view of a Stirling, the RAF's big bomber. Also on hand was a motion picture camera team, commanded by Captain John Ford. They had been sent to England to cover aspects of American involvement in the European war and cooperation with other forces.

Our Flight Commander was to do the briefing for the operation later that afternoon, after a meal. I remember we had pork and red cabbage, such a wonderful change from 'bangers and mash', followed by real ice-cream of various flavours and colours. I later learned that this was shipped in powder form from America, then mixed and poured into containers. These would be loaded into a B-24 which would be sent up on an air test at high altitude for a couple of hours, to freeze the mixture!

Bowsers arrived to refuel our Stirlings, and our flight engineer, Frank, was in charge of our aircraft and directing movements from atop the wings. As the last tank was being filled, a mistaken signal sent the vehicle off, trailing the pipe from which fuel was still pouring, thus soaking Frank. Although he soon dried out, he was no fun to be near for the next few hours, as the smell lingered on.

Now it was time for our briefing for the night's operation. We trooped into a Nissen hut (which is still standing at Harrington, and now turned into a museum after restoration), where we were met by many Americans smoking cigars whilst getting into their flying and para gear. Cameras had been set up on tripods, strong lights were on and sound equipment was whirring, for the briefing was to be recorded on film. However, it was rather undisciplined, with no 'Attention, senior officer!', but plenty of smoke. Our Flight Commander started the briefing, to be followed by their weather man, and then Lieutenant Colonel Obolensky, who was to lead the American para team.

So, briefing finished and all prepared, we made our way out to the three Stirlings. With the film crew following and still shooting film, Obolensky and his boys got on board our aircraft. We took off at 2330 hrs, loaded with twelve US paras. The lads settled down on the floor, but as we crossed the English coast a few at a time were allowed up front to view

Squadron Leader 'Bertie' Wallace DFC delivers his briefing at Harrington, 5 August 1944. (*801st/492nd Bombardment Group Assn, via 190 & 620 Sqns Archive*)

An RAF sergeant assists an American soldier as he fits his parachutes at the start of Operation 'Donald'. (*801st/492nd Bombardment Group Assn, via 190 & 620 Sqns Archive*)

Lieutenant Colonel Obolensky is given a helping hand as he boards one of the lorries taking the 'Donald' troops to the 620 Squadron Stirlings.
(*801st/492nd Bombardment Group Assn, via 190 & 620 Sqns Archive*)

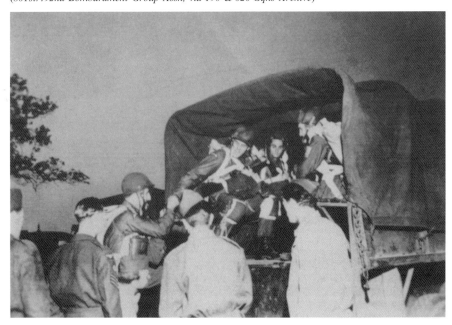

the scene from the astrodome. As we got over the Channel, it began to build up with cloud, which became thicker towards the French coast.

It did not take us long to get to our allotted DZ position but we could see nothing, as there was no break in the clouds. Obolensky was assuring us they'd be OK and would drop blind. We made three or four circuits of the area, hoping for a break in the cloud and identification from the ground, but we had no luck, and had to bring them all back to Harrington. Poor old Obolensky was beside himself, wanting us to go straight back to France after refuelling, but dawn was almost upon us and we could not drop in daylight. So we returned to Fairford and went to bed.

Flt Sgt de Rome's aircraft had been the first to take off from Harrington that night, followed a few minutes later by Fg Off Murray's. The third aircraft, captained by Fg Off Bunce, was accelerating along the runway when its port outer engine failed. As the take-off was aborted, a tyre burst, causing damage to the Stirling's undercarriage, so this aircraft was unable to continue.

In spite of the weather, Murray and his crew were successful in dropping Lt Hirtz and Lt Kern with nine of their men at 0130 hrs on 6 August. These troops all landed safely, along with explosives and ammunition packed in six containers, and other supplies in panniers. With Lt Hirtz acting as liaison officer, they made contact with the *Maquis* and proceeded to their objective, the railway viaduct near Guimiliau. There they mounted a guard for three days, until the American ground forces reached them.

Having completed their primary task, even though their party had been reduced in number, the 'Donald' troops moved on to the port of Roscoff, where they

Flying Officer Bunce and his 620 Squadron crew. Standing, left to right: Flight Sergeant Brian Allen (wireless operator), Warrant Officer Plum Warner RAAF (air gunner), a member of the ground crew, Pilot Officer Ross Bunce (pilot), Flight Sergeant Jack Farmer (bomb aimer) and Flying Officer Doug Simmins (navigator); kneeling, four members of the ground crew, and far right, Pilot Officer Jack Svensson (flight engineer). *190 & 620 Sqns Archive*)

supervised the German garrison's surrender. This was negotiated with the enemy troops by making them well aware that nearby artillery units would go into action, unless they came out within twenty minutes – which they did, thus avoiding any bloodshed. The 'Donald' troops then carried out further patrols in the Roscoff area, before making their way to Cherbourg, from where they were flown back to the UK on 19 August.

Two days after their operation from Harrington, Flt Sgt de Rome and his crew returned, taking ground crew personnel to repair Fg Off Bunce's aircraft. Lieutenant Colonel Obolensky, who had been so frustrated at being unable to jump from de Rome's aircraft on the night of 5/6 August, did get to France a few days later, as leader (now code-named 'Butch') of OG 'Patrick'. This unit operated successfully in the Indre *département* for the next month or so.

On the night of 5/6 August, 620 Squadron also sent eight aircraft from Fairford to three SOE DZs, plus one to a 'Dunhill' DZ for the SAS. All except one of these aircraft were successful, although some had to divert to Tarrant Rushton and Keevil on their return. No. 620 Squadron took part in more SOE drops on 6/7 August, when a total of five aircraft went to 'Salesman' (SOE circuit operating in the area around the Haute-Vienne), 'Pimento' and 'Shipwright' DZs. Four of these aircraft were successful.

Two nights later, on 8/9 August, there was widespread activity by 38 Group. Ten aircraft from 190 Squadron went to 'Dick' (south-west of Chartres), 'Mark' (northeast of Châtellerault), 'Percy' and 'Pimento' DZs for SOE. Conditions were clear over the English Channel, but across France the weather was generally very poor. No reception signals were observed at DZs 'Dick 93' and 'Percy 48'. Fg Off Pascoe and his crew, who flew to the latter DZ, had a particularly difficult time. After takeoff, they were unable to retract their aircraft's twin tailwheels, and on their way to the DZ they ran into thunderstorms, in 10/10ths cloud that extended down to 300 feet above ground level. Having abandoned their attempt to drop, the starboard inner engine started to issue sparks and smoke and had to be shut down, following which the RPM gauge for the port inner engine fell out of its panel. There was yet another problem, as the Gee equipment packed up, so the remainder of the navigation on this eventful flight had to be done by dead reckoning. The two aircraft that went to 'Mark 17' were able to carry out their drops, but some containers remained on board one of them, captained by Fg Off Siegert. Back at base, it was discovered that the bomb doors under the port wing of this aircraft could not be opened, because a drive chain had broken.

On the night of 8/9 August, Fairford Stirlings also took part in a tactical bombing operation, the first of the handful of occasions that they were used in this role. The target was a *château*, which was occupied by the *Gestapo* and situated near Fauillet, to the south-west of Bordeaux. Six crews, drawn in equal numbers from the 'A' Flights of 190 and 620 Squadrons, took part in this operation, the preparations for which had included the dropping of practice bombs on the Marcham range, near Abingdon, over the previous few days. The aircraft captains included both the Squadron Commanders, with the Station Commander, Gp Capt Wheeler, flying as Wg Cdr Harrison's co-pilot.

Late in the evening of 8 August, the six Stirlings took off from Fairford, carrying between them fifty-two 500 lb high-explosive bombs, plus containers of 40 lb GP (General Purpose) bombs and 4 lb incendiaries. Passing over the English coast at Bridport, they crossed the Channel and then let down to fly across France at low level. The first of the 620 Squadron crews ran into bad weather over central France.

They made two runs over what was thought to be the target area, but could not identify the *château*, and returned to Fairford with a full bomb load. The first of the 190 Squadron crews also ran into thick cloud and failed to find the target, but elected to jettison their bombs in the Channel on the way back, rather than land with them still on board. However, the crews of the other four aircraft reported that visibility was good as they approached the target from the north-west. Flying at 500 feet in bright moonlight, they followed the valley of the River Garonne until the *château* came into view.

The first bombs were dropped at 0230 hrs, as Wg Cdr Lee led the attack. On leaving the target area, he encountered a small amount of flak in the vicinity of Tonneins, but after that the return flight was uneventful. Flt Lt Hannah was two minutes behind his CO, and also bombed successfully. He was followed by the remaining two aircraft from 190 Squadron. By the time Sqn Ldr Gilliard approached the target it was brightly illuminated by fire. This provided a clear aiming point for his stick of bombs, which straddled the *château* as they fell. The last aircraft was flown by Wg Cdr Harrison, who arrived to find the *château* engulfed in flames. Members of his crew observed a huge red explosion as their bombs fell on the left-hand side of the target. The final blows of this sudden and devastating attack were struck by their gunner, Flt Lt Davidson, who fired 1,500 rounds into huts alongside the *château.*

On the night of 9/10 August, 190 Squadron sent sixteen aircraft on SOE operations, to destinations which included 'Hugh' and 'Ian' DZs. Eleven of these aircraft were successful, though some encountered heavy flak. Fg Off Chesterton's aircraft, LK431 'F', dropped containers and panniers on a DZ in the Limoges area, before making a slow return journey after the starboard outer engine had to be shut down and its propeller feathered. When this aircraft became overdue, Flying Control at Fairford called for IFF (Identification Friend or Foe) plots from other stations, to determine its position, but 'F-Fox' eventually landed safely at base. Chesterton's air gunner, Flt Sgt Ron Shaw, remembered this was a very alarming flight:

In August 1944 we flew on an SOE 'op' over France, before which we were warned off flying over the Cherbourg Peninsula, since the Americans were in heavy fighting there and would treat all aircraft overhead as hostile.

On the return flight, after a successful drop, one of the engines developed a fault and caused great vibration in the fuselage, especially at the rear. George, the skipper, and Dougie, the bomb aimer, had great difficulty in flying the aircraft. However, the most direct way home was across the Cherbourg Peninsula, where we met heavy 'Ack Ack', presumably from the Americans, despite our firing the 'colours of the day'.

We had some very near misses, one of which blew the lower escape hatch in. The skipper then warned us to be prepared to bale out. My 'chute was stowed at the rear of the fuselage, behind the gun turret, but after centralising the turret, I found its doors had jammed. With help from Jimmy, the wireless operator, I managed to free the doors and decided to leave them open, in case they jammed again. I found it very cold and draughty, as we had no Perspex panel in the front of the turret (the gunners on the squadron had all agreed to have these panels taken out, for clearer visibility). Happily, we did not have to jump and returned safely.

The following morning I was sent for, to go to the hangar, where 'F for Fox' was having an engine change and service. The Armoury Sergeant then showed

Stirling 'F-Fox' of 190 Squadron. It bore the inscription 'Ferdinand el Taurus' on its nose.
(*G.H. Chesterton*)

me where all except one of the bolts securing the gun turret to the aircraft had sheared off, owing to the vibration.

The same night, 9/10 August, 620 Squadron sent four aircraft to the Saône-et-Loire area. They were carrying French paratroops of 3 SAS, possibly as part of the effort to set up Operations 'Barker' and 'Harrod'. The DZ arrangements were made by 'Ditcher', an SOE circuit operating to the north-west of Lyon. However, no reception signals were observed, so the troops could not be dropped. Fg Off Neale's aircraft, EF237 'W', carrying seven paratroops, ran into a concentration of searchlights over Bourges and was hit by flak. This damaged the electrical system for operating the flaps, which then had to be lowered manually before landing, using a long and laborious procedure that required numerous turns of a crank handle.

The code name of 620 Squadron's DZ that night turned out to be an apt but unfortunate one when Fg Off Bell's Stirling, EF256 'C', ditched in the Channel after being hit by anti-aircraft fire. It has been suggested that this aircraft was another victim of 'friendly fire' from the American forces, but – perhaps not surprisingly – there is nothing in official records to confirm this.

Jim Viney, 620 Squadron, recalled:

After being shot down somewhere between Jersey and the French mainland, Bill 'Dinger' Bell and his crew got 'Purple Hearts' because they spent the night in one of the US hospitals under observation. They tried to forgo the pleasure of wearing the decoration and only did so under orders. 'Dinger' and his Aussie bomb aimer, 'Ace' Tod, were very large sheep farmers who, I understood, pulled the aircraft out of its dive by brute strength alone; they were also great drinkers of ale.

Flying Officer Neale's 620 Squadron crew: in doorway, top, Flying Officer Ted Wheeler (navigator); in doorway, left, Sergeant Norman Thompson (wireless operator), and right, Sergeant Ken Keenan (flight engineer); standing, left to right, Sergeant John Marshall (air gunner), Pilot Officer Ted Cutts (bomb aimer) and Flying Officer George Neale (pilot).
(*190 & 620 Sqns Archive*)

Two of the paratroops on board Stirling EF256 were drowned. While some sources give the date of their deaths as 12 August 1944, it is clear from the handwritten entries in the RAF Fairford Watchkeeper's Log that EF256 was lost on the night of 9/10 August. In addition, the following message was received at Fairford from 32 Air Sea Rescue Unit at Calshot, late in the evening of 11 August:

> All the crew are safe. F/O Bell, F/O Bradshaw, F/Sgt Bridges and Sgt North-field and dispatcher Sgt Brown are at RAF Calshot near Southampton. F/Sgt Tod flew home from Cherbourg today and is 'somewhere in England'. The rear gunner, F/Sgt Dutton is in hospital in Cherbourg. Three French paratroops brought back to Calshot. Two paratroops (Selles and Dastis) were killed at time of ditching.

Flight Sergeant Stan Dutton, the air gunner in Flying Officer Bell's crew, who ended up in hospital after the ditching of Stirling EF256 during the night of 9/10 August 1944. (*190 & 620 Sqns Archive*)

On the night of 10/11 August, eight aircraft from 190 Squadron were sent to 'Giles' and 'John' DZs for SOE. Six of these aircraft were able to drop. There were fourteen aircraft from 620 Squadron operating for the SAS that night, twelve of which were successful. One of the unsuccessful 620 Squadron crews returned early with an unserviceable Gee set, only to find that the cloud base at Fairford had fallen to less than 500 feet. They managed to land at Brize Norton, but when the rest of the Fairford aircraft returned they had to be diverted much further east, to land at Bourn, Methwold, Newmarket Heath, Tempsford and Waterbeach.

The next night, 11/12 August, Fairford was asked to provide twenty aircraft for SAS and SOE drops. After various cancellations, eight aircraft from 620 Squadron went to a 'Hippodrome' DZ for SOE, and all were successful. This was a record night for 38 Group, in respect of the number of special operations sorties flown, with fifty-six aircraft dropping a total of 935 containers and sixty-nine packages.

As they were flying on operations night after night, the Fairford aircrews had to adjust to a routine of catching up on their sleep during the mornings, and carrying out training flights or air tests in the afternoons. Don Mason described how his crew had some hair-raising experiences when they air-tested their Stirling after one repair job:

It was customary to be at the flights at 7.30 to 8.00 am in the morning. We would take a look at the Daily Routine Orders (DROs) and Personnel Occurrence Reports (PORs – called Piccadilly Occurrence Books by all and sundry), and if we were not wanted would go out to the aircraft on dispersal to check equipment and, if necessary, carry out an air test. On an operational squadron a close bond was developed with one's ground crew, many of whom never left dispersal from the time the aircraft departed until it returned. Before the ground crew handed the aircraft over, the Form 700 had to be examined and signed. This was a mandatory procedure, strictly enforced.

On one operation, our aircraft had suffered some flak damage to the port tailplane. This was changed and we had to air test the aircraft. All was well until on take-off we experienced a severe vibration, passing right through the aircraft, a most disconcerting experience. We were too far along the runway to abort the take-off, so we did a tight circuit, landed, taxied back to dispersal and put the aircraft 'u/s' on the Form 700.

Later we were told the aircraft was serviceable, but another air test produced an even more severe vibration. This happened three times until finally we refused to air test again. By this time, our Squadron Engineer Officer, Flt Lt

# GENTLEMAN

GIVENCHY

PARIS

Une signature boisée à la sensualité affirmée.
Le charme explosif et envoutant de l'Iris.

A woody scent full of confident sensuality.
The explosive and captivating Orris charm.

**LA NOUVELLE INTENSITÉ POUR HOMME**
**A NEW INTENSITY FOR MEN**

**EAU DE PARFUM**

# GENTLEMAN

## GIVENCHY
PARIS

EAU DE PARFUM

9

INGREDIENTS: ALCOHOL, PARFUM (FRAGRANCE), AQUA (WATER), ETHYL
HEXYL METHOXYCINNAMATE, ALPHA-ISOMETHYL IONONE, LIMONENE,
BENZYL SALICYLATE, COUMARIN, LINALOOL, BUTYL METHOXYDIBEN-
ZOYLMETHANE, BUTYLPHENYL METHYLPROPIONAL, HEXAPRADU, BHT,
CINNAMAL, OXI, CITRONELLOL, CITRAL, GERANIOL, HYDROXYCITRONELLAL,
GERANIOL, EUGENOL.

3 274872 368057

Butcher, was involved and he refused to believe that we had a problem. We said 'OK, we will air test it again, but you will have to come with us'. Indeed he did, but his face blanched on take-off and he shouted to us to get it down. Subsequently we discovered that although the large nuts and bolts securing the tailplane to the fuselage had been lock-wired, they had not been tightened to the correct torque and were loose. This showed that sometimes people and aircraft could have been lost through causes other than enemy action, for we might well have lost the tailplane in flight had we not persisted in locating the problem.

If all were well at dispersal, we would go back to the flights. This was to see if ops were on that night, and whether we were on the battle order which was usually put up at midday. The ops main briefing usually occurred at 2.00 pm, with final briefing at maybe 6.00 pm. Then, apart from meals, it was sort out your kit ready for take off. All aircrew members had their own particular parts to play in preparations; the navigator would do his flight plan, pilots would get any specific flight information, the wireless operators would obtain ciphers, colours and letters of the day, etc.

If there were no ops that night, we were stood down or had to report for training, maybe learning about new equipment, performing parachute or dinghy drills, or PT, for there was always something to be done.

On the night of 12/13 August, twelve aircraft from 190 Squadron, and four from 620 Squadron, delivered the advance parties for Operations 'Loyton' and 'Barker', which were to be carried out by troops of 2 SAS and 3 SAS, respectively. Together

aking advantage of a sunny day in the summer of 1944, aircrew personnel of 190 Squadron practise 'dinghy drill'
a flooded gravel pit near Fairford. (*G.H. Chesterton*)

with a Phantom signals team and Jedburgh team 'Jacob', the 'Loyton' troops were dropped in the Vosges mountains. There they fought alongside the *Maquis*, but faced unexpectedly fierce opposition from enemy forces determined to hold this strategically important area close to the German border. A substantial number of 'Loyton' troops were captured, but few lived long as POWs.

'Barker' was established to the south-west of 'Loyton', with the similar intention of co-operating with the *Maquis*, but was a much smaller operation. Nevertheless, 'Barker' caused considerable disruption to enemy communications in the Saône-et-Loire *département*. Operation 'Harrod' was also carried out by 3 SAS in this area, and succeeded in working with the *Maquis* to break down the enemy's transport links. There were also drops to an SOE DZ, 'John 137', during the night of 12/13 August. Three aircraft from 190 Squadron carried these out.

The third week of August was an especially busy one for 38 Group, as 459 sorties were flown. Fair weather during the first half of the month was followed by a dull spell with frequent drizzle, but most days were flyable and there were only a few late cancellations of operations. On the night of 14/15 August, five aircraft from 190 Squadron were detailed to carry out drops for the SAS, and three were successful. One of these aircraft went to DZ 'Gain 24', while the other four were carrying troops and supplies at the start of 'Jockworth'. This was another operation carried out by the French 3 SAS, which in this case had been given the job of disrupting enemy communications in south-east France. The same night, 190 Squadron sent two aircraft to an SOE DZ, 'Dick 93', and both were successful.

It was 620 Squadron's turn the next night, 15/16 August, as two aircraft dropped SAS troops, and seven others went to SOE DZs. There were thunderstorms across France, but the crews persevered and all were successful. WO Keogh and WO Dawe, the captains of the two aircraft making SAS drops, subsequently received a message from the AOC 38 Group, congratulating them on the completion of their sorties under such adverse conditions. During the night of 16/17 August, three aircraft from 620 Squadron succeeded in dropping SAS troops on three DZs in France, in the face of further bad weather.

The next day, Fg Off Bill Chappell and his 190 Squadron crew learned that they had reached the end of their very long tour.

Thomas Higgins' diary:

17 August
I am *screened*. Boy! thirteen months, and at last through an operational tour. Only two crews left from our 'Con' unit, Cottingham's crew and ours. Plenty of luck all way round. Two weeks' leave – look out London!

In spite of his understandable relief at finishing his tour, Flight Officer Thomas Higgins volunteered for further operational duties as soon as he was posted back to the USAAF. He went on to serve as a bombardier in B-29 Superfortresses. His final mission, a bombing raid over Japan on 14 August 1945, was cut short when all aircraft were recalled, as news of the Japanese surrender had just been received.

On the night of 17/18 August, 190 Squadron sent a total of five aircraft on operations, to 'Messenger' and 'Percy' DZs for SOE, and to a 'Jockworth' DZ for the SAS. Three of them were successful. Aircraft from 190 Squadron were on operations again the next night, 18/19 August, as three of them went to SAS DZs, and ten to SOE DZs. This time eight were successful.

There was to be no let-up in the pace set for the Fairford Stirlings. On 19 August, twenty-one aircraft were detailed for operations, but these were later cancelled on

Flight Sergeant Ron Miller RAAF with members of his 620 Squadron crew. (*190 & 620 Sqns Archive*)

account of the weather. On 20 August, twenty-nine aircraft were requested, with the intention of dropping to 'Bob', 'John' and 'Mongrel' DZs for SOE, and 'Houndsworth' for the SAS. After various sorties had been cancelled, eleven aircraft from 190 Squadron, and four from 620 Squadron, flew over France in some very difficult conditions. Only six of them were successful. One of the 620 Squadron aircraft, EF296 'K', captained by Flt Sgt Miller, carried out its drop, but an engine caught fire on the return journey, about 50 miles from the English coast. This aircraft diverted to Weston Zoyland in Somerset for an emergency landing.

During the afternoon of 21 August, there was a spectacular accident at Fairford, involving Stirling EF275 'N' of 620 Squadron. As this aircraft was taking off for a flight to St Athan, no reading appeared on the airspeed indicator, so the Australian pilot, Fg Off Scanlon, closed the throttles and attempted to stop. However, he was unable to prevent it from running off the end of the runway, across a road, and into some logs.

Although EF275 was extensively damaged, only two of the eleven men on board were seriously injured. The air gunner, Flt Sgt Riddle, sustained a compression fracture of a vertebra, and the bomb aimer, Flt Sgt Franklin, broke a bone in his right leg.

Eric Titterton, 6620 Servicing Echelon, recalled:

One of our machines had not been performing as required, and it was decided to send it down to the Maintenance Unit at St Athan in South Wales for further tests. In our billet was an LAC Osgood who was going on leave and had hitched a lift.

When the plane left the bay, the pitot head cover had been inadvertently left on, and the airmen in the caravan at the end of the runway gave the pilot the

137

Stirling EF275, photographed by Flight Sergeant Noel Chaffey shortly after its crash. In fact, this aircraft was not written off, but was repaired and returned to service with 570 Squadron at Rivenhall, though one wonders how much of the original airframe was retained. (*N.R. Chaffey*)

green light for take off, followed almost immediately by a red, as they spotted the cover was still in place. However, the red light was not seen by the crew and the plane started to roll. I was watching, and saw it swerve from side to side, then hop over a hedge at the end of the runway, before piling up into a field, on the other side of the public road.

The plane was a write-off, but fortunately no one was killed, though one crew member had an injured back. Before the rescue services arrived, Osgood was told to beat it, as he was not an official passenger, and gathering up his 'Goon' bag, he did just that.

'Ossie' Osgood, 6620 Servicing Echelon, recalled:

I had been on night ops and was asleep in the billet when one of the lads came in at about 11 am and told me that 'Bluey' Scanlon was taking an aircraft up on an air test, during which he would be landing at St Athan. As I lived less than 10 miles away from there, at Barry, I went to the Officers' Mess to see if I could persuade 'Bluey' to give me a lift home. He agreed to take me in spite of the fact that there would be a Shorts boffin with us, together with an aircrew member going to see his brother who was in hospital at St Athan.

Anyway, we got onto the runway and just as 'Bluey' let the brakes off I noticed a ground crew corporal running and waving his arms. However, we were at full throttle by then, and went on to plough across the road, writing the kite off. Five minutes later the Wingco arrived and he asked if 'Bluey' had got out, only to find him trying to smoke two cigarettes at once!

All good stories have a happy ending, and I did get home that afternoon. Right after we had got the injured aircrew off to the sick bay, an RAF van, with two WAAFs in it, pulled up by me and asked me how to get to Gloucester. It turned out that they were going to Cardiff so I still got home in time for tea!

The subsequent investigation confirmed that EF275's pitot head cover had been left in place. Fg Off Scanlon and two ground crew corporals were held to be jointly responsible for the accident, through not having ensured that the cover had been removed when the pre-flight inspection was carried out. Disciplinary action was taken against the two corporals, but Scanlon had paid a much higher price by the time the investigation was complete, for he was killed at Arnhem on 20 September 1944.

On 21 and 22 August, operations were planned for the Fairford Stirlings, but cancelled in the evening on each occasion. On the night of 23/24 August, 620 Squadron sent ten aircraft to SAS DZs set up by the 'Houndsworth', 'Loyton' and 'Hardy' operations, and two others to an SOE DZ, 'Peter 38', near Bordeaux. Although thunderstorms were encountered over France, all except two of the aircraft were successful. It was always good for morale to know when an operation had

Flying Officer Athol 'Bluey' Scanlon RAAF (right) with members of his crew, and two of their ground crew. (*190 & 620 Sqns Archive*)

gone well, and this time, the troops at 'Hardy 9' were able to send a message, congratulating Fg Off Deacon and his crew on an 'excellent drop'. 'Hardy' was a 2 SAS operation, established initially to gather intelligence in an area to the north-west of Dijon. Its base was later used by 'Wallace', also a 2 SAS operation.

On 24 August, a total of thirty-five Fairford aircraft were requested for operations to 'John', 'Mongrel', 'Paul' and 'Percy' SOE DZs, and 'Haggard', 'Houndsworth', 'Kipling', 'Loyton', 'Moses' and 'Rupert' SAS DZs. After cancellations, there were twelve aircraft from 190 Squadron, and fourteen from 620 Squadron, flying that night. For a change, the weather was good and only two of the aircraft were un-successful. Operation ''Haggard' had commenced on 10 August and was carried out by troops drawn from B Squadron of 1 SAS. They had been given the task of harass-ing the retreating Germans forces in the area between Nevers and Gien. French troops of 3 SAS later provided reinforcements for 'Haggard', which remained active until late September. C Squadron of 1 SAS was assigned to 'Kipling', which started three days after 'Haggard'. Deployed in an area to the west of Auxerre, the 'Kipling' troops carried out offensive patrols for several weeks. Some of them later took over from the 'Houndsworth' troops of A Squadron, 1 SAS, in the Morvan. 'Moses' was a 3 SAS operation, which proved to be successful in disrupting road and rail links around Poitiers.

The night of 25/26 August was another busy one, as the 38 Group squadrons carried out drops across France and also over Luxembourg for the first time. Sixteen aircraft from 190 Squadron, and seven from 620 Squadron, were on SOE oper-ations, with four others from 620 Squadron going to 'Kipling' and 'Harrod' DZs for the SAS. To start with, the weather was generally good and some of the crews could see flares and gun flashes in the Seine valley, where fierce fighting was going on. During the night, the weather over the UK deteriorated, necessitating the diversion of several of the Fairford Stirlings to other airfields, including Brize Norton and Hampstead Norris. One of the 190 Squadron aircraft failed to return. This was LJ827 'S', which crashed at Villebougis, to the south-east of Paris. It was captained by an Australian, Fg Off Norman Port, whose crew that night included a 2nd flight engineer, Sgt Bussell, on an attachment from 1665 HCU at Tilstock. There was only one survivor, the bomb aimer, Flt Sgt Fulcher. News reached Fairford on 4 September that he had been repatriated and was in a Devon hospital.

During the morning of 26 August the diverted Stirlings returned to Fairford, but there was little time for their crews to rest, since thirty-one of the station's aircraft were requested for the next round of operations. After cancellations, 190 Squadron sent eleven aircraft to SOE DZs during the night of 26/27 August. Five were suc-cessful in dropping. The crews of the other six aircraft either encountered bad weather or did not observe any reception signals at their DZs. No. 620 Squadron aircraft sent fifteen aircraft to SOE DZs that night, of which eleven were reported to have been successful. There was also one 620 Squadron aircraft, captained by WO Keogh, dropping troops of 2 SAS at the start of 'Wolsey'. This was an intelligence-gathering operation conducted by a small team in the area around Soissons and Compiègne, in north-east France. Later on, a message was received from 'the field', confirming that this SAS drop had been successful, except for a 'hang up' of one container. One of the 620 Squadron aircraft ran into problems when part of its starboard outer engine cowling lifted into the airflow. This made the Stirling very difficult to control, and its captain, Plt Off McKenzie, considered landing on an airstrip in France. However, no contact could be made with anyone on the ground, so he brought the aircraft back to Tangmere in Sussex for an emergency landing.

On the night of 27/28 August, 190 and 620 Squadrons sent eleven and thirteen aircraft, respectively, to various SOE and SAS DZs, including ones set up by 'Diplomat' (SOE circuit in the Aube *département*) and 'Glover'. Most of these aircraft were successful, in spite of some very bad weather, which included thunderstorms. The commitment for the Fairford Stirlings was reduced the next night, 28/29 August, as only three aircraft were requested from each of the two squadrons. In the end, a single sortie was flown to an SOE DZ, by a 620 Squadron aircraft. During the morning of 29 August, four aircraft from 190 Squadron were detailed to carry out drops to an SAS DZ, 'Loyton 12'. Late in the afternoon, these drops were cancelled, along with most of the other operations planned by 38 Group for the night of 29/30 August. The only ones that did go ahead were 'psychological warfare' flights, dropping propaganda leaflets over the Channel Islands, which were still occupied by the Germans.

On 30 August, thirty-six aircraft were requested from Fairford for SOE operations over France. The main task required mass drops on two DZs situated close to the Swiss border, but early in the evening these were postponed. When they went ahead the next night, 31 August/1 September, 38 Group set a new record, as 136 aircraft were dispatched. 190 Squadron sent seventeen aircraft to 'Director 95'. Nine of these were successful, seven failed to drop because of bad weather, and one jettisoned its load near Cabourg as it returned with engine trouble. No. 620 Squadron sent seventeen aircraft to a DZ for 'Marksman', a circuit operating on the high ground of the Ain and Haute-Savoie *départements*, but twelve were unsuccessful, owing to the weather. In addition, 190 and 620 Squadrons each sent one aircraft to 'Loyton 14A' for the SAS, and both of these dropped successfully.

During August 1944, the Fairford Stirlings had flown 394 sorties, often in weather that was unpleasant, and particularly so when low cloud obscured many of the DZs towards the end of the month. However, none of the operations flown from Fairford could have taken place without the untiring support of 6190 and 6620 Servicing Echelons. On 1 September, the dedication of ground crews throughout 38 Group was acknowledged in a special message from the Air Officer Commanding, AVM Hollinghurst:

> This Group has recently put out a very large number of aircraft on operations, and we have had comparatively little technical trouble apart from damage by enemy aircraft. I know that the conditions under which the maintenance personnel work are far from ideal, which makes me appreciate their efforts all the more. I am sure they will continue the good work of keeping No. 38 Group on the top line.

On the night of 1/2 September, 620 Squadron sent three aircraft to SAS DZs, which were in the Dijon area, close to retreating enemy forces. Two of the aircraft, captained by Fg Off Cox and Flt Sgt Miller, dropped troops, containers and panniers on their DZs. Fg Off Marshall and his crew dropped six paratroops on their DZ, but then encountered vigorous enemy opposition, so they had to leave the area without dropping their supplies. In their own words, it was 'a very warm spot'. Two of these three aircraft diverted to Woodbridge, in Suffolk, on their return.

Apart from air tests, there was not much flying out of Fairford until the night of 5/6 September, when fourteen aircraft from 190 Squadron took troops and supplies to SAS DZs in France and Belgium, and twelve aircraft from 620 Squadron went to SOE DZs in France. There was an accident at Fairford on 6 September, when Stirling EF296 'K' of 620 Squadron, captained by WO Keogh, burst a tyre as it landed at the end of an air test. The aircraft swung violently, breaking off one of the wings. Fortunately, there were no serious injuries to the any of the crew.

On the night of 6/7 September, 190 Squadron sent three aircraft to SOE DZs, one of which was successful in dropping. The squadron also sent three aircraft to SAS DZs that night. One aircraft dropped twelve troops, plus containers and panniers to 'Abel 9'. One of the pair of aircraft sent to 'Loyton 17' dropped sixteen troops, but the crew of the other failed to observe any reception signals and brought their troops back. 'Abel' was an operation carried out by the French 3 SAS in the Vosges and Jura mountains. Five aircraft from 620 Squadron went to France and Luxembourg on the night of 6/7 September, but poor weather prevented them from dropping to their SOE DZs.

On 7 September, there were no special operations planned for 190 and 620 Squadrons, because they now needed to be at full strength, in readiness for a massive airborne assault in Holland.

# CHAPTER 6

# Battle Over Arnhem

## September 1944

For several weeks after D-Day, the Allied forces consolidated their positions in Normandy, while fending off German counterattacks. At the end of July 1944, they broke out from the beachhead area, although enemy opposition remained fierce at this stage and casualties were heavy on both sides. A month later, the Allies were beyond the River Seine, with the German forces in Paris having surrendered on 25 August. The troops of the British Second Army soon swept into Belgium, liberating Brussels in due course. To their left, the Canadian First Army cleared the way towards the Channel ports, and to their right the United States First and Third Armies pushed through to the Ardennes and the Vosges. However, by the beginning of September, movement of the battlefront was slowing down, partly because it was limited by the rate at which supplies could be transported over long overland routes from the port of Cherbourg. Further progress across Holland and into Germany was also going to be impeded by the Maas, Waal and Lower Rhine rivers, all of which provided the enemy with natural lines of defence.

It was within this scenario that Field Marshal Sir Bernard Montgomery, Commander of 21 Army Group, made his case for an airborne operation that might take control of the river crossings at Nijmegen and Arnhem, and therefore expedite the final advance into northern Germany. Over the years, much has been written about the wisdom of the decision to proceed with this operation, 'Market Garden'. Its concept was certainly a bold one, not least because of the sheer scale of the airborne component, 'Market', which involved the transport of some 35,000 troops – more than double the number delivered by air to Normandy on D-Day.

The RAF's 38 and 46 Groups had sufficient aircraft to take the British 1st Airborne Division to Arnhem, but its troops would also require resupply drops until they were relieved by ground forces. The USAAF's IXth Troop Carrier Command would transport the American 82nd and 101st Divisions, whose primary objectives were the canal and river bridges along the road between Eindhoven and Nijmegen. The opening up of this route would enable the ground forces, comprising the 'Garden' component of the operation, to advance north-east to Arnhem. There, the main task of the 1st Airborne troops was the capture of the road bridge over the Lower Rhine. They were also expected to secure the railway bridge that crossed the river to the west of this, and a pontoon road bridge.

Many of the personnel who took part in 'Market' have often wondered why only one lift of paratroops and gliders was carried out on the operation's first day, 17 September. By the time the second lift started on 18 September, the Germans were reacting with considerable force. Furthermore, both these lifts were carried out in broad daylight. The start of 'Market' was therefore quite different from the D-Day landings, during which the two main airborne assaults, 'Tonga' and

'Mallard', had been completed within twenty-four hours, in darkness and daylight, respectively.

However, the plan for 'Market' had been preceded by one that bore a much closer resemblance to the sequence of events on D-Day. No. 38 Group Operation Order No. 524, issued on 6 September 1944, was for Operation 'Comet'. If things had been done according to the 'Comet' plan, British airborne forces would have captured the bridges at Nijmegen and Grave (which were taken by the Americans during 'Market'), as well as the ones at Arnhem. The attacks on these bridges would have been made in darkness, at 0430 hrs, by troops landed in gliders from Harwell. Key stages of the 'Comet' plan that would have involved 190 and 620 Squadrons were:

1. Twelve Fairford Stirlings to drop Pathfinder paratroops at 0730 hours, in order to secure, and designate, the LZs for the main glider landings;
2. The first glider lift, to include thirty-eight Horsas towed from Fairford, landing at LZ 'U' from 0911 hrs onwards.
3. The second glider lift, also on the first day, to include nineteen Horsas towed from Fairford, landing on LZ 'U' from 1847 hrs onwards.

In the 'Comet' plan, LZ 'U' was south-east of Nijmegen, and just north of the River Maas. The British airborne forces had also been allocated LZs 'L' and 'Z', and DZ 'Y', which were situated in the same area, close to transport routes between Nijmegen and bridges over the Maas. The positions of LZ 'S' and DZ 'X', west of Arnhem in the 'Comet' plan, were retained for 'Market'.

When it came to rejecting the night glider landings, during the change of plan from 'Comet' to 'Market', two major risk factors were taken into account. First, Operation 'Tonga', the initial lift on D-Day, had shown that identification of unmarked DZs and LZs was very difficult at night, even for the most practised and proficient of aircrews. Second, the Germans had developed a formidable air defence system in response to the RAF's night bombing campaign. Consequently, night-fighters and radar-directed anti-aircraft guns presented threats over Belgium and Holland that were far more potent than the opposition experienced during 'Tonga' (though this had been bad enough for 620 Squadron, which lost three Stirlings in the early hours of D-Day). It was decided, therefore, that all landings during 'Market' would take place in daylight, with Allied fighters maintaining air superiority along the routes to and from the DZs and LZs. However, a major flaw in the 'Market' plan was introduced by the decision not to carry out both main lifts on the first day, even though this sequence would have been quite feasible, during the hours of daylight, in late summer.

On 7 September, everyone at Fairford realised that a major airborne operation was imminent, as the camp was sealed from the outside world. Although it was becoming very cloudy, the Stirlings of 190 and 620 Squadrons were air tested, before being marshalled on the airfield with the Horsa gliders. The aircrews were briefed, so that they would be ready to go to Holland early the next morning, but at 2200 hrs the operation (still 'Comet' at this stage) was postponed because of the weather forecast. Conditions improved on 8 September, and the tugs and gliders were re-marshalled, only for the operation to be postponed again at 2200 hrs.

Most of the Fairford Stirlings were air tested on the morning of 9 September, but this time in preparation for special operations. Taking advantage of a spell of fine weather, there was considerable activity throughout 38 Group for five successive nights. Between 9 and 14 September, 190 and 620 Squadrons flew a total of eighty-seven sorties for SOE and the SAS, more than three-quarters of which were successful. Their destinations included SOE DZs for 'Bob' (Besançon area), 'Glover' (south-east of Chaumont) and 'Wrestler' (north of Châteauroux) in France, and 'Rummy' to the west and north-west of Emmen, in northern Holland. There was at least one supply drop on an Osric DZ, at an unspecified location in Belgium, while operations to SAS DZs, near Épinal and Dijon, were probably for 'Abel' and 'Loyton'.

After the operations carried out during the night of 13/14 September, the weather remained fine, but there was to be practically no flying by the Fairford Stirlings over the next three days, as maximum serviceability was demanded of them again. The decision to proceed with 'Market', the amended airborne plan for the Arnhem operation, had been taken on 10 September, a week before its start date. Details of the plan were presented to RAF Station Commanders at a briefing held at the Troop Carrier Command Post at Eastcote, in Middlesex, on 15 September, a day before the Operation Order for 'Market' was issued to the squadrons.

During the night of 15/16 September, a dozen aircraft from 38 Group were sent to SAS DZs, but neither 190 nor 620 Squadrons took part in these operations. On 16 September, daylight operations to SAS DZs were flown out of Fairford for the first time. These were carried out by three Stirlings from 1665 HCU at Tilstock, and one from 299 Squadron at Keevil. Their DZs were 'Dickens 20', 'Haggard 15' and 'Spenser 1'. All four aircraft were successful in dropping their supplies, which included containers, panniers and bundles of vehicle tyres. 'Spenser' was a short-lived but successful operation, which involved troops of 4 SAS, who harassed the German forces retreating through the area around Bourges.

On 16 September, the camp at Fairford was sealed. During the early evening, the aircrews of 190 and 620 Squadrons were briefed on the tasks they were to carry out the next morning, dropping paratroops and delivering gliders to zones on the west side of Arnhem.

George Chesterton, 190 Squadron, recalled:

When the plans were made known for a major airborne operation, intended to carry troops over the Rhine in Holland, there was a general feeling of optimism. We had done it before, on D-Day, so why should it not be done again? There was, I remember, a feeling of pride that it was the 1st Airborne who were to be given the furthest target, and to be carried in British aircraft.

Rightly or wrongly, the paratroop and RAF briefings were held independently, so we had little or no contact with the troops before take-off. The briefings were brisk and efficient, but not as detailed as they had been before D-Day. The intelligence briefing led us to believe that there would be little or no anti-aircraft resistance and that Arnhem was held by garrison troops of low morale.

As had been predicted by a favourable five-day weather forecast, it was fine for the start of Operation 'Market' on 17 September 1944. Fifty Stirlings from Fairford took part in the first day's lift, with 190 and 620 Squadrons providing equal numbers of aircraft. The initial wave consisted of six aircraft from each squadron, carrying 180 Pathfinder paratroops of the 21st Independent Parachute Company.

George Chesterton continued:

It was difficult not to feel emotion as the paratroops boarded the aircraft. The hardened regulars apparently took the whole enterprise as one almost of

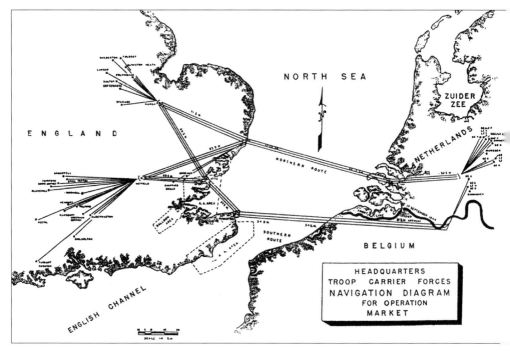

The 'Market' air routes. (*190 & 620 Sqns Archive*)

routine and at the other end of the scale there were the unashamedly white-faced, lip-biting young troopers.

No. 620 Squadron's LJ930 'A', captained by Sqn Ldr 'Dickie' Bunker DFC and Bar, was the first Stirling to take off, at 1010 hrs. Eight minutes later, twelve aircraft were airborne with the Pathfinder paratroops. Theirs was an essential task, since they were expected to secure DZ/LZ 'X' and LZ 'Z', before setting up Eureka beacons and visual markers to guide in the aircraft of the main lift, later that day. Zones 'X' and 'Z' were next to each other, south of the Arnhem to Utrecht railway line, and north of Heelsum. Zones 'L', 'S' and 'Y' were north of the railway. The selection of this area for the landings, with the most westerly zone, 'Y' being some 12 kilometres from the main road bridge at Arnhem, was determined by the lack of large, open spaces close to the city centre, together with the need to avoid the heavily defended *Luftwaffe* airfield at Deelen, just to the north.

Two air routes to Arnhem had been carefully chosen, taking into account the threat from the enemy defences. The northern route took the aircraft across the North Sea to the coast of Holland, but then over some heavily defended areas. It would require extensive cover by Allied ground-attack aircraft, in order to suppress enemy flak positions. The southern alternative crossed Belgium, before turning north-east towards the LZs. Although this route was the longer one, it involved a shorter time over enemy-occupied territory.

Both northern and southern routes were used on the first day of 'Market'. The Fairford Stirlings flew along the northern route, for which the main assembly point was overhead Hatfield in Hertfordshire. From there, a huge fleet of aircraft formed

thfinder paratroops of the 3rd Platoon, 21st Independent Parachute Company, gather up their kit at Fairford, ·ly in the morning of 17 September 1944. (*Imperial War Museum, CL 1154*)

thfinder paratroops board a Stirling at Fairford, 17 September 1944. (*Imperial War Museum, CL 3985*)

into three parallel streams, one and a half miles apart, before passing over the Suffolk coast at Aldeburgh. They crossed the sea at 2,500 feet, and made their landfall at Schouwen. The Germans had deliberately flooded large areas of the low-lying Dutch countryside, which made it difficult for the aircrews to obtain navigational pinpoints. Continuing east, they reached their Initial Point, 'Ellis', located near 's-Hertogenbosch, where a turn was made onto a north-easterly heading for the run-in to the Arnhem DZ/LZs. As aids to navigation, Eureka beacons and coded lights had been set up at the turning and assembly points in England and also on board ships positioned along the route.

Larry Siegert, 190 Squadron, recalled:

Ours was to be the lead aircraft of the 12 Pathfinder Stirlings. 17 September was a Sunday, and I remember seeing people going to church, as we headed across England. We went low over the North Sea and across Holland where we had lots of fighter escorts and ground-attack aircraft hitting any anti-aircraft posts. The field at Arnhem was empty as we came across the Rhine and flew over, dropping our paratroops in near-perfect conditions. I remember as we turned away, looking back at the field; their parachutes looked like a line of mushrooms across the field and already the second Stirling was running in to drop.

At this stage of the operation, the weather was reasonably good along the whole of the northern route, but visibility was limited by haze to about six miles. Although there was broken cloud over Holland, this was at 2,500–3,500 feet and caused no problems as the Stirlings ran in at 500 feet to drop the Pathfinders. The return route was flown on reciprocals of the outbound legs, at 5,000–7,000 feet, well above the cloud.

The view from the astrodome of a Stirling on the runway at Fairford, as the tow-rope is attached to its Horsa glider 17 September 1944. The faint speck towards the top right of the picture is a Dakota towing a glider. (*Imperial War Museum, CL 1155*)

1 Parachute Brigade, 1 Air Landing Brigade and various support units were scheduled to arrive at the DZ/LZs as soon as there had been sufficient time for the Pathfinders to set out the various homing and identification aids. At Fairford, little time was wasted in starting the glider lift, once the Stirlings carrying the Pathfinder troops were away. Within fifty minutes, thirty-eight tugs were airborne with their Horsas, which were carrying troops, jeeps, trailers, motorcycles and even bicycles.

Malcolm Mitchell, 190 Squadron, recalled:

On the airfield at Fairford we joined the ever-growing stream of Stirlings lining up, each awaiting its turn to taxi onto the runway. There we were to have our Horsa glider hooked on, and then take off. In the air, we manoeuvred to line up and join the great flow of aircraft and gliders heading out towards Holland. It was a bright, sunny day and looking down at the green fields of England, giving way to the splashing sea over which our airborne armada passed, put me in a happy mood.

We then crossed the Dutch coast, and seemingly with no opposition made our way towards Arnhem and our landing zone. Here the scene was of a confused mass of gliders lying in the fields, others coasting down to land, and many more behind us, being towed in. Finally, with a waggle of its wings, our glider released to join the others making their way down. We took a last look at the scene – my own view was somewhat restricted as I was looking out of the astrodome – and saw the tugs behind us, with their gliders, stretching far into the distance. We then dropped our tow-rope, turned and settled down to an uneventful flight back to our Fairford base.

Jim Marshall, 620 Squadron, recalled:

All our operations up until then had been night ops, so we were in for a new experience. We had been briefed for the Arnhem operation some time before it actually took place, then it was off, on again, off again, on again. Our first task was to tow Horsa gliders to the landing zone. The glider which our aircraft towed carried a jeep, a field gun, a trailer and six soldiers. The two glider pilots had joined us at briefing when the immensity of the operation was expounded, and we were told about the weather expected, the form-up details and the route. Each navigator had a formula which applied to his aircraft; this involved timing our heading to the west after take-off, then turning to the east which brought us in formation with the other aircraft.

We crossed over England and the North Sea without incident, except for the odd glider breaking its tow-rope. However, we ran into flak from a barge while going parallel to the River Rhine. Fighters quickly dived on it and set it on fire. Some of the anti-aircraft fire was very close and both of our glider pilots were wounded. They assured us that they could hold on as we could still talk to them over the intercom. They released as we approached the landing zone and we had our gunner give us a report on the success of their landing. We swung away, out of the route of the following aircraft and dropped our tow-rope in a specific field (the Germans must have ended up with an awful lot of rope), and then we joined the gaggle of aircraft homeward bound.

David Evans, 620 Squadron, recalled:

Our job as a crew was to tow a Horsa glider carrying twelve men, a jeep and a trailer containing mortars and ammunition to Arnhem. We took off and

A Fairford Stirling casts a shadow on Down Ampney airfield, as it flies overhead at the start of Operation 'Market'. On the runway are two lines of Horsa gliders, with the Dakotas of Nos 48 and 271 Squadrons being taxied in from either side to link up with them. (*190 & 620 Sqns Archive*)

headed out west from Fairford until we were over the Bristol Channel, before turning onto the heading east towards Holland. As I watched the column of aircraft from the astrodome, it disappeared from my sight whether I looked forward or aft. It was a memorable and spectacular scene. The fighter cover was so good that we saw flak-barges on the Lower Rhine being literally blown out of the water by rocket fire from Typhoon fighters. Our Horsa cast off and landed, then we jettisoned the tow-rope. As we circled to leave we could see the gliders on the landing zone looking like cars parked in a massive field.

Mike Dauncey, Glider Pilot Regiment, Fairford, recalled:

On 17 September 1944, I took part in the first lift of the Arnhem operation, when Fg Off Pascoe was the captain of the Stirling bomber which towed us. As his debriefing report stated – it was a 'very successful trip – uneventful'. I can still remember seeing the little Dutch farm, in a triangle of land, straight in front of us, as we approached our landing zone, 'Z', exactly as planned. The navigation was brilliant.

Not all the Fairford Horsas on the first lift reached Arnhem. The glider towed by 190 Squadron's Stirling EF316 'Z', captained by Plt Off Middleton, made a forced landing near South Cerney airfield, about five miles west of Fairford. It had released the tow-rope when it climbed into a very high position, relative to the tug, as they flew into cloud. The gliders towed by 620 Squadron's LJ873 and LJ875, captained

Horsa gliders lie scattered across one of the Arnhem landing zones. This photograph appeared in British newspapers on Tuesday 19 September 1944. 'A field in Holland has sprung a new crop', according to one reporter. (Imperial War Museum, CL1173)

by Fg Off Gawith and Plt Off Kidgell, respectively, were also still in the local area when they broke their tow-ropes. One of these gliders landed at Down Ampney, and the other at South Farm, Castle Eaton.

The glider towed by 620 Squadron's LJ899, captained by Fg Off 'Bluey' Scanlon, broke its tow-rope when the combination entered cloud over Holland, but it landed safely, south-west of 's-Hertogenbosch. The glider towed by LJ588, captained by Plt Off Clement of 620 Squadron, was also lost over Holland, but in this case it appeared have been hit by flak before crashing near Fijnaart. It was later reported that the two glider pilots, Sgt Cook and Sgt Rowland, had been killed, along with their four passengers from the Royal Artillery.

Stirling crews from Fairford reported seeing several gliders down in the sea. Dinghies were dropped to them, and their positions passed to the Air Sea Rescue service, so that launches and Warwick aircraft could be sent to provide further assistance. A few gliders were observed in fields, short of the LZs, but the first glider lift to Arnhem appeared to be a success overall. After the mishaps *en route*, thirty-three of the Fairford Horsas made it to their LZ, identified by a white letter 'Z', red flares and purple smoke. The wind was very light, which created an unforeseen problem as the glider pilots set up their approaches, since some of them tended to overshoot the touchdown area. This led to congestion, and a number of collisions on the ground towards the northern end of the LZ. There was little opposition from the enemy, in the area around LZ 'Z', and as the Stirling crews looked down they could see Dutch civilians waving and greeting the troops as they landed. However, both flak and small arms fire were encountered over the rope-dropping area. This was about three kilometres beyond the LZ, and not far south of Deelen airfield. Some of the Fairford Stirlings on the first lift sustained minor damage.

Stirlings of 620 Squadron, flying high as they return from Arnhem on 17 September 1944. The aircraft nearest t camera is LJ566 'E-Easy', captained by Flight Lieutenant Gordon Thring DFC. (*190 & 620 Sqns Archive*)

RAF Fairford's Station Commander, Group Captain Allen Wheeler, listens as Wing Commander Graeme Harrison, CO of 190 Squadron, describes his flight on the first day of Operation 'Market'. (*Imperial War Museum, CL 1148*)

On 17 September, a number of the Fairford Stirlings carried War Correspondents who, according to the 620 Squadron diarist, later 'gave glowing and not entirely accurate accounts of their experiences.'

Jim Marshall, recalled:

At debriefing, a war correspondent was allowed to sit in as his aircraft had been forced to return when it lost its glider over the UK. The story he wrote was ours except that he padded it out and put words in my mouth which I had a hard time living down at home – I ask you – did you ever hear a Scotsman say 'Mighty Fine', like John Wayne?

During the late afternoon and early evening of 17 September, the aircrews of 190 and 620 Squadrons were briefed for the next day's operation. Forty-three of the Fairford Stirlings were going to tow gliders carrying more troops, whose task was to establish a perimeter around Arnhem. At this stage, it was still assumed that the ground forces coming from the south-west would arrive in the town by the end of the second day of the operation. It was also expected that troops of the Polish Paratroop Brigade, who were waiting to be dropped on DZ 'K', south of the river, would provide reinforcements.

By the evening of 17 September, the landings by the American airborne forces appeared to have gone according to plan, so it was hoped that the road from the south-west would soon be opened up, thus allowing the British ground forces to start their advance towards Arnhem. In the western suburbs of Arnhem, there was

153

Pilot Officer Doug Sellars and his 190 Squadron crew: standing, left to right, Sergeant F. Kempton (flight engineer), Flying Officer W. Mowat RCAF (navigator) and Pilot Officer D.S. Sellars RCAF (pilot); kneeling, left to right, Warrant Officer I.S. Armstrong RCAF (air gunner), Flight Sergeant C.G. Hill RAAF (bomb aimer) and Warrant Officer R.M. Palmer RCAF (wireless operator). (*190 & 620 Sqns Archive*)

fierce fighting as the 2nd Parachute Battalion moved in to capture the northern end of the main road bridge over the river, but this objective was achieved by dusk. The 1st and 3rd Battalions were faring less well. They had run into unexpectedly stiff opposition, which included armoured vehicles of the II SS Panzer Corps.

On 18 September, the Fairford Stirlings were to use the northern route again, but the weather had deteriorated overnight, so they were not cleared to take-off until 1125 hrs. The Horsas they towed were carrying loads that included troops, jeeps, trailers, six-pounder guns and a motorcycle. Three of these gliders failed to leave the UK. Plt Off Sellars, in Stirling 'U' of 190 Squadron, cast off his glider over South Cerney airfield, when the tug's starboard outer engine failed just after forming up, and Flt Lt Jack, in LJ917 'L' of 620 Squadron, lost his glider when the tow-rope broke, also near South Cerney. Stirling 'Y' of 190 Squadron, captained by Plt Off Bebarfald, landed at Woodbridge, as did its glider, after their tow-rope broke over Suffolk. An Oxford aircraft was sent from Fairford to Woodbridge with a spare rope, enabling the Stirling and Horsa to return to base later the same day.

Flying in formation, it was difficult for the pilots to maintain station as their aircraft were buffeted by the slipstream of others. A number of gliders were lost *en route*, owing to this hazard. Flt Sgt Herger's 190 Squadron Stirling was forced close to a Dakota by the slipstream of another aircraft, but as Herger dived to avoid the Dakota, his glider pilots tried to climb, and the tow-rope snapped. This glider landed safely in Holland, as did the one towed by Fg Off Farren of 190 Squadron, after its tow-rope broke, also as a result of slipstream turbulence.

George Chesterton recalled:

Although the second day of Operation 'Market' was not as quiet as the first, all went well. Again flying in loose formation, tug and glider combinations made the rendezvous on time and then straggled out in an impressive string. Take-off had been delayed because of fog over the Allied fighter airfields in Belgium, a delay one has subsequently learnt was fortuitous since patrolling German fighters then needed to return to their bases to refuel. The occasional combination broke up, usually when a tow-rope snapped, but the gliders appeared always to come safely to rest. As we approached the landing zone a fair amount of light flak was in evidence, but there was an added problem; our starboard inner engine was rapidly losing oil pressure and it would be touch and go as to whether we would make the last mile or two. However, all was well, and with a bellow of 'goodbye and good luck' the glider cast off and was seen by our rear gunner to settle heavily but safely amongst the rapidly accumulating force. At cast-off the Stirling would surge forward almost as though unchained, but on this occasion the starboard inner had immediately to be feathered and the climb away was sluggish enough to cause anxiety. The return journey was therefore slower than expected, and a very indifferent landing that used up every inch of the runway was greeted with derision by the Wing Commander and our Flight Commander as they were walking away from dispersals. Three days later both these splendid men were dead.

Stirling outbound for Arnhem (with glider in tow) on 18 September 1944, photographed by Flight Sergeant Noel Chaffey of 620 Squadron. He was flying in Stirling LK127, which was shot down two days later. (V.R. Chaffey)

Photographed above the clouds by Flight Sergeant Noel Chaffey, a Stirling returns from Arnhem on 18 Septembe
1944. (*N.R. Chaffey*)

Having delivered most of their gliders safely to the LZ, all the Fairford Stirlings returned from the second lift, but there had been much more flak than on the first one, and several aircraft were damaged. In the early evening of 18 September, the Fairford crews were briefed for the next day's flights to Arnhem. In addition, six aircraft of 190 Squadron were requested for SOE operations to Holland that night. However, five of these sorties were later cancelled, leaving a single aircraft, captained by Fg Off Connell, to carry out a drop of containers and a pannier.

Although the second lift had generally gone according to plan, the enemy was now responding vigorously. Conditions were becoming decidedly unpleasant on the LZs, which were under fire from small arms and mortars. The 1st and 3rd Parachute Battalions, brought in on the first day, made a determined effort to reach the centre of Arnhem, but heavy casualties were inflicted among them by the German armoured vehicles. The troops who arrived on the second lift, with the intention of forming a perimeter around the town, also became caught up in fierce fighting and were unable to achieve their objectives. The northern end of the road bridge was still in British hands, but it was looking unlikely that reinforcements would arrive in time to prevent it from being retaken by the Germans.

By the third day, 19 September, the situation on the ground at Arnhem had worsened to the extent that the British troops were constantly under attack. They had now formed a defensive perimeter around the 1st Airborne Divisional HQ, which had been set up in Oosterbeck, a western suburb of the city. There was still no sign of the Second Army, coming from the south-west, so any prospect of re-inforcing the troops at the road bridge was fading rapidly.

On 19 September, the southern route to Arnhem was used, though the weather forecast for the northern route was better. This decision was taken for 'tactical reasons', since it was thought unwise to use the northern route on three successive days. The southern route took the aircraft over North Foreland, Ostend and Ghent, and past Antwerp, to the Eindhoven area, from where they made a straight run-in to Arnhem. Owing to the weather, the air support crews had another frustrating wait all morning, before operations could begin. With most of the glider force delivered, Fairford was sending only two Stirlings from 190 Squadron, and one from 620 Squadron, as tugs. They took off at approximately 1230 hrs. Troops, jeeps and trailers were carried in their gliders, two of which were successful in reaching the LZ. The third glider was lost after its tug, piloted by Fg Off Bebarfald of 190 Squadron, ran into low cloud. The glider started to overtake the Stirling and nearly forced it into the sea, before the tow-rope broke. After ditching approximately five miles from the Belgian coast, three men were seen to escape from the glider and climb into a dinghy, but it is believed that both glider pilots died. A message giving the glider's position was passed to a Motor Torpedo Boat, in the hope that it might rescue the survivors.

At 1300 hrs, the Fairford Stirlings commenced their resupply flights to Arnhem. Nos 190 and 620 Squadrons each had seventeen aircraft detailed to take part in this operation, but LK513 'G' of 190 Squadron, captained by Plt Off Atkinson, swung on take-off and its port undercarriage collapsed. Flying in 'vics' of three, the rest of the aircraft ran into some bad weather that afternoon, though conditions did improve towards the DZ. There were further problems when unsatisfactory communications with the Allied fighter escorts led to a mix-up over timing at a rendezvous point. Although the Fairford crews did not see any hostile fighters, the absence of Allied fighters meant that enemy anti-aircraft fire could not be suppressed. This was almost certainly a factor in the marked increase in the number of Stirlings and Dakotas shot down by the ground defences that day. As the aircraft were running in for their drops, the opposition became intense and was kept up as they departed to the north of the DZ.

The Fairford Stirlings delivered 742 containers and 129 panniers on 19 September. Most crews managed to drop on the designated area, 'V', but some reported that they had been forced to drop from a greater than usual height, because of other aircraft crowding them out.

Jim Marshall recalled:

Our next lift took place on the 19th September. We carried twenty-four containers on the bomb-racks and had four panniers for pushing out of the hatch.

Flying Officer Jim Marshall in the cockpit of his 620 Squadron Stirling.
*(190 & 620 Sqns Archive)*

Soldiers of the Royal Army Service Corps were on board to assist with the dispatching of the panniers. This lift did not go as smoothly as our first. We were a long line of Stirling in pairs following each other, but we didn't see the fighter support this time and quite a bit of flak was coming up en route. The streams of aircraft started to merge and we would see Stirlings all over the sky. The odd aircraft would be hit and we could see it go down and cartwheel on the ground or crash in a mushroom cloud. Each time this happened the pairs seemed to ease away from each other so that by looking you could see where the trouble was and avoid flying over that spot. We now had several separate lines of aircraft. At the DZ it was amazing, as I seemed to spend my time dodging panniers and containers being dropped from aircraft which were higher than the briefed dropping height. The flak from the ground was bad but the chances of being hit by a pannier full of landmines seemed greater. I certainly breathed a sigh of relief when our load had gone and we were able to swing away from the area.

Unfortunately, the aircrews' brave efforts on 19 September were largely wasted, for it was later learned that the DZ was in enemy hands by the time they arrived over-head. The British troops on the ground knew this to be the case, but had been unable to get messages back to the UK. The best they could do in this desperate situation was to lay out ground marker strips and set up a Eureka beacon, on an open area nearby. Because this improvised DZ was partly obscured by trees, the troops also fired Very lights into the air as an aid to recognition. However, when the aircrews spotted these signals, they had to decide very quickly whether to drop on this DZ, or on the original one as briefed.

George Chesterton recalled:

The last 20 miles were like going through a shooting alley, and an aircraft next to me just blew up in the air. We were lucky and got away with it, but the sickening thing was that practically everything we dropped went to the Germans. What still bugs me to this day, is that at every briefing we were told 'You must stick to the dropping zone as arranged, don't be misled, the Germans are trying to persuade us that the dropping zones are in their hands'; well of course they were, but we continued to drop where we were told.

Two of the 190 Squadron Stirlings failed to return on 19 September. EF263, captained by Flt Sgt Coeshott, was hit by flak and crashed about 50 kilometres south-west of Arnhem, at St Michielsgestel. All six members of the crew were killed, together with the two RASC dispatchers. LJ939, captained by Sqn Ldr Gilliard, reached the DZ but was hit by shells, which severed some of the control cables. Gilliard gave the order to abandon the aircraft, and Fg Off Cullen (bomb aimer), Fg Off Lawton (navigator), Flt Sgt Byrne (flight engineer), Plt Off Lane (wireless operator) and Sqn Ldr Bantoft (listed in the 190 Squadron Operations Record Book as 2nd pilot) managed to jump. The stricken Stirling then crashed just west of Oosterbeck, killing Sqn Ldr Gilliard, Fg Off McEwen (air gunner) and Drivers Breading and Taylor (RASC dispatchers). Byrne and Lane were taken prisoner. Lawton and Cullen also landed behind enemy lines, but they evaded capture and eventually returned to the UK.

Reg Lawton, 190 Squadron, recalled:

I was navigator to Sqn Ldr John Gilliard, and was last with 190 Squadron on 19 September 1944. We took off from Fairford at midday on an Arnhem re-supply flight and were shot down at low level over the target. Some in the plane were killed by gunfire but I managed to jump and landed in a heap of soft sand in a tiny clearing in a forest, just as my parachute was opening. When I got back to England, after about a fortnight, the squadron was almost folding up, as it had experienced so many losses.

An Air Force officer (ground type) had invited himself along for the ride and got more than he bargained for. I understand he survived the jump and some-how got back to his office (somewhere in London, I think) in very quick time. The two army men were standing by the open door at the rear, ready to push out the panniers on parachutes. They were killed, as was Norman McEwen, rear gunner and one-time Sports Editor of the *Glasgow Herald*. It is possible the intercom was cut and they didn't get the message to bale out.

On 19 September, many of the Fairford Stirlings came back peppered with holes from shrapnel and small arms fire. The ground crews set to work immediately, carrying out battle damage repairs as best they could. There had been no casualties among the 620 Squadron crews, but WO Pelletier, the Canadian wireless operator in Fg Off Pascoe's 190 Squadron crew, was wounded, as was one of the army dispatchers in their aircraft.

Malcolm Mitchell recalled:

On the 19 September our crew was stood down, the only flying for us being an air test of a Stirling. The aircraft briefed for the resupply drop at Arnhem left without fuss or worry on the part of their crews, as far as I could see. The first indication we had that things were going wrong was when the aircraft returned, many showing signs of flak damage. In due course, those of us who had stayed behind met their crews in the mess, and then we learned of the reception they had met. There had been anti-aircraft fire all over the shop – and some of the crews, friends of mine, people who slept in my billet, had not returned.

It went without saying that those who had returned, and those of us who listened to them, were definitely not happy about the prospect of going to Arnhem again on the morrow. Many men stayed in the mess, drinking to cheer themselves up. I, however, have never been much of a drinker and I soon left, to go to my billet and read until lights out.

As 20 September dawned, there was fierce fighting at the Arnhem road bridge, and also further west, around Oosterbeck. The Waal bridge at Nijmegen had been captured by American troops of the 82nd Airborne, but this objective was achieved 48 hours later than planned. It had become clear that even if reinforcements did manage to reach Arnhem, via the road from the south-west, they would be far too late to save most of the British airborne troops.

At 1000 hrs the Fairford Stirling crews attended the briefing for their next re-supply operation. By this time, news had been received of DZ 'V' having fallen into enemy hands. The drops were therefore to be made on a new DZ within the shrinking British perimeter. Later in the morning, it was decided to postpone the departure time at Fairford by two hours, so it was not until 1440 hrs that the first of seventeen aircraft from 620 Squadron took off. They were followed by a similar number from 190 Squadron. All the resupply flights would follow the southern route from now on. The Fairford Stirlings had been instructed to fly in pairs, but visibility was very poor, making it difficult for them to keep in formation. After crossing the coast at Ostend, the weather improved slightly, fighter escorts arrived as planned, and there was no sign of enemy fighters. However, there was low cloud over the DZ, with visibility still only two to four miles, and as before, the flak was intense. In spite of this, many of the supplies did get through, but the troops, pinned down by enemy fire, could not do much to retrieve them until nightfall. A few aircraft from 38 Group were ordered to drop on another zone, 'Z', which most did successfully, or so they thought, since it was later learned that this one had also fallen into enemy hands by the time they arrived overhead. Five out of the thirty-four Fairford Stirlings sent to Arnhem on 20 September failed to return and many others were seriously damaged.

Malcolm Mitchell recalled:

We could see Arnhem, with the aircraft ahead of us flying into the flak. One exploding shell sent a piece of shrapnel flying through our bomb aimer's compartment, passing just to the left of his head and smashing some of the electrical equipment fixed to the aircraft's side. I walked forward to look down into the compartment, to see Bob grinning up at me and pointing to the damage. I had then to leave my post by my instruments and go to the rear of the aircraft. One of the duties of a flight engineer was to act as a dispatcher. On this occasion my task was to help push out two panniers, filled with supplies. By the weight of them, they must have contained ammunition, as I could hardly move them with my hands. The large exit in the floor of the aircraft had by this time been opened and I lay down on the deck, to push the panniers out, when we were given the green light signal.

Therefore, I did not see the scene as we crossed the Rhine and made for the dropping zone. But I was aware of the anti-aircraft opposition, for the air was full of the noise of exploding shells and I could hear the sound of shrapnel hitting our aircraft. But our luck held and we were not hit in any vital part. Soon the green light came on and, by thrusting with my legs and straightening my knees, I was able to push out the first pannier. Then I moved over and in a similar fashion disposed of the second one. Having done this I quickly made my way back to my own position by the astrodome. Our pilot, 'Ikey', had opened the throttles and we were climbing steeply. Below I caught a glimpse of the battlefield, but my attention was directed mainly towards the Stirling which was following us, for its port outer engine was smoking and on fire. We watched as the aircraft slowly stopped climbing, turned and began to go down. Then the parachutes started to come out and we counted them as the aircraft descended – one, two, three, four, five – but no more. The pilot had obviously held on whilst his crew got out, but had no time to jump himself.

Three of the Stirlings lost on 20 September belonged to 190 Squadron. LJ829, captained by Fg Off Matheson, was probably one of the many brought down by flak. All seven members of the crew were killed (a 2nd pilot was on board), along with the two RASC dispatchers, when this aircraft crashed south of the DZ, at Doorwerth.

Fg Off le Bouvier's aircraft, EF260, was hit by flak and its port wing caught fire. All the crew members, the two army dispatchers and Mr Edmund Townsend, a *Daily Telegraph* War Correspondent, baled out before the aircraft crashed south of the Rhine. Flt Sgt Kershaw and Flt Sgt Martin were captured, but the others managed to reach the Allied lines to the south-west. On his return to the UK, le Bouvier submitted the following report:

We took off from Fairford in a Stirling aircraft at about 15.10 hrs, 20th Sept 1944. We were scheduled to drop supplies to the First Airborne Division at Arnhem; but about 15.30 hrs we were hit by flak near Oosterbeek. We were then flying at about 900 feet and were hit in the port wing. I came in, dropped the supplies and then climbed. At about 2,000 feet the crew baled out. After they had gone, I got out and landed a few miles north-east of Elst. I was immediately picked up by Dutch peasants, given an overall and hidden in a ditch. At about 21.00 hrs, a Dutchman came back and took me to a farm on the northern outskirts of Elst on the main Elst-Arnhem road. There I met a member of the First Airborne Division, Private Stephen Danby, who had reached Elst the day before from Arnhem. We were given civilian clothes and hidden in the farm. The Germans were concentrating in the area and there was a sort of advanced HQ the other side of the road.

On 22 September, the farm came under fire from the British artillery and that night the family decided to evacuate and advised us to do the same, preferably in the opposite direction. On 23 Sept., we were all ready to go, when at 07.15 hrs, a German platoon turned up at the farm. We managed to get away through a cellar corridor in the back of the farm and headed roughly due west in an attempt to reach the bridgehead west of Nijmegen.

At about 11.30 hrs, we met an advanced platoon of the Worcesters on reconnaissance. We were sent to HQ and I was able to tell them the position of the German concentrations near Elst which they immediately attacked by artillery. At the HQ I was told that the following members of my crew were reported to be safe further to the north: F/Sgt Sanders, the two Army despatchers and Mr Townsend. We were then sent to Nijmegen, where I left Pte Danby. I then continued to Eindhoven where I spent the night. On 24 Sept I flew to Brussels and from there to UK.

In contrast to Fg Off le Bouvier's matter-of-fact report, an article by Mr Townsend was written with a spirit of adventure that may not have appealed to aircrews who had witnessed so many horrific losses over Arnhem by the time it was published in the *Daily Telegraph* on 26 September. Townsend described how he had been sitting in the co-pilot's seat when Stirling EF260 was hit by flak and caught fire. After baling out, he landed in a ploughed field to the south of the Rhine, and was assisted by a local family, before being escorted across country by the Dutch Resistance.

Townsend soon joined a group of RAF evaders, including four others from le Bouvier's crew. With an RAF officer from another squadron, he made his way to a village that had just been liberated by British ground troops advancing from the south-west. There they met more RAF personnel and British airborne troops. This group, numbering about twenty, attempted to get to Valburg, but ran into German patrols, and were forced to go into hiding in nearby woods, in order to avoid sniper fire. Following an overnight stay in a farmhouse, the evaders set out again for the British lines. In spite of German shelling, they were successful in reaching a British HQ before nightfall. From there, transport was arranged for their return to the UK.

Fg Off Robertson and his 190 Squadron crew, in Stirling LJ831, failed to return to Fairford on 20 September, but it was soon learned that they had made an emergency landing in Belgium. Over the DZ, their aircraft had been hit by flak, as they dropped twenty-four containers from 1,000 feet. The wireless operator, Flt Sgt Thompson, was wounded in the right shoulder, and the rear fuselage and tailplane of the aircraft were seriously damaged. Robertson's personal report, submitted when he got back at Fairford, on 23 September, tells the story of what happened next:

As soon as we were hit over DZ a/c went into a steep dive, control regained at about 400 feet. I gave orders to fit parachutes. Finding myself unable to hold aircraft due to elevator trim tabs being shot away, I called for my Bomb Aimer, (F/Lt Rosenblade) and between us we got the aircraft level. I got a course from the navigator who was unable to find a pinpoint, so we flew very shaky D.R. [dead reckoning] as far as GHENT. On the last leg the aircraft became very hard to control. I gave the crew an opportunity to bale out, but, discovering the W/Op was wounded, all decided to stay with the aircraft which I landed fairly smoothly at GHENT. I should like to comment on the good show put up by my W/Op (F/Sgt Thompson) who, although wounded, stuck to his job and saw that the proper messages were sent out before having himself attended to.

Two aircraft from 620 Squadron were shot down on 20 September. LK127, captained by Fg Off 'Bluey' Scanlon, was a victim of flak. Scanlon and his crew had flown to Arnhem on 17 and 18 September in LK299 'O', but this aircraft was badly damaged on the latter sortie, so they took LK127, which was a spare aircraft, on 20 September. There had been changes to Scanlon's crew after the crash of Stirling EF275 at Fairford on 21 August. Flt Sgt Franklin was replaced as bomb aimer by a Canadian, Flt Sgt Lamont, and for the Arnhem operations, the air gunner, Sgt Marshall, was on loan from Fg Off Neale's crew, the rest of whom were fortunate to be away on a battle training course at this time.

Scanlon's navigator was Fg Off Eric Dane:

On the 20th, we dropped our cargo, including skips containing jerricans of petrol, which had to be pushed manually out of the opening in the floor towards the rear. Climbing and banking to port, we were caught by heavy flak and the port wing just burst into flames. Orders to abandon were given, the bomb aimer went out, then the flight engineer, Bill Murray. I remember clipping Bluey's parachute on him, and him patting me on the shoulder and telling me to go. The rear gunner, Johnny Marshall, did not reply to the abandon order, but Ted McGilvray, our wireless operator, didn't have a chance. He was with the two Army dispatchers, closing the rear doors when the order came to 'Bale out', and I think he was off intercom, so he went in with the plane.

I am afraid that, out of the seven of us on board, only two made it, Bill Murray and myself. I learned from the Dutch later that we were only about 1,000 feet up when we jumped, so it didn't take long to come down. When the skipper left the aircraft it was diving and he was too low for his 'chute to open properly. Although he was still alive when a Dutchman got to him, he died soon after.

Stirling LK127 crashed into marshy ground at Heteren, on the south bank of the Rhine, to the west of Arnhem. It was reported that the air gunner, Sgt Marshall, baled out, but then descended into the Rhine. It is possible that the bomb aimer, Flt Sgt Lamont, who has no known grave, also went into the Rhine, since Fg Off Dane saw him jump from the aircraft. The remains of one of the dispatchers, Cpl Fowler, were recovered for burial, but the other dispatcher, Dvr Hadley, has no known grave, so it is not known whether he perished in the crash, or may have baled out and drowned in the river. Fg Off Dane and Flt Sgt Murray evaded capture, and were among the group of RAF and Army personnel with whom the *Daily Telegraph*'s Mr Townsend reached the British lines.

The other 620 Squadron aircraft shot down that day, LK548, captained by Plt Off McHugh, was hit by flak and crashed near Vorstenbosch, which is about 25 kilometres south-west of Nijmegen. Flt Sgt Gascoyne, Flt Sgt Hume and Sgt Evans survived, but the other three crew members and the two RASC dispatchers were killed.

A Stirling runs in for a resupply drop at Arnhem. This photograph was taken from a garden in Heteren, by a member of the family that assisted Flying Officer Eric Dane after he was shot down. (*190 & 620 Sqns Archive*)

David Evans recalled:

On Wednesday 20 September we were again required to deliver containers, but because of poor weather conditions take-off was delayed for two or three hours. As we approached Arnhem from the southerly direction the flak appeared much heavier than the previous day. Incendiary bullets tore into the trailing edge of the starboard wing setting it alight, and from my position in the astrodome I could see the flames. I discussed the extent of the fire with Tom Vickers, the rear gunner, who could view the underside of the wing from his position in the turret. We concurred eventually that the fire had been blown out in the slipstream. Minutes later I was momentarily blinded by dust as a cannon shell pierced the wooden frame of the astrodome, within an inch of my nose. I was shocked to note that my position had been straddled by cannon fire which had made very neat holes about 18 inches apart in the floor of the compartment. This must have happened just as the bomb-aimer released the containers and our army colleagues were pushing out the baskets. We then climbed and were heading south for home, when we were again hit. This time it was an 88 mm shell that went through a main petrol tank in the starboard wing, fortunately without exploding. I saw the hole appear in the wing, followed instantly by a fountain of high-octane fuel which became a roaring jet of fire. Within seconds the flames were inside the aircraft. My pint-sized fire extinguisher had no effect and I knew the aircraft was doomed.

I picked up my parachute pack and clipped it onto my harness as I made my way forward to the escape hatch in the bomb-aiming compartment. Jock Hume, the navigator, was ahead of me and I helped him to remove his helmet as he made his way down the steps into the bomb-aiming compartment. As Nick Gascoyne, the bomb-aimer, opened the hatch, the navigator went on his way, to be followed by myself. Foolishly I went out feet first, clasping the rip-cord handle, which I pulled when I felt I was clear of the doomed aircraft. As the parachute pack opened it caught my chin with such force as to render me unconscious. By the time I regained consciousness I had hit the ground, and was surrounded by about a dozen people, two of whom supported me as I stood up. I was in RAF blue battledress which, being stained and faded, looked similar to German field grey. The first question asked of me by a young English-speaking girl was 'Are you English?' I replied 'Yes' and enquired if she was Dutch, to which they all shook their heads. I then thought I had landed across the border in Germany, but they had thought I had asked if they were 'Deutsch', their word for German. When I finally realised who they were I took out a packet of 'Players' cigarettes which finally clinched my nationality. I was then taken across a field to a farmhouse and made to sit at a table for some food. The kind farmer and his wife gave me a boiled duck-egg, some bread and a mug of tea. In my concussed state I did not feel hungry, but felt obliged to eat because of the hospitality shown to me. Indeed, I had to eat a second egg and was glad when a young man arrived at the farmhouse and announced that he would take me to the British Army. As I got up from the table I looked around the room and saw several young faces in every window, and I thought to myself that all the children of the village had come to gaze at the strange parachutist. It was only long after the war was over that I learnt that the farmer had twenty children!

The young man who had called for me was a member of the resistance organisation and wore an orange band on his sleeve. He mounted his light-weight motorcycle and bade me sit on the pillion, at the same time handing me the German rifle he was carrying, advising me to beware of snipers. Very soon we were meeting the vanguard of a column of British tanks, and there was bewilderment on the faces of the soldiers as they peeped out of their turrets. I am sure they did not expect to see an RAF sergeant, capless and with his face all bloody, riding pillion on a miniature motorcycle.

My destination, a large building like a town hall, was quickly reached and as I walked to the door I noticed a row of civilians. They had their hands up against the wall of the building, so that they could be easily searched, and I was promptly told that they were collaborators whom had been rounded up as soon as the Germans left. There to greet me as I entered the hall were my two fellow crew members, namely Flight Sergeants Hume and Gascoyne. They were having cuts and bruises attended to by some nursing sisters of a religious order. Jock Hume was almost unscathed in spite of the fact that his parachute had only been attached to his harness by one strap. Nick Gascoyne had a cut above an eye but otherwise was in one piece, although in his haste he had forgotten to fasten the side straps of his parachute harness, and could easily have fallen out of the harness. Of the eight crew members we were the only three to escape.

We learned that those who were expected to deliver us from the enemy were in fact 12 RAF Regiment men and their CO, a young Flight Lieutenant. They were occupying a large house on the eastern outskirts of the town of Uden at which we had arrived. They welcomed us as reinforcements and found us a motley array of weapons, since we were all three unarmed. I recall being handed a revolver, but was glad that I did not have to make use of it. Some time during the night we had a visit from our Dutch allies who were very keen to get to grips with the enemy who had suppressed them for so long. I think they were a little disgusted with us when we suggested that perhaps we should wait until more help arrived. The RAF Regiment group had the task of organising the repair of a local airfield, so that it could be used as a forward base by fighter aircraft. Having fallen out of the sky so unexpectedly we were ill prepared to carry out the simplest ablutions, but with the help of our newly found colleagues we were able to make ourselves presentable the following morning. This was fortunate because the Flight Lieutenant announced that he and the three of us were invited out to breakfast with the Underground leaders for the district.

We were led to a big house, indeed a mansion, and breakfast was served in a large room which had windows opening out onto a garden with a stream at the bottom. All I can remember of the meal after all these years is that we were served with a large glass of gin, and no doubt we drank toasts to all our allies, or at least pretended to drink, because the drink was not entirely to my taste at such an early hour. After the meal we all went out onto a balcony overlooking a square where a large crowd had gathered, and then proceeded to cheer us. Souvenirs were exchanged such as Dutch and English coins, buttons, insignias, brevets and postcards. Whilst we were being feted by the newly liberated towns-folk of Uden, our resistance friends were busy arranging to evacuate us to Eindhoven and on home to England. One problem that morning was that our route south was being shelled by enemy artillery, but by about 2.00 pm it was considered safe for us to leave. A large Chevrolet car arrived, driven by a heavily-armed Orange man who announced he and his colleague would take us to Eindhoven.

The journey was not easy because we had to make our way against the tide of British Army vehicles that were surging towards Nijmegen along just one available road. So heavy was the traffic that some vehicles were using the fields alongside as extra tracks. The countryside was littered with shattered and still-burning corpses of cows and horses, splintered trees, burnt-out tanks and vehicles. There were also newly-dug graves, marked by the helmets of dead Germans.

As we arrived in Eindhoven our first sight was of the Philips factory, then only a tangled mass of steel girders. We were taken to one of the few intact buildings, which was being used as the headquarters of the Dutch Resistance in the area. Our companions were made to hand over their weapons, much to their disgust, and told to return home. After a few questions we were taken to a civilian lorry of the type used for carrying hay and straw. The deck of the lorry was already occupied by a group of American glider pilots who had landed at the Grave and Nijmegen bridges. We joined them and after a wait for some more American stragglers we were on our way to Brussels. There we arrived at the Hotel Angleterre, just as the daylight faded, and bade farewell to our American allies. The British then proceeded to take charge of our immediate needs. The food comprised some atrocious captured German 'ersatz' rations, so before going to sleep we decided to taste some Belgian food and drink. Money was no problem, as what little Dutch money we had been given was enough to allow us to sample some Belgian beer. We were made very welcome in our Air Force blue uniforms, which contrasted with the khaki of all the other uniforms to be seen in newly-liberated Brussels. Although the food at the Angleterre was bad, the beds were comparatively luxurious. After breakfast, transport to the airfield was arranged and before long we were aboard an RAF Dakota, but feeling a little apprehensive without parachutes. The flight to England was un-eventful, our fellow passengers being other RAF aircrew who had spent various periods of time in hiding after being shot down over occupied Europe. They thought us very fortunate, being able to escape so easily.

On arrival at Northolt we were ushered through Customs with nothing to declare, our dishevelled state enough to indicate our status. My battledress sleeve was torn, my face carried the scars of the parachute straps, and my cap was missing. Nick had a nasty gash above his left eye, and on his feet were German jackboots. The RAF authorities at Northolt issued us with travel warrants and we caught the tube to Paddington railway station where we had to wait for a train to Fairford via Oxford. This gave me an opportunity to telephone home – my mother answered and you can imagine the joy there was to learn I was safe. She had received a telegram, announcing that my aircraft had failed to return, but that there was a chance that I was alive and in captivity.

We caught the last train from Oxford to Fairford and reported to the guard-room about midnight, to be told that a new crew had taken our billet, and that we should report to the sick-bay. The following morning we enjoyed a sleep-in before we were visited by our CO, Wing Commander Lee, who was very anxious to learn about the situation over Arnhem, since he was to go on the next operation. Little did he realise then that he also would become a casualty by crash-landing. Later we were debriefed and then collected our personal effects which had been impounded, this being normal procedure when crews went missing on operations. On Sunday 24 September we collected leave passes and were on our way north in an old Singer saloon car owned by Jock Hume. I drove it as far as Bangor-on-Dee where Jock's girlfriend lived. On reaching Bangor I then hitched a lift towards home and eventually arrived in Ruthin to meet loved ones.

By the evening of 20 September, the Battle of Arnhem was all but lost, since the last of the gallant defenders at the road bridge had neither food nor ammunition left. The following morning they were overwhelmed as German tanks moved northwards across the bridge. Meanwhile, the troops within the shrinking perimeter around the 1st Airborne Divisional HQ remained under heavy fire.

For the RAF, 21 September 1944 turned out to be the most disastrous day of Operation 'Market'. Resupply drops were flown in four waves, and although fighters escorted the first and second waves, those assigned as cover for the third and fourth remained on the ground, owing to poor weather over their bases. Among the unescorted Dakotas and Stirlings were ten aircraft from 190 Squadron, and eleven from 620 Squadron, which had taken off from Fairford just after midday. Over Ostend, conditions were murky, beneath an overcast sky, but visibility improved to several miles in the Arnhem area, under a 2,500 ft cloud base. Once again, the flak was fierce and accurate.

Jim Marshall recalled:

Our next flight to Arnhem was on 21 September. As the Fairford aircraft were starting to taxi out, the armourers reported a short circuit in my bomb-racks, so I was held up. I still hoped to catch up with the stream but the CO drove onto the runway ahead and stopped me from rolling. It had been decided that I would rendezvous with a Dakota squadron over Eindhoven, where we would have the cover of a Thunderbolt fighter wing for our run-in to Arnhem. During the trip to Eindhoven everything seemed normal and I circled there awaiting the Daks; they arrived but there were no fighters. So I took up a position ahead of them and started my run-in. Our DZ was on the front lawn of a large house which apparently was about all we still held. On the way in, one did not require a bomb aimer to map read as the trail of burning Stirlings and Dakotas pointed the way. The DZ seemed to be surrounded, with the German tanks using their '88's as anti-aircraft guns. They were hitting us, and I even saw German soldiers behind trees with Schmeissers and they too were hitting us. Looking back I could see the Daks taking an awful pasting and one, which was on fire, held course until its crew had pushed out their panniers over the DZ and then it crashed in flames. Another Dak looped the loop before going nose first into the roof of a house.

With all the fighter strength available on the continent, I think that some-body had their finger in, for we did not see any friendly fighters and it appeared that the main stream, which I had been delayed from joining, had run into fighters from Deelen, a German base just north of Arnhem and so close that they could almost shoot us down as they did circuits of their own field. Fortunately, they were all refuelling when we came in.

There were some shell holes in our aircraft and I think they later counted two hundred bullet holes, but the four engines kept turning as we raced home. At one stage, I looked back and saw Al Boardman, our flight engineer, jumping from side to side, dodging shrapnel as it came through the floor and sides – he

Flying Officer 'Archie' Andrews RCAF (far left) with the members of his 620 Squadron crew, examining the damaged tailplane of their Stirling, LJ980 'K-King'. (*190 & 620 Sqns Archive*)

looked so funny, I think I laughed. As we sped at low level, Dai Booth, our gunner, was feeling frustrated, since he still had some ammo left, and as we crossed a railway signal box covered in plate glass he couldn't resist shattering it. He remarked 'They are supposed to be on strike anyway'. One dispatcher had a bleeding knee where some shrapnel had scraped it and that was the total of our casualties.

On our return to Fairford we were told to taxi the aircraft to the dump. I think it was 'Archie' Andrews, an American in the RCAF, who landed at the same time as I did – a body could stand upright in the holes in his tail. However, things were not good at base; in the Officers' Mess the girls were all in tears and they even gave me a hug as I walked in. I lived on a site that was towards the gate – one of the aircrew officers' sites – I was alone, there was nobody left on the site. I walked around the different Nissen huts hoping to find someone, but no. The following night we were the only operational crew assigned and my crew hardly talked to me. I think they thought I had volunteered.

Sgt Arthur Moody, 620 Squadron, recalled:

On 21st September we were going to Arnhem again with supplies in containers and panniers. But this was not to be our day. When we arrived at our Stirling, 'K-King', we found the containers had been accidentally dropped from the bomb bays onto the tarmac, when someone tripped a switch. The other crews were taking off, but we had to wait until the ground crew had winched the containers back up. Our pilot, 'Archie' Andrews, himself an American who had enlisted in the RCAF, had been told to join the Americans in their formation once we were ready. Eventually we took off and joined them, a strange sight, a Stirling flying in a Dakota stream.

When we reached Holland the flak was getting heavy and I saw some Dakotas go down. We carried on to our DZ and the two RASC dispatchers went to the hatch, ready to push out the panniers. Then all hell let loose from the ground. Our bomb aimer released the containers, then I heard the Skipper talking on the intercom to the rear gunner, Geoff Wright, who was saying that

rgeant Arthur Moody (wireless operator, on t) and Flight Sergeant Geoff Wright (air nner), of Flying Officer Andrews' 620 uadron crew. (*190 & 620 Sqns Archive*)

the panniers were stuck in the hatch. The Skipper called me and said 'Go and have a look, see what's going on'. I took my parachute pack with me, 'just in case', but the kite was twisting and turning to evade the stuff coming up, and trying to walk down the fuselage was most difficult, I put my 'chute on the floor of the plane and helped to release, and then drop, the panniers out of the hatch. By now the plane was being raked with bullets and shrapnel and I turned to pick up my parachute, only to find it was being soaked in hydraulic oil. Then, when I went to close the trap door, the handle, which was on a long arm, had been shot off, so I leaned over and pushed the door down hoping it wasn't damaged, and secured it. I then decided to plug in my intercom but at this point something like a hammer struck me on my thigh; it was a piece of shrapnel, but fortunately it caused little injury to my leg.

When we landed we could see the full extent of the damage to our Stirling, with lots of pieces missing from the tailplane and fuselage, but at least we did come back.

One by one, damaged Stirlings limped into Fairford during the late afternoon of 21 September. Many of their crews told of encounters with enemy fighters, as well as flak. Other Stirlings had diverted to other airfields because they either were too badly damaged to risk the flight back to Fairford, or had wounded crew members on board. Among the latter aircraft were two belonging to 620 Squadron. LJ892 'T' made an emergency landing at Woodbridge, with Flt Sgt Kay (captain), Flt Sgt Cleaver (flight engineer) and Plt Off Gosson (bomb aimer) all wounded. Fg Off Deacon landed LJ580 'X' in foggy conditions at Manston in Kent. His gunner, Fg Off Smith, had a bullet wound through one of his lungs and was admitted to the Manston Station Sick Quarters in a critical condition. Flight Sergeant John Everitt was the wireless operator in this aircraft:

We flew to Arnhem on the 17, 19 and 21 September. We suffered a bit of flak damage on the 19th, but on the 21st things really got nasty. Our Canadian gunner was wounded and we heard him shout from the rear turret, 'I've been hit Skip'. At that time we were down to about 500–600 feet and weaving all over the place to avoid the flak. As soon as we were away from the area I went to the rear turret and hauled our gunner out into the fuselage – he had been shot in the left side of his chest. I stemmed the bleeding with field dressings and got his mouth open to let him cough up blood. I used the radio to code a message to RAF Manston requesting an emergency landing. They were equipped with FIDO, fog dispersal equipment that used gigantic flares along either side of the runway.

169

Flying Officer Deacon's 620 Squadron crew: left to right; Flight Sergeant Charles Kempster (bomb aimer), Fligh Sergeant John Everitt (wireless operator), Flying Officer Paul Deacon RCAF (pilot), Flying Officer Hugh Jam RCAF (navigator), Sergeant 'Jock' Keiller (flight engineer) and Flying Officer Gordon Smith RCAF (air gunne (*190 & 620 Sqns Archive*)

We had lost some of our systems, including the flap controls. Without flaps we needed all the very long runway, as the heat from FIDO tended to keep us airborne, but after we floated through that area we then came down with an almighty thump. The ambulance was keeping abreast of us along the runway and its crew were very quickly aboard and lifted our gunner out – we also made a hasty exit for fear of fire. You can imagine my dismay when the ambulance crew lifted 'Smithie' out and there was the biggest pool of blood I shall ever want to see. The bullets had passed right through poor 'Smithie' but because of his parachute harness I hadn't seen all the wounds. I'm more than pleased to say he eventually recovered.

Of the ten Stirlings sent to Arnhem by 190 Squadron on 21 September, only three returned. The members of Fg Off Siegert's crew in 'T-Tommy' were particularly lucky to survive, although the wireless operator and both RASC dispatchers were wounded, and the aircraft was seriously damaged. They managed to drop twenty-four containers and four panniers, but were hit by flak over the DZ, before being pounced on by Fw 190 fighters.

Larry Siegert recalled:

We had a rest on 20 September, but set out again on the 21st to resupply the troops at Arnhem. We flew in loose formations of three aircraft. We were behind our commanding officer, Wing Commander Harrison, and two others. I remember seeing a formation of fighters coming in to meet us as we neared Arnhem. I thought they would be friendly fighter escorts, but as they banked to attack I could see the Maltese crosses on their wings. We dived for the DZ, which was covered by a wall of flak. Although hit we dropped our supplies and headed away but were followed by two Fw190 aircraft which attacked us and fired repeatedly. However, we dived down to a very low level and did a succession of steep turns away from the pursuing fighters. Our rear gunner, Flight Sergeant Jack Welton, succeeded in shooting down one of them and the other eventually gave us away. We continued back to Fairford, though our wireless operator, Warrant Officer Jim Thomson RNZAF, was badly wounded, as were the two army dispatchers who were hit by the German cannon shells, which couldn't quite get those of us up front.

The fighter attacks on Fg Off Siegert's aircraft lasted about eight minutes. During that time, Flt Sgt Welton expended some 4,000 rounds of ammunition, while keeping up a running commentary that enabled Fg Off Siegert to carry out evasive manoeuvres to the best effect.

The other two 190 Squadron Stirlings that returned from Arnhem on 21 September were also badly damaged. Plt Off Middleton's aircraft made an accurate drop, but over Oosterbeck it was hit by light flak and machine-gun fire, which damaged the starboard inner engine and started a fire. Having shut down the engine and extinguished the flames, the crew of this Stirling returned to base nearly two hours after the other survivors from 190 Squadron. Their struggle to fly on three engines was made even worse because the propeller on the damaged engine could not be feathered.

Flt Lt Gardiner's 190 Squadron aircraft also dropped successfully, but lost a one-foot square area from the starboard aileron when it was hit by light flak near the DZ. The crew of this aircraft reported seeing a Stirling blowing up as it hit the

Pilot Officer Middleton's 190 Squadron crew: standing, left to right, Flight Sergeant Ralph Beck (navigator), Flying Officer Alex Bossley (bomb aimer), Pilot Officer Bill Angus (air gunner) and Sergeant Jack Drury (flight engineer); kneeling, left to right, Warrant Officer Harold Cretney (wireless operator) and Pilot Officer Bob Middleton (pilot). Apart from Sergeant Drury, all the members of this crew were Canadian. (*H.B. Allan*)

ground south of Oosterbeck. Fg Off Siegert's crew had observed a Stirling exploding in mid-air over the DZ, two crashing near the DZ, and another crashing near Valberg. In addition, they saw a Stirling in the River Waal, to the east of Winssen, with its dinghy floating on the water.

Among the missing 190 Squadron Stirlings was that of the CO, Wg Cdr Harrison. His aircraft, LJ982, was hit by flak and crashed at Zetten, south-west of Arnhem. The crew of seven (a 2nd pilot was on board) and the two dispatchers were all killed. Flt Sgt Herger's aircraft, LJ943, was also hit by flak and crashed at Zetten, just south of Wg Cdr Harrison's aircraft. Five members of LJ943's crew were killed, as were the two dispatchers. The flight engineer, Sgt Hillyard, and air gunner, WO Thomas, were wounded, but baled out and were captured.

Les Hillyard, 190 Squadron, recalled:

We dropped the supplies and put the nose down to get a bit of speed as we had been flying at about 1,000 feet and were nearly stalling as we carried out the drop. At about 800 feet there was a terrific bang. All my instrument panel disappeared, and I got pieces of shrapnel in my right arm and left leg. We were terribly on fire and then there was another bang, as I was trying to put the fire out. This time, I think that the main tanks must have blown, because I suddenly found myself in mid-air. The aircraft crashed about 100 yards from where I landed by parachute, so we were very low when it blew up. The only other survivor was our air gunner, WO Jack Thomas, who like the other members of the crew was Canadian. Also killed were two RASC laddies, and Fg Off Thornington, another air gunner, who only flew with us that day for experience. In 1945 I found he came from Folkestone and I went down to try and explain to his widow what had happened. After landing, I was captured straight away and taken to a hospital in Arnhem. I was later at the *Dulag Luft* interrogation centre, then *Stalag Luft* VII, and finally *Stalag Luft* III in Silesia, after a forced march from January to February 1945. What a terrible march that was, in thick snow and blizzards, without food, or proper clothing and shoes.

Over Elst, Fg Off Bebarfald's 190 Squadron aircraft, LJ881, was badly holed by flak and its supplies were jettisoned. Six enemy fighters then attacked the Stirling, setting it on fire. As the aircraft started to disintegrate, the order to bale out was given, but only Flt Lt Munro (wireless operator), WO Morris (air gunner), and one of the dispatchers, Dvr Hughes, managed to jump in time. They were given shelter in a village and eventually reached the British lines. It is thought that the other dispatcher, Dvr Jones, may have survived the crash, but died later of wounds. The remaining four members of the crew were killed when the Stirling hit the ground, north of the River Waal at Andelst.

Flt Lt Anderson's 190 Squadron aircraft, LJ833, was also hit by flak and attacked by fighters. The Stirling caught fire and then broke up as it was ditched in the River Maas near Ravenstein. Sgt Smith (flight engineer), and Flt Sgt Orange (bomb aimer), got into the dinghy with dispatcher Dvr Bloomfield and were helped to the riverbank by some local men. The rest of the crew, including the other dispatcher, were presumed to have drowned.

Over the DZ, Fg Off Farren's 190 Squadron aircraft, LJ823, sustained flak damage to the gun turret. Three fighters then attacked the Stirling and the order to bale out was given. Flt Sgt Cairns (bomb aimer) and Flt Sgt Skewes (wireless operator) were reported to have been killed when they baled out too low for their parachutes to open. A second bomb aimer on board, WO Billen, was also killed. Flt

Sgt Stone (flight engineer) and Flt Sgt Brown (air gunner) were injured and taken to hospital, but the navigator, Flt Sgt Ross, landed safely and later returned to Fairford. The two dispatchers, Dvr Poole and Cpl Woodley, also baled out without serious injury. Farren was still in the aircraft when it crashed near Haren. He was taken to hospital with back injuries, after being thrown through the windscreen.

More fortunate were Fg Off Hay and the members of his 190 Squadron crew, in LJ916, who all survived a crash-landing, to the east of Tilburg. Fg Off Pascoe and his crew also had a lucky escape after their aircraft, LK498, was hit by flak over the DZ. With the port wing on fire, and the rudder controls severed, the Stirling was almost out of control, but Pascoe pulled off a successful belly landing behind enemy lines at Grave. The members of Pascoe's regular crew were all unharmed, as were the 2nd pilot, Flt Sgt Buckley, and the two dispatchers, Dvrs Fitzhugh and Richardson. Many years later, the following account was written anonymously, but it is believed to be the work of 'Taff' Hughes, the flight engineer in Pascoe's crew:

At about noon on 21 September 1944, at RAF Fairford, there were lined up five Stirlings of 'A' Flight, 190 Squadron, loaded with containers of supplies to be parachuted to our beleaguered forces in Arnhem. It was to be a fateful day; none from this Flight was destined to return. Also assembled were the aircraft of 'B' Flight and, on the other side of the perimeter track, the Stirlings of their sister squadron, No. 620.

On board aircraft 'F for Fox' was Sgt 'Taff' Hughes, the Flight Engineer. This was his fourth sortie to Arnhem. For him Operation 'Market Garden' had started four days earlier, on 17 September. On the first day his aircraft 'K for King' carried a load of paratroops. There was little enemy opposition, and the mission proved uneventful. On the following day the sortie consisted of towing a large Horsa glider filled with troops and equipment. Though the Stirling crew observed signs of increasing enemy activity, again they had returned unscathed to Fairford.

The third day was more eventful. The mission this time was to drop supplies, and on the run-in to the DZ the aircraft was hit many times by flak. One shell burst in the rear fuselage, which filled with acrid smoke. Taff Hughes grabbed a fire extinguisher and went aft to deal with any fire that may have started. The aircraft was then again hit by flak, this time in the forward compartment, causing injuries to the face and head of the wireless operator, 'Snowy' Pelletier. The aircraft completed its run-in and dropped its load. As it turned for home Snowy's injuries were attended to with supplies from the first aid kit. On arrival back at Fairford priority landing permission was given to the aircraft, and as soon as it had taxied in, a waiting ambulance took Pelletier off to nearby Wroughton Hospital.

The next day the crew of Stirling 'K for King' rested, their aircraft being badly in need of repair. On the following day, 21 September, the crew were allotted 'F for Fox'. On that day the wounded wireless operator, Pelletier, was replaced by Plt Off Booth. On learning that the sortie was to be in the same area as the last three, the crew not unnaturally had some misgivings. The crew could be categorised as 'old hands' as they each had now completed twenty operations, but they were remarkably young in age, the oldest being Reg Walker at twenty-three years of age, and the youngest Taff Hughes who was nineteen.

On the approach to Arnhem it was very evident that the reception was going to be hot. The sky was patchy and dark with flak bursts; smoking aircraft could be seen falling headlong out of the sky, and enemy fighters, Me 109s and Fw 190s, were much in evidence. To say the least, the crew knew they were in for a rough time, and the captain, Frank Pascoe from Sydney, devout Roman Catholic that he was, crossed himself. Taff Hughes muttered his Protestant bit: '*Ie, pe rhodiwn ar hyd glyn cysgod angau, nid ofnaf niwed . . .*', the Welsh words of the 23rd Psalm.

The pilot reduced height to tree-top level, to make the expected fighter attacks less easy. At this height the aircraft was a large but fleeting target for enemy machine gunners – the rattle of bullets hitting the aircraft sounded like heavy hail against a window pane. The rear gunner, Len Armstrong, roared into action with bursts of fire from his four Brownings against enemy troops lining the hedgerows. They were easily distinguished, particularly by their helmets. Fortunately, no member of the crew was hit, though the aircraft was holed in a number of places. As the aircraft made its run-in, the bomb-aimer, Les Couch, requested the captain to gain sufficient height for the parachutes attached to the supply containers to open. The DZ was found and the supplies dropped, save some which failed to leave the aircraft due to damage to the release mechanism.

After the drop, the navigator, Reg Walker of Melbourne, called on the intercom to give the captain the course to steer for home. He turned to take up the new course but, by mischance, he turned too far. His repeater compass was giving a false reading because the gyro unit, to which the repeater was connected in the rear of the aircraft, had been damaged by flak.

Once again the aircraft was subjected to everything that the enemy could bring to bear – fighter attack, flak, and heavy machine-gun fire. Taff Hughes decided to take a look from the astrodome at his four Hercules engines which, up to that time, had given no trouble. To his dismay he saw that both starboard engines were on fire. On the intercom he informed the captain, and then went aft to shut off Nos 2 and 4 tanks, supplying those engines. The captain operated the Graviner fire extinguisher system to the two starboard engines, and then feathered them. The fire abated momentarily, but soon burst back into life.

It was obvious now that the aircraft was doomed, but it was too low for the crew to make their escape by parachute and there would not be sufficient power from the two port engines to gain height quickly, if at all. Frank Pascoe coolly announced over the intercom that he would put the aircraft down, and ordered the crew to their crash positions.

The aircraft skimmed along very low; it lightly lopped a few trees, struck a farm building or two, and finally belly-landed in a large cultivated field, carving out a deep furrow. As it screeched to a halt, the caked Gloucestershire mud on the aluminium floor rose into clouds of choking, blinding dust which filled the aircraft. Hughes found his way through it to the rear door and made a quick getaway from the burning aircraft, for there remained a lot of fuel in the tanks which might explode at any moment. It was also possible that some of the hung-up containers in the bomb-bay were packed with live ammunition – not a place in which to hang around. He was quickly joined in a nearby ditch by the wireless operator and the rear gunner. A few shouts brought over the navigator and the bomb-aimer, but where was the captain, Frank Pascoe? Was he trapped in the wreckage? After a few moments he calmly emerged from the far side of the burning aircraft and, on hearing their shouts, joined the other crew members in the ditch. Some minutes were spent in congratulating Frank Pascoe on

Flying Officer Pascoe's 190 Squadron crew; left to right, front: Pilot Officer Reg Walker RAAF (navigator), Warrant Officer 'Snowy' Pelletier RCAF (wireless operator), Flying Officer Frank Pascoe RAAF (pilot) and Flight Sergeant Les Couch (bomb aimer); standing, in front of tailplane, Sergeant 'Taff' Hughes (flight engineer); standing, on tailplane, Warrant Officer Len Armstrong (air gunner). (*190 & 620 Sqns Archive*)

his superb feat of airmanship in bringing the stricken aircraft safely to a halt. Quick thinking and a cool brain as well as supreme flying skill combined to save the entire crew from injury. They were safe and could spend the next few minutes relaxing before deciding what their next move should be.

Unhappily their period of relaxation was short-lived. From the comparative safety of their hiding-place, they now witnessed the appalling sight of unarmed and defenceless Dakotas being shot down by enemy fighters. As these transport aircraft held steady on the run-in to their DZs they were sitting ducks, and the minor weaving that they were able to do was to no avail. Very few parachute escapes could be seen from this aerial carnage.

As the one-sided aerial combat died down, the crew noticed a number of men and boys gathering round their wrecked aircraft. Despite their warning shouts to keep away, some of them remained in the vicinity. A few actually entered the wreckage and carried off the rear-gunner's belts of .303 ammunition, while others endeavoured to remove the Browning guns from the rear turret. They were Dutch, these brave people. Patriotic as they were they must surely have known the great risks they were running, but they seemed determined to take the guns and ammunition for their own use, or at least to deny them to the enemy. They were able to render invaluable assistance to the crew, since being local people, they knew the area well and the disposition of the enemy troops. At great risk to their own lives, and by devious routes, they guided the crew to the British lines not far away. One Dutch lad, about twelve years old, proudly displayed his belt containing the Boy Scout emblem which he normally kept well hidden as the Scout organisation was not encouraged by the Germans.

That night the crew slept at Eindhoven and the next day they hitched a lift to Brussels, which was still celebrating its liberation. They were not slow to join in, and they found that the money in their escape packs, in various currencies, was acceptable everywhere. Their celebrations were however short-lived. Being hatless and wearing battledress uniforms having a far from smart appearance, they attracted the attention of the eagle-eyed Military Police, who, on learning their story, had them conveyed to Evere airport. There they were unceremoniously bundled into an Avro Anson bound for Blighty. But they rejoined their squadron at Fairford too late to do any more 'market gardening'. Their captain, Frank Pascoe, was subsequently awarded the Distinguished Flying Cross. Could anyone have deserved it more?

620 Squadron lost two of its Stirlings on 21 September, both to flak. Plt Off Carey and his crew all survived when they made a belly landing in LJ946, at Bennekom, and Fg Off McLeod's aircraft, LJ830, crash-landed in flames near Renkum, on the north side of the Rhine. The gunner in the latter aircraft, Fg Off Thomas, was killed, apparently as a result of falling from his badly damaged turret. It is thought that the two army dispatchers on board also died, possibly because they either fell or deliberately jumped from the rear of the blazing Stirling before it crashed. Fg Off 'Nipper' McLeod and his bomb aimer, Flt Sgt Bate, were taken prisoner, but Fg Off Newton (navigator), Fg Off King (wireless operator), and Sgt Haig (flight engineer) evaded capture and returned to the Allied lines in October 1944.

On 21 September, later in the day, American C-47s took off from their Lincolnshire bases with the intention of dropping paratroops of the Polish Parachute Brigade on a DZ at Driel, to the south of the Rhine (this was some way west of the DZ, 'K', originally allocated to them). Bad weather forced a number of these

Flying Officer Jack Thomas RCAF, the air gunner in Flying Officer 'Nipper' McLeod's 620 Squadron crew, who was killed on 21 September 1944. (*190 & 620 Sqns Archive*)

This photograph of the 'McLeod crew' was taken in Shropshire, when they were converting to the Stirling at Tilstock, early in 1944. (*190 & 620 Sqns Archive*)

aircraft to turn back, while the rest ran into horrendous flak as they approached the DZ. In any case, the Polish paratroops who did make it to the DZ had little hope of providing effective support for the 1st Airborne troops, trapped north of the river, unless enough boats or amphibious craft could be delivered overland from the south-west.

As 22 September dawned, the perimeter around the 1st Airborne troops at Arnhem continued to shrink. During the morning, eighteen Fairford aircraft were detailed to carry out resupply drops, but the weather was poor and shortly after midday this operation was cancelled. Meanwhile, troops of the British XXX Corps and the US Airborne Divisions were keeping the route via Nijmegen open, as units of the 43rd Infantry Division fought their way towards the Polish positions at Driel, which they reached in the early evening.

While the 38 Group squadrons were stood down during the afternoon of 22 September, an investiture parade was held at Netheravon. The Military Governor of Paris, General Koenig, presented the *Croix de Guerre* to Plt Off Fogarty, WO Willis and Flt Lt Robertson of 190 Squadron, and Flt Lt Jack, Plt Off McNamara and Flt Sgt Coysh of 620 Squadron, in recognition of their efforts towards the liberation of France. There had been some other good news that morning, when it was learned that Flt Sgt Les Brown of 620 Squadron, missing since he took off from Tarrant Rushton on 11 April 1944, was safe and back in the UK.

On 23 September the 1st Airborne Division reported itself to be 'in desperate need of reinforcement'. At Fairford, seven crews from 190 Squadron, and eleven from 620 Squadron, were briefed and ready to go, but there was then a delay as they waited for the weather to improve, so the first Stirling did not take off until 1410 hrs. Although conditions were misty *en route*, visibility was good at the DZ, beneath a 2,000–3,000-foot cloud base. With P-47 Thunderbolts covering this operation, enemy fighter activity was slight, but heavy flak was encountered on the run-in to the DZ, particularly in the area between Eindhoven and Hertogenbosch.

Noel Chaffey, 620 Squadron, recalled:

We had been shaken by what we'd gone through on two previous sorties to Arnhem but there were even bigger scares for us on 23 September. We'd changed crew positions for this one, Bryan, our bomb aimer, having left his position in the nose of the Stirling to take up a co-pilot role. As the radio would not be needed much, I occupied the bomb aimer's position, from where I could provide visual assistance to Ben's navigational plots and give directions to Derek, our pilot.

On this mission I had chosen to wear my parachute all the time (not comfortable when lying on one's stomach), whilst I also kept my foot firmly on the release catch of the escape hatch in the floor, ready in case we had to bale out. On the run-in, my hand was on the container release button, which I pushed as we arrived over the DZ. The dial on a machine to my left whirled as the twenty-four containers were released and a green light then showed 'bomb-bay all clear'.

We turned and climbed as the bomb-bay doors were closing, but were being trailed by radar-predicted flak, with great black puffs of smoke around us. Suddenly, the Stirling took a nose dive and turned to starboard – so this was it, I thought, shall I kick open the hatch now? Then Derek's very quiet English voice came over the intercom, 'Sorry lads, we're going down to the deck and hedge-hopping home – everyone OK?' It turned out that the pilots on the squadron had previously got together and all agreed that the best way to avoid being shot down by predicted flak was to get below the radar, and so we were successful in flying back to the Dutch coast at only 50 feet.

Over the DZ, the Stirling captained by Flight Officer Bliss, a USAAF pilot serving with 190 Squadron, was hit by machine-gun fire, which set the starboard inner engine alight. Fortunately, the flames went out after about thirty seconds. Bliss's flight engineer was Sergeant George Fairweather, who remembered this flight well, their fourth to Arnhem.

We were wakened at 7.00 am and told to get our aircraft ready for Holland. Whilst half asleep we looked at empty beds in the hut that belonged to four of our friends who went down on the previous mission, and we wondered if our beds would be vacant the following morning. After briefing we knew what to expect and as we made our way to the aircraft, one or two lads expressed themselves as being 'scared to death' but they would stick it no matter what happened. One pilot told me he had a strong feeling that he would never return but hoped the supplies would get through first. He delivered the goods but did not come back.

After taking off, the trip went without a hitch until we were about 10 miles from Arnhem. At this point Joe Missaubie, our French Canadian Indian gunner, shouted 'Hello Jock, have you said your prayers today?' I looked at what lay ahead of us and replied, 'You bet I have'. This is all that was said but I wondered if he got any comfort from my reply. Straight ahead of us I could see a black cloud which was formed by shell bursts, as it hung over our supply dropping area.

On the ground were hundreds of anti-aircraft guns, all pointing towards us. By this time I could see the front of the stream of aircraft as they flew through what the press described as 'murderous flak'. Some were shot down in flames while others simply disintegrated in the air. A few minutes later we were in the thick of it and the flak sounded like being in a tin hut and several boys pelting stones at it, as it passed through the kite.

The sky was packed with Stirlings dropping containers on parachutes, and I could see an occasional airman who was fortunate enough to bale out, dangling at the end of his 'chute. Intermingled in this chaos were bullets and bursting shells. As we were dropping our supplies, two shattering explosions occurred under our right wing, and to our horror we saw black smoke and flames belching from the starboard inner engine.

Our height was 500 feet, which was too low for a parachute to be of service, and to attempt to land whilst on fire with several tons of petrol still on board is seldom done more than once. We were each convinced our end had come as we went into a screaming dive at a speed higher than our instruments could record. I had to push on the roof with my hands to keep my feet on the floor, whilst the logs and charts made their way to the roof. As I watched the ground racing towards us, I remember saying 'Lord I am coming beside you', then after a few spits and bangs the damaged engine suddenly roared into action and the fire disappeared. With this extra power our pilot was able to pull out of the dive and we skimmed over the ground. In the dive we had passed under a shower of supplies and had to do a steep climb in order to ascend over another lot.

Half an hour later we were above the clouds, laughing and joking about our experience as we joined our other mates. During the first part of the return

Flight Officer Craig Bliss and his 190 Squadron crew at debriefing. This photograph was probably taken 17 September 1944, the first day of 'Market'. (*Imperial War Museum, CL 1158*)

journey we flew round each other to see who had the most holes in their kite, then signalled messages to each other. As we came in to land we took our crash positions and waited for the first bump to see if the kite would stay in one piece, which it did.

At their debriefing on 23 September, Bliss and his crew reported having seen a Stirling, also with its starboard inner engine on fire, making a crash landing near the DZ (this was probably a 570 Squadron aircraft from Harwell) and another, flying over the DZ, with its port inner on fire. They also observed a Stirling lying intact on the ground, at a position estimated to be three miles south of Grave.

On 23 September, many of the Fairford crews found that supplies parachuted from aircraft flying above them presented an extra hazard over the DZ, and WO Macmillan's 190 Squadron aircraft was actually hit by a container. Through trying to avoid these objects, Plt Off Sellars was forced to make a second run over the DZ, only to find that two of his containers had hung up because of flak damage to the bomb racks. Unfortunately, the DZ that day was confined to a very small area and no more than 10 per cent of the supplies seem to have reached the British troops who needed them so urgently.

All the 190 Squadron crews sent to Arnhem on 23 September returned. However, following the tragic loss of 190 Squadron's Wg Cdr Harrison, two days earlier, 620 Squadron was now also without a CO, since Wg Cdr Lee and his crew were missing. Fortunately, they had survived a crash-landing at Oss in Stirling LJ873, and everyone on the squadron was relieved to see them again in the evening of 24 September, after they had been flown back to Fairford in an Anson.

Ernest Fletcher, 620 Squadron, recalled:

During the Arnhem operation my pilot was ill, so some of us flew with other crews. Our navigator, F/Sgt Eric Pratt, flew with our squadron commander, Wing Commander Lee, and was shot down somewhat short of Arnhem on their

...is Stirling, burning in a Dutch field, is probably LJ873, the aircraft crash-landed by Wing Commander Donald ... DFC, 620 Squadron's CO. (*190 & 620 Sqns Archive*)

fourth trip. To quote Eric, 'the Wingco made a great crash landing' and all the crew left the aircraft safely. Almost as soon as they had evacuated the aircraft a Dutch farmer appeared and indicated – Americans this way, Germans that way. They went the right way and were quickly rescued by US troops and returned safely to the UK. When Eric got back to the crew, after survivor's leave, we had a terrific celebration and that was the first time that I ever finished the evening the worse for drink – not drunk, but decidedly merry!

As the stream of RAF aircraft headed for Arnhem on 23 September, to carry out their resupply drops, they had passed a fleet of American C-47s towing Waco gliders to LZs south-west of Nijmegen. This glider operation, to reinforce the US Airborne Divisions, had been postponed for several days, the victim of bad weather. It came too late to have an effect on the outcome of 'Market Garden'. On 24 September, air support to Arnhem from UK bases was halted by the weather, though a small number of 46 Group Dakotas, operating from an airfield near Brussels, did get through to make resupply drops.

After an eventful week, which had seen so many tragic losses, there was a gradual return to more normal life on the station at Fairford. A Sunday evening dance took place in the NAAFI on 24 September, and local flying resumed the next morning.

Flight Sergeant Eric Pratt, the navigator in Flying Officer Herbert's 620 Squadron crew, flew four times to Arnhem with Wing Commander Lee, and was shot down on the last of these occasions. (*190 & 620 Sqns Archive*)

There were replacement aircraft waiting for acceptance air tests, and also many new aircrews needing to be checked out. Fg Off Ken 'Tug' Wilson and his crew had been posted from 1665 HCU to 620 Squadron while 'Market' was going on:

> We arrived at Fairford on 20 September just as the disaster of the Arnhem operation became all too abundantly and painfully clear. The number of RAF crews on the airfield was suddenly depleted and the few aircraft that returned were in a sorry state. The Mess was empty, the huts were empty, and morale was wearing a trifle thin, until slowly, chaps began to trickle back – all with amazing stories of baling out or walking away from crash landings at Arnhem.

The Fairford Stirlings had flown the last of their operations to Arnhem, but were very soon back in action, this time on behalf of SOE. On the night of 24/25 September, five aircraft from 620 Squadron took off for drops to DZs 'Bob 296' and 'Messenger 42' in France. Only one of these aircraft was successful; three others found no reception, probably because of other activity going on close to the DZs, and one returned early with its Gee set unserviceable. Over the next few days and nights, the Fairford Stirlings also carried out paratroop and container drops at the Netheravon DZ whenever the weather permitted.

From 25 September, UK-based squadrons played no further part in resupply operations to Arnhem. During the night of 23/24 September, Allied troops had reached the south bank of the Rhine and made contact with the survivors of the 1st Airborne Division beyond the river. Many of the 1st Airborne troops were evacuated across the Rhine during the night of 25/26 September, but by the morning there were still several hundred on the north bank, including the seriously wounded, awaiting their fate as POWs.

Important lessons were learned from the failure of Operation 'Market Garden'. These were taken into account when 'Varsity', the airborne crossing of the Rhine, was being planned in detail from October 1944 onwards. It had become quite clear that an airborne assault, however large, needed to be carried out in one day, and should only go ahead if land forces were able to provide reinforcements swiftly. The air support squadrons had also found that resupply drops, onto small DZs close to enemy forces, were liable to go badly wrong, unless there were good communications with the troops on the ground.

Above all, air superiority had to be maintained, in order to suppress enemy fighters and flak, if heavy losses of air support aircraft were to be avoided. The total casualties suffered by 190 and 620 Squadrons through the spring and summer of 1944 had been fewer in number than those of 620 Squadron alone, when it was bombing in the latter half of 1943. However, during 'Market Garden', the loss rates for Stirling and Dakota squadrons soon reached levels that would have been intolerable over a longer period. 190 Squadron fared particularly badly, since it lost twelve aircraft, more than any other RAF squadron operating over Arnhem. Yet, even when faced with mounting losses, the aircrews of 38 and 46 Groups had pressed on, again and again, throughout that fateful week. Their courage and determination should be long remembered.

# CHAPTER 7

# They Also Served

## The Ground Crews, 1943–6

As the autumn of 1944 was ushered in by calm, misty mornings, 190 and 620 Squadrons were able to look back on six very eventful months at RAF Fairford. They had trained for, and taken part in, the successful D-Day landings and the ill-fated Operation 'Market', as well as numerous covert operations for the SAS and SOE. In all these tasks, the 320 or so aircrew members of the two squadrons relied on the support and teamwork of more than 2,000 other personnel on the station. Naturally, some of the closest bonds were forged between the aircrews who flew in, and the ground crews who looked after, the Stirlings of 190 and 620 Squadrons.

For airmen who had just finished technical training, the flexible pattern of working adopted by ground crews on an operational station usually came as a bit of a surprise. As a newly qualified Flight Mechanic, Eric Titterton had been posted to 620 Squadron at Chedburgh:

> I reported to the engineering officer, a Flight Lieutenant Butcher, who told me how badly I was needed, and ordered me to report without further ado to Flight Sergeant Clarke at the 'B' Flight Office, which I duly did. I was allocated to aircraft 'Q-Queenie' and introduced to the ground crew, comprising a Corporal Withers, two riggers, and two flight mechanics. They were snugly ensconced in a bell tent, and enquired earnestly if I played solo. The answer being in the affirmative, I was invited to join in a game. This was only interrupted by the arrival of the NAAFI wagon, bringing tea and wads to the weary workers (to me it seemed like a holiday camp!). All this seemed very strange to me, but what I did not realise then was that the aircraft was serviceable, and that was all that mattered. On an operational squadron everything was geared to this, and as long as this was so, no one cared what we did. If however the plane was u/s you worked without a break until it was serviceable.

At Fairford, the ground crews serving with 190 and 620 Squadrons were reorganised into 6190 and 6620 Servicing Echelons, respectively. Out at the dispersals, they generally worked as small teams on particular aircraft and soon got to know the crews who flew in them. Major servicing was managed along more centralised lines, so the personnel involved in this task might find themselves working on aircraft from either of the Fairford squadrons. Having joined 190 Squadron at Leicester East, Flight Sergeant Ivan Fairfax made the administrative move to 6190 Servicing Echelon at Fairford:

> At Fairford the two Servicing Echelons were part of the Technical Wing on the station, the other two wings being Flying and Administrative. The Technical

Wing staff soon became augmented with personnel from the Women's Auxiliary Air Force and the Royal Navy's Fleet Air Arm. My Electrical Section was allocated half of a very large Nissen hut with the Instrument Section at the opposite end, and electricians were also employed in the Station Workshop and the Motor Transport Section. WAAF electricians worked alongside airmen in the battery charging room, and also in Flying Control, where they maintained runway lighting and other equipment.

Our largest single commitment was the servicing and repair of the Stirling aircraft. Most of the scheduled work was performed inside a hangar but lack of space inevitably meant that servicing also had to be carried out at the aircraft dispersals when it came to priority jobs. Dispersing the work force increased the problem of supervision because every job had to be signed for by the airman involved, and then countersigned by an NCO.

Supply of replacement equipment often created problems when servicing the aircraft. At Fairford, a generator shortage developed, so in desperation I made an unannounced visit to a maintenance depot where I found a large number of aircraft power plants waiting to be serviced. With the approval of a very helpful warrant officer, I removed about a dozen generators from them, and fortunately every one was found to be serviceable when checked in the electrical workshop at Fairford. However, the Equipment Officer was a little bemused when I presented the paperwork to him, as I had short-circuited the stores system.

A typical day for the ground crews began at 0630 hrs as they rose from their beds, of which there were often more than twenty in each Nissen hut on the domestic sites. After ablutions and breakfast, the usual drill was for a very informal roll call to take

rsonnel of 6190 Servicing Echelon at Great Dunmow. (*190 & 620 Sqns Archive*)

A Daily Inspection being carried out on a Stirling at Great Dunmow. (*N. R. Chaffey*)

place outside the flight office, before those allotted to individual aircraft made their way out to the dispersal points. If they were lucky, they might hitch a lift on a truck, otherwise they had to walk along the perimeter track to their aircraft. Later on, many personnel were issued with bicycles, to save time when travelling around the airfield.

If an aircraft had flown on operations the previous night, it would need to be inspected for damage and attention would also be paid to any snags noted in the aircraft's Form 700. In any case, a Daily Inspection had to be completed before the aircraft could be signed off as serviceable for the next flight.

At the dispersals, the day-to-day work on a Stirling's Hercules engines was carried out by Flight Mechanics, while overhauls or more complex rectification tasks were the responsibility of airmen with the trade of Fitter II (Engines). After gaining experience as a Flight Mechanic, Bert Heald was able to take advantage of further training to qualify as a Fitter:

I served with 620 Squadron at Fairford as a Fitter II (Engines), though I was first trained as a Flight Mechanic which meant looking after one engine on an aircraft. When I went on a Fitter's course, this was a jump up from being a Flight Mechanic, and the work became more technical. This involved major overhauls on the engines at intervals, and while engine changes were mainly done in a hangar, many other jobs were carried out in the open. I flew in

lot Officer Herbert and his 620 Squadron crew, with their ground crew, atop a Stirling at Fairford. It is easy to see at a fall from a wing could well result in serious injury. (*190 & 620 Sqns Archive*)

Stirlings a few times, particularly after engine changes, if only to give the air-crew complete confidence that the ground engineering staff had done a good job.

The Stirling aircraft was enormous for its day; inevitably there were accidents and my initiation came when I slipped on some oil on the wing and finished up on the tarmac, fortunately landing on some engine covers which cushioned the fall. I was not injured (apart from my pride) and all my mates had to say was 'What do you do for an encore?' 'Chiefy' (the Flight Sergeant) came over, very concerned, and said I was a bloody fool, suggesting I should join a circus if I wanted to do acrobatics!

As a Flight Mechanic with 6190 Servicing Echelon, Eric Wadman worked on the Stirlings of 190 Squadron's 'B' Flight. He was assigned to 'U-Uncle', which was usually flown by Flight Officer Bliss of the USAAF:

In 1944, a group of us were posted to 190 Squadron at Fairford from 54 Operational Training Unit in Scotland. Having worked on Beaufighters, we presumed we had been posted because we were used to the Bristol Hercules engine, which also powered the Stirling. Starting sequences on the Stirling were therefore familiar – check that chocks were under wheels, wheel brakes on, fuel cocks selected, cooling gills turned to fully open. Usually engines were turned first by hand, with a cranking handle (those used on the Stirling were about 12 feet long, with a double crank at the bottom, so that two airmen could work together). This was to clear any oil collected in the lower cylinders of these

187

radial engines; if an engine was started with a pool of oil in a cylinder, the hydraulic pressure produced could blow the cylinder head off.

Engines could be started using trolley accumulators to avoid draining the internal aircraft batteries. To start up, each engine was turned twice on the electric starter, pressing the starter button with one hand, and using the other to operate a 'Kigass' pump, which primed the engine by injecting 100 octane fuel directly into the inlet manifold. The magneto switches were then put on and the throttle opened slightly, so that when the engine fired there would be sufficient revolutions for the engine to pick up to slow running. Now the starter was again turned, combined with further priming, after first giving signals to the assisting crews on the ground, calling 'Contact'. Once the engines were running, with the alternators charging the aircraft batteries, the ground/flight switch was turned to 'flight', and the trolley accumulator disconnected and wheeled away.

On cold days, the oil was thick, so when you started up the oil pressure would often jump up 'off the clock' and you quickly had to reduce the engine revs, and allow the engine to warm up before continuing with the run-up. Having started up all engines, I was able to climb up into the pilot's seat to do the ground run proper.

The throttles and propeller levers were operated to check the boost pressures and engine revs, and then the magnetos were checked. Each engine had port and starboard magnetos, and two spark plugs to each cylinder. At 1,500 revs, cruising revs, and maximum take-off revs, you switched off briefly first the port mag, and then the starboard mag. If while doing this there was a large fall in revolutions, you knew that you had an electrical fault in the ignition system still switched on. This usually required a change of some spark plugs, or sometimes there was condensation inside the distributor block, which could also cause backfiring, as electrical tracking through the moisture sent current to a plug in a 'wrong' cylinder.

A ground run would show up any such snags, and on a very cold day, I warmed the engines up for the mechanics before they worked on them, for most servicing was done out in the open. The engine cowlings had to be 'dropped' for visual and manual checks to be made for oil or fuel leaks, tightness of nuts, security of control linkages, etc. In addition, fuel or other pipe connections had to be bridged by strips of brass, to avoid a build-up of static electricity in flight – a break in one of these links could lead to sparks and possibly start a fire. Usually we had two of us to an aircraft, one taking the port engines and the other the starboard ones. There was also an aircraft rigger, to check wheels, flaps, ailerons, rudders and elevator, and a crew of armourers, electricians, radio and instrument mechanics, who all had to do their own checks.

Often, before shutting down the engines on completion of a ground run, the armourers or radio people would ask for 1,500 revs on port and starboard inners, to provide power to swing the rear turret, or for a radio check. While ground running I usually operated the flaps and moved all the flying controls, so that our rigger could see that they all worked correctly as he walked around the aircraft, and also operated the landing lights, which came down out of the port wing, at the move of a lever.

When engine runs and visual inspections had been completed, fuel and oil were topped up, and entries were then made in the aircraft's Form 700 in the Flight Hut. This had to be done by all trades each day. When everything was correct, and signatures in place on the Form 700, a senior NCO would add his signature, and our aircraft letter 'U' could then be placed up on the service-ability board, in chalk, along with 'S' for serviceable. If a fault was found, and work had to be done, the letters 'U/S' were chalked on the board, signifying unserviceable. A quick look at the board would show our Flight Sergeant how many of our 13 'B' Flight aircraft were serviceable and available for operations.

The ground crews would normally be working on the Stirlings for most of the morning, with a break when the NAAFI wagon visited each dispersal point to dispense refreshments, which were particularly welcome when working outside in the cold. Even in good weather, the ground crews' working conditions at Fairford were far from ideal, because the station had not been built to take heavy bombers. In particular, the area of paved surfaces, used for moving equipment and jacking up aircraft, was insufficient for the needs of the two squadrons based there.

Eric Wadman recalled:

When tyres were to be changed, we worked with our rigger to jack the aircraft up. This needed the erection of trestles and screw jacks and padded top beams to take the weight off the offending wheel by supporting the appropriate wing. Painted on both sides of the wheel, between tyre and hub, was a yellow line. This was checked on Daily Inspections, and at the end of the runway, if an aircraft made two or three successive take-offs and landings, towing gliders on 'circuits and bumps'. For this type of operation a team would be stationed at the runway and check if the yellow hub marks were still aligned, since the sudden thrust of landing could turn the tyre around the wheel hub and shear off the valve, causing the tyre to deflate. If the marks had moved any appreciable distance the take-off could not proceed. They also checked the smooth surface of the tyres, moving the aircraft slowly forward by hand signals to see if any stones had become embedded.

Mobile platforms were required for work on the Stirling's Hercules engines.
(*190 & 620 Sqns Archive*)

By lunchtime, it would be known whether or not the aircraft were required for operations that night. If they were, details of loads to be carried would be passed to the armourers. The jobs they had completed during the morning included cleaning the machine-guns, replenishing ammunition, and check-ing the Fraser Nash gun turrets for correct operation and freedom from defects such as hydraulic leaks. Another important task was to clean thoroughly the glazing of the turrets, though the centre windows were usually removed to ensure the gunners had un-obstructed vision between their guns.

The armourers also looked after the air-craft's flare chutes and bomb gear. If oper-ations were planned, winches were collected from the armoury during the afternoon, and teams of three or four men set to work, loading supply containers into the Stirlings'

An armourer working on 620 Squadron's LJ580 'Yorkshire Rose' at Fairford. (*N.R. Chaffey*)

Two of the refuellers at Great Dunmow.
(*190 & 620 Sqns Archive*)

bomb-bays. They usually finished around teatime, but sometimes it was necessary to work well into the evening, since there were no hard and fast rules and everyone stayed with the aircraft until the job was done. After the others had finished work, an engine fitter and an airframe fitter always remained available as Duty Crew, in order to attend to any visiting aircraft, and to deal with refuelling or minor rectification work that might be called for during the night. Eric Titterton remembered the sense of teamwork that emerged when night operations were being flown:

Life was very different for us, compared with the Mechs on non-operational stations, for we had our own machine to look after, our own aircrew whom we knew intimately, and minimal discipline. At our reunions our aircrews have said, 'You were always there to welcome us back, whatever the hour', and of course this was true, but we did take it in turns to do night flying duties, which consisted of checking that the pilot signed the Form 700, and seeing the aircraft safely out of the bay and onto the perimeter track. After the planes had left we would make our way to the cookhouse for supper, and then back to the flight hut to await their return. Our relationship with the airborne troops was always cordial, but minimal, as they usually messed separately and were brought to the aircraft in vehicles, and taken away immediately after landing from exercises.

John Scott was also a Flight Mechanic working with 620 Squadron. He remembered the lighter moments off the camp, as well as the long periods of waiting for aircraft to return from operations:

Life was, I suppose, what one would expect in our job – little was ever said about any target or destination, and an aircraft's fuel load was sometimes changed several times to suit the task or weather. Then there was the horrible job of de-icing the wing and prop leading edges with a sort of clay mixture which seemed to get all over you. Finally, on winter nights, we had to apply de-icer spray, of which the aircraft got its fair share and the operator nearly as much. If your turn came for night flying duties, to see the aircraft off and to wait for its return, we had little self-erected huts in some places, if not the Chief's Nissen hut, in which to shelter. When on these duties one would leave for an early tea at the cookhouse and it was from here that we took slices of bread and chunks of margarine, and we would also arm our goon bags with Betox (a vegetable extract) and Bournvita purchased from the local 'Woollies' while on leave. After the departure of our aircraft it was customary to read books and polish brass models of Spitfires, Stirling or Halifax aircraft, or work

Decorating Stirlings with 'Nose Art' was a popular pastime among the ground crews. This photograph shows 620 Squadron's 'I'm Easy II', its operational tally denoted by stencilled beds, instead of the more usual bombs, gliders or parachutes. Pilot Officer C.W. Walker lends scale to the huge mainwheels. (*190 & 620 Sqns Archive*)

on a tatty Austin Seven or an old motor-bike, until a phone call came through informing us of the aircraft's return. A cancelled op, or a 'Stand down' called by Chiefy, provided good cause for a cycle race back to the billet to change into best blues for a trip to the local pub, village hall dance or a gig at the Land Army Girls' hostel, while a day off was usually spent in Cirencester or Swindon, either at the pictures or the roller skating rink. On an evening off, one got a train from Fairford to Witney, followed by a walk around the town and a few jars of ale before coming back on the train which was always packed. This

Pilot Officer 'Tom' Herbert in the cockpit of Stirling LJ875 'B-Beer' at Fairford.
(*190 & 620 Sqns Archive*)

railway was single track and as the train pulled into Fairford a rather ancient
porter with a hurricane lamp stood at the barrier to collect the tickets. His
efforts were not entirely wasted as a few WAAFs and a couple of Station HQ
blokes usually handed their tickets in. To get to camp was a long walk from the
station to the village, then up the hill to the camp. However, some bright spark
had found a better way to empty the train, alighting from the opposite side of
the carriage onto the track then going through the fence along the side of the
quarry, past the Aircrew Site, across the road and into Site 1 and our Hut 12 –
and you kept your ticket!

All the 'Nose Art' photographs in this chapter show 620 Squadron Stirlings.
Although many of the 190 Squadron aircraft were also decorated individually, few
photographs of their artwork seem to have survived. Eric Titterton's artistic talent
was much in demand on both squadrons, but his creations did have to be toned
down sometimes!

As a bit of a side line I used to paint insignia on the planes, for instance on
'Z-Zebra' I painted a zebra booting Adolph, but was asked by Squadron
Leader Hannah if I would mind painting out the Führer – for who would want
to be shot down displaying such an insult to the German leader?

Pilot Officer Ron Clement sitting in the cockpit of Stirling EF256, 'The Joker', at Fairford. The 'T2' hangar in the background is still used by the United States Air Force. (*190 & 620 Sqns Archive*)

Stirling EF268 'R', inscribed as 'Frevermore'. Flying Officer Caskey, his crew and their paratroops were killed in this aircraft on D-Day.
(*190 & 620 Sqns Archive*)

'Finger II' – Flying Officer Ross Bunce's Stirling LJ872 'V' at Great Dunmow. (*190 & 620 Sqns Archive*)

Flying Officer Frank Cox's Stirling LJ865 'D-Dog', biting the *Führer*, at Great Dunmow. This aircraft displayed an impressive record of parachute-dropping operations, plus glider tows to Arnhem on 17 and 18 September 1944. (*190 & 620 Sqns Archive*)

Stirling EF303 'Q-Queen', shortly after the move to Great Dunmow. This aircraft was also a 'veteran', whose operations included a glider tow on D-Day and two tows to Arnhem. (*190 & 620 Sqns Archive*)

# CHAPTER 8

# Moving Eastwards
## September to December 1944

As the enemy's grip on western Europe loosened during September 1944, there was a marked reduction in the number of SAS and SOE sorties flown to France by the 38 Group squadrons. They then stepped up their activity over Holland, although it was accepted that the success rate for covert drops of agents or supplies to the Dutch Resistance was never going to be high, mainly because the flat, low-lying landscape made it very difficult to conceal DZs from the occupying forces. Following widespread infiltration of Dutch Resistance networks by the Germans earlier in the war, SOE was now trying to set up secure operations for intelligence gathering. The involvement of the Resistance in these operations was likely to be more effective, in terms of hastening the end of the war, than their taking direct action, such as sabotage of roads and railways used by the enemy. It was true that the latter approach had worked in France, but this was partly because the *Maquisards* could quickly go to ground in its spacious and varied landscape, after carrying out attacks.

On the night of 24/25 September, five Stirlings from 620 Squadron took part in SOE operations to northern Holland, though only one of these aircraft was successful. Of the others, one returned early with Gee trouble, and three were unable to drop because no reception signals were observed at their DZs. Two nights later, 190 Squadron was also back in action. Seven of its aircraft took off on SOE operations to France, but all had to bring their loads back, since the weather was bad and no reception signals could be seen.

On 27 September, 190 and 620 Squadrons were told that they would soon be moving eastwards, to take over the USAAF base at Great Dunmow in Essex. But for the time being, operations from Fairford continued as usual, and on the night of 28/29 September, 620 Squadron sent seven aircraft to SOE DZs in eastern France. Five dropped their supplies successfully, in conditions of bright moonlight. The same night, another aircraft from 620 Squadron carried out the last SAS sortie to be flown from Fairford. It made a successful drop to a DZ near Épinal. On the night of 30 September/1 October, 190 Squadron sent nine aircraft on SOE operations to Holland. The DZs were near Amsterdam and Utrecht, and to the east of Arnhem. Five of these aircraft were successful in dropping supplies.

During the first week of October 1944, the squadrons in 38 Group were busy with preparations for their moves to bases in Essex. The only exceptions were 298 and 644 Squadrons, which were to remain at Tarrant Rushton. In order to stay close to the majority of its airfields, HQ 38 Group was also to move, from Netheravon to Marks Hall, at Coggeshall. On 1 October, Sqn Ldr Bunker was promoted to Wing Commander and posted from 620 Squadron, to succeed the late Wg Cdr Harrison as CO of 190 Squadron. On 9 October, Wg Cdr Lee left 620 Squadron, which he had commanded since its formation in June 1943. He was granted the acting rank of Group Captain and remained in 38 Group, as he was posted to Tilstock. Wg Cdr Geoffrey Wynne-Powell DFC succeeded him as CO of 620 Squadron.

On the night of 3/4 October, two aircraft from 620 Squadron were detailed for SOE drops near Utrecht and Amsterdam. However, they were unable to carry these out, since the weather was poor and no reception signals were observed at either of the DZs, 'Draughts 2' and 'Marmosette 1'. On 5 October, an advance party, totalling seventy-four officers and other ranks, travelled by road from Fairford to Great Dunmow. Most of the personnel at Fairford were to follow them within a fortnight, but there was one large-scale operation planned for the Fairford Stirlings before they departed for their new base. This was Operation 'Molten', which required thirty-two Horsa gliders to be towed to Italy. It is believed the gliders were requested by the Mediterranean Allied Air Force for possible landings in Yugoslavia, though there is no record of their actually having been used for this purpose.

On 9 October, thirty-three Stirlings and thirty-two Horsas took off from Fairford, heading for the south of France. They landed at Istres, near Marseilles, where they were to stop overnight. The tugs had been provided in equal numbers by 190 and 620 Squadrons, and there was an extra Stirling from 620 Squadron, available as a spare tug, if needed. This aircraft went ahead of the others, carrying a small advance party, whose task was to set up Eureka beacons at Istres and Ciampino, near Rome. Eighty-five ground crew personnel travelled with the main party, taking tools and spares, in order to make 'Molten' as self-sufficient as possible.

Twenty-seven of the Fairford combinations arrived over Ciampino airfield on 10 October. The gliders were released there, but the Stirlings then flew south-east and landed at Pomigliano, near Naples. There had been several glider losses along the way, fortunately without any casualties. One had broken away from its tug shortly after taking off from Fairford, but landed safely near Swindon. Its tug, Stirling 'Y' of 620 Squadron, returned to base. Stirlings 'H' of 190 Squadron, and 'R' of 620, became unserviceable at Istres, while 'M' of 190 diverted to Bayonne airfield after its glider broke away south of Poitiers. At Istres, two of the gliders sustained some damage on landing, and were unable to proceed to Ciampino.

Stan White, 620 Squadron, recalled:

The first leg was from base to Istres in France, a flight of five and a half hours. Because the airfield at Istres had only recently been liberated there were no facilities for us. We had to sleep in the aircraft and feed on what were known as iron rations. After a restless night and a breakfast of rock biscuits and tea (made with pressed tea cubes and condensed milk), we were ready to start the second leg of the journey.

From Istres we flew to Ciampino airfield near Rome, where the gliders were landed. The towing aircraft flew on to land at Pomigliano near Naples. We slept on board a British naval ship in Naples harbour. We were allocated a hammock each below deck, but after falling out of mine three times I gave up and went up on deck where I spent the rest of the night chatting to a sailor on duty.

On the 12 October we were transported back to our aircraft, and after a short briefing we took off to fly back to base, carrying a number of ex-prisoners of war, and sick and injured servicemen.

ying Officer Geoff Gawith and his 620 Squadron crew 'brew up' at Istres. (*190 & 620 Sqns Archive*)

Malcolm Mitchell, 190 Squadron, recalled:

In October 1944 we took off, towing a glider, to fly to Naples in Italy. Our first leg carried us over France, having crossed the coast near Cherbourg. The flight across France, in clear, warm, sunny weather, was uneventful, and as the droning hours passed we fell into a very relaxed state. Suddenly 'Ikey' called me through the intercom, 'Malc, the controls have jammed!' At this, I jumped up and began hurriedly to trace back the flight controls to the wings and the tail. I could find nothing wrong, so I plugged in my intercom at the back and told him so. 'It's OK now,' he replied, 'it was the automatic pilot, I fell asleep and put it in with my elbow.' Remember, we were towing a glider, while at that time having no control over the aircraft at all – that certainly woke us all up for the rest of the flight! We continued past Toulouse, to the airfield at Istres, close to the Mediterranean Sea. Having landed, fed, etc, we all drove down to the nearby town of Istres, to spend the evening in a café, relaxing over some wine.

The next day, we continued our journey, flying across the Mediterranean to Corsica, then across the Tyrrhenian Sea, to arrive over Italy, where we descended for a good view, and then flew south to Rome, where the gliders were released. We circled over the Vatican, as most unusual sightseers, went on to look at Vesuvius, and finally landed near to Naples. We were put up in a ship there and proceeded to explore the town, finding the people most friendly. One young girl insisted on blowing the whistle attached to my battledress (to be used if lost in a dinghy at sea, etc), which entailed her head being in close proximity to mine! We spent some time in a classical palace, which had been acquired as a NAAFI for servicemen, and spent an evening at the Scala Opera House, to see 'Tosca'. Some of the lads, either drunk on the wine, or trigger happy (having

Vesuvius emerges from the morning mist, viewed from the wing of a Fairford Stirling at Pomigliano airfield. (*190 & 620 Sqns Archive*)

never used a pistol in anger), and being in a country formerly our enemy, were a little aggressive. In the evening, as we walked back to the ship, we passed a shuttered shop. In the gloom behind sat two men. The lads saw something suspicious in this, and ordered them out. This they refused to do (or did not understand the order), so one lad attempted to shoot the lock off the shutters. The bullet ricocheted up the road, missing people walking along the top. At this we managed to get our people to leave, to join the ship. This welcome break soon ended, and we returned to Britain, flying over the Alps on the way.

Stirlings 'X' of 190 Squadron, and 'F' of 620 Squadron, had released their gliders over Ciampino, but were declared unserviceable at Pomigliano. On 12 October, the remaining twenty-five Stirlings at Pomigliano took off on their return journey to the UK, but one of them had to make a precautionary landing at Versailles after two of its oil coolers developed problems. The twenty-four aircraft that arrived at Fairford were carrying 170 passengers, mainly from the RAF and Army, but with a few also from the American forces and the French *Armée de l'Air*. Customs and Excise clearance was quickly arranged, so that the passengers could proceed with their onward journeys.

It was the beginning of November before all the Stirlings involved in 'Molten' returned to the UK. By then, 190 and 620 Squadrons and their respective Servicing Echelons had moved to Great Dunmow. This 'new' RAF station, which had been under the command of Group Captain K.J. McIntyre OBE since 11 October, lay to the north-west of Great Dunmow town, but was in fact closer to the village of Little Easton. During 1943, the construction of the airfield for the USAAF deprived the Easton Lodge estate of much of its parkland and necessitated the felling of a large number of mature trees. Easton Lodge had formerly been one of the homes of Frances, Countess of Warwick. Popularly known as 'Darling Daisy', she was often visited there by the Prince of Wales (later King Edward VII). The large house, on the north side of the airfield, was requisitioned to form part of the wartime camp, which otherwise comprised temporary hutted accommodation. As at Fairford, there were just two 'T2' hangars on the airfield.

During the morning of 12 October, some of the Fairford Flying Control personnel moved to Great Dunmow, in preparation for the main transfer of the aircraft.

Noel Chaffey, 620 Squadron, recalled:

I took off from Fairford as a passenger with Flight Sergeant Peter Jordan and his crew, taking the control tower personnel to set up their systems at Great Dunmow. From there, we went to Manston, where I rejoined my own crew. We then flew more equipment up to Great Dunmow, before returning to Fairford.

Whilst unloading at Great Dunmow, we took the chance to have a quick look around. Our aircraft was parked right by the control tower, which was

reat Dunmow airfield, 30 May 1944. The 386th Bomb Group, equipped with B-26 Marauders, operated from here tween September 1943 and October 1944. (*English Heritage (NMR) USAAF Photography*)

Easton Lodge, photographed by Flight Sergeant Noel Chaffey in the autumn of 1944. The main part of the buildi
was demolished shortly after the war. (*N.R. Chaffey*)

close to Easton Lodge, the 'Big House'. The front walls were overgrown with
Virginia Creeper and appeared alive with a deep red colour. But we left
exploring the house until later and rushed off to look over the 'hut' sites. The
Sergeants' Mess was closed but of a similar pattern to ours at Fairford, as were
the other Nissen huts, though there were slit trenches in between every second
hut. These were necessary as we were now in 'Doodle Bug Alley', with the V1
Flying Bombs coming over us to get to London.

In some of the huts, I was amazed at all the items left on the shelves by the
Americans. There were radios, brand new bedding, tins of biscuits and boxes of
chocolate bars; heaven only knows what other goods they left in their 'PX'
store. However, when we returned a few days later and commandeered a hut,
not a single comfort was to be seen. The locals from the village had got word of
the changeover and had raided the huts, leaving us with bare shelves – but who
could blame them!

On 14 October, the weather was fine, but breezy, as most of the 190 Squadron
Stirlings flew to Great Dunmow, carrying their squadron personnel and some of the
ground crews. The rest of the personnel from 6190 Servicing Echelon, together with
those of No. 3 Glider Servicing Echelon, made their way to Great Dunmow by rail,
the same day.

Eric Wadman, 6190 Servicing Echelon, recalled:

By the autumn of 1944, there were rumours of a move, and then ground crews
started leaving Fairford by road with equipment for our new station. We
learned that some of us would be flying down in our allotted aircraft, with our
kit, including tools and cycles, and even the flight hut tables and chairs.

0 Squadron's LJ875 'B-Beer', with Flight Sergeant Ken Hillier standing above his gun turret. In the background the 'Marauder Graveyard'. (*190 & 620 Sqns Archive*)

I enjoyed this first opportunity for me to fly in one of our Stirlings, and as soon as we were airborne I was given permission to go down into the bomb aimer's position. It was exhilarating to pass over towns and villages, and to see the traffic moving along the main roads leading into London. At one point, I saw a flight of nine Dakotas, 'sliding' across below us, and a little later, a formation of three Spitfires came climbing up to have a look at us, and then were quickly lost ahead.

As soon as I heard the change of propeller pitch, I knew we were preparing for landing, and I went back, to settle on the floor by the centre section. The wheels rumbled as we landed, and then we taxied around the perimeter track to the new dispersal point of 190 Squadron 'B' Flight at Great Dunmow.

The skeleton crews of the advance party saw us in, and on climbing out, I noticed that the American 'Stars and Stripes' were still flying from the control tower. In the far corner of the airfield, in the direction of the tower of Little Easton Church, I noticed the 'Graveyard', containing the remains of twin-engined Marauder bombers. They had fought a hard battle, against the German fighters and anti-aircraft fire, on their many missions over enemy-occupied territory.

Ivan Fairfax, 6190 Servicing Echelon, recalled:

It was a dry and sunny morning when our convoy moved out from Fairford. On arrival at Great Dunmow, the airfield appeared to be deserted, the sun was about to set and the temperature very low. We found a domestic site at the bottom left corner of a sloping area which appeared to have been a wood until recently. In this area there were numerous Nissen huts, all in darkness and apparently uninhabited. The next day threw light upon many things. Three of

Personnel of the Electrical Section, on the steps of Easton Lodge. (*190 & 620 Sqns Archive*)

the larger buildings were messes, and there were more sleeping quarters and other miscellaneous buildings.

Attached to the old house was a more recent building that became the residence of the Station Commander. Across the road, and almost opposite the main entrance to Easton Lodge, was a railway halt, which had been used by the Prince of Wales when he visited the Countess of Warwick.

The Electrical and Instrument Sections were allocated the west wing of Easton Lodge, which the Countess had used as her summer residence. The Instrument Section occupied a conservatory and other small outbuildings, at the back of which was a cobbled courtyard complete with a fountain. On both sides of the courtyard were high walls that during the summer months were in the shade of mature pear trees. The wall on the left side, facing the entrance gated wall, had a coach house and stable, inside of which the floor was cobbled, below a vaulted ceiling.

John Smith, 6190 Servicing Echelon, recalled:

The Electrical Section at Dunmow was quite something. Instead of being in a Nissen hut, our workshop was in the day room that had been used by the lady of the estate. The entrance was from the courtyard through a tunnel into this large room, which had a ceiling some 25 feet high. At one end was an internal balcony with a large window looking out over the lawns. The Electrical Officer chose this for his office, having hardboard fitted from the balcony rail up to the ceiling, to give some privacy. The top half of the inside wall had a mural painted on it, depicting a sunken Italian garden, actually the real one in the grounds. What a place to call a workshop! It did wonders for morale.

:aston Lodge's formal lawns and Italian sunken garden were designed by Harold Peto. Two gardeners were :tained during the war years, and they made an excellent job of looking after these features, as can be seen in ese photographs, taken in 1944. (*190 & 620 Sqns Archive*)

The Station Headquarters building at RAF Great Dunmow. Partly visible in this photograph are Spitfire, Ti[
Moth and Oxford aircraft of the Station Flight. The Oxford, DF336 (on the right), soldiered on for a furtl
decade, and was one of the last in service with the RAF. Its 'Finest Hour' was in 1953, when it represented N[
Advanced Flying Training School at the Coronation Review of the RAF, held at Odiham. (*N. R. Chaffey*)

On 16 October, a number of 620 Squadron's Stirlings were ferried to Great
Dunmow, where they were greeted by low cloud and rain. The weather was slightly
better the next day, when most of the 620 Squadron personnel, plus some ground
crews, were flown to Great Dunmow. No. 6620 Servicing Echelon's main party,
No. 4 Glider Servicing Echelon, and Station HQ personnel followed them by train.

A few Horsas were towed from Fairford to Great Dunmow on 19 October, but
the following day brought high winds, which delayed the completion of this task.
The glider tows resumed on 22 October, when eighteen gliders were transferred,
leaving seventeen at Fairford, waiting to be flown across the next day. The glider
fleet was still depleted after the Arnhem operation, so a number of new Horsas were
later ferried to Great Dunmow by Albemarle tugs.

Eric Wadman recalled:

At Great Dunmow (or Easton Lodge, as we first knew it), we soon started to
settle down into the flight routine, with all ground crew members doing their
Daily Inspections of the Stirlings, and us fitters our engine runs. Within a day
or so of our arrival, the 'Stars and Stripes' flag on the Flying Control building
was pulled down and the RAF Ensign flew in its place. The 'Works and Bricks'
Flight was busy, bringing the living sites up to RAF standards. Concrete paving
slabs were laid across the site to the Nissen huts, with posts and whitened ropes
fencing off the pathways to give the grass a chance to recover, and to prevent
too much mud and dirt being taken into the billets. There had been long, open
rows of toilet pans in the ablutions, but these soon had walls and doors to
separate them, to give a little more privacy.

There were about 2,500 personnel within the camp bounds. The dormitory sites of Nissen huts were dispersed amongst the trees, and fairly central to these was 'The Communal Site'. Here the main buildings were larger Nissen huts, around the edge of an open stretch of grass, with a few scattered trees, in part of what had been the park at Easton Lodge. To the left was the Airmen's Mess, with the Sergeants' Mess to the right. There was also the all-important NAAFI building, comprising the usual canteen facilities, billiard and reading/writing rooms. On off duty evenings, the NAAFI was the central meeting point for most of the 'erks'. Nearby was a large mess hall, which the Americans had converted into a cinema and concert hall.

Days off were usually once a week, and could be any day from Monday through to Sunday. Bishops Stortford was the only town of any size within easy reach, and our facilities on camp surpassed what could be found in Great Dunmow, unless you were an ardent drinker and wished to indulge in a pub crawl.

Although the autumn weather at Great Dunmow was not particularly good, the Stirlings made a swift return to operational flying. On the night of 22/23 October, three aircraft from 620 Squadron flew to SOE DZs 'Draughts 5', 'Rummy 16', and 'Rummy 18', in western Holland. It was a dark night, and identification of the DZs was made even more difficult by flooding of the surrounding Dutch countryside. No reception lights were seen and the loads had to be brought back.

This photograph illustrates the comradeship that existed at RAF Great Dunmow, with flying and ground crew personnel enjoying a drink together. Third from left is Flight Lieutenant Bill 'Dinger' Bell DFC RNZAF of 620 Squadron, who had survived a ditching in the English Channel a few weeks earlier. (*T. T. Owen*)

On the night of 25/26 October, five aircraft of 190 Squadron flew on SOE operations to 'Black Widow', 'Bluebottle', and 'Draughts' DZs, at widespread locations in Holland. Three were successful in dropping, in spite of some very bad weather. Another aircraft from 190 Squadron dropped to a DZ in northern Holland. This was 'Fabian 3', set up by a small party of Belgian troops belonging to 5 SAS, whose task was to gather information on V2 rocket launch sites. Owing to the weather, two aircraft diverted to Manston on their return, but the others managed to land at base.

Between operations, continuation training at Great Dunmow followed a pattern similar to that organised previously at Fairford. One of the main activities was glider towing, carried out whenever the weather permitted. The first Group Exercise to be planned after the move was appropriately named 'Essex', orders for which were issued on 23 October. This should have consisted of a long cross-country glider tow to Wiltshire and back, via several turning points over southern England, with a further cross-country by the tugs, after releasing the gliders. However, following several postponements because of the weather, 'Essex' was finally cancelled on 29 October.

At Great Dunmow, the flying programme was not helped by the poor state of the airfield. This urgently required repairs and additions to the lighting system, while the lights that did work were often obscured by mud thrown onto them by aircraft and vehicles. Interference between radio transmissions from Great Dunmow and the airfields at Rivenhall and Wethersfield, which had also been taken over by 38 Group, was another technical problem that needed to be solved. As a result of all the rain during the autumn of 1944, the grass areas at Great Dunmow and these neighbouring airfields became too waterlogged to be usable, as noted in the 38 Group Operations Record Book at the time: 'The slightest excursion from the perimeter track and you're sunk – literally.'

SOE operations resumed on the night of 1/2 November, as three aircraft from 190 Squadron, and six from 620, were sent to various Dutch DZs ('Bluebottle', 'Criena', 'Draughts', 'Dudley', 'Event', 'Nico' and 'Rummy'). On this occasion, there was a temporary improvement in the weather and all six of the 620 Squadron aircraft were successful. Two of the aircraft from 190 Squadron did not drop, because no reception signals were observed, but the third one dropped twenty-four containers and two packages.

On 4 and 5 November, the Great Dunmow Stirlings took part in Air-Sea Rescue searches, but they were unable to find the crew of an aircraft that was thought to have ditched in the North Sea. During the afternoon of 5 November, Great Dunmow reverberated once more to the sound of American bombers, as thirty B-17 Flying Fortresses of the 401st Bomb Group were diverted there. Two of these aircraft were damaged in a collision on the ground, and had to be left behind when the others took off at dusk to return to their base at Deenethorpe in Northamptonshire.

Ernest Fletcher, 620 Squadron, recalled:

Whilst stationed at Dunmow, on many cold mornings the sky overhead would be filled with condensation trails as Flying Fortresses gained operational height before setting course for Europe. One day, on returning from a bombing mission, some were diverted to land at Dunmow. I recall that quite a number of us were watching as they came into land; one touching down, one in the middle of the runway and one about to turn off onto the perimeter track. We watched fascinated until, alas, they got a bit too clever, one wasn't quite quick enough

American B-17, taxiing past the Stirlings at Great Dunmow. (*N.R. Chaffey*)

clearing the runway and the aircraft behind caught up and ran into it. There was plenty of damage to the two aircraft but the crews were OK.

On the night of 6/7 November, there were SOE operations, with four Stirlings of 190 Squadron going to 'Draughts', 'Dudley' and 'Podex' DZs in Holland. Three aircraft returned, but were diverted to Earls Colne. None of them had been able to drop. The fourth aircraft, LK195 'A', which had been destined for 'Dudley 3', east of the Zuider Zee, was missing. Its crew, captained by a Canadian, Fg Off Edwin Hodgson, had been among the replacements posted from 1665 HCU to 190 Squadron in September 1944, following the heavy losses suffered at Arnhem. This was their first operation together, although Hodgson had flown as 2nd pilot to Flt Lt Chesterton on an unsuccessful attempt to drop at the same DZ, 'Dudley 3', on the night of 1/2 November. There was the faintest of hopes that the missing crew might have survived, after a Mosquito pilot reported seeing a light flashing from the North Sea, which he thought was possibly a torch in a dinghy. During the morning of 7 November, six aircraft from 190 Squadron made a thorough search of the area, but they came back without finding any trace of the missing crew, who had actually crashed near Enkhuizen, on the west bank of the Zuider Zee.

Although the promotion of a resistance campaign in Holland presented SOE with many problems, the rugged landscape of Norway was well suited to the setting up of covert DZs, and one in which targets of military importance were vulnerable to attack. Earlier in the war, the Norwegian Resistance organisation, *Milorg*, had directed its efforts towards intelligence gathering, misinformation and civil disobedience, but by the end of 1944 sabotage of transport links and industrial plants was taking place with SOE's backing. As they tried to suppress these destructive actions, the German forces maintained a large presence in Norway, which had the secondary effect of reducing their resources at the main European battlefront.

The night of 6/7 November was the first occasion that the Dunmow Stirlings took part in SOE operations to Norwegian DZs. Two 190 Squadron aircraft were sent to 'Halter 1' and 'Reins 2', south-west of Oslo, but both were unsuccessful, since one crew failed to identify the DZ and the other was unable to see any reception signals. These operations to Norway would prove to be some of the most arduous carried out by 190 and 620 Squadrons, for the elements often seemed to be more of an enemy than the Germans.

Malcolm Mitchell recalled:

Our transfer to Dunmow put us a little nearer to Norway, but this was still about four hours' flying away. Navigation became more difficult, especially when Norway had cloud, for the sea provided no location points. But we had a very good navigator in Ross Vincent and never became lost. I do however remember some swift map work on one trip, when we crossed the Norwegian coast unexpectedly. My main problem was fuel, as the trip took nearly eight hours, mostly over the sea.

If we were fortunate, we would catch a glimpse of the coast of Denmark, off the starboard bow, giving the navigator and bomb aimer a reference point. However, we were just as likely to miss it and to carry on until we hit the coast of Norway. Our target lay amongst the mountains to the north of Oslo usually, where the Norwegian Resistance hid and operated. On one occasion, we crossed the coast near to Oslo and turned towards our target, this bearing taking us past a German airfield, Gardermoen. We were disconcerted to see the profile of a Junkers 88 flying across our path and below us, but the crew must have been concentrating on their approach and landing, for they did not see us. And so, on to our DZ in a valley in the mountains, where we made a successful drop after the mutual recognition signals. Then up to 10,000 feet and away, back to the Skaggerak and home, past a flak ship, which did us no damage. Clearing the Skaggerak, we obtained a fix from the last corner of Norway and crossed the dark, wide, North Sea.

Returning like this on a similar operation, and flying at 10,000 feet, we soon entered cloud, and the temperature dropped rapidly. Being fearful of ice, I pushed my head and an Aldis lamp into the astrodome and looked out towards the wings, lit by the lamp. Ice was indeed beginning to form there, which, if allowed to build up, would destroy the aircraft's lift. I therefore asked our pilot, 'Ikey', to descend to a warmer altitude. However, the ice kept increasing, so we had to go on descending through the cloud, until we were only 200 feet above the sea. We flew on until the ice finally disappeared and we were able to climb again. But these manoeuvres had left us short of fuel, as I reported to 'Ikey'. We then altered course for the nearer coast of Scotland, and made landfall with enough fuel to get to the RAF base at Kinloss, where we thankfully landed. We went to Norway many times, but the other operations, whilst long, hard and tiring, passed off without incident.

However, one did not have to be on an operation to be in danger, when flying. On a clear late autumn day, we took W-Willie (our usual aircraft) up for an air test. We climbed steadily and levelled out at 10,000 feet. At my instrument panel I was amazed to see the engines begin to fail, as their oil pressure (normally 80 lb per square inch) dropped to about half of this, with the cylinder temperatures rising alarmingly. When the oil pressure on one engine went down to 35 lb per square inch, and it was in danger of seizing up, I called to 'Ikey' for it to be stopped and the propeller feathered. Soon another engine became dangerous and had to be feathered, and yet a third. We really went to panic stations when the last engine also overheated. It was then necessary to get down as soon as possible, so I asked for the flaps and the undercarriage to be lowered and the remaining engine to be throttled back and the propeller set to fine pitch, to take the strain off it. When that had been done, we practically fell out of the sky. Reaching a lower altitude, I ventured to restart an engine. Its condition

...nusual view from a Stirling on an exercise over Essex, with the starboard inner engine stopped and its propeller ...hered. (*190 & 620 Sqns Archive*)

stabilising, I tried starting the third engine, successfully. By this time, we were near enough to the airfield to attempt a landing, which we did on three engines safely. The next day, my ground crew told me the reason for our problem – they had omitted to fix the winter baffle plates to the oil coolers, and in the high, cold air the oil had frozen, putting them out of action (through what was referred to as 'coring'). The bypass valves had then returned hot oil straight back to the engines, overheating them and reducing the oil pressure. I'd had no idea what was wrong, but luckily my instinctive actions had saved the engines and allowed the oil to thaw.

On 8 November, fourteen aircraft from 190 Squadron, and fifteen from 620 Squadron, towed gliders to Tarrant Rushton, from where they were to take part in Group Exercise 'Bear'. Bad weather caused this exercise to be postponed until 10 November, and when it did go ahead there was still a strong wind. A few gliders cast off on the way to the LZ, which was at Chilbolton airfield in Hampshire, but most released according to plan and landed safely. Ground mist, encountered *en route*, was used to advantage by the Mosquito crews who were providing fighter affiliation practice. They were able to hide in the mist, then climb out of it to intercept the Stirlings, taking their gunners by surprise. The exercise also provided some air experience for troops of the 6th Airborne Division, who were carried as passengers. Having fought almost continuously since D-Day, they had recently returned to the UK and were now taking part in further training.

On the night of 10/11 November, a single aircraft from 190 Squadron, captained by Fg Off Siegert, flew to Holland and made a successful delivery to an SAS DZ, 'Fabian 7'. A special message was later sent by the recipients, 'paying tribute to the accuracy and excellence of the drop'.

The weather then put a stop to all 38 Group operations until the night of 15/16 November. The only squadron active that night was 620, which sent twelve aircraft on SOE operations to 'Draughts', 'Dudley', 'Event', 'Marmosette', 'Mongoose', 'Podex' and 'Sculling' DZs in Holland. The DZs were covered by mist and low cloud, but seven aircraft were successful in dropping. One aircraft returned to Great Dunmow early because of problems with icing, but the other eleven had to be diverted to Tarrant Rushton on their return, owing to poor visibility at base.

Over the next few days, there were few operations by the 38 Group squadrons, and none at all by 190 and 620. On 19 November, there was some good news for Fg Off le Bouvier of 190 Squadron, when he learned that his bomb aimer, Flt Sgt Martin, and air gunner, Flt Sgt Kershaw, who had baled out near Arnhem on 20 September, were now known to be safe, albeit as POWs.

During the evening of 21 November, four Stirling crews were practising night circuits and landings with Horsas at Great Dunmow. The weather was fair to start with, but it soon deteriorated and only four lifts were completed. One of the tug aircraft was LK276 'Y' of 190 Squadron, captained by Fg Off Ian Kidgell, an Australian. On this flight, Fg Off Walter 'Wattie' Brain, a New Zealander, was occupying the co-pilot's seat. This aircraft released its glider, then jettisoned the tow-rope, before clearance to land was requested at 2113 hours. Clearance was not given, and the aircraft was instructed to stand by. There were no further transmissions from the aircraft, which crashed in the circuit at Newton Green, at approximately 2120 hrs. The aircraft hit some small trees, passed under an overhead cable, and skidded along the surface of a ploughed field for a short distance before the rear

Flying Officer Ian Kidgell (in dark blue RAAF uniform), with members of his crew. This photograph was taken while they were at 1665 HCU, Tilstock, before being posted to 190 Squadron. (*Mrs M. Kidgell via 190 & 620 Sqns Archive*)

fuselage broke away. The remainder of the aircraft continued moving until it crashed into a bank and exploded. There was no sign of any fire before this final impact. Only the air gunner, Flt Sgt Reid, was found alive at the scene of the crash. He was unconscious and died on the way to hospital.

Examination of wreckage at the crash site indicated that Stirling LK276 had a low rate of descent, a shallow angle of bank, and all four engines developing normal power, when it came into contact with the ground. The Investigating Officer was of the opinion that there had been no structural failure or damage to the aircraft in the air. The air gunner was not in his turret when found, so he might have moved forward to assume his 'crash position', but there was no reason to suspect that the captain of the aircraft anticipated any danger. The subsequent Court of Inquiry did not set out to apportion any blame, but it did consider the possibility that LK276's crash may have been caused by the captain being distracted from his instrument flying, while trying to keep the airfield lights in view, under conditions of increasing haze. However, this was only put forward as a theory, and the main conclusion was that the cause of the accident could not be determined.

Eric Wadman was one of the airmen who had worked on Stirling LK276 shortly before its crash:

During the day of 21 November 1944 a ground crew on 'B' Flight, 190 Squadron, was detailed to do the daily inspections on Stirling 'Y-Yorker'. I was one of the two engine fitters involved. Not having worked on this aircraft before, I took the two port engines and my mate the two starboard ones, but working together to drop the cowlings, for our visual checks. I then personally did the full ground run of all four engines.

When all was completed, we all went up to the flight hut, and signed our names in the Form 700, then carried on back to the aircraft. We were not instructed to 'stand by', for any immediate daytime operation or exercise, so our job was done for the day on that particular aircraft.

It was to be my day off on the 22nd, so when the day shift had finished at 5.30 pm, we returned to the airmen's mess for tea, and went back to our billets for the rest of the evening. Meanwhile, other members of 'B' Flight, having had their tea at the airmen's mess, would have to return to the flights, if they had been detailed for night flying ground crew duties. I had an 'early night', and though next to the airfield, you became so familiar with take-off and landing noise that once in bed, the engine sound never disturbed your sleep.

Next morning, washed and shaved, and in my Best Blue uniform, I went to the mess for breakfast, then hurried to catch the red double-decker bus that would ferry me to

Flying Officer Walter Brain, who was killed with Flying Officer Kidgell and his crew on 21 November 1944. (*Mrs M. Kidgell via 190 & 620 Sqns Archive*)

Bishops Stortford, without a care in the world, and anticipating an enjoyable day in town. It was still early, with some service people on the upper deck, and a few local civilians getting on in Great Dunmow. We pulled away and as we rounded a corner, heading into the countryside, I had the sight which shocked me to the core.

To the right of us, in a field, were the towering fin, tailplane, and rear fuselage of a Stirling aircraft, but ahead of it nothing but a jumbled mass of broken, twisted bits of metal. I only recall small outer bits of wing, and four hunks of metal, which had once been the engines, as recognisable among these. I had been running those engines a few hours earlier, for the fuselage bore an ominous, tall 'Y', painted on its side. There had been no talk in the mess hall that morning of a night crash, so the news came to me in that split second as we rounded that corner. My day off had turned into a nightmare.

Next day, on the flight, all those whose names had been on the 'Y-Yorker' Form 700 were assembled, and we were taken to the Court of Inquiry. There we stood outside, in case any of us were called to answer any questions. To my relief, it transpired that the aircraft had hit the ground with all engines under power, so there was no question of engine failure having contributed to the crash.

Although the Court of Inquiry considered the crash of Stirling LK276 to be purely accidental, there is an intriguing twist to this tragic story, because it has been alleged that the aircraft was shot down by an intruder. At first sight, this idea may appear

is impression of Stirling LK276's crash site is taken from a watercolour, in which Eric Wadman portrayed the
ne he witnessed while travelling on the bus to Bishops Stortford. (*E. Wadman via 190 & 620 Sqns Archive*)

far-fetched, since many of the German night-fighters in Western Europe had been
redeployed to bases in France during the summer of 1944, in response to the
Normandy invasion. There was then very little intruder activity over the UK until
early 1945. Moreover, there are no entries in the Great Dunmow Watchkeeper's Log
that indicate any enemy air activity in the vicinity of the airfield during the evening
of 21 November 1944. Any such occurrences would normally have been worthy of
note, and close examination of this original document reveals no evidence of any
alterations or deletions. Nevertheless, there are accounts from witnesses, both on
and off the RAF Station at Great Dunmow, that are inconsistent with the evidence
presented by the Investigating Officer to the Court of Inquiry.

Larry Siegert, 190 Squadron, recalled:

On 21 November 1944 Fg Off Brain was checking out Fg Off Kidgell on night
towing of the Horsa. It was a clear night, and myself and two of my crew,
navigator Fg Off Vince Willis and bomb aimer Plt Off Leonard Pepperell, were
playing bridge in our Nissen hut at the dispersal site where we lived at night. We
went outside, I think towards 9.00 pm, and a Stirling passed over us at circuit
height with its navigation lights on. Tucked in behind it and very close was a
smaller aircraft without nav lights. As they flew away we heard the cannon
which next day we realised was the shooting down of Kidgell and Brain. We
knew nothing of the inquiry into the 'accident', otherwise I am sure we would

have discounted the pilot blame theory. The small aircraft we saw behind the Stirling was obviously a German intruder aircraft. It wasn't a glider because that would have had nav lights on, and been towed well back from the tug aircraft, with the rear gunner always in his turret during towing to acquaint the pilot of the glider's situation, i.e., high tow or low tow. I understand that when they found the crashed Stirling the rear gunner was not in his turret.

Donald Tranter had lived with his family in London until 1941, when their house received a direct hit from a German bomb. They were then evacuated to Woodgates End, which is to the north-west of Great Dunmow airfield. Mr Tranter's description of LK276's crash is as follows:

The farm we lived on had two large fields which backed right up to the airfield. As a boy of 14, I spent every moment I could at the perimeter fence, watching RAF aircraft land and take off. In early 1944, an American construction unit had installed a very complicated landing light system to guide aircraft onto the runway. We had about 150 wooden posts criss-crossing our fields, about 10–15 feet tall, with coloured lights pointing different ways.

I remember this particular aircraft crash as if it happened today; in my mind's eye it is so clear and also so very sad, only a few more minutes and it would have landed on the north-south runway. It was a cold clear night. My mother and I had gone outside to a big shed in which we stored apples for winter use. We could hear this four-engined aircraft on final approach, and by its sound we knew it was a British aircraft. Stirlings had been up and down all day with Horsa gliders in tow. The runway/approach lights were on and we could see the aircraft's black outline and the glow of its exhausts as it came low and slow over our heads.

Without warning we heard twenty to thirty loud bangs, a bit like fireworks, and the aircraft caught fire on its right wing and engines. My Mum said 'A Jerry fighter has got her!' At the same instant, we could hear the sound of another aircraft, very fast, gone in an instant.

The runway lighting was switched off and the local anti-aircraft guns opened fire, and at the same time the air raid warning sounded. The Stirling, we could see it so clearly now, passed over towards Easton Lodge, but it seemed to gain height and it flew on over the runway and came down at Newton Green. After school the next day I visited the crash area and was told by the soldiers on guard that there were no survivors.

The morning after the crash, it was business as usual at Great Dunmow, since operations were planned for the night of 22/23 November, but these were later cancelled because of the weather. The following night, 23/24 November, six aircraft from 190 Squadron were detailed for SOE operations to 'Draughts', 'Dudley' and 'Necking' DZs in Holland. However, the lead aircraft, Fg Off le Bouvier's 'U-Uncle', burst a tyre while taxiing and was unable to proceed. The other aircraft had to be manoeuvred around the obstruction created by 'U-Uncle' and were delayed in taking off. They arrived some thirty minutes late over their DZs, but two of them dropped successfully.

On the night of 27/28 November, 190 and 620 Squadrons each had six aircraft taking part in SOE operations to 'Bit', 'Crupper', 'Reins', 'Tail' and 'Thrush Red' DZs in the south of Norway. Two aircraft from 190 Squadron failed to take off, after one developed radio trouble and the other a fuel leak. Only four of the

Dunmow crews were able to drop, the others having failed to observe any reception signals. Although conditions were generally clear over Norway that night, there was a lot of low mist in the valleys, which could have obscured the lights on some of the DZs. Anti-aircraft fire was encountered over the Norwegian coast and around the Oslo Fjord, but all the Dunmow aircraft came back safely.

Morgan Thomas, a bomb aimer with 620 Squadron, recalled the tense atmosphere that preceded these long-distance operations:

> Some of the most memorable times were as we travelled around the airfield to our aircraft. We set out in darkness in a three-ton truck, though they called it the crew bus. It had a row of seats down each side and another double row down the centre where aircrew sat back to back. Each crew member got on the bus loaded with safety and navigational equipment so it was rather crowded. It was always very dark in the bus and one rarely knew who one was sitting beside, but small talk went on for a short time. Not knowing who you were sitting by could be a blessing, because the following day you might discover that the person next to you had not returned. You then realised that you might have been the last person, apart from his crew, who had spoken to him.
>
> After a short time, silence would prevail and then someone would try to start up a song, such as 'Bless 'em all'. Suddenly the bus would stop and the driver

embers of Flight Sergeant Dann's 620 Squadron crew, in and around the cockpit of their Stirling, 'S-Sugar': in e cockpit, left to right, Sergeant 'Mac' McKenzie (navigator) and Flying Officer 'Tommy' Thomas (bomb aimer); top of the cockpit, left to right, Sergeant Jack Harris (wireless operator), Sergeant Ken Copping (air gunner), ight Sergeant George Dann (pilot) and Sergeant Monty Shaffer (flight engineer). (*M. Thomas*)

would shout out an aircraft letter and the respective crew would disembark. Off again in silence, until someone would try another song. As each crew got off the bus the silence became unbearable and it was a great relief when your aircraft letter was called. Once at your aircraft, with tasks to be carried out, the sense of loneliness disappeared. It was here that we met the aircraft ground crew, who always seemed pleased to see us and we would have a short chat with them. They stayed until we taxied out from dispersal and would always give a 'cheerio' wave as we departed. They would be there to welcome us when we returned hours later – it must have been a long wait for them.

As far as possible, Norwegian operations were planned for nights with bright moonlight, because the Stirling crews navigated by a combination of dead reckoning and map reading on these long flights, which went beyond the useful range of Gee transmissions. But the crews were only too well aware that good visibility also helped the German night-fighters based in Norway.

Henry Hooper, 620 Squadron, recalled:

After Arnhem we continued dropping supplies, making three trips to Norway, a part of the world with very different terrain from the rest of occupied Europe. On one bright moonlit night with the ground snow-covered, everything was so clear yet featureless. It caused our engineer, who was looking out of the astro-dome, to remark: 'Skipper, do you know what we would look like, if someone spotted us from above? We would look like a dirty fly crawling over an iced cake.'

On 29 November, 190 and 620 Squadrons each sent seven aircraft on Exercise 'Cru', in which paratroops of the French Forces of the Interior were dropped on DZs at two locations south of Reims, near to their Headquarters in France. The same day, both squadrons sent some of their less experienced crews to Tarrant Rushton to pick up paratroops, for dropping during Exercise 'Castle'.

During November 1944, there had been announcements of decorations for gallantry in the skies over Arnhem. These included the DSO for Wg Cdr Bunker, CO of 190 Squadron (and formerly with 620 Squadron), the DFC for Flt Lt Robertson, Fg Off Pascoe, Fg Off Siegert and Plt Off Sutherland of 190 Squadron, and the DFM for Flt Sgt Thompson of 190 Squadron. The DFC was also awarded to Fg Off Bunce of 620 Squadron.

At the beginning of December 1944, the weather took a turn for the worse, but the resultant lull in flying did allow some more time for recreation, including football matches between Dunmow teams and those from other local RAF and Army units. The station cinema showed its first film during December, and there were usually dances in the NAAFI on Sunday nights. There were also, from time to time, performances by visiting ENSA Concert Parties.

Eric Wadman recalled:

These ENSA shows were usually at weekends, and held in the camp cinema. They typically contained a couple of comedians, male and female singers (frequently of the pantomime star type) and with a good sprinkling of curvy dancing girls, to cheer up the 'boys in blue'. Ground and air crews all joined in the fun, and often contributed to it, with spontaneous humour, such as a Cockney shout from the back of the hall, when a shapely singer was on the stage, 'Wrap it up, I'll have it!'

The 620 Squadron soccer team. Back row (standing), left to right, Compton, McLeod, Wing Commander Wynne-Powell (Squadron Commander), Bridges, Berry, Curtis; front row, Hodgen, Evans, Lomas, Dutton (Captain), Beale and Davis. (*190 & 620 Sqns Archive*)

'Liberty Runs' were organised regularly, to take off-duty personnel into Chelmsford (a ticket for this bus transport cost 6d). However, during the war, there were often occasions when travelling on leave, or just going for a night out, could turn into a bit of an adventure, even if one did break a few trivial rules along the way!

Noel Chaffey recalled:

Now that we were stationed in Essex, London was only an hour away by train, from Bishops Stortford. We had rail passes on our official leaves, but many times a quick trip to the big city for a dance or a show was a possibility, and it was always fun trying to get there on the 'cheap'.

A quick duck under the barbed wire fence, by the gatehouse of Easton Lodge, led us onto the main road. Heading west, we'd look out for a passing American jeep and cadge a lift to the railway station. No matter how laden they were, there was always room for a 'little un'.

On our return to camp the unofficial way, we could get on the perimeter track and await a pick up by the crew trucks on the station. Our aircraft pad was very close to the fence, whereas to go via the guardroom it would mean walking miles, through the village and then up the hill to the main gate.

Elizabeth Robson, MT Section, recalled:

I was a WAAF driver then and knew the gardens at Easton Lodge extremely well. They were actually out of bounds, but a good deal of courting went on there, and as I had a dog (quite illegally) I used to walk there a lot and explore.

219

WAAF airwomen of the MT Section at RAF Great Dunmow. Elizabeth Robson is at the back, second from left sitting on the balustrade of the Italian sunken garden at Easton Lodge.
(*Elizabeth Robson via 190 & 620 Sqns Archive*)

It was fascinating place; my grandmother had told me a lot about 'Darling Daisy', who had lived there. The WAAF quarters were between the rose garden and the lakes, then almost hidden under hogweed. There must have been about twenty to thirty huts, and an ablution hut or two. A road ran down to our quarters and to the Officers' Mess. A lot of rabbit shooting went on there at night in the car lights – though they were hardly brilliant in the blackout! I remember the rabbits were quite often black, descendants of pet ones Lady Warwick had once let out.

At one time I was Group Captain McIntyre's driver. He was a very nice giant of a man, who on returning to the Officers' Mess used to suggest that I and my dog could take a short cut home to our Nissen hut via the gardens. He would give me a leg up to the wall surrounding them, even though they were out of bounds. One night I jumped down, straight into the arms of an RAF Police corporal – 'Allo, allo – what's this then?' – who took a lot of convincing that McIntyre had pushed me up and over. Luckily, he eventually recognised the Station Commander's voice from the other side of the wall; very authoritative it was!

Eric Wadman recalled:

On one occasion, when returning from seven days' leave in Bristol, the train was held up at dusk for a long while outside London, owing to attacks by V1 flying bombs and V2 rockets, which meant that I missed the last train from London to Bishops Stortford. The leave pass stated that personnel had to be back at camp by midnight.

I found a group of Great Dunmow ground crews at the station and we went to the RTO (Railway Transport Officer). Knowing the cause of the delay, he stamped our passes, but informed us there were no more trains until the milk train in the early hours of the morning. We eventually arrived at Bishops Stortford, at 0530 hrs, but still with nine miles between us and the guardroom. It was imperative that we got there at the latest by 0800 hrs, as it was a rule of the station that all personnel returning from leave had to report to the Sick Bay for inspection.

The nine of us knew we had to get moving, so we formed into a small squad and set out on foot, keeping in step to maintain a steady pace. After a sleepless night and no breakfast, we only had our spirits and comradeship to keep us going. It was with great relief that we saw the gate and red brick pillars of what would have been the entrance to the old coaching drive into Little Easton Estate. However, we still had to walk along the drive, through the woods, and past the Horsa gliders parked in there under cover, before reaching the airfield perimeter track. Although we could now see the admin site, it was strictly forbidden to take short cuts across the airfield.

We made it to the guardroom by one minute to 0800 hrs. The Sergeant's only remark was 'You ran it a bit fine! Better get on up to Sick Bay right away!' That was another half mile on, hidden in the trees, past the Airmen's Mess, so there was to be no breakfast today. After about an hour's wait in Sick Bay, we then had to return to our billets to change into our working blues. We found that our mates had made up our beds the evening before, but we had to strip and stack our 'biscuits' (the three square palliasses which made up the mattress for the service beds) and blankets ready for Orderly Officer's Inspection of huts later in the morning. However, I found a flask of tea and a 'wad' (NAAFI cake) left by my mate, which went down well.

It was a joy to find my bicycle safe in the small ablutions hut, to be able to pedal the last half mile up to 'B' Flight, to report at the Flight Hut and to check on which aircraft I had been assigned to. It was my 'U-Uncle', but by the time I arrived, one of my mates had already taken my two port engines and signed for the Daily Inspections, and within 10 minutes the morning NAAFI van had arrived with steaming hot tea and 'wads'. God bless the NAAFI girls!

Operations to Norway were planned for the night of 4/5 December. These were later cancelled because of the weather, but one aircraft of 190 Squadron did manage to drop to an SOE DZ, 'Rummy 20', in western Holland. On 6 December, aircraft from 620 Squadron took part in Group Exercise 'Vigour', dropping SAS paratroops at Great Sampford, a nearby grass airfield that had recently been made available for use by 38 Group. The following day, another Group Exercise, 'Recurrent', took place. As part of this, twenty Stirling-Horsa combinations took off from Great Dunmow on a cross-country flight, which included fighter affiliation with Spitfires and Mustangs, before the gliders were released to land at Great Sampford. The usual flying programme of air tests, cross-countries, glider towing, parachute dropping and fighter affiliation continued whenever the weather was good enough. However, during December 1944 the overall number of aircraft movements at Great Dunmow was down by 40 per cent, compared with the previous month.

The damp conditions throughout the autumn of 1944 had exacerbated a problem of glue deterioration in the Horsa gliders. There were now about 100 of these at Great Dunmow, in the three flights of 'G' Squadron, GPR (Glider Pilot Regiment).

New Horsa Mk II gliders were being delivered, but there were some examples of the Horsa Mk I that were spending their third winter in the open. The Horsa's wooden airframe was simply not designed for long exposure to the British climate and a programme of inspections revealed that quite a few of the gliders were in need of serious remedial work.

Towards the end of 1944, glider pilot numbers were still below full strength because of the losses at Arnhem. On the other hand, it had become apparent that the overseas flying training programme was providing the RAF with an aircrew surplus. It was decided, therefore, to post RAF pilots to GPR units, including 'G' Squadron at Great Dunmow. Each Wing of the GPR was to remain under the command of an Army Officer, but with an RAF Officer as his second in command; Army and RAF Officers, in equal numbers, were to serve as Squadron and Flight Commanders, each with an officer of the other service as his second in command. Having been trained to fly powered aeroplanes, most of the RAF pilots posted to the GPR took a very dim view of this scheme. They were given assurances that they would later return to RAF flying duties, but this depended, of course, on their surviving the operational tasks that might be required of them. British glider pilots were not only expected to fly to the battlefield, but also to fight on it.

Everyone at Great Dunmow felt they were now in the firing line, since the station was only 30 miles from London, which was suffering badly from attacks by V1 flying bombs and V2 rockets. As their launch sites in France were overrun, the Germans took to releasing V1s from He 111 bombers, which were based in Holland and operating over the North Sea. Many of these air-launched V1s passed over Essex on their way to London.

Eric Wadman recalled:

One autumn morning, I saw a V1 flying bomb passing over our living sites, at dawn. At first I thought it might be a Liberator with an engine on fire after an early take-off, until it flew over me at about 400 feet, to explode a few minutes later, in the direction of Stansted airfield. On one occasion, after being on leave, I came back to stories of a V1, which having apparently been put off course by a fighter attack, had started to circle the airfield, too near to the NAAFI, where a pay parade quickly scattered.

At this time we could also hear four regular explosions each day, as V2 rockets hit the ground. In typical German fashion, the regularity could be commented on; 8.00 am, 9.30 am, 11.00 am and 12.30 pm, then they finished for the day. On 'B' Flight one morning, our ground tradesmen were coming in to sign up the Form 700s, certifying that they had completed their daily inspections, when there was one almighty bang and dust showered off the roof of the Nissen hut. There was a rush for the door to see what had caused it; right in line with the door, and in the centre of the field adjoining our flight perimeter fence, a tall straight column of smoke and clods of earth reached skywards. A V2 had come down from a height of 60 miles at supersonic speed, and no sound had been heard before its arrival. Nothing could stop the V2, once launched, the only defence being the heavy bomber attacks on their launch sites.

Ten Years On – this photograph shows Noel Chaffey (proudly wearing the 620 Squadron crest on his blazer) on the main runway when he visited the disused airfield at Great Dunmow in 1954. Flying from the airfield ceased soon after the departure of 620 Squadron in January 1946. It was then taken over by the Army and used as a storage depot for thousands of surplus military vehicles. The site was derequisitioned in 1958. Its runways and other hard-standings were eventually torn up, to be used as rubble in the motorway building programme of the 1960s and 1970s. Apart from a few Nissen huts, which have been kept for agricultural use, there are now very few signs of the busy RAF Station that once occupied this part of Essex. (*N.R. Chaffey*)

# CHAPTER 9

# Winter and Rough Weather

## December 1944 to March 1945

After the single successful drop by 190 Squadron to a Dutch DZ at the beginning of December 1944, there were no operational flights from Great Dunmow for over three weeks. Bad weather and the waning of the moon conspired against efforts to press on with the long-distance operations to Norway, while persistent, low-lying fog put a stop to further drops over Holland.

On Christmas Day 1944, the Airmen's Dinner at Great Dunmow was served in the customary RAF style by the officers and senior NCOs, to the accompaniment of music from the Station Band. A Christmas operation was planned for 190 and 620 Squadrons, with the intention of ferrying troops to the continent, along with some seasonal supplies for those already there. Half the aircrews were stood down on

Christmas morning at RAF Great Dunmow, 1944. Left to right: Flight Sergeant Bill Hall, Flight Sergeant 'Jock' McLeod, Pilot Officer Jake Etkin and Flight Sergeant Les Pountney, all of them members of Pilot Officer 'Lucky' Jordan's 620 Squadron crew. (*190 & 620 Sqns Archive*)

The disused hunting lodge, used as a shelter by the ground crews. (*N.R. Chaffey*)

Christmas Day, but the others were unlucky enough to be called to the flights at 0500 hrs, only to be told that the operation had been postponed for 24 hours because of thick fog. They were ready again on Boxing Day morning, but then faced another postponement. It looked as though the Dunmow Stirlings would be able to take off on the following day, 27 December, but an improvement in the weather was short-lived, so the Christmas deliveries to the continent were finally abandoned.

Noel Chaffey, 620 Squadron, recalled:

Our Christmas Day was a white one. We were not flying that day, and the other members of our crew had gone on leave for 48 hours. I took the opportunity to spend Christmas Day walking around the outskirts of the station, going into the woodland areas with my camera to record some winter photographic memories. I was very pleased with one or two of the photos and had some nice enlargements done for my albums. I'd already filled four Canadian albums and was now working on my second English one.

As winter showed its white coat, our ground crew had discovered for themselves a super little spot in the woods, close by the dispersal point. Here was an abandoned hunting lodge, thatched and with lots of canvas covering the gaping windows and doors. They had a fire in the grate for their 'brew-ups', so the NAAFI van didn't do much business at this section, except for the 'wads', which were always in demand.

On some crisp, cold, clear days earlier in December, we had been on a variety of flights, including exercises with gliders, and dropping paratroops at Great

225

This elderly Spitfire Mk VB, BL692, still wore the markings of 234 Squadron when it was one of a pair used by the Station Flight at Great Dunmow. It crashed near the 'Blue Gates', at the southern entrance to the grounds of Easton Lodge, on 2 March 1945. Its pilot, Flight Lieutenant Owen, injured his back and broke an arm in the accident. (*190 & 620 Sqns Archive*)

Sampford. We went out over the sea for air firing at flame floats and aluminium markers, and there was fighter affiliation with a Spitfire based at Great Dunmow, to give the rear gunners a chance of sharpening up their actions.

On the night of 28/29 December, 190 and 620 Squadrons each sent six aircraft on SOE operations to 'Tail' and 'Thrush Red' DZs in Norway. Visibility was excellent under a full moon, so the frozen lakes of Norway were easily identified. Some of the crews also reported that the patterns flashed by lighthouses on the Norwegian coast were useful aids to navigation. All except one of the 190 Squadron aircraft dropped their containers and packages, plus some propaganda leaflets, to the north of Kristiansand, although there were a few container hang-ups because of electrical faults. Two of the crews found it impossible to open their aircraft's floor hatches, as these were jammed by ice, so they were forced to bring their packages back to base. Some flak was experienced along the route, with the greatest concentration coming from ships in the Oslo Fjord.

Sadly, this resumption of operations was marred by the loss of one of the 620 Squadron aircraft, LJ970 'S', captained by Fg Off Jack McNamara RAAF. This aircraft had been destined for 'Tail 2', SSE of Oslo. Flt Lt Chesterton of 190 Squadron was flying to 'Thrush Red 2', in the same area, when he saw a bright explosion in the sky. He almost certainly witnessed the destruction of LJ970, since there were no other aircraft lost on operations to Norway that night. As will be related in the next chapter, a chance discovery by a 620 Squadron crew, just after the end of the war, revealed that LJ970 had been shot down near Sande by a night-fighter of the *Nachtjagerstaffel Norwegen*. The eleven Dunmow aircraft that re-turned from Norway in the early hours of 29 December were diverted to Marston

lying Officer Jack McNamara RAAF (fourth from left, standing) and his 620 Squadron crew, with members of their ground crew. (*190 & 620 Sqns Archive*)

Moor and Rufforth in Yorkshire. Four out of the five remaining aircraft from 620 Squadron had been successful in dropping their supplies.

The next SOE operations flown by the Dunmow Stirlings were on the night of 30/31 December. One aircraft from 190 Squadron went to Holland and dropped two agents, containers and packages, on 'Rummy 28', west of Utrecht. Another lone aircraft, from 620 Squadron, dropped supplies to 'Draughts 5', situated near Hoorn, on the west side of the Zuider Zee. Six aircraft from 190 Squadron were sent to 'Flank', 'Pommel' and 'Puffin' DZs in Norway, but only one crew observed reception signals and carried out their drop. Serious icing was encountered when the aircraft entered cloud, and Flt Lt le Bouvier returned early, after shutting down an engine because of oil cooler 'coring', brought about by the extremely cold conditions. Five out of six 620 Squadron aircraft sent to 'Crupper', 'Flank' and 'Pommel' DZs in Norway dropped successfully. The remaining one was unable to drop, since there were no reception signals. Although visibility was very good that night, navigation proved difficult on the way to Norway because of an unexpectedly strong wind, which drifted the aircraft towards the Danish coast.

Noel Chaffey recalled:

On the SOE operations to Norway we had very long flights over the rough winter North Sea. Icing up was a particular problem in storm clouds – the bases were often too low for us to fly under them, and we tried going above them, but our heating arrangements and oxygen supplies were limited. If you were in those clouds laden with ice and electricity, it was almost as bad as flying through flak from enemy AA guns. I saw the Stirling outlined in blue electrical 'St Elmo's Fire' a few times, which was very scary. However, I used to tune into the BBC, and switch the broadcasts to all stations in the aircraft. 'Can I do yer

Warrant Officer Noel Chaffey's Stirling 'D4-Y', in the winter of 1944–5. No. 620 Squadron aircraft bore the un code 'QS' at Chedburgh, Leicester East and Fairford; at Great Dunmow, and later, in the Middle East, 'QS' an 'D4' codes were used concurrently. At Leicester East, and for a time at Fairford, 190 Squadron aircraft carrie individual aircraft letters, but no unit codes. Later, at Fairford, the 190 Squadron code was 'L9'; at Great Dunmo 'L9' and 'G5' codes were both used, the latter not to be confused with '5G', used by 299 Squadron Stirlings. (*N.R. Chaffey*)

now, sir?', 'Don't forget the diver' and 'Don't mind if I do', from Tommy Handley's show, all got a laugh. Those comedy programmes were a great relief, and helped to make the war seem far away.

Late on New Year's Eve, 190 and 620 Squadrons each sent four aircraft on SOE operations, to 'Bit', 'Crupper' and 'Snaffle' DZs in Norway, but two other aircraft failed to take off. One had a jammed throttle, and the other got bogged down on the muddy airfield. The weather was initially much better than had been forecast, and aided by bright moonlight the crews made accurate landfalls when they reached the Norwegian coast. A Eureka beacon had been set up on the 'Bit 7' DZ and was used to good effect, as its signals were picked up at a range of 40 miles. Seven of the Dunmow aircraft were successful in dropping, but during the night the weather closed in at base. Four aircraft diverted to Carnaby in Yorkshire, but owing to a signals mix-up, 190 Squadron's LK275 'V', captained by Flt Sgt Dickens, proceeded to Bungay in Suffolk and was very low on fuel when it arrived there. As LK275 was on final approach to land (in a downwind direction), it manoeuvred suddenly, to avoid a collision with another aircraft, and in doing so, struck a tree. LK275 touched down safely, but was then deliberately ground-looped in an attempt to stop it going off the end of the runway. This action resulted in a collapsed undercarriage, fortunately without causing any injury to the crew.

However, there was much worse news as New Year's Day dawned, for 620 Squadron's LJ914 'R', captained by Fg Off Frederick Waring, was posted as missing. This Stirling failed to reach its DZ, 'Crupper 30'. It was claimed as shot down by a night-fighter crew of the *Nachtjagerstaffel Norwegen*, although reports from other Stirling pilots indicate that flak played a part in its destruction.

Larry Siegert, 190 Squadron, recalled:

On 31 December 1944, the 620 Squadron Stirlings took off ahead of us. Going across the North Sea at low level I was horrified to see streams of tracer going up ahead of me and then an aircraft on fire, plunging down into the water. We veered to the north to avoid the flak and crossed the Norwegian coast near Kristiansand, before we successfully dropped among the mountains north of Oslo. It was quite scary, dropping there at night, as it was difficult to tell how close you were to the snowy peaks, so we tended to drop a bit high to allow for misjudgement of distance.

Ken Wilson, 620 Squadron, recalled:

In all, I did eleven ops with 620 Squadron, the worst being the trips to Norway. These were very long hauls across the North Sea, flying at 500 feet to avoid detection by the German radar. The greatest danger in that area was from the flak ships, which lay in wait as we approached the Norwegian coast. They changed their positions continually and therefore it was pot luck if you were unlucky enough to fly over them – it was rare that one even saw them in time to take avoiding action.

On New Year's Eve, a few miles to our starboard, at the mouth of the Skaggerak, there was suddenly a very fierce display of tracer fire and flak bursting at low altitude, which marked the end of my very dear friend Freddie Waring and his crew. We had tossed up for who should take off first – and Freddie won! The aircraft went down in a ball of fire with not a hope of survival for the crew in the freezing waters of the North Sea. This was an ominous start to an eventful trip, which ended over 10 hours later when we were diverted to land in FIDO at Carnaby. What a start to the New Year for Freddie's wife, who was pregnant with their first child – I had the daunting task of telling her the sad news.

ying Officer Ken Wilson's Stirling, LJ935 'P-Peter', at a very muddy Dunmow dispersal.
*90 & 620 Sqns Archive*)

The New Year's flying at Great Dunmow started with some air tests and the return of the aircraft that had diverted to Carnaby early in the morning. On 2 January 1945, HQ 38 Group issued orders for 'Quiver', an exercise intended to polish the dead reckoning skills of the navigators. This actually comprised a series of flights, to be arranged by Station Commanders when other commitments permitted. The usual task, on this exercise, was to find the tiny island of Rockall, which lies 300 miles west of the Scottish mainland, without any recourse to radio aids.

On 6 January, three of the Dunmow Stirlings took part in an Air-Sea Rescue search, looking for a dinghy in the North Sea. Two of them diverted to Westcott in Buckinghamshire, and the other to Hutton Cranswick in Yorkshire, as the weather closed in. The next day, ten of the 190 Squadron Stirlings flew on a glider-towing exercise, which should have ended with the gliders landing at base. Only five of the gliders had been released over the airfield by the time a snowstorm swept in, forcing the rest of the combinations to divert to other airfields in Essex and Hertfordshire.

The freeze persisted at Great Dunmow for the best part of a week, in the course of which there were just a few Stirling air tests, plus a diversion of American B-17s. As the snow melted, heavy rain started to fall, but 190 Squadron was able to send five aircraft on operations to Holland during the night of 14/15 January. Two of these were going to SAS DZs, set up by 'Fabian' and 'Gobbo'. The latter was an intelligence-gathering operation involving Belgian troops of 5 SAS in northern Holland. The other three aircraft went to SOE DZs 'Podex 3', 'Rummy 20' and 'Rummy 21'. Plt Off Isaacson and his crew dropped containers and packages to 'Rummy 20', assisted by a Eureka beacon set up on this DZ, which they were then able to identify visually through a break in the cloud. None of the other Dunmow crews were successful that night, since there were no reception signals at 'Podex 3', and low cloud completely covered 'Rummy 21' and the SAS DZs.

The snow and rain were followed by gales, with gusts of up to 100 mph on the night of 18/19 January. These caused substantial damage to aircraft parked on the 38 Group airfields in Essex. Seven Stirlings were damaged at Great Dunmow, as were a number of Horsa gliders.

A Horsa at Great Dunmow, turned upside-down by a gale. (*190 & 620 Sqns Archive*)

At the start of January 1945, it had been decided that 38 Group would add to the pressure on the retreating German forces by sending up to thirty aircraft on tactical bombing operations each night. While these were intended to be concentrated attacks, in practice they were unlikely to have been effective except as nuisance raids, owing to the methods used. Bombers of 2 Group dropped markers over some of the targets, but Gee was generally used to determine the release points for the bombs. These were dropped from heights between 3,000 and 10,000 feet, to give stick lengths of 1,500 yards. The targets were up to 50 kilometres beyond the British and Canadian lines, chiefly at key positions on road and rail routes.

190 and 620 Squadrons prepared for this role by dropping small practice bombs on the ranges at East Hatley in Cambridgeshire, Leysdown on the Isle of Sheppey, and Dengie Flats in Essex. Their first bombing operation was on the night of 21/22 January, attacking targets to the west of Mönchen-gladbach. Five aircraft from 190 Squadron and one from 620 Squadron were sent to drop 500 lb bombs and 4 lb incendiaries at Neder Krüchten, while four aircraft of 620 Squadron took similar loads to Arsbeck. The low air temperature that night led to coring of the Stirlings' oil coolers, but all the aircraft dropped their bombs, except for 'A' of 620 Squadron, captained by Sqn Ldr Berridge, who had to shut down an engine and return early. A similar bombing operation was planned for the next night, 22/23 January, with ten Dunmow aircraft requested, but this had to be cancelled because of the weather.

On 23 January, snow fell again at Great Dunmow, and this time it was followed by fog, which made flying practically impossible over the next few days. Although SOE operations to Norway were planned for both 190 and 620 Squadrons on the night of 29/30 January, these were subsequently cancelled because it looked unlikely that any airfields would be open for the aircraft on their return. The forecast was shown to be correct the following morning, when there were four inches of snow at Great Dunmow.

Dennis Gibson, 620 Squadron, recalled:

My personal memories of Great Dunmow include the cold weather, frozen ablutions and toilets, lack of fuel for the billet stove and the endless walk from the domestic site to the mess and squadron offices, the roads always deep in mud. The one person I envied was the airman in charge of the blanket store. He was never short of fuel and always had a red-hot stove, which he was quite happy to share with anyone who dropped in.

Eric Wadman, 6190 Servicing Echelon, recalled:

The east wind swept across Essex, and it became bitterly cold. Working on the

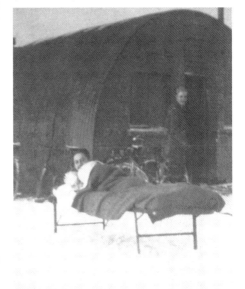

Flight Sergeant Ken Watson was the flight engineer in Flying Officer Geoff Gawith's 620 Squadron crew. Said to have been a loud snorer, Watson awoke one winter morning to find that the others in his Nissen hut had carried him outside, so they could get a good night's sleep. (*190 & 620 Sqns Archive*)

'Taffy' the Crew Chief (kneeling, centre), with the ground crew of 620 Squadron's 'K-King', in freezing fc January 1945. (*190 & 620 Sqns Archive*)

aircraft, up on the tall engine gantries, we were exposed to the wind, and at times you could not even feel the hexagon heads of nuts and bolts, when trying to put them together. We had only the one flight hut, for the paperwork and records kept on 190 Squadron's 'B' Flight dispersal, which held thirteen Stirlings, so we utilised the small makeshift wood and corrugated iron shacks that had been put up by the American ground crews. Armed with aircraft axes, we made forages to the nearby hedgerows, looking for firewood, or sometimes we used small cans, filled with earth or sand, into which we poured a little dirty fuel used for engine cleaning purposes, and lit it, to give a low flame, around which we warmed our frozen hands.

By 1 February, much of the snow at Great Dunmow had melted and there was a busy flying programme, which included air tests, fighter affiliation, air-to-sea firing and formation cross-countries. During the afternoon there was an aircrew fatality, as a result of an incident involving Stirling LJ832 'U' of 190 Squadron. While flying from Tarrant Rushton to Tilstock, where members of a 190 Squadron crew were waiting to be collected, LJ832's pilot experienced control difficulties and believed the aircraft was icing up. At 8,000 feet, the aircraft entered cumulus cloud, control was lost and the order was given for the crew to bale out. Fg Off Wilsdon (bomb aimer), Flt Sgt Newcombe (navigator) and Plt Off Macdonald (air gunner) jumped, but the next member of the crew became caught in the escape hatch and was unable to leave. As the aircraft descended at high speed, a number of access panels broke away and hit other parts of the airframe. In spite of this damage, the pilot regained control of the aircraft, which was pulled out of its dive at only 900 feet. The man stuck in the hatch managed to free himself and climb back in, before an emergency landing was made at Honiley in Warwickshire.

Wilsdon and Newcombe landed safely by parachute, apart from Newcombe sustaining a sprained ankle. Plt Off Robert Macdonald, a Canadian, was found dead at Tibberton, near Worcester. He was still attached to his parachute, which appeared to have functioned correctly. When examined, Macdonald's harness was found to be slack, and it was concluded that this, combined with deployment of the parachute at a high airspeed, had produced an opening shock that was severe enough to break his neck.

Stirling LJ832 remained at Honiley while repairs were carried out, and was ready for ferrying back to Great Dunmow on 6 March. However, this aircraft's sorry tale was not quite over, for the members of the next 190 Squadron crew to fly in it were very lucky not to become casualties.

Larry Siegert recalled:

I was sent with my crew to Honiley to return Stirling 'U-Uncle' to Great Dunmow, with Fg Off Hoskyns delivering us there in 'O-Oboe'. On take-off from Honiley, I could barely control the aircraft because the elevator trimming controls were fitted the wrong way round. When I thought I was trimming nose down in our normal take-off checks, the aircraft was actually being trimmed nose up. As a result, when we lifted off the nose went up and we climbed with me and my bomb aimer trying to push the control column forward and any work on the trimmer made it worse. We both had our feet on the control column to push forward to avoid stalling the aircraft, which was climbing madly. Fortunately the penny dropped and I reversed movement on the trim handle and got the trimmer back to neutral.

We gingerly flew back to Essex but owing to some problem in the circuit at Dunmow, Flying Control suggested we land at RAF Matching. There we made a safe landing and our engineers sorted out the defect.

A small number of 38 Group aircraft went to Holland for SOE on the night of 2/3 February. Among them was a Stirling from 620 Squadron. This aircraft was to have dropped to 'Dudley 8', but it came back early after fumes appeared in the cabin. Tactical bombing was also carried out that night. Eight aircraft from 190 Squadron, and seven from 620 Squadron, were detailed to bomb targets at Grevenbroich, an important point of intersection for roads, railways and a river, to the south-west of Düsseldorf. The weather was generally good, but fog over the target made visual identification difficult. The crews therefore had to rely entirely on Gee to determine their bomb-release points. A load of twenty-four 500 lb bombs was dropped by each of the Dunmow Stirlings, except for one that was unable to do so because its Gee equipment became unserviceable a few minutes before it reached the target area. Although flak was expected on this operation, none was encountered.

The Dunmow Stirlings were next in action on the night of 7/8 February, when targets at Kalkar, Uedem and Weeze were bombed. This operation was done in support of troops belonging to the Canadian First and British Second Armies, who were clearing the west bank of the Rhine, to the north-west of Wesel. Visibility over the target was poor, with 10/10ths cloud that extended up to 7,500 feet and produced icing conditions. Matters were not helped by the conflicting times and positions that had been issued during briefings and it was only by good fortune that no aircraft were lost through mid-air collisions. There was opposition from flak that night, and a number of unidentified aircraft were observed, including one climbing very fast, thought to be an Me 163 rocket-powered fighter. Several crews also reported seeing the trails of V2 rockets leaving their launch sites. Ten aircraft from 190 Squadron,

Stirling LJ973 'QS-T' of 620 Squadron being 'bombed-up'. This aircraft was captained by Flying Officer Da
McKenzie on the bombing operation during the night of 2/3 February 1945. (*190 & 620 Sqns Archive*)

and eight from 620 Squadron, took part in this operation. All returned safely, and
apart from one aircraft with Gee failure, which jettisoned its bombs over the sea, all
reached their targets. Another problem, familiar to the Stirling crews from their
experience of dropping supply containers from the bomb racks, was the hanging-up
of bombs as a result of electrical faults. On this occasion, a number of bombs had to
be brought back to Great Dunmow, where the aircraft carrying them were landed
carefully.

Ken Wilson recalled:

On 7 February 1945 we carried out some tactical bombing on German targets.
This turned out to be something of a shambles with a horrifying number of
aircraft blundering around over the targets due to a cock-up in the briefing of
the timing and Gee co-ordinates. I took Lieutenant Tiny Kidner as an unauthorised passenger – he was an SAS officer who had been badgering me to
take him for a trip for ages. I thought him quite mad as he leaned out of the

window taking photographs, oblivious of the flak which was too close for comfort. He thought it all great fun until we came in to land back at base, when to my horror (and his) the elevators jammed and we made more of an arrival than a landing.

In addition, five aircraft from 620 Squadron were sent on SOE operations during the night of 7/8 February. They went to 'Draughts' and 'Cubbing' DZs in Holland, but only one crew was successful in dropping. The others did not observe any reception lights, though the weather was good over their DZs.

From 8 to 11 February, 190 and 620 Squadrons were standing by for further bombing operations, but each day these were cancelled because of the weather. This cleared up sufficiently for other 38 Group squadrons to bomb during the night of 13/14 February, when the only Dunmow aircraft operating were three from 620 Squadron, heading for Dutch DZs. There was a second attempt at dropping to 'Dudley 8' for SOE, while the other two aircraft went to 'Fabian 24' and 'Ruskin 2'

'Tug' Wilson's 620 Squadron crew. Standing, left to right, Flying Officer Dougie Cummins (navigator) and Flight Sergeant Ben Lewis (air gunner); sitting, in doorway, Warrant Officer Clive Mathieson (wireless operator); standing, right, Flying Officer Ken Wilson (pilot); kneeling, left to right, Sergeant Steve Lydon (flight engineer) and Warrant Officer 'Andy' Anderson (bomb aimer). (*190 & 620 Sqns Archive*)

for the SAS. No reception signals were observed at any of these DZs, so all the aircraft had to return with their loads.

The following night, 14/15 February, two aircraft from 190 Squadron took off on SAS operations to Holland. This time, Wg Cdr Bunker and his crew made a successful drop of containers and a pannier to 'Fabian 25'. Although it was suspected that the 'Ruskin' ground party might have been captured the previous night, a further effort was made to drop to them. In the event, Plt Off Middleton and his crew did not see any reception signals at the DZ, 'Ruskin 3'. On the night of 14/15 February there was also a tactical bombing operation, which involved eight aircraft from 190 Squadron, and seven from 620 Squadron. The target was Rees, a town of strategic importance on the Rhine. Twelve of the Dunmow crews dropped their bombs, but the other three were unable to do so, owing to Gee failures (serviceability of this navigation aid was essential to the operation, which went ahead in the knowledge that there would be full cloud cover over the target). Some flak was encountered, but no damage was done to any of the Dunmow Stirlings.

The 38 Group squadrons were out in force on the night of 20/21 February, as 103 aircraft took part in SOE operations. With the liberation of France, Belgium and Luxembourg complete, and that of Holland in sight, the Norwegian resistance fighters now provided SOE with its main means of striking at the enemy in Europe. On the night of 20/21 February, all the DZs were in Norway, except for 'Dudley 8'. A 190 Squadron aircraft made a third and final attempt at dropping to this Dutch DZ, but was unsuccessful, defeated this time by low cloud. Nos 190 and 620 Squadrons each had ten aircraft detailed to fly to Norway, but one of the 620 Squadron Stirlings was unable to take off because of a technical defect. The weather was good over the whole route for the remaining nineteen aircraft, twelve of which dropped to 'Crupper' and 'Flank' DZs set up at remote locations in the mountains to the west of Hønefoss. Flak ships were encountered about 25 miles off the Norwegian coast, but all the Dunmow Stirlings returned safely. Among them was the 190 Squadron aircraft captained by Fg Off Bickford, who had to shut down an engine when it caught fire on the way back from a successful drop.

There were further bombing operations over Rees the next night, 21/22 February, but these were carried out by Stirlings from Shepherd's Grove. Two of the 196 Squadron aircraft from that station failed to return. Another was attacked by a German night-fighter and crash-landed in flames on its home airfield, killing the air gunner. This resurgence of *Luftwaffe* intruder activity served as a warning that aircraft operating from East Anglian bases remained vulnerable to attack at night, even at this late stage in the war.

On the night of 22/23 February, Norway was the destination. Nos 190 and 620 Squadrons each sent ten aircraft on SOE operations to 'Crop' and 'Pommel' DZs, with instructions to return to Kinloss, because poor weather was forecast for Great Dunmow in the early hours of the morning. The weather over Norway turned out to be very good, which left the Dunmow Stirlings wide open to the attentions of searchlights and flak in the Oslo area, but eight aircraft from each squadron dropped successfully. In the clear air that night, the enemy airfields in Norway were seen to be lit up well. Flt Lt le Bouvier of 190 Squadron was given a 'green light' to land, when passing an airfield to the north-east of Oslo, but he understandably declined the invitation. Several enemy aircraft were sighted over Norway, but none of the returning crews reported attacks by them.

By 0430 hrs on 23 February, nineteen of the twenty Dunmow Stirlings had landed at Kinloss. The missing aircraft was 190 Squadron's LK566 'G', captained by WO

Stanley Currie. Over Kristiansand, Flight Officer Bliss of 190 Squadron had seen an aircraft being subjected to intense flak, before it fell in flames and continued to burn on the ground. As there were no other 38 Group aircraft lost that night, this was almost certainly LK566, which had been destined for 'Crop 25', a DZ just north of Oslo. However, LK566 was later claimed as another victim of a night-fighter belonging to the *Nachtjagerstaffel Norwegen*. Regardless of which weapon dealt the final blows, the crew of this Stirling stood no chance of survival as it crashed on high ground near Langang. The loss of its navigator, Flt Sgt Donald Hollinrake, came as a second terrible shock to his family, since his younger brother, Keith, a sergeant flight engineer with XV Squadron at Mildenhall, had been killed in a Lancaster crash seven months earlier.

Ken Wilson recalled:

> 20 and 22 February saw two more Norway ops, 9 hours 25 minutes and 11 hours 40 minutes flying respectively, with no second pilot and indifferent 'George' [automatic pilot]; ruddy cold, oil coolers coring up, with wheels and flaps down to reduce speed and raise the oil temperatures – a sitting target at 120 mph in broad moonlight. At one stage we were frightened something rotten when one of the first German jet fighters made several passes at us off the Danish coast. We were flying so slowly he overshot and eventually gave up.

As the crews at Kinloss took off and headed back to base during the afternoon of 23 February, others at Great Dunmow were preparing for operations to Norway that night, again with the intention of landing at Kinloss on their return. There was low cloud and rain as three aircraft from 190 Squadron, and six from 620 Squadron, took off for 'Crupper' and 'Flank' DZs, but over Norway the weather was excellent and enemy opposition negligible. All the 190 Squadron aircraft, and three of those from 620 Squadron, were successful in dropping, though some of the crews had trouble dispatching packages because the floor hatches were jammed by ice.

The next couple of days were uneventful at Great Dunmow, except for a minor accident on 25 February. This involved one of 190 Squadron's Stirlings, LJ826, which damaged its tailwheel assembly while landing in a gusty crosswind, after carrying out a glider lift.

On the night of 26/27 February, 190 and 620 Squadrons each sent five aircraft on operations. They were going to 'Bit', 'Crupper', 'Flank', 'Reins', 'Snaffle' and 'Vet' DZs in Norway. The weather was variable that night, with a good deal of low cloud over some of the DZs, whereas others were quite clear. Three aircraft from 190 Squadron, and two from 620 Squadron, were successful in dropping. Fg Off Whiteley of 190 Squadron observed light flak from ships to the east of Kristiansand, followed by what he thought was an aircraft going down in flames over the sea. A Stirling from 138 Squadron at Tempsford, which had been destined for 'Crupper 37', was subsequently reported missing.

Notwithstanding all the dangers of Norwegian operations, there had been surprisingly few operational losses of 38 Group aircraft since the start of 1945, so all the Halifax and Stirling air support squadrons were near to full strength at the end of February. Planning for 'Varsity', the airborne component of the Rhine crossing operation, was now at an advanced stage. Each of the Stirling squadrons in 38 Group was expected to have thirty-four serviceable aircraft, and crews to fly them, by 15 March.

In the meantime, 190 and 620 Squadrons continued their operations for SOE. The night of 1/2 March saw a return to Holland, as two aircraft headed for DZs located

Stirling LJ826 of 190 Squadron. The aerial wire, seen here thickly coated with frost, is part of the aircraft's I (Identification Friend or Foe) system. This photograph also shows clearly the Stirling's unusual twin tailwh arrangement, damaged when this particular aircraft made a crosswind landing on 25 February 1945. (*N.R. Chaffey*)

to the west of Utrecht. It was a cloudy night, but the 620 Squadron aircraft captained by Sqn Ldr George Whitty DFC was successful in dropping to 'Cubbing 4'. This was Sqn Ldr Whitty's first operation since joining 620 Squadron as a Flight Commander. The 190 Squadron aircraft operating that night was captained by Fg Off Lewis. It was carrying containers and a consignment of thirty carrier pigeons. Its crew did not observe any reception signals at the DZ, 'Checkers 1', which was surrounded by extensive flooding. On the way back, an order to the two army dispatchers was misunderstood, with the unfortunate result that the pigeons were thrown out over the sea.

On 2 March, 190 and 620 Squadrons each had twelve aircraft taking part in Group Exercise 'Riff Raff', during which they towed gliders around a cross-country route before releasing them at Great Sampford. Six aircraft from 190 Squadron, and five from 620 Squadron, were on operations that night, 2/3 March. Fg Off le Bouvier and his 190 Squadron crew went to 'Rummy 30', in the same part of Holland as the previous night's DZs. Their containers and packages were dropped successfully, in spite of squally conditions throughout the flight. The other ten aircraft went to four different 'Crupper' DZs in Norway. They encountered strong winds and rain over the North Sea, but clearer conditions towards Norway. Nevertheless, the air was still very bumpy over the high ground surrounding the DZs, situated to the west and north-west of Hønefoss. Visibility in this area was excellent under a bright moon and the crews were guided to the DZs by Eureka beacons, which they found to be effective out to a range of about 30 miles. All of them reported successful drops, but two of the 620 Squadron aircraft had narrow escapes from attacks by night-fighters, with one of them sustaining slight damage.

Since most of Great Dunmow's operational work now took the form of supply drops over Norway, it was appropriate that there should be an official visit to the station on 3 March by the C in C Norwegian Forces, General Hanstein. He was accompanied by the AOC 38 Group, AVM Scarlett-Streatfeild, and the C in C Airborne Forces, Major General Gale. The occasion was marked by the attendance of the Central Band of the Royal Air Force, which gave performances in the Sergeants' Mess and in the NAAFI, and also in the Officers' Mess and Station Cinema the next day.

There then followed nearly a fortnight with no operational commitments, as 38 Group prepared for 'Varsity'. At this time, a heightened state of alert was put into effect at RAF stations, in response to recent night attacks by enemy intruders. Personnel at Great Dunmow were reminded that a complete blackout needed to be maintained during the hours of darkness, even though many of the civil blackout restrictions had been relaxed in September 1944. Throughout the nights of 3/4 and 4/5 March there were warnings of intruder aircraft and 'Divers' (V1 flying bombs), with many of the latter passing just south of Great Dunmow. The 38 Group stations were also told to expect 'Scram' diversions of Bomber Command aircraft, if these were unable to land at their home airfields because of intruder activity.

Although the weather was changeable at Great Dunmow during March 1945, training hours increased markedly and more glider lifts were carried out than in any month since April 1944. On 7 March, 190 and 620 Squadrons each contributed twelve glider-towing aircraft to Group Exercise 'Riff Raff II', which was organised along the same lines as 'Riff Raff I', carried out a few days earlier. On the night of 9/10 March, six crews from 190 Squadron, and six from 620 Squadron, were

Stirling, after a belly-landing on the grass at RAF Great Dunmow (Easton Lodge is visible on the horizon, and the aircraft's starboard wingtip). The direction of the shadows cast by the aircraft indicates that this photograph was taken early in the morning. Unfortunately, it has not been possible, from either the Ministry of Defence's accident record forms, or the Squadron and Station Operations Record Books, to identify this aircraft or the cause of its mishap. (*190 & 620 Sqns Archive*)

involved in Group Exercise 'Flot', taking along new pilots, bomb aimers and wireless operators for experience in night dropping, as they delivered French paratroops to three DZs in the New Forest. There was a minor accident at Great Dunmow on 13 March when Stirling LJ935 collided with LJ927 while being marshalled on the ground. Both aircraft appear to have been quickly repaired and returned to service with 620 Squadron.

On 14 March, Great Dunmow was visited by the C in C Fighter Command, Air Marshal Sir Roderick Hill (38 Group had been placed in Fighter Command, when this re-formed in October 1944). The same day, 190 and 620 Squadrons each had eighteen aircraft taking part in Group Exercise 'Vulture', a large-scale rehearsal for 'Varsity'. This exercise also provided glider loading practice and air experience for troops of 6 Air Landing Brigade, who were flown in the gliders. Glider-towing formations from all the 38 Group stations followed cross-country routes, before combining in a single stream for a run-in to a rendezvous point over Stow-on-the-Wold in Gloucestershire. The formations then split and returned to their home airfields, where mass glider landings were carried out. During 'Vulture', there were a few broken tow-ropes *en route*, and a number of gliders landed outside the airfield at Great Dunmow, where fog was forming as they returned.

A further Group Exercise, 'Token', was completed on 17 March. This was principally a 'paper exercise' for the benefit of the Army, and Great Dunmow's flying contribution was confined to 190 and 620 Squadrons each providing two glider-towing aircraft. In the days running up to 'Varsity' there were only a few SOE operations carried out by the squadrons in 38 Group. None of these tasks involved

A tow-rope is moved into position behind a 190 Squadron Stirling at the start of a glider lift. (*190 & 620 Sqns Archive*)

... tow-rope is attached to the Stirling ... (*190 & 620 Sqns Archive*)

... and to the Horsa. (*190 & 620 Sqns Archive*)

As the 'Green light' is given, the Stirling and Horsa start their take-off run. (*190 & 620 Sqns Archive*)

the Dunmow Stirlings, whose flying programme at this time was concentrating on 'circuits and bumps' with the Horsa gliders.

On 20 March, a practice night drop was arranged for a 620 Squadron aircraft. It was scheduled to arrive over the Great Sampford DZ at 2100 hrs. Before they took off on this detail, Sqn Ldr Whitty and his crew were briefed by Capt Slater, the SAS Liaison Officer at Great Dunmow, who was to fly with them in Stirling LK116 'A'. The aircraft made its run over the DZ, and was returning to Great Dunmow when the sirens sounded on the ground, at about 2110 hrs. Five minutes later, Great Dunmow Flying Control received a message confirming that a hostile aircraft had crossed the coast and was approaching North Weald airfield. A 'Bandit' warning was transmitted to all Stirlings on local flights out of Great Dunmow, but LK116 was shot down shortly after this, at about 2120 hrs. Over the next few minutes, three other hostiles were plotted near Bury St Edmunds. Mosquito night-fighters were scrambled, and succeeded in shooting down a Ju 88 off the Norfolk coast. However, they were unable to prevent other German intruders from sweeping in and attacking a number of aircraft flying in the vicinity of East Anglian airfields. Although this was the last night that intruders destroyed Allied aircraft over the UK, it was a costly one for 38 Group, since a Halifax from 1665 HCU at Tilstock was also shot down, near Wittering in Cambridgeshire.

Eric Wadman recalled:

Late take-offs had enabled local flying to be carried out in darkness, with the aircraft coming back at around 9.00 pm. Several were in the circuit, and making their landing approaches. Then we heard the drone of a distant aircraft out beyond Dunmow, coming in on a long approach. A group of us, off the late bus, were just approaching the hangars, close to our living site, but still rounding the last bend on the perimeter track. Suddenly, we saw a line of lights making a lazy curve in the sky, followed some seconds later by a series of sharp cracks. We at first dived for the grass, not knowing what it was. Was it a V1 Doodlebug, just being released from a Heinkel 111 bomber, with its reaction motor starting up? Suddenly, there was a flame, which grew longer, like a curving comet in the sky, but the increasing sound of racing engines soon told us one of the Stirlings had been attacked by a night intruder, and we watched in dismay as the aircraft continued in its downward dive, to erupt in massive flames, somewhere out beyond Dunmow, to the east.

Ken Hillier, 620 Squadron, recalled:

My flight engineer, Ernie Fletcher, and I were visiting friends in Great Dunmow that evening, when we heard low-flying aircraft and gunfire. We ran outside and saw a Stirling in flames, just clearing the houses. It was obvious it would crash very close, so we jumped on our bikes and followed it down the Colchester Road, where it crashed in a bight of the small river, about a quarter of a mile away, still in flames. We were able to get into the fuselage through the aft hatch. The rear turret was empty and ammunition was exploding. The body of the gunner was on the ground by the rear of the aircraft. We tried to get into the cockpit, which was burning, but the mainspar had collapsed and it was impossible to get past it.

There was just one survivor from the crew of Stirling LK116, the flight engineer, Flt Sgt Cramp, who baled out and was taken to the Saracen's Head public house in Great Dunmow after his ordeal.

Tony Cramp, 620 Squadron, recalled:

The night we were shot down we had an Army Airborne Officer with us on an exercise to check some new DZ lights at a small airfield not far away. It was a bright moonlit night, and when we got back to Dunmow we were warned of an intruder in the area. The runway lights were out and almost immediately we were attacked from underneath. All our lights went out, the batteries were hit and with a port engine on fire, we were only at about 800 feet when we got the order to bale out. Normally as a crew we never wore parachute harnesses on local flying, but as I was cold I had put my harness on just after take-off, so I was the first to go out. I landed in a field not far from the road out of Dunmow and got a lift from a passing motorist who took me to a pub from where I was picked up by transport from the station. After this I did no more ops, and was not on the Rhine Crossing operation, but as a spare flight engineer I did local flying and instruction on Stirlings and Halifaxes.

The loss of Stirling LK116 must have seemed doubly ironic when the list of casualties became known, for among them were two survivors of previous crashes that involved fatalities. Capt George Slater had been flying as a passenger in the 196 Squadron aircraft, LK126 'N', which had been destroyed at Shepherd's Grove a month earlier, after being attacked by an intruder. LK116's Canadian air gunner, WO Paul Bell, had been on board LJ882 when it crashed in France on 23 July 1944, while taking part in an SAS operation with 190 Squadron. The sole evader from LJ882's crew, he returned to 190 Squadron in October 1944, and was posted to 620 Squadron in January 1945. There he joined the crew being formed by Sqn Ldr Whitty, the new commander of 'A' Flight. When Flt Lt Bill Gardiner went back to Canada in January 1945, four members of his 190 Squadron crew (Plt Off Ames, Flt Sgt Cramp, Flt Sgt Douglas and WO Williams) were transferred to 620 Squadron to complete Sqn Ldr Whitty's crew. Flt Lt Gardiner's Irish gunner, Flt

Sgt Jack Coghlan, remained with 190 Squadron but was killed in a flying accident on 11 May 1945.

'Varsity' was imminent, and at noon on 21 March the camp at Great Dunmow was sealed, and patrols set up, to prevent anyone from communicating with persons outside, except on official business. Air tests were the main flying activity at this stage, but 'Spoof' exercises were also flown by the 38 Group squadrons. Ten aircraft from 620 Squadron flew on these exercises throughout the morning of 22 March, with five from 'A' Flight as solo aircraft, and five from 'B' Flight towing gliders. They made radio calls appropriate to a normal flying programme, while most of the aircraft were of course firmly on the ground. During the afternoon of 22 March, 190 Squadron took over the 'Spoof' task at Great Dunmow. A further deception measure was provided by the order issued for Exercise 'Meteor'. This was actually a cover for the movement of 46 Group Dakotas from Blakehill Farm, Broadwell and Down Ampney to the Essex airfields they would use during 'Varsity'. There were few flights out of Great Dunmow on 23 March, the eve of the big operation. The Stirlings of 190 and 620 Squadrons were ready, and this time, nothing had been left to chance.

# CHAPTER 10

# From Varsity to Victory

## March to May 1945

Operation 'Varsity' was scheduled to start early in the morning of 24 March 1945, by which time Operation 'Plunder' (the crossing of the River Rhine by ground forces) would be well under way. 'Varsity' required some 21,000 troops of XVIII Airborne Corps to be landed east of the Rhine in a single lift. This would be achieved through a combined effort by the RAF and the USAAF, with nearly 1,800 transport and tug aircraft, and over 1,300 gliders, taking to the air. XVIII Airborne Corps came under the command of the British Second Army, and comprised the British 6th and US 17th Airborne Divisions. Their troops would land in an area extending northwards from Wesel to the River Issel, but not until ground troops of the British Second and US Ninth Armies had crossed the section of the Rhine between Wesel and Emmerich. The 6th Airborne troops were expected to secure the village of Hamminkeln at an early stage, and also to seize road and rail bridges over the River Issel, in the area between Hamminkeln and Ringenberg.

Nos 3 and 5 Para Brigades, of the 6th Airborne Division, would be carried in American C-47 aircraft. They had the job of protecting the northern flank of the

ꞏsas in the glider park at Great Dunmow, being prepared for Operation 'Varsity'. (*190 & 620 Sqns Archive*)

Comrades in arms at Great Dunmow: left to right, Flight Sergeant 'Ken' Kendrew (flight engineer, 190 Squadron), Staff Sergeant Bruce McAlister Hodge (Glider Pilot Regiment) and Kendrew's pilot, Flying Officer Hugh Allan RCAF. Allan and his crew towed Hodge's glider during both the 'Market' and 'Varsity' operations. (*H.B. Allan*)

airborne landings, and would themselves be dropped on DZ/LZs 'A' and 'B', to the north-west of Hamminkeln. The RAF's Stirlings, Halifaxes and Dakotas would be towing 434 gliders, carrying troops of 6 Air Landing Brigade to DZ/LZs 'A' and 'B', and also to LZs 'O', 'P', 'R' and 'U', closer to Hamminkeln. South of these were the DZs and LZs for the American troops of the 17th Airborne Division. Their main objective was the wooded high ground of the Diersfordter Wald, to the north-west of Wesel. This town, situated on the north-east bank of the Rhine, incorporated the junctions of major road and rail routes, and was next to a large road bridge over the river. It therefore constituted a key position that needed to be in the hands of the Allied ground forces by the time the airborne troops arrived. Enemy resistance in this area had already been weakened by artillery bombardment, and Wesel itself would be practically destroyed by RAF bombing during the night of 23/24 March.

There was not much peace for the personnel at Great Dunmow as they tried to grab a few hours' sleep before the start of 'Varsity'. The air raid sirens were activated at 0311 hrs on 24 March, as an 'Attack Warning RED' was issued in response to V1 flying bombs passing near the airfield, so nearly everyone was awake at 0345 hrs, when 'Reveille' was sounded. By 0500 hrs, the ground crews of 6190 and 6620 Servicing Echelons were making final checks on their sixty Stirlings, which would be towing Horsas loaded with troops, jeeps, guns and other equipment.

Eric Wadman, 6190 Servicing Echelon, recalled:

The evening before 'Varsity', we had to marshal all twenty-six aircraft of 190 Squadron, and twenty-six of 620, plus eight pool aircraft brought in, on the perimeter track. Facing in the opposite direction, and meeting the Stirlings at the main runway, were the Horsa gliders.

We had to be at the runway, with our starter trolleys, chocks etc, before dawn on 24 March. Two lines of gliders had already been arranged abreast the end of the main runway, and on the grass beside them the same number of Stirlings, half to the left, and half to the right, in long 'crocodiles'. Ahead, two sets of traffic lights had been erected on the grass, each manned by a controller.

As it became lighter, the Glider Pilot Regiment crews arrived first, for final briefing, while the troops of the Airborne Division stood by their gliders. The Stirling crews also began to arrive, but by then we had already warmed up the

Dunmow Stirlings, (top) awaiting Operation 'Varsity', and (bottom) marshalled on the perimeter track, ready
ɔ. (*190 & 620 Sqns Archive*)

engines. Once the Stirling crews were on board, on a given order the engines of one aircraft after another started up.

Now the first aircraft were marshalled onto the runway, to line up in front of the gliders on the left-hand side of the runway, the traffic lights showing red. The towing cables were attached, and when the amber light shone, each tug moved slowly forward, its controller watching the cable – as soon as it was taut, he signalled green, and the tug pilot applied full power and took off. As the Stirlings moved in pairs onto the end of the runway from the right, two Crossley wagons, each with a glider in tow, followed on behind, and more tug aircraft and gliders were swiftly hooked up. The lights went again from red to amber, amber to green, and one after another, the aircraft and glider combinations took off and followed the long stream of ahead of them.

Although visibility was poor, the weather forecast for the continent was good, as the first of the Dunmow Stirlings, captained by 190 Squadron's CO, Wg Cdr Bunker, took off at 0630 hrs with its glider. This combination was followed by the others at a rate of nearly one a minute. However, shortly after becoming airborne, the fifth Stirling, LJ826 'J', of 190 Squadron, developed an engine problem. Its pilot, Fg Off Connell, cast off his glider, and landed as soon as he was cleared to do so. He and his crew boarded a spare aircraft, 'B', and joined the queue to take off again. Their second flight that day was successful.

Just over an hour later, all but one of the Dunmow Stirlings were away according to plan. The last few departures had been delayed because of an accident involving 190 Squadron's LJ997 'H', captained by Fg Off Lewis. On its take-off run, LJ997's port outer engine had misfired badly and the aircraft swung, causing the undercarriage to collapse. The pilots in the Horsa it was towing were able to cast off and land safely, and everyone on board the Stirling was unhurt, apart from the navigator, Fg Off Weldon, who sustained a small cut. Lewis and his crew boarded another spare aircraft, 'P', and this time went on to deliver their glider successfully. Stirling LJ997 was so badly damaged that it was formally 'struck off charge' five days later. It was found that the spark plugs in its faulty engine were very oily, probably because of the long time the aircraft had been taxiing (it was number fifty-five in the queue of sixty aircraft).

Eric Wadman recalled:

We must have had most of the combinations away, when one of 190 Squadron's aircraft, halfway down the runway with its glider, had a problem, with an engine starting to misfire. The pilot passed instructions to the glider, to 'cast off and clear the runway', while he turned the aircraft the other way to also take it clear of the runway. In doing so, the long-legged Stirling undercarriage snapped, and with a heavy crunch, she broke her back. Both tug and glider had actually cleared the runway in use, but the Stirling, with its very high tail unit, was judged to be still too close to the following aircraft as they took off. Therefore, an order was given to taxi all the remaining aircraft onto another runway, while the Crossley wagons swiftly moved the gliders, ready for the new take-off direction. In view of the mishap, it was surprising how quickly the combinations were taking off again, but now making a starboard turn as they departed, to follow those already airborne.

When the last pair had taken off, the station was suddenly quiet and empty. Not knowing quite what to do, small groups of ground crews started to drift back to the familiar area of our flight dispersal. All was so peaceful, with only the sound of the skylarks, and other birds in the distant hedgerows. A NAAFI van pulled up by the Flight hut, and we suddenly realised we needed that mug of tea, and some cake. We stood around talking for what seemed an age, when suddenly, we could hear a very distant drone of engines coming in short waves. All eyes were turned to the west, the noise slowly but steadily rising in volume, until someone with sharp eyes suddenly pointed them out to us, a long way off, looking like a swarm of bees.

After take-off, our aircraft had travelled west, before steering back over Dunmow, and forming up into three long lines of tug and glider combinations. There was a sudden rush to get a better vantage point, on the top platforms of our engine trestle trolleys, and from these we watched the steady progress of this huge, three-pronged Armada, the noise getting louder and louder, until it filled the whole air with its vibration. I had never before seen such a single mass of aircraft at one time, and as they wheeled to the south, we wondered what the people of the London suburbs would make of all this. Eventually the tail end of the formation passed over the airfield, the sound gradually diminishing, as it passed into the distance, until all was quiet once more. Hardly a word was spoken, but then there was another sound. Suddenly, there were formations of fighters, American and British, Spitfires and Tempests, Thunderbolts, Mustangs and Lightnings, all flying fast and low, to pass under our massive formation, and going on to play havoc with the German forces by the time the gliders and paratroops arrived across the Rhine.

Overhead their home airfield, the Dunmow Stirlings and Horsas set a course that took them across Kent, to rendezvous with the other RAF tugs and their gliders over Hawkinge airfield. After crossing the Channel, they joined the Americans over Belgium, to form two parallel streams, with the Stirlings, Halifaxes and Dakotas towing their Horsas and Hamilcars to port, and the USAAF C-47s their Waco gliders to starboard.

Malcolm Mitchell, 190 Squadron, recalled:

By this time we were well trained in the technique of towing, and the take-off and forming up for 'Varsity' was done smoothly, without fuss. However, when we were over the sea, heading towards the continent, my starboard inner engine developed a fault. Oil pressure dropped and cylinder head temperatures rose alarmingly. I told 'Ikey' that it would have to be feathered and switched off. It was quite possible for a Stirling to tow a glider whilst flying on three engines, but we were on an operation, towing a glider full of troops to battle, so our cautious pilot decided to abort the flight and return to base.

Plt Off 'Ikey' Isaacson cast off his glider over Great Dunmow, then landed his Stirling, 'W'. Two of the 620 Squadron aircraft, 'O' and 'V', had lost their gliders shortly after take off, when the tow-ropes broke, and these tugs also returned to base. 'O' took off with another glider, as did 'Q' of 620 Squadron, the latter being the replacement for 190 Squadron's 'W'. However, neither 'O' nor 'Q' was able to catch up with the stream by the time Brussels was reached, and both turned back at that point, as laid down in the orders covering this eventuality.

Despite these setbacks at the start of 'Varsity', the rest of the Dunmow Horsas made it across the Rhine. Most of them were destined for LZs 'P' and 'R', with smaller numbers going to LZs 'A' and 'B'. The fighter cover provided by the 2nd Tactical Air Force proved very effective, so there was little or no opposition from

This photograph was taken by Warrant Officer Noel Chaffey during Operation 'Varsity'. Seventeen gliders can counted on LZ 'P', which was clearly visible from the air at this early stage of the operation. (*N.R. Chaffey*)

In contrast to the previous photograph, this one – taken from a 190 Squadron Stirling – gives an indication of murky conditions that developed as battlefield smoke drifted across the Rhine. (*H.B. Allan*)

enemy fighters. Eureka beacons marked the turning points *en route*, but these navigation aids were scarcely needed, since the visibility over the continent was about eight miles. Over the DZs, visibility was also good to start with, but deteriorated rapidly as battlefield smoke added to dust haze that had been generated by the bombing attacks of the previous few hours. This caused some anxious moments for the later arrivals among the glider pilots, who had practically no sight of the ground as they released from their tugs.

Although the enemy anti-aircraft guns were heavily suppressed by air attacks and artillery fire, there was still a formidable barrage of flak in some areas around the DZs and LZs. The C-46 and C-47 transports of the US IXth Troop Carrier Command suffered particularly heavy losses (amounting to fifty aircraft shot down), as they ran in at low level to drop paratroops. Many of the RAF Stirlings, Halifaxes and Dakotas sustained damage as they towed their gliders at a height of 2,500 feet, but only eight of these tugs were destroyed. It was estimated that up to 80 per cent of the gliders were damaged by flak or small arms fire before they landed, and there were many casualties among the British glider pilots, whose fatalities included approximately sixty RAF pilots seconded to the Glider Pilot Regiment.

190 and 620 Squadrons did not lose any aircraft during 'Varsity', but several of their crews reported seeing a Halifax crashing in flames near one of the LZs, and two Stirlings on fire to the west of the Rhine. Several of the Dunmow Stirlings returned with minor flak damage, including Plt Off Middleton's 190 Squadron aircraft, 'Z', which was hit in one of its petrol tanks, fortunately without catching fire.

Ken Wilson, 620 Squadron, recalled:

The final 'big' operation we carried out was the Rhine Crossing. Flying Stirling 'P-Peter', I towed a glider piloted by Staff Sergeant Bennett, released him over LZ 'B', and returned to Dunmow in one piece. The nasty part of the trip for us was when a V1 flew right through our stream of aircraft as we were forming up over Essex – amazingly, no one broke radio silence. We could not believe our luck as we crossed the Rhine, with relatively little opposition from fighters and light flak, which was quite a relief as we were all anticipating another 'Arnhem' type op with its attendant carnage. The operation was a huge success and no follow-up resupply trips were called for. The Mess bar did great business that night!

Shortly after the glider lift had been completed, American B-24s carried out a supply drop to the airborne troops east of the Rhine. The next day, 25 March, thirteen Stirlings of 190 Squadron, and twelve of 620 Squadron, were ready to carry out further drops, if they were needed. Orders for these were cancelled late in the afternoon, because units of the British Second and US Ninth Armies had already broken through to relieve the Airborne Divisions.

There were no more operations for 190 and 620 Squadrons until the night of 30/31 March, when each sent four aircraft on SOE tasks to 'Crupper' and 'Flank' DZs in Norway. Flights from Great Dunmow to several other Norwegian DZs had been cancelled because of gale warnings, but the weather was actually much better than forecast. All the Dunmow aircraft were able to drop containers to DZs that were clear of cloud and designated by Eureka beacons, though Fg Off Lewis and his 190 Squadron crew were unable to dispatch packages to 'Flank 2' because the floor hatch of their aircraft iced up. After dropping their containers they observed a Ju 88 night-fighter passing them head-on, and then, about three minutes later, saw an aircraft catch fire and explode in mid-air. This must have one of the five Stirlings lost by other 38 Group squadrons operating over Norway that night.

Fg Off Andrews and his 620 Squadron crew could very easily have joined the list of casualties on the night of 30/31 March. On the way back, they had just passed the Norwegian coast when their aircraft, LJ871 'M', was attacked by a night-fighter. Its opening shots put the Stirling's gun turret out of action and cut off the inter-com to its occupant, WO Wright. The enemy aircraft was extremely persistent, as it made a series of attacks over a period of about thirty minutes. Fortunately, no one on board the Stirling was wounded, although considerable damage was done to the airframe. Large portions of the port aileron and the bomb doors were shot away, there were punctures to the tailwheels and one of the mainwheels, and the gyro compass was disabled. As he nursed the aircraft back to base in this precarious state, Andrews transmitted a request for the emergency vehicles to stand by. His Stirling's arrival turned into a crash-landing, as the starboard undercarriage collapsed, but the crew remained unharmed. Luck had certainly been on their side that night.

Fg Off Ken Wilson had a rude awakening as he returned to base, early the same morning:

> On the 30 March, we took off on another operation to Norway, but we were at last given 2nd pilots – I was lucky enough to get one Tony Edgecombe, a Rhodesian ex-flying instructor who had never flown anything more than Oxfords. After a long and hairy trip, I handed over to Tony and promptly fell asleep. Three hours later, as dawn was breaking I found us over Dunmow with him shaking me and saying 'How do you land these bloody things, "Tug"?'

'Tug' Wilson and crew, with their 'chalk-marked' Stirling. (*190 & 620 Sqns Archive*)

Squadron's Stirling 'QS-M'. The damage to the port aileron (top), and under-fuselage bomb-doors (bottom),
ws that Flying Officer 'Archie' Andrews and his crew had a remarkable escape from a German night-fighter on
night of 30/31 March 1945. (*190 & 620 Sqns Archive*)

On 1 April 1945, all operations in 38 Group were cancelled on account of the weather, but the Dunmow squadrons each sent six aircraft to take part in an Air-Sea Rescue search, looking for downed aircrew. When the Stirlings returned, encrusted with salt from the stormy North Sea, their crews reported having seen a number of dinghies, all empty, unfortunately.

On the night of 2/3 April, fifty aircraft from 38 Group took part in SOE operations across Holland, Denmark, Germany and Norway. Nos 190 and 620 Squadrons had each been requested to provide seven aircraft for operations over Norway, but the weather forecast led to the cancellation of sorties to the more westerly DZs. As a result, only four Dunmow aircraft took off, heading for 'Crupper' and 'Stirrup' DZs. One of the two 620 Squadron aircraft was successful, but the other was unable to drop because of poor weather and failed navigational equipment. One of the 190 Squadron aircraft, captained by Flt Sgt Driscoll, was unable to drop, as no reception signals were seen at its DZ, 'Crupper 33'. The other 190 Squadron aircraft, 'G5-Q', captained by Fg Off Wren Hoskyns, failed to return from its operation to 'Stirrup 16', and was presumed to have been lost in the North Sea. As well as the crew of six, there were two RASC dispatchers on board. The serial of this Stirling is noted as EF242 in the 190 Squadron Operations Record Book, but Aircraft Record Cards indicate that it was in fact PK227.

The next night, 3/4 April, six aircraft from 190 Squadron flew on SOE operations to 'Cubbing', 'Nico' and 'Rummy' DZs, near Gouda in Holland. One dropped to 'Cubbing 3' and two to 'Rummy 23', while the crews of the other three aircraft did not observe any reception signals. On 5 April, 190 Squadron and its engineering support unit, 6190 Servicing Echelon, took part in a parade, at which the AOC 38 Group, AVM Scarlett-Streatfeild, presented the new 190 Squadron crest to Wg Cdr Bunker. This comprised 'A cloak charged with a double-headed eagle displayed' (derived from the City of Arnhem's coat of arms) and the motto *Ex Tenebris* (Out of Darkness). The design was therefore inspired by the squadron's determined efforts during Operation 'Market', as well as its many night operations flown for the SAS and SOE.

During the evening of 5 April, orders were issued for Operation 'Amherst'. This was due to commence on the night of 6/7 April, with 38 Group dropping 720 paratroops of the French 3 and 4 SAS to DZs near Coevordon, Groningen and Zwolle, in Holland. 'Amherst' was intended to disorganise the German forces, and thus prevent them from putting up an effective defence against the Canadian First Army, which was advancing north-eastwards into this area. Specific objectives for the SAS patrols included bridges and an airfield (at Steenwijk), all of which needed to be kept intact for use by the Allies. As its contribution to this operation, Great Dunmow was asked to provide sixteen aircraft, each of which would carry fifteen paratroops.

During the morning of 6 April, a further six aircraft were requested of Great Dunmow, this time to take part in Operation 'Keystone'. This involved troops of 2 SAS, who were to be dropped to DZs south of the Zuider Zee. The main aim of 'Keystone' was to capture bridges over the Apeldoorn canal, in order to halt enemy movements across this waterway. Shortly after midday on 6 April, both 'Amherst' and 'Keystone' were postponed, because bad weather was forecast. If these airborne operations did go ahead, it now seemed likely that they would be the last major ones supported by 190 and 620 Squadrons before the end of the war in Europe. In early anticipation of this, the Station Commander at Great Dunmow gave a lecture on 6 April, spelling out the good behaviour that would be expected of all ranks when Victory in Europe was announced.

But for the time being, SOE operations continued as usual. On the night of 6/7 April, five aircraft from 620 Squadron took off for 'Draughts', 'Necking' and 'Whimper' DZs in Holland. All had to return with their supplies, and in the case of the aircraft that went to 'Necking 8', the two agents on board. Four of the crews found no reception (probably because of enemy convoys near their DZs), while the fifth encountered ground mist, which prevented the DZ from being located. There was some enemy opposition and one aircraft was hit by small arms fire.

On 7 April, 'Keystone' was postponed once more. At Great Dunmow, there was not much flying that day, but eight aircraft from each squadron were being prepared for 'Amherst', since the weather seemed to be improving. After being loaded, one of the 620 Squadron aircraft became unserviceable with an electrical fault and was not replaced. During the evening, eight aircraft from 190 Squadron, and the remaining seven from 620 Squadron, took off and headed for Holland, only to find that their eight 'Amherst' DZs were completely covered by low stratus cloud. No visual pinpoints were obtainable, so the drops had to be carried out 'blind' from 1,500 feet, using Gee to establish the DZ positions. The Dunmow Stirlings dropped 222 paratroops, four SOE agents and eighty-four containers, and some of the aircraft also dropped 'simulators' (dummy paratroops) in an area to the north-west of the real DZs. In the air, no enemy opposition was encountered, and all aircraft returned safely, leaving the French SAS troops to carry out an operation that was generally successful in helping to break up the German defensive lines.

Jim Marshall, 620 Squadron, recalled:

On 7 April 1945 we had an interesting operation with 15 French SAS troops. We were dropping them in the northern part of Holland but on the way up we were dropping dummy parachutists which were rigged to set off firecrackers when they landed. All of the aircraft on this operation were doing this on different routes, so the situation must have been somewhat confusing to the German commanders as they wouldn't know which ones were going to be the real live troops.

On the night of 8/9 April, two Stirlings from 620 Squadron were detailed for further SAS drops to DZs in Holland. Plt Off Jordan and his crew were unable to drop, as no reception signals were observed at their DZ, 'Amherst 26'. 'D-Dog', captained by WO Marriott, dropped sixteen French troops and ten containers at DZ 'Dopey 4'. Both aircraft were diverted to Tempsford on their return, since Great Dunmow was obscured by cloud with a base of only 300 feet.

The weather put paid to operations on the night of 9/10 April, but the next night, 10/11 April, seven aircraft from 190 Squadron were sent to 'Cubbing', 'Dopey', 'Draughts', 'Medico', 'Necking' and 'Whimper' DZs, set up by the SAS and SOE in Holland. Five out of the six aircraft on SOE drops were successful. Fg Off Sellars and his crew identified their SAS DZ, 'Dopey 4', but then observed mortar flares close by. The DZ lights were quickly extinguished, so they were unable to proceed with the drop and had to return with their two paratroopers, twenty-four containers and three packages still on board.

Operation 'Keystone' finally went ahead on the night of 11/12 April. Five aircraft from 620 Squadron were sent to two DZs, carrying forty-three troops, ten containers and one pannier. There was no reception for the three aircraft going to 'Keystone A', but the other two dropped seventeen troops and two containers to 'Keystone B'.

Warrant Officer Norman Marriott RNZAF (standing, third from left) with his 620 Squadron crew and members c their ground crew, in front of Stirling LJ865 'D-Dog'. (*190 & 620 Sqns Archive*)

The following night, 12/13 April, four aircraft from 190 Squadron took off with further SAS troops to be dropped at the 'Keystone B' DZ. Two of these aircraft were then going to make a second drop, of containers, on 'Whimper' DZs for SOE. No reception signals were seen at any of the DZs, so the paratroops and supplies had to be brought back to base. The same night, Dunmow Stirlings went on SOE operations to Denmark for the first time. The ten crews (five from each squadron) found that Eureka beacons set up at the 'Tablejam' DZs gave a useful homing range of about 15 miles as they ran in at a height of 500 feet. Nine of the crews were successful in dropping containers and packages to the DZs, but Fg Off Connell of 190 Squadron was forced to turn back after making two attempts to cross the Danish coast in the face of intense and accurate flak. At their debriefings, the crews commented on the lack of an effective blackout in Denmark. Various towns were clearly marked by streetlights, and a large POW camp was also seen to be well lit.

Although many successful operations had been carried out by the 38 Group squadrons equipped with the Stirling, this aircraft's days were numbered, since it had been decided that the Halifax would replace it in the air support role. On 13 April, four of 620 Squadron's Stirlings were ferried to Northern Ireland for disposal, but it would be several more weeks before all of them were gone from Great Dunmow.

In the meantime, there was plenty of work for the Stirlings. On the night of 13/14 April, four aircraft from 190 Squadron, and three from 620 Squadron, went on SOE operations to Denmark again. The weather was good and the illuminated POW camp (the same one as the previous night) provided a useful aid to navigation, along with the Eureka beacons at the 'Tablejam' DZs. Of the four 190 Squadron aircraft, two were successful in dropping, and one reached its DZ but was unable to drop as no reception signals were seen. Having failed to pinpoint their position when they reached the Danish coast, the crew of the fourth aircraft were caught by searchlights on two occasions, and subjected to persistent light flak, before abandoning their

Pilot Officer C.N. Jones RCAF, the gunner in Warrant Officer Marriott's crew.
(*190 & 620 Sqns Archive*)

sortie. One of the three aircraft from 620 Squadron dropped. Another got to its
DZ, but no reception signals were observed. The third aircraft, captained by WO
Marriott, failed to reach its DZ and was hit by light flak, which slightly wounded the
gunner, Plt Off Jones. Three of the Dunmow Stirlings diverted to Tarrant Rushton
on their return.

On the night of 14/15 April, the Dunmow squadrons each sent five aircraft on
SOE operations to Norway, having been briefed to drop containers from medium
level to DZ 'Blinkers 2'. One of the 620 Squadron aircraft was unable to take off
because of a generator problem, but the crews of seven out of the other nine reported successful drops. After dropping, 190 Squadron's LK335 'G5-Q', captained
by Flt Sgt Bailey, was illuminated by fighter flares, just before a twin-engined
aircraft was observed. This made four passes, apparently without firing any shots,
though the Stirling's gunner, Sgt Stewart, managed to fire two short bursts at it.
Later on, members of the same crew saw a bright orange glow on the sea, to the west
of Norway, and about 20 miles away to their left. This probably marked the
destruction of 190 Squadron's TS265 'L9-H', captained by Fg Off Jimmy Lewis.
The seven members of TS265's crew (a 2nd navigator was on board) have no known
graves. Although the weather was reasonable over Norway that night, the returning
aircraft encountered electrical storms and low cloud over the North Sea, and only
one landed at Great Dunmow. The others diverted far and wide, to land at
Acklington (Northumberland), Langham (Norfolk) and Madley (Herefordshire).

Also, on 14/15 April, a 190 Squadron aircraft, captained by Fg Off Insley, made
a third attempt to drop to SAS DZ 'Dopey 4' in Holland. The aircraft circled for
some time, after locating the DZ area using Gee, but there was complete cloud cover
at about 1,000 feet and the drop had to be abandoned. On 15 April, redundant

Many of the Dunmow Stirlings sent to Northern Ireland for disposal in the spring of 1945 were 'veteran' aircraft. LJ952 'Yorkshire II' had been on many operations with Flying Officer Derek de Rome and his crew since the summer of 1944. When this aircraft left 620 Squadron in April 1945, the 'Yorkshire II' motif was taken over by LJ566 (seen here), which had also flown on many parachute-dropping operations, as well as glider tows to Arnhem and across the Rhine, and two tactical bombing operations. (*N.R. Chaffey*)

The 'de Rome crew', with Stirling LJ566 'D4-Y' at Great Dunmow. On the left, standing, Flight Sergeant Bryan Garwood; sitting, in doorway, Flying Officer Basil 'Ben' Crocker; standing, left to right, Flight Sergeant Frank Pearman and Flying Officer Derek de Rome; kneeling, left to right, Warrant Officer Noel Chaffey and Flight Sergeant Pete Griffin. (*N.R. Chaffey*)

Stirlings were flown out of Great Dunmow by four crews from 190 Squadron and three from 620 Squadron, who were brought back from Northern Ireland in two other Stirlings belonging to 190 Squadron.

On the night of 17/18 April, 620 Squadron had five aircraft flying on SOE operations to Norway. They were all successful in dropping containers to 'Crupper' and 'Bit' DZs. Over the next few days, the other 38 Group squadrons continued their covert operations to Denmark, Holland and Norway, but 190 and 620 Squadrons were about to take on a different role. Earlier in April, HQ 38 Group had advised its Stirling squadrons that they would soon be transporting much-needed petrol supplies to the continent. Various loading methods were tried out, before deciding to pack 4½-gallon jerricans in wicker panniers, thus enabling each Stirling to carry 535 gallons of petrol inside its fuselage. Whenever possible, aircraft delivering this cargo would return to the UK with Allied POWs, who were now being freed in large numbers.

During the morning of 18 April, 190 and 620 Squadrons each dispatched ten empty aircraft to airfield B58 (Melsbroek/Brussels). They collected ex-POWs, who were brought back to Wing in Buckinghamshire. Stirling 'L9-L' of 190 Squadron burst a tyre on landing at Brussels and its crew, captained by Fg Off Connell, had to return as passengers in a Stirling based at Rivenhall. In the afternoon, each of the Dunmow squadrons sent ten Stirlings, loaded with petrol, to airfields used by 83 Group, which formed part of the 2nd Tactical Air Force. The 190 Squadron aircraft landed at B120 (Lanenburg/Hannover), and those of 620 Squadron at B116 (Wunstorf/Hannover).

On 19 April, 190 and 620 Squadrons each had ten aircraft detailed to deliver petrol to Lanenburg, before proceeding to Brussels to pick up ex-POWs. A strong crosswind prevented all but one of these aircraft from landing at Lanenburg. The diverted aircraft landed at either Wunstorf or Brussels. Passengers who boarded at the latter airfield were flown back to Wing and Westcott. The next day, 20 April, twelve aircraft from 190 Squadron delivered petrol to B108 (Rheine), and twelve from 620 Squadron took a similar cargo to B116 (Wunstorf).

Malcolm Mitchell recalled:

During this period, towards the end of the war, our crew was given the chance to see a little of what was left of Germany, after the devastation wrought by the RAF and the Americans. My main memory of this was the sight when we flew close to Hannover. The centre of the town had literally disappeared, turned to rubble. Around the centre was a ring of largely untouched suburban buildings. The Germans had certainly 'Reaped the Whirlwind'.

Noel Chaffey, 620 Squadron, recalled:

We made two flights to B116 (Wunstorf) with petrol. The second one was on 20 April, when we took a packed lunch, which we ate whilst sitting on the grass just off the perimeter track on this much-damaged airfield near Hannover. As we were eating our Spam sandwiches and consuming our Thermos flasks of tea, a jeep came whizzing along, with some British soldiers, asking if we'd like some souvenirs of war: flags, helmets, arm and hat bands etc. We accepted some and I collected a piece of shrapnel from one of the nearby bomb craters and was satisfied with that and a red observation balloon (not inflated!). I took a colour photo of the crew on this occasion, sitting alongside our aircraft – wearing

On the way to Wunstorf airfield, Warrant Officer Noel Chaffey took this photograph of the devastated city of Hannover. (*N.R. Chaffey*)

The 'de Rome crew', at Wunstorf airfield. (*N.R. Chaffey*)

enemy helmets. This was my first 'Kodacolor' colour film, sent by friends in California. It still makes good prints, even today.

George Dann, 620 Squadron, recalled:

On the 18 and 20 April we were running petrol to Wunstorf. Any trepidation about carrying large amounts of petrol on board was increased by the fact that we were landing very heavy Stirlings on a runway of grass covered with metal 'Sommerfeld' trucking! A somewhat dicey operation, to say the least.

While the Stirling crews were doing this hazardous job of transporting petrol, some of them gave in to the temptation to obtain a few gallons, in order to keep privately owned motor vehicles on the road at a time when fuel rationing was strictly enforced. The illicit petrol then had to be carefully hidden from the prying eyes of the RAF Police.

Anon, 620 Squadron, recalled:

At Dunmow there was a lake in the wood. This lake was used to hide the jerricans, which were immersed, each with a line with a little label identifying a particular crew member.

During the afternoon of 20 April, the Dunmow Stirlings at Wunstorf and Rheine proceeded to Brussels. The plan was for them to fly ex-POWs from Brussels to Odiham in Hampshire, and to Wing. However, there were not enough passengers to fill all the aircraft at Brussels, so several returned empty, direct to base. Four of the 190 Squadron aircraft came back with passengers, three of them to Wing, and one to Odiham.

The 190 Squadron Stirling that landed at Odiham during the early evening of 20 April was LJ930 'L9-A', captained by the CO, Wg Cdr 'Dickie' Bunker, DSO DFC and Bar. Once the passengers had alighted, the engines were quickly restarted, for the flight of sixty or so miles to Great Dunmow. While the aircraft was taxiing

ɔrmer POWs wait to board a 620 Squadron Stirling at Brussels on 20 April 1945. (*190 & 620 Sqns Archive*)

In this line-up of 190 Squadron Stirlings, the CO's aircraft, LJ930 'L9-A', is the one on the far left, chalk-mark '183'. (*190 & 620 Sqns Archive*)

towards the runway, Odiham Flying Control transmitted a message to let the pilot know that its tailwheel tyres appeared to be deflated. This message was not acknowledged, so an airman was sent across the airfield to intercept the aircraft and signal that something was amiss. He succeeded in doing this, but received a 'thumbs up' from the pilot, who then lined up on the runway.

As the Stirling accelerated for take-off, the tail lifted quickly, taking the weight off the tailwheels. However, the wheel hubs, which were made of a flammable magnesium alloy, had already been set alight by friction with the perimeter track and runway surfaces. The aircraft lifted off and climbed away, leaving a trail of smoke, before a mass of flames erupted from the rear fuselage. In the intense heat, the gun turret broke free and fell to the ground. Parts of the elevators and their control linkages either melted or fractured, following which the aircraft entered a shallow dive and crashed at Broadway Green Farm, south of Windlesham in Berkshire. Stirling LJ930's final flight had lasted just four minutes. Personnel from RAF Blackbushe soon arrived at the crash site and recovered six bodies. A seventh was found about one and a half miles away, close to the gun turret.

Examination of the Stirling's wreckage revealed that five jerricans were still on board when it took off from Odiham. At least two of these containers would have been full of petrol, since seals on their caps had not been disturbed. A quantity of German large-calibre ammunition was also found among the wreckage. The subsequent Court of Inquiry decided that while the flat tyres were the primary cause of the accident, it was likely that ignition of the highly flammable agents inside the fuselage led to the catastrophic fire and loss of control. After recording their findings, the authors of LJ930's accident report concluded by noting how unfortunate it was that Wg Cdr Bunker, who had completed numerous Bomber Command operations before serving with 620 and 190 Squadrons, should have died in this way.

The crash of Stirling LJ930 deprived Flt Sgt H. Smith of the five members of his 190 Squadron crew, who had been detailed to fly with the CO that fateful day. Flt Sgt Bagley, the flight engineer in the CO's regular crew, was also on board LJ930, hence seven men were killed in all. A quite understandable repercussion of this tragic accident seems to have been that Stirling crews became very cautious if any tailwheel damage arose. Over the next few weeks, there were numerous instances of crews declaring aircraft unserviceable for this reason. For example, the crews of five out of eighteen Stirlings sent from Rivenhall to Brussels on 16 May signalled that they were unable to return because of tailwheel problems.

On 21 April, eleven aircraft from 190 Squadron flew to Rheine with petrol, and returned via Brussels, where they picked up 271 ex-POWs for the return journey to Westcott. Eleven of 620 Squadron's Stirlings were also taking part in the same round trip, but during the afternoon one of these aircraft, LJ627 'QS-E', captained by WO Johnson, swung off the runway at Rheine while landing in a strong crosswind. The starboard mainwheel of this aircraft ran into a bomb crater, as a result of which its undercarriage collapsed and the starboard wing was torn off. Thankfully, there were no injuries to the crew, who returned to base in another 620 Squadron aircraft that evening.

Members of Flight Sergeant George Dann's 620 Squadron crew pose for the camera outside an *estaminet*, after landing at Vitry-en-Artois on 22 April 1945. (*M. Thomas*)

On 22 April, the Dunmow squadrons each sent fifteen aircraft to airfield B50 (Vitry-en-Artois), and from there they transported RAF personnel of 226 and 80 Squadrons to B77 (Gilze-Rijen), near Tilburg in Holland. Ex-POWs boarded the Stirlings at Gilze-Rijen, to be flown back to Westcott, and Dunsfold in Surrey.

Noel Chaffey recalled:

On 22 April we took off from Great Dunmow for station B50 in France and then went on to Tilburg, Holland, filling up with thirty ex-POWs and bringing them back to Westcott. There I got a couple of photos of the POWs in front of our Stirling, 'Y'.

During the morning of 23 April, six aircraft from 190 Squadron took off for Brussels, and were followed by six more in the afternoon. The ex-POWs they collected were brought back to Dunsfold and Westcott. Twelve aircraft from 620 Squadron also flew ex-POWs from Brussels to Westcott that day. These were the last of the

American ex-POWs with Stirling LJ566 'D4-Y', at Westcott, 22 April 1945. (*N. R. Chaffey*)

repatriation flights to be carried out by the Dunmow Stirlings for the time being, but their crews could look back on a job well done, having brought home nearly 3,400 men in less than a week.

Ken Wilson recalled:

As hostilities in Europe were nearing an end, we spent the most heart-rending, yet heart-warming, days of the war, flying loads of poor devils home to England, some of whom had been in the bag as prisoners of war for four or five years. Many of them broke down in tears when they saw the white cliffs of Dover as we crossed the coast.

On 24 April, Wg Cdr Geoffrey Briggs DFC was posted to Great Dunmow, to assume command of 190 Squadron.

'Buster' Briggs, 190 Squadron, recalled:

I was an instructor at the School of Air Support at Old Sarum, near Salisbury, when I received an order from Group Captain John McIntyre to report to RAF Great Dunmow, to take command of 190 Squadron, as the former CO had been killed. I went there and took over, and at the same time learnt to fly Stirlings, since I had previously been with 298 Squadron at Tarrant Rushton, flying Halifaxes for eighteen months.

On 11 April, orders for Operation 'Jubilant' had been received at Great Dunmow. The requirement for this operation had grown out of a fear that the enemy might harm POWs through violence, starvation or lack of medical treatment, or use them as hostages, before their camps in northern Germany could be liberated by Allied ground forces. It was decided, therefore, to prepare for an airborne operation, in which troops of the British 1st Airborne Division, the US 13th Airborne Division and the US 501st and 508th Parachute Regiments would, if necessary, be landed by parachute and in Horsa gliders, in order to seize command of the camps.

The decision whether or not to proceed with the full 'Jubilant' operation would depend on intelligence gathered by small parties of covertly dropped paratroops, whose instructions were to keep certain camps under observation, and to assess any threats to their inmates. These paratroops belonged to the Special Allied Airborne Reconnaissance Force (SAARF), which reported to Supreme Headquarters Allied Expeditionary Force. The SAARF personnel were drawn from the American, Belgian, British, French and Polish forces. Their operational units were similar to the Jedburgh teams, insofar as each comprised three members, one of whom was a signaller. However, most of the SAARF teams had members of a single nationality, whereas the 'Jeds' were usually mixed.

The Operation Order for deploying the SAARF teams used the code name 'Vicarage', but a specific operation carried out by 190 Squadron on the night of 25/26 April was known as 'Violet'. Three Stirlings were each to drop two three-man teams, plus eight supply panniers, to DZs near *Stalag* XIA at Altengrabow, to the east of Magdeburg. Permission was given for these teams and their supplies to be 'blind dropped', if necessary. The aircraft captains, DZ designations, and team nationalities and names were: Sqn Ldr Fisher, 'Violet 1', with a British team ('Eraser') and a French team ('Briefcase'); Fg Off Bickford, 'Violet 2', with a British team ('Pennib') and an American team ('Cashbox'); and Fg Off Allan, 'Violet 3', with an American team ('Sealingwax') and a French team ('Pencil').

On the night of 25/26 April, the 'Violet' aircraft encountered searchlights and light flak in the area of the DZs, but visibility was good, apart from a slight ground haze,

crew who flew to DZ 'Violet 3', on 190 Squadron's last operational task: left to right, Flight Sergeant 'Brad' dbrook (wireless operator), Flying Officer Bill Summers RCAF (navigator), Warrant Officer Ted Cunningham AF (bomb aimer), Warrant Officer 'Chuck' Randall RCAF (air gunner), Flying Officer Hugh Allan RCAF ot) and Flight Sergeant Ken Kendrew (flight engineer). (*H.B. Allan*)

and all three dropped their teams. Unfortunately, the members of the French 'Pencil' team, dropped from Fg Off Allan's aircraft, landed in the midst of enemy forces. They evaded capture by the Germans, only to have the misfortune to be detained and interrogated by the Russians. However, they eventually managed to escape, and returned to the UK in June 1945. Members of the 'Eraser', 'Briefcase' and 'Cashbox' teams were captured by the Germans and taken to *Stalag* XIA. There, they gained the co-operation of the Camp Commandant, and were able, by radio, to advise their HQ that the situation was stable at Altengrabow. Subsequent communications ensured that food and medical aid were provided by American forces as soon as they reached the camp. British, American, French and Belgian POWs were evacuated from the camp before its control was handed over to the Russians, at which point the SAARF troops also had to move out and head for the American lines.

Although small in scale, 'Violet' was worthy of note, because it turned out to be the last operation in which paratroops were dropped behind enemy lines in Europe. On 26 April, four crews from 620 Squadron were detailed to take part in a further 'Vicarage' task, with the intention of dropping five teams of SAARF paratroops and twenty-one panniers. Three of the sorties were later cancelled, leaving a single aircraft, LJ977 'QS-C', captained by Fg Off Andrews, to fly to a DZ situated between Hannover and Berlin. The weather was very bad, but one pannier containing food was dropped successfully.

As the preparations were being made for the 'Vicarage' drop on the night of 26/27 April, a large fire broke out in the Great Dunmow bomb dump, which was situated on the south-east side of the airfield. By the late afternoon of 26 April, huge explosions were throwing pieces of shrapnel more than a quarter of a mile, posing a risk to parked gliders. National Fire Service tenders were called in to assist the RAF fire service, but loud bangs continued to be heard throughout the night, as more bombs detonated. It took two days to extinguish the fire completely. This incident, which caused considerable disruption to the flying programme at Great Dunmow, was followed by some very unseasonable weather, including snow showers. This put a stop to most flying, and all operations, by the squadrons in 38 Group, until the night of 2/3 May, when six Stirlings from Tempsford flew to SOE DZs in Norway. These were the last operations carried out by 38 Group during the Second World War, although its squadrons continued to train for their air support role, regardless of the impending end of hostilities in Europe.

Having been postponed for 48 hours because of the weather, Group Exercise 'Amber' went ahead on 3 May, with 200 tug-glider combinations taking part. Great Dunmow contributed a total of thirty-nine combinations, which soon ran into bad weather. After their planned cross-country flight was cut short, the Stirlings of 190 and 620 Squadrons formed up in preparation for a glider release over base. In the course of this exercise, four aircraft from 620 Squadron lost their Horsas, and the crew of one of these gliders sustained minor injuries as it crash-landed.

Each of the Dunmow squadrons had ten aircraft detailed to take part in a re-supply drop on 4 May, as a continuation of Exercise 'Amber'. All except one successfully dropped on a DZ near Sudbury in Suffolk. The remaining aircraft, LK196 'B' of 190 Squadron, swung on take-off. Its pilot, Fg Off Atkinson, deliberately ground-looped in an attempt to stop, but this caused the Stirling's undercarriage to collapse. The six crew members and two passengers were very lucky to escape unhurt, since their aircraft narrowly missed the Flying Control building and finished up only a few yards from two parked aircraft. Atkinson had been with 190 Squadron for less than a fortnight, and had logged only four hours' flying time on Stirlings. Following this accident, the AOC 38 Group criticised the practice of converting some pilots onto the Stirling after they were posted to the squadrons, rather than at 1665 HCU, where this training was still available.

Nos 190 and 620 Squadrons took delivery of several Halifax III and VII aircraft during the first week of May 1945. For the time being, Stirling transport and training flights would continue, alongside the type conversion programme for the new aircraft. After an initial phase of general handling and circuits, the exercises carried out in the Halifax aircraft were similar to those flown in the Stirlings, and included glider towing, low-level cross-countries and fighter affiliation.

Late in the afternoon of 4 May, the camp at Great Dunmow had been sealed, and all flying stopped, as forty-two Stirlings of 190 and 620 Squadrons were made ready for Operation 'Schnapps'. This involved the transport of personnel and supplies to Denmark. However, Great Dunmow's commitment to this operation had been cancelled by the time it went ahead, on 7 May, the day that news of the German surrender was received.

'Victory in Europe' was officially announced by the Prime Minister, Winston Churchill, on 8 May 1945. Nos 190 and 620 Squadrons were stood down and a Thanksgiving Service was held outside the Flying Control building at Great Dunmow. Throughout the rest of the day, transport left at regular intervals, taking

...ling LK196 'B-Bull' of 190 Squadron, after its accident on 4 May 1945. The mangled tubular frame is from one ...he platforms used when servicing the Stirlings' engines. (*190 & 620 Sqns Archive*)

personnel to Chelmsford. The officers served lunch to the airmen and airwomen who remained on the camp. A comic football match took place, and there were free performances at the Station Cinema during the afternoon and evening. A Grand Victory Dance (with free beer) was also held in the evening. But not everyone at Great Dunmow was able to take part in a full day of celebrations, for there were some jobs that could not be left undone.

Ron Remfry, 6620 Servicing Echelon, recalled:

VE Day, 8 May 1945, came. All flying and work on the aircraft was cancelled for the day, provided that the aircraft were serviceable and ready to fly if needed. It shows how trusting we were that we were prepared to act as if hostilities had not actually ceased. Unfortunately, one kite was not serviceable and I drew the job of fixing it. Each engine had a unit which kept the airscrew turning at a constant speed by adjusting its pitch as the power setting was changed. All I had to do was to replace this unit with a fresh one and check that it was operating efficiently. The trestle was put under the engine, the duff unit removed and a new one fitted. The trestle was taken out of the way, the engine started, run up, and the constant speeding tested. No good, it was not working properly. So cut the engine, put the trestle back in place, remove the faulty unit, go back to stores and obtain another one.

So back to the aircraft, installed the new unit, remove the trestle again, start up the engine and test again. Still duff. This was repeated again with a third

Warrant Officer Noel Chaffey of 620 Squadron managed to get to London on VE Day and took this photo of crowds in Whitehall. (*N.R. Chaffey*)

unit. Still duff. So as a last resort the original unit was fitted back. It worked perfectly. That took from 9.00 am until 3.00 pm. What a glorious VE day, when almost everyone else was celebrating. I imagine that there must have been a small piece of dirt or grit in one of the oilways and the continual running of the engine and the unit managed to flush it out. After that it was straight to the NAAFI for a drink, clean up, a quick evening meal and then out into Dunmow for an evening of celebration. According to my recollection my pints went well into double figures. I had borrowed 'Shiner' Moon's bicycle to get into town and had to ride it back to camp. I don't think it knew the way. At every turn I came to, I managed to make the turn, but the bike went straight on. Naturally we came a cropper each time. I arrived back at camp quite OK, but the bike was a little the worse for wear!

On 9 May, it was back to work for everyone at Great Dunmow, in preparation for Operation 'Doomsday', which had been postponed for 24 hours because of the celebrations. The purpose of this operation was to transport troops of the 1st Airborne Division to Norway. Their task was to supervise an orderly handover of power from the Germans, who had approximately 300,000 military personnel in the country, still armed and under the command of their own officers. The Stirling and Halifax aircraft of 38 Group would be joined in this operation by American C-46 transports, based at Barkston Heath in Lincolnshire.

There were twenty-five Stirlings from 190 Squadron, and twenty-three from 620 Squadron, among the 210 'Doomsday' aircraft that took off on 10 May. Loaded with troops and supply containers, for delivery to Gardermoen, the Dunmow aircraft left very early in the morning. By 0700 hrs, many of their crews were reporting that they had run into bad weather over the North Sea and were turning back, but a couple more hours elapsed before 38 Group sent a general recall signal to its aircraft. Of the twenty-two aircraft that did get through to Gardermoen, fourteen were Stirlings from Great Dunmow. Their crews had navigated mainly by dead reckoning, since their Rebecca sets were unable to obtain a clear response from a Eureka beacon set up on the airfield at Gardermoen. Two aircraft from 190 Squadron landed at other airfields on the continent: 'G5-Q', captained by Flt Sgt Bailey, put down at Vaaler, to the north-east of Oslo, and 'L9-X', captained by Flt Sgt Insley, made an emergency landing at Eindhoven, following a mechanical failure of its starboard outer engine. Three of the Dunmow aircraft that turned back were diverted to Peterhead in Aberdeenshire.

This left four Dunmow Stirlings reported as overdue, but it was soon confirmed that two of these were safe. One had in fact landed at Gardermoen, while the other, 'QS-K' of 620 Squadron, was also in Norway, at Eggemoen. Flt Sgt Stan White was the air gunner in the latter aircraft:

On the 10 May we were detailed to ferry seventeen airborne troops to Gardermoen. The weather was expected to be reasonable over Norway, but it deteriorated rapidly during the early morning. A recall signal was sent out and those aircraft that had not yet taken off were held at base. We did not receive this message. We hit a severe snowstorm as we crossed the Norwegian coast and our skipper decided to climb above the cloud to avoid it. As we neared Oslo the bomb aimer spotted a break in the cloud and saw a lake beneath it. He suggested to the skipper that we should go down through the cloud and continue our run into Gardermoen below the cloud, which was quite low now. Three times in the next few minutes the skipper narrowly avoided a collision with a mountainside by putting the aircraft into a steep climbing turn. It's just as well that the troops we were carrying couldn't see what was going on at the time, though they must have known that the flying was a bit erratic.

Our bomb aimer drew the skipper's attention to a landing strip in a clearing at the edge of a wood and identified it as Eggemoen near the town of Hønefoss, to the north-west of Oslo. The skipper flew a low pass along the landing strip and decided it was long enough for us to land and take off again. As we touched down we realised that the military base adjacent to the landing strip was still occupied by the *Luftwaffe*, though there were no aircraft visible.

A German vehicle followed us down the runway and as we came to a halt it overtook us, the driver indicating that we should follow him. He led us to a concrete pad in a clearing in the wood, where the skipper shut down the engines and we all got out. Almost immediately a squad of about twenty Germans came marching towards us. They were carrying rifles and our airborne troops lost no time in setting up two or three tripod mounted machine guns. An agitated passenger jumped out of a vehicle and explained in English that he was the Commandant's interpreter and that the armed men were not going to attack us, they were merely coming to guard our aircraft. The officer in charge of the airborne lads told the interpreter that we didn't need their guards and instructed him to tell the armed men to withdraw. The interpreter promptly complied and the armed men about turned and disappeared.

Warrant Officer Miller's crew at Eggemoen, with local reporter Laura Lyngved. Left to right, Flight Serge Gordon Husband (flight engineer), Flight Sergeant Idwal Davies (bomb aimer), Warrant Officer Jack Ho (navigator), Flight Sergeant Don Veitch (wireless operator), Flight Sergeant Stan White (air gunner), L; Lyngved and Warrant Officer Ron Miller (pilot). (*190 & 620 Sqns Archive*)

utenant Colonel Cook of the South Staffordshire Regiment salutes as the Norwegian National Anthem is played
Iønefoss. Members of Warrant Officer Miller's crew are in the crowd behind him.
*J & 620 Sqns Archive)*

A German staff car then arrived, carrying the commandant. He asked for the senior air force officer, through his interpreter, and our skipper explained that Lt Col Cook, the officer in charge of the airborne men, was the senior officer. However, the commandant explained that he wanted to hand over the airfield, but only to the senior air force officer, so our skipper, Ron Miller, who was a Warrant Officer, was put in charge.

The skipper asked the interpreter to inform the Norwegians of our arrival and request from them transport to take the troops to Oslo. An hour or so later a busload of police arrived from Hønefoss, followed by a female reporter named Laura Lyngved from a local newspaper, *Ringerikes Blad*. The police loaned us the bus and driver to take the airborne troops to Oslo.

At this time communications in Norway were difficult and we were not able to contact our base until mid-morning on the 11 May. On that day, the weather was much better and we able to take off for our return to base, via Peterhead for refuelling.

The AOC 38 Group, AVM James Scarlett-Streatfeild, had chosen to go to Gardermoen in one of the two 190 Squadron Stirlings that were still missing. It had been intended that he should fly with Wg Cdr Briggs, 190 Squadron's CO, in aircraft 'L9-J', along with General Urquhart and a Brigadier of the 1st Airborne Division. Owing to the limited number of crew seats in the Stirling, there was then a fateful change of plan:

'Buster' Briggs recalled:

On 10 May, I flew General Urquhart of the 1st Airborne Division to Norway. At the last moment the AOC 38 Group had come up to me and asked 'Buster, can I fly there with you?' I replied that I already had the General with me and that the Stirling only had one comfortable seat (the co-pilot's). He then asked me who else was going, and I replied 'Squadron Leader Robertson, commanding "A" Flight'. 'OK', replied the AOC, 'I know Robbie. I'll go with him.'

The weather across the North Sea was terrible, and all the mountains in Norway were covered in cloud. My navigator, Flt Lt Bob Seymour, with whom I had flown for almost three years, said it was impossible to land, but that he could put us within a mile of the airfield as our navigational system, called 'Rebecca', was working intermittently. I therefore offered the General and his staff our RAF type parachutes, and said I would let him bale out from 2,000 feet above the ground! He declined, so we turned for home.

After about another 10 minutes my navigator said that the 'Rebecca' was working better, and he thought he could get us in. So I turned back – in trepidation – and made a descent through cloud, which we broke out of at about 200 feet, in a valley with fir trees above us on each side and with the runway straight ahead. So I landed the General safely, together with his staff, but it was a very near squeak.

The next news of the two missing aircraft came on 12 May. Fg Off Eric Atkinson and his crew had survived a ditching in LJ899 'L9-Z', along with fourteen of their eighteen passengers, who were soldiers of the King's Own Scottish Borderers, under the command of a Canadian officer, Major Donald Hartt. Fg Off Atkinson, who had crashed at Great Dunmow six days earlier, still had very limited experience on Stirlings when he took off on 'Doomsday' (at the time of the ditching he had thirteen hours on type). LJ899 had gone out of control, in very turbulent conditions, after some fabric on the port wing had come loose. Atkinson did well to recover from this situation, but the aircraft had descended to a height of about 500 feet and the port wing was nearly stalling. He therefore elected to put down in Røgden Lake, which is on the border between Norway and Sweden, and near the Swedish town of Torsby. The aircraft struck a pine tree on the eastern side of the lake, then it went into the water. As it did so, the rear fuselage broke, and four of the soldiers in that part of the aircraft were drowned. Their bodies were recovered by the Swedish authorities, and buried on 16 May at Fryksände churchyard in Torsby, although their graves were later moved to Kviberg Cemetery. The Stirling crew and the remaining troops were allowed to make their way overland to Norway, where the bomb aimer, Fg Off Long, was admitted to Middel Skole Hospital, in Oslo. Two of the soldiers were also slightly injured.

The last 'Doomsday' aircraft to be accounted for was LK297 'G', captained by Sqn Ldr Robertson, and carrying AVM Scarlett-Streatfeild and seventeen troops. The wreckage of this Stirling was not discovered until 21 June. It had flown into high ground to the north of Oslo, killing all on board. The casualties were buried at the Vestre Gravlund, Oslo, on 2 July, with Group Captain McIntyre and two former members of 190 Squadron being among the 38 Group personnel who flew to Norway to attend the funeral.

The 'Doomsday' flights to Gardermoen resumed on the morning of 11 May, with 190 and 620 Squadrons each sending twelve aircraft loaded with troops, motorcycles and supply containers. The weather was now much improved and all the

artime view of Gardermoen airfield. (*Arne Egner via 190 & 620 Sqns Archive*)

tirling lands at Gardermoen during Operation 'Doomday'. (*Arne Egner via 190 & 620 Sqns Archive*)

Stirling LK250 'QS-F' of 620 Squadron at Gardermoen, viewed from underneath the nose of 'Bitter Sweet' (LK124 '5G-B' of 299 Squadron). (*Arne Egner via 190 & 620 Sqns Archive*)

...atroops of the 1st Airborne Division, flown to Gardermoen in 620 Squadron's 'D4-N', captained by Flying ...cer de Rome. (*N.R. Chaffey*)

Dunmow Stirlings arrived safely, including the one from 190 Squadron that had stopped overnight at Vaaler.

Malcolm Mitchell recalled:

On the 11 May we flew to Gardermoen again. This crossing of the North Sea was interrupted by having to conduct a square search of an area of sea where two of our aircraft were believed to have ditched the day before, but we found nothing, unfortunately. We then flew on to Gardermoen with our supplies.

George Dann recalled:

At Gardermoen, supply containers were dropped by each Stirling first, and then airborne troops were landed. Later we had the spectacle of German soldiers filing along in a queue, dumping their weapons in heaps, under the watchful eyes of the Paras.

There were Ju 88s of II/KG 26 and IV/NJG 3, and Ju 188s of III/KG 26, scattered around Gardermoen airfield (the *Nachtjagerstaffel Norwegen* had been renamed as IV/NJG 3 in March 1945). While they were exploring the *Luftwaffe* camp at Gardermoen, Flt Lt Marshall and his 620 Squadron crew made a strange discovery, which explained what had happened to their comrades who were in Stirling LJ970 'QS-S', the only Allied aircraft lost over Norway on the night of 28/29 December 1944.

Jim Marshall recalled:

The photograph of our crew gathered around a machine-gun does have a story – we landed at Gardermoen as the Germans were being moved into holding

Troops of the 1st Airborne Division gather up the supply containers dropped by parachute at Gardermoen. (*Imperial War Museum, CL2639*)

camps and when we crossed behind some barracks a fire attracted our attention. We pulled out this machine-gun which had belonged to an aircraft of 620 Squadron that had been shot down over Norway. On the side the *Luftwaffe* had painted: '*Abschuss am 28.12.44. Hauptmann Vogt*'. I guess they were trying to destroy evidence though I do not know why – perhaps Vogt was concerned that we would be vengeful.

This machine-gun was one of the four that had been manned by Flt Sgt Billy Hughes, the gunner in Fg Off Jack McNamara's crew. *Hauptmann* Vogt (or Voigt)

Flight Sergeants Eddie French, Ernie Fletcher and 'Jock' Johnson of 620 Squadron, with a Ju 188 night-fighter, which would have been one of their adversaries over Norway, not long before this photograph was taken on 11 May 1945. (*190 & 620 Sqns Archive*)

Flight Lieutenant Jim Marshall and his crew examine the Browning machine-gun from 620 Squadron's 'S-Sugar', shot down on 28 December 1944. (*190 & 620 Sqns Archive*)

The inscription on the machine-gun from 620 Squadron's 'S-Sugar'. (*190 & 620 Sqns Archive*)

had been in command of the IV/NJG 3 detachment at Gardermoen. It was later learned that he had taken a Ju 88 and flown to Hamburg shortly before the arrival of the 'Doomsday' force.

On 11 May, there was another tragic accident, linked to 'Doomsday'. Arrangements were made to fly Fg Off Insley and his 190 Squadron crew, who were stranded at Eindhoven, back to the UK in an American C-46. This aircraft's crew failed to receive the message asking them to provide the Stirling crew with transport, and took off without them. The latter crew therefore accepted an offer of a flight in a Wellington of 69 Squadron, but this aircraft swung on take-off and crashed into a building. Insley was seriously injured, and was admitted to a British Army Hospital at Eindhoven. His bomb aimer, Flt Sgt Sharp, escaped with minor injuries, but the other crew members, Fg Off Vanular, WO Coghlan, WO Hay and Flt Sgt Dexter, were all killed.

Operation 'Doomsday' continued on 12 May, with fifteen aircraft from 190 Squadron, and sixteen from 620 Squadron, taking off from Great Dunmow. Two of the Stirlings experienced technical problems and turned back, but the rest were successful in delivering a varied load of troops, supply containers and panniers, motorcycles and bicycles to Gardermoen. The next day, 13 April, 190 and 620 Squadrons each sent a further thirteen aircraft to Gardermoen, carrying containers and petrol.

Malcolm Mitchell recalled:

The third time that we flew to Gardermoen, on 12 May, we were allowed to stay for a while, so a group of us decided to make our way down to Oslo. We found the road and started to walk down it. Soon we heard the sound of a vehicle behind us. We gathered across the road, to see a German truck, fuelled by a gas bag on its top, coming towards us. Waving our guns, we forced it to stop, and, despite the driver's grumbles, we made him drive us into Oslo, one of us sitting in the driver's cab, with a pistol trained on him! In Oslo, having been given military money, we all piled into a restaurant – quite an experience, as the meal was very basic and primitive. We then began to stroll through the town, followed by a number of admiring young girls. Also wandering aimlessly through the town were a number of Russian POWs, whom the British forces had liberated. I was able to have some conversation with them, using the Norwegian girls as interpreters.

Finally, we made our way to the station, for the train back to Gardermoen, only to find that the next train to go there was leaving the following morning! However, after speaking to the station master, we were given permission to sleep in a waiting room, on benches. The next morning we queued at the ticket office, and I was approached by a young ex-POW Russian, who fully intended to buy a ticket back to Russia! He had seen, and wanted, a hammer and sickle star badge that I always wore – illegally – on my uniform. I told him, 'No, me a Communist', pointing to myself. He then brought out a rouble note, with the picture of Lenin on it. At this, I pointed to the picture, gave the 'thumbs up' sign, and accepted the trade. I still have the note.

So we got back to Gardermoen, a small settlement which looked rather like a town of the American West, with raised wooden sidewalks and wooden buildings, the roadway not being made up. We walked back to the airfield, to find that supplies had been dropped by parachute, and that there were a number of parachutes lying about. We grabbed these and cut them up to make

Ju 88, bogged down and abandoned at Gardermoen. (*Arne Egner via 190 & 620 Sqns Archive*)

knickers for our ladies. I then strolled over to a Junkers 88, climbed on, and managed to remove an instrument, as a souvenir. Later I was reunited with my crew, and we flew back to Dunmow. Thus ended my experience of Norway.

Noel Chaffey recalled:

On 13 May, we flew again to Gardermoen, this time with ten containers and eighty-four jerricans of petrol. We stayed for the day and had time to look around. We went outside the airfield area into the scenic countryside and saw the buildings of the enemy camp amongst the pine trees. We approached the Officers' Mess, a large building with an open-spaced verandah and a great staircase leading to the front door, but after seeing a couple of enemy soldiers approaching from the woods we made a polite retreat back to the safety of the airfield.

The containers we dropped had 'chutes made of nylon and these were all collected and brought back to our aircraft to be returned to stores at Great Dunmow for repacking. However, they were minus one, from which we had discarded the webbing and shroud strings over the North Sea. Frank took the nylon home, so that his wife Flo could make square scarves for each of us, with our initials embroidered in the corner – I still have mine!

The flights on 13 May completed Great Dunmow's contribution to 'Doomsday', which had taken 36 hours longer than expected, mainly because of the bad weather at the start of the operation. There were further supply flights to Gardermoen on 15 May, when five aircraft of 620 Squadron transported mail and rations. The same day, three others from 620 Squadron carried out Air-Sea Rescue duties over the North Sea, while 190 Squadron ferried eight of its Stirlings to Maghaberry in Northern Ireland for disposal. Three Dakotas were provided to fly crews back to Great Dunmow, during the time that these ferry flights were taking place.

On 18 May, ten aircraft of 620 Squadron flew American ex-POWs from Brussels to Chilbolton in Hampshire. Plans for similar flights over the next three days could not be implemented, owing to bad weather. No. 620 Squadron had five aircraft ready to take food to Norway on 21 May, but the weather delayed their departure. They took off on 23 May, only to be recalled to base as conditions worsened again.

At one of Great Dunmow's dispersals, Warrant Officer Noel Chaffey poses in the spring sunshine for the camer Flight Sergeant Frank Pearman. The Stirling in this picture, LK294 'D4-V', was with 620 Squadron fr September 1944 to June 1945. It was eventually struck off charge in 1946, as a result of a flying accident w serving with 299 Squadron. (*N.R. Chaffey*)

Finally, on 24 May, they succeeded in reaching their destination. Meanwhile, 190 Squadron concentrated on conversion to the Halifax, with the last of its Stirlings being ferried to Northern Ireland on 26 May.

On 30 May, 620 Squadron took troops to Brussels and brought back ex-POWs to Dunsfold. The squadron also transported troops to Brussels the following day, but two of its Stirlings were unable to return, after one taxied into another, causing serious damage to both.

At the end of May 1945, there were signs of the transition to a much smaller, peacetime Royal Air Force, as the first lists of personnel to be released from the service were issued. But the Allies were still at war with Japan, and on 24 May it was announced that 620 Squadron would be transferring to the Far East Air Force, along with the Halifax squadrons from Tarrant Rushton, Nos 298 and 644. In the end, only 298 Squadron made this move, because there was a change of plan, which meant that 620 and 644 Squadrons would remain in the UK for a few more months, before going to the Middle East instead.

# CHAPTER 11

# Keeping the Peace

## June 1945 to August 1946

At the beginning of June 1945, the 190 Squadron aircrews were busy with their Halifax conversion programme. Meanwhile, the 620 Squadron Stirlings were being used for trooping flights to Brussels, but their crews were also able to carry out a few Halifax conversion flights, when not fully engaged in their transport tasks. On 1 June, an administrative change, which affected 190 and 620 Squadrons, was the transfer of 38 Group from Fighter Command to a more logical placing in Transport Command.

After a day's stand-down at Great Dunmow on 6 June, to mark the first anniversary of D-Day, 620 Squadron continued the trooping flights to Brussels. These were completed on 10 June. There was not much flying on 12 and 13 June, as 190 and 620 Squadrons interchanged many of their aircrews. Quite a few of those posted from 190 Squadron to 620 Squadron had already converted to the Halifax, so they were ready to fly this type as soon as the latter unit phased out its Stirlings. 190 Squadron then resumed its Halifax conversion programme, for the crews posted across from 620 Squadron. Over the next few days, there were no transport flights for either of the Dunmow squadrons, but they did take part in a number of glider-towing exercises, by both day and night, as well as container drops, cross-countries and fighter affiliation work.

und crew personnel, with a Halifax of 620 Squadron at Great Dunmow. (*190 & 620 Sqns Archive*)

On 19 June, seven aircraft from 190 Squadron, and ten from 620 Squadron, took part in Group Exercise 'Renaissance', towing Horsa Mk I gliders. These were being ferried to Thruxton in Wiltshire, where they would eventually be scrapped, but their final flights also served a useful purpose, since some operational training was carried out on the way. For Sgt Roy Gould, an RAF pilot seconded to 'M' Squadron, Glider Pilot Regiment, this exercise turned out to be an alarming one, as he later reported:

In order to obtain maximum benefit the flight was planned as a cross-country and named Exercise 'Renaissance', with a fighter affiliation exercise at some point *en route*. Horsa HG802 was flown by Flying Officer K.W.E. Loman and Sergeant R. Gould, Squadron Intelligence Officer and Sergeant respectively. The formation initially followed a northerly course towards the King's Lynn area, where a mock attack by Tempests took place, the fighters zooming up through the formation, giving the tug rear-gunners little opportunity to flash a warning to the gliders. Shortly after this, the Horsa became laterally unstable and difficult to hold in position behind the tug. The glider was carrying a number of screw pickets for the purpose of securing it on arrival and the second pilot went back to see whether they had moved to cause the instability. There had however been no movement but as a precaution they were moved to one side in an effort to alleviate the problem, but with little effect. During this time, there had been no communication from the tug, but this was not unusual because the intercom wire through the towing cable frequently broke under tension.

The interior of Horsa HG802, after its crash-landing at Thruxton. (*R. Gould*)

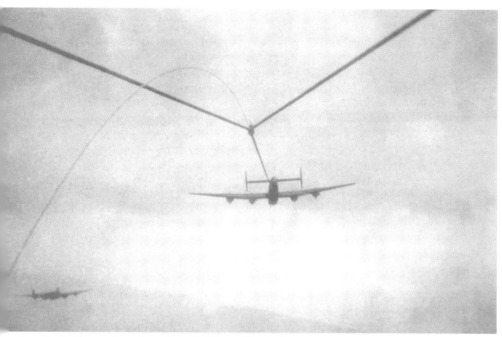

view of a Halifax tug from the cockpit of a Horsa glider in the 'low tow' position. The thin, curved line is the ercom cable between the tug and glider. (*R. Gould*)

However, on release from the tow at Thruxton the glider became extremely unstable, yawing to the right but at the same time dropping the left wing. All the strength of both pilots was required to maintain some semblance of control. The situation was made worse when the flaps were lowered, with the aircraft stabilising momentarily, then swinging in the opposite direction. Partially raising the flaps gave a degree of control, but it still required the efforts of both pilots. The very erratic approach resulted in a heavy touchdown and a series of bounces, culminating in the nosewheel leg coming up through the cockpit floor and the aircraft sliding across a runway. The smell of burning wood prompted a very rapid evacuation.

Subsequent examination revealed that the fabric covering the joint between the starboard wing and the centre section had come loose and jammed the flap on that side in the half-down position (the flaps on the Horsa were lowered by compressed air and raised by bungee cord). The result of an examination by the Station Engineer Officer was even more disturbing, for he announced that in his opinion the aircraft was in Category 'E' condition (i.e. a write-off) when it was handed over to the crew and that the wing had been moving in flight. The Horsa was only fitted with lap belts with the result that both pilots jack-knifed on impact and sustained severe abdominal bruising.

Fg Off Loman and Sgt Gould had gained their 'Wings' overseas before being posted to the Glider Pilot Regiment, and shortly after their Horsa accident they both returned to the RAF to complete their training at a (Pilot) Advanced Flying Unit. Sadly, Ken Loman and another former 'M' Squadron glider pilot were killed during this training, when their Oxford aircraft flew into high ground at night. After being

283

demobbed, Roy Gould went on to have an interesting career in non-destructive testing of aircraft structures and components.

During the latter part of June, the flying programme at Great Dunmow was taken up mainly with further training flights, but five Halifaxes from 190 Squadron flew to Brussels on 25 June, and returned to Dunsfold with troops coming home on leave. On 29 June, three of 620 Squadron's Stirlings were sent to Northern Ireland for disposal, and six Halifaxes were collected from Tarrant Rushton. Having been postponed for two days because of poor weather, Exercise 'Residue' took place on 30 June. This was run along the same lines as 'Renaissance', with 190 and 620 Squadrons towing the last of 'M' Squadron's Horsa Mk I gliders to Thruxton.

Wg Cdr Briggs had been posted from 190 Squadron to 620 Squadron on 25 June. He succeeded Wg Cdr Wynne-Powell as 620 Squadron's CO on 1 July, the same day that Wg Cdr L.C. Bartram took over as CO of 190 Squadron. However, the recent redistribution of aircrews at Great Dunmow had left 190 Squadron with a shortfall. In order to return 190 Squadron to its full complement, now set at twenty crews, it was necessary to post in some personnel from the Operational and Refresher Training Unit. This was based at Matching, a few miles south of Great Dunmow, and had also recently converted from Stirlings to Halifaxes. By this time, most of the aircrew personnel from the Dominions of the Commonwealth were either on their way home or awaiting embarkation. One of the Australians who bade his crew farewell was Flying Officer Noel Chaffey of 620 Squadron:

> During my last phase of flying with 620 Squadron, I'd been requested to attend an interview at Group HQ, as the result of which I was commissioned as a Flying Officer, a lowly rung on the ladder of promotion for an officer, but at least my pay was increased.
>
> I didn't really have time to get used to the Officers' Mess or duties, though whilst still a Warrant Officer I had gained some experience as Station Orderly Officer. For example, one day I inspected the Mess huts for cleanliness and the standard of food. I advanced into the dining hut of the Sergeants' Mess, preceded by a Flight Sergeant orderly NCO, who yelled, 'Any complaints?' and they stood *en masse*. As it happened, they had fish, but it sure was on the turn. The cook, a fat slob of a sergeant, came forward as ordered and was asked to explain why and how the meal was so bad – 'I can only do my best with what they give me' – was the reply, much to the laughter from the standing mass. Had I not been there with pistol ready, just in case, the cook could well have been left steaming in one of his vats. Ah, the joys of authority!
>
> Soon after that, we had news of postings. The Commonwealth members of the squadron were all to return to their countries and others were to re-crew as necessary. We had a final parade on the Station, when Free French General Koenig presented *Croix de Guerre* medals from a grateful France for our help to the *Maquis*. Letters of thanks and congratulations were received too from other countries, including Belgium, Holland, Denmark and Norway, and later some of our boys would be personally awarded medals from Heads of State.
>
> So I said goodbye to my crew, Pete Griffin being the last to see me. His bed was next to mine, and I'd called back to the hut to get the last of my gear after saying goodbye to others on site. We parted with a handshake and 'I'll be seeing you, Pete'. But I never did; he died some time after the war, with a brain tumour, but not before he had two boys and a girl. The eldest, Brian, is the spitting image of his Dad so he would never die for me.

During the first few days of July 1945, 620 Squadron sent its remaining Stirlings to Northern Ireland. Meanwhile, 190 Squadron's Halifax aircraft were moving both freight and passengers to and from the continent, and visited various UK airfields, including Tarrant Rushton, Dunsfold and Warmwell, on these trips. By the third week of July, 620 Squadron was also up and running with its new aircraft, and becoming involved in a wide range of transport tasks. Other flying details formed part of a monthly training syllabus, which had been drawn up for both the Dunmow squadrons. This included instrument approach procedures, glider towing, parachute dropping, fighter affiliation and formation flying. There were also some long cross-country exercises, for improving 'crew efficiency and endurance'. Relying mainly on dead reckoning for navigation, these flights often lasted over ten hours.

On 13 July, twenty aircraft from 620 Squadron towed gliders during Group Exercise 'Angus', with P-47 Thunderbolts of the USAAF playing the part of the enemy. The gliders were released to land at Rivenhall, from where they were retrieved later the same day. On 24 July, 620 Squadron also took part in Exercise 'Release', towing gliders to Earls Colne. On 30 July, the squadron took part in Exercise 'Barry', dropping paratroops in Scotland.

Gp Capt McIntyre handed over command of Great Dunmow to Gp Capt H.A. Purvis DFC AFC on 16 July. A couple of days later, there was a stand-down for the Station Sports Day, but both squadrons were back in the air immediately after this break, carrying out transport flights to destinations that included Brussels, Gardermoen and Schleswig.

Towards the end of July, the Dunmow flying programme concentrated on further training flights, including a 190 Squadron versus 620 Squadron night cross-country

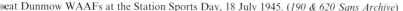

…eat Dunmow WAAFs at the Station Sports Day, 18 July 1945. (*190 & 620 Sqns Archive*)

and container-dropping contest. On 27 July, Wg Cdr Briggs was posted to take command of 570 Squadron at Rivenhall. He was succeeded as 620 Squadron's CO by Wg Cdr K.R. Slater AFC.

On 1 August, fourteen aircraft of 190 Squadron were scheduled to fly from Great Dunmow to Prague, but their departure was delayed by wet weather. The rain had cleared the next day, so they were then able to proceed, carrying 123 Czech military and civilian personnel, plus some 'special freight'. For the crew captained by Fg Off Britten, this was their first transport flight with 190 Squadron, which they had joined a few days earlier. Their air gunner was Flt Sgt Howard Whitehead:

> On 2 August we set off from Great Dunmow in a Halifax, to carry freight to Prague. The flying time was 3 hours 55 minutes and we arrived in the afternoon. I believe ours were the first Allied aircraft to land there since the end of hostilities with Germany. At that time, the Russian military forces were still in occupation of Czechoslovakia, and, as we learned later, much to the annoyance of the civil leaders and population. There was no love lost between the two parties. The Russian Air Force controlled the airfield, and as our aircraft came to a halt at the dispersal point we had the surprise of our lives. We were besieged by dozens of Russian Air Force personnel, who looked more like brigands than airmen. They were as determined to enter the aircraft as we were to keep them out. Quite a task!
>
> We were eventually welcomed by civic dignitaries, after being taken to a hotel for a wash and brush-up – with no soap provided. We were then taken to a night club for food and drink. There were speeches of welcome and thanks for delivering the 'freight', which we believed was bullion. It had been in three wooden crates in the aircraft and guarded by armed soldiers during the journey.
>
> During the celebrations everything suddenly went quiet. The reason for this was a visit by the Russian Military Police. They walked around with an air of importance. Our hosts remained completely silent as a protest to their presence – the Russians eventually left. The celebrations recommenced. We raised our glasses to each other. Our hosts shouted '*Selio*' and threw their empty glasses against the wall, I think in disgust and annoyance at the Russians being in their country.

Over the next few days, both 190 and 620 Squadrons were occupied with air tests, in preparation for a variety of transport tasks to Belgium, Norway and Denmark. The conversion from Stirlings to Halifaxes at Great Dunmow had been remarkably trouble free, with only a couple of incidents, which resulted in nothing more serious than damaged tailwheels. However, on 5 August, Halifax NA450 'D4-Q' of 620 Squadron crashed while attempting to take off at Warmwell, after completing a troop-ferrying flight to this Dorset airfield. When all the fuel warning lights came on (probably because of an electrical fault), the pilot, Fg Off Simpson, had no option but to abort the take-off. He tried to avoid overshooting the runway by deliberately ground-looping the aircraft, but it struck a hedge and the undercarriage collapsed, fortunately without causing any injury to the six crew members.

On 11 August, two aircraft from 190 Squadron flew servicing personnel and equipment to Brussels, where they were to set up a staging post for 'Hellas'. This operation was organised in order to repatriate Greek displaced persons, many of whom were in very poor shape after years of slave labour under the Nazis. The Dunmow crews were briefed for 'Hellas' on 13 August and seven aircraft from 190 Squadron, and eight from 620 Squadron, went to Brussels the next day, 14 August.

The start of the operation was then postponed, as Japan's surrender had just been announced.

15 August 1945 was VJ Day. In the expectation that celebrations might start very early, the Station Commander at Great Dunmow issued orders at 0020 hrs, to the effect that all MT vehicles were to be immobilised and all pyrotechnics, arms and ammunition locked away. At 0250 hrs, the operations block received a message, stating 'the WAAF site has been raided by irresponsible airmen' and that the Station Commander was proceeding there to quell the disturbance. Ten minutes later, the Duty Clerk in the operations block recorded that the building was now being 'invaded by a number of irresponsible aircrew and glider pilots with their female accomplices'. Everything was quiet again by daybreak, and later in the morning all available motor vehicles were being used to provide transport from the camp to Great Dunmow town and Chelmsford. Free cinema performances were staged throughout the day, which ended with a Grand Victory Dance and free beer for all ranks in the NAAFI.

As these celebrations were going on at Great Dunmow, the aircraft at Brussels were taking off on the first wave of 'Hellas' flights, transporting freight as well as passengers. Their route to Hassani airfield, near Athens, took in refuelling stops at Istres and Foggia. The return journey was made via the same staging posts, but landing in the UK at St Mawgan in Cornwall, rather than at base. The 'Hellas'

The members of a 620 Squadron crew visit the Acropolis, after landing at Athens. Standing, left to right, Flight Sergeant Anderson (2nd pilot), Flight Sergeant Hughes (wireless operator) and Flying Officer Rostron (navigator); sitting, left to right, Flight Sergeant Venning (flight engineer), Flying Officer Harrison (pilot) and Flying Officer Kitchener (air gunner). (*190 & 620 Sqns Archive*)

flights were to continue into the first fortnight of September, while there were also many shorter flights to continental destinations by both the Dunmow squadrons. All this activity meant that plans to work a 5½-day week at Great Dunmow, with flying being kept to a minimum at weekends, soon had to be shelved.

Malcolm Mitchell, 620 Squadron, recalled:

> One task given us was the ferrying of 'Displaced Persons' back to their home countries. We took some to Greece, dropping in on Italy to refuel on the way. We were then fortunate enough to spend a few days billeted by the Aegean Sea, after flying down the length of the Corinth Canal, its sides level with the wings of our aircraft. The Aegean was a marvellously clear sea, in which we swam, looking down at the rocks below. One day we drove to Athens, noticing people lying in hovels like slit trenches by the side of the road. I then saw the Acropolis high on its hill, whilst driving into town. Athens seemed untouched by the war, and quite a busy city.

On 2 September, a 620 Squadron Halifax, NA411 'QS-K', was badly damaged in an accident at Great Dunmow. As the pilot attempted to take off on a cross-country flight, he found the ailerons could not be moved. He closed the throttles and applied the brakes, but these actions came too late to prevent a crash off the end of the runway. A fire that broke out around the starboard outer engine was quickly extinguished, and the crew vacated the aircraft safely. Examination of the aircraft at the scene of the accident suggested that the control locks might not have been disengaged during the pre-flight checks. The captain of the aircraft was subsequently tried by court martial. He was defended by a civilian barrister, Mr Bernard Gillis KC, and acquitted of the charges brought against him.

On 1 September, thirteen aircraft from 190 and 620 Squadrons had taken off from Brussels, carrying displaced persons to Athens. They were expected to return on 3 September, bringing soldiers home on leave. At Hassani airfield, one of the 620 Squadron aircraft, PN298, swung to starboard as it attempted to take off. It then crashed into some staging post buildings, killing an airman. The crew of the Halifax and their fifteen army passengers all escaped without any serious injuries. The pilot of the Halifax was immediately grounded, and soon declared redundant by the RAF.

In September, Wg Cdr Slater was succeeded as CO of 620 Squadron by Wg Cdr R.I. Alexander DFC. The weather put a stop to most of the flying at Great Dunmow on 14 September, but in the afternoon there was a parade, at which Wg Cdr Alexander received 620 Squadron's squadron crest from the AOC 38 Group, Air Vice-Marshal R. Ivelaw-Chapman CBE DFC AFC. The crest comprised 'In front of a demi-pegasus couped, a flash of lightning' and the motto: *Dona ferentes adsumus* (We are bringing gifts). The AOC took the salute as the ceremony ended with a march-past. On Saturday 15 September, the first of the annual Battle of Britain air displays took place at RAF stations. Halifaxes towed gliders from Great Dunmow to displays at Aldergrove, Chilbolton, Fairwood Common, and Holmsley South. Three aircraft from 620 Squadron also went to Holland, to demonstrate a container drop at the Hague.

Ken Wilson, 620 Squadron, recalled:

> One of the jobs I did with a Halifax was to give an air display at Chilbolton. Before the flying programme commenced, the great British public were invited to climb aboard and inspect the aircraft. While the crew had lunch in the Mess,

local ground crew personnel were supposed to keep an eye on things in the cockpit; it seemed, however, they failed to notice some grubby little nipper busy unscrewing the escape hatch over the pilot's seat.

As the show started I took off down the runway, then at 200 feet, with max boost and revs, the hatch blew off and I was immediately blinded by the dust blowing up from the floor. Unable to see very much, and deafened by the slipstream, I did a very hairy low level circuit and pulled off a horrendous landing after bouncing the length of the runway. What a disgraceful display after winning the war! At the end of the show a local farmer turned up with my battered hatch, which still fitted well enough for me to be able to fly back to base and explain myself!

On 17 September, six aircraft from 620 Squadron flew to Manston, where they were to take part in Exercise 'Rookie'. This consisted of a series of air experience flights for paratroops. As it landed at the end of the first wave, Halifax PN291 'D4-T' burst a tyre, then its undercarriage collapsed and the starboard outer engine caught fire. All seven crew members and fifteen passengers safely evacuated the aircraft, which was later struck off charge.

The next day, 18 September, seven aircraft from 190 Squadron, and eight from 620 Squadron, flew to Colerne in Wiltshire, to collect further gold bullion for the Czech Government. Two of the 620 Squadron aircraft, 'D4-S' and 'QS-O', were involved in a taxiing collision at Colerne, so two more had to be sent as replacements. Bad weather delayed the start of the operation until 20 September, when the fifteen aircraft took off for Prague, carrying between them 30 tons of gold and forty-one passengers, including a number of armed guards. Four more aircraft, two from each of the Dunmow squadrons, flew out with bullion the following day.

On 21 September, 190 and 620 Squadrons took part in Group Exercise 'Womnud'', which ended with 110 gliders making a massed landing at Great Dunmow. Over the next few days, several 620 Squadron crews flew to Pershore and Kinloss to pick up new Halifax aircraft. Although the weather was not particularly good in September 1945, the many transport tasks and a busy training programme resulted in more hours being flown by 190 and 620 Squadrons than during the previous month.

There were no transport commitments for the Dunmow crews on 1 October, but there was yet another accident, this time involving Halifax PP341 of 620 Squadron. This aircraft struck a hangar while taxiing. Its captain faced a court martial, demonstrating that the post-war Air Force could afford to take a hard line when dealing with accidents allegedly caused by aircrew error.

On 3 October, twenty Halifax-Horsa combinations took off from Great Dunmow, as part of Group Exercise 'Doofah'. The gliders landed at Earls Colne on this occasion. Over the next few days, 190 and 620 Squadrons flew freight to Egypt and Palestine, as well as various European destinations.

A signal was received on 9 October, instructing 620 Squadron to get ready for a move to Tarrant Rushton, along with its engineering support unit, which had recently been renumbered as 4620 Servicing Echelon. Later in the month, it was decided to send 190 Squadron to Tarrant Rushton, instead of 620 Squadron, which would now wait to be transferred overseas. In preparation for this, 620 Squadron started ferrying its Halifaxes to various airfields, including Hawarden, High Ercall, Kinloss and Pershore, where they were exchanged for 'tropicalised' aircraft. Meanwhile, there were the usual training exercises at Great Dunmow, including 'Share-out', which ran from 16 to 20 October and included dropping of paratroops at Great Sampford. There were also dispatcher training flights for wireless operators, and further 'Rookie' air experience flights for paratroops, though the flying programme was slowed down during the last week of October, first by gales and then by rain and fog.

On 1 November, eight aircraft flew an advance party of 190 Squadron and 4190 Servicing Echelon personnel to Tarrant Rushton. The main party and eighteen aircraft followed four days later, with the final two aircraft completing the move the day after that. As 190 Squadron was arriving at Tarrant Rushton, 644 Squadron was exchanging the last of its old Halifax Mk III aircraft for Mk VIIs and preparing to fly out to Qastina, in Palestine. 'C' Squadron of the Glider Pilot Regiment left Tarrant Rushton on 14 November and was replaced the next day by 'G' Squadron. On 16 November, Group Captain W.M.C. Kennedy was posted from Leicester East to take over as Station Commander at Tarrant Rushton, where 190 Squadron was soon engaged in a training programme that included paratroop drops and the towing of 'G' Squadron's enormous Hamilcar gliders, each of which had an all-up-weight more than twice that of a Horsa.

By 1 December, 644 Squadron's move to Palestine was practically complete, leaving 190 Squadron to operate out of Tarrant Rushton on various transport tasks over the next few weeks. Among these tasks was long-distance towing of gliders, including seven Hamilcars taken to France on 30 December. These were loaded with 'BABS' radio equipment for delivery to staging post airfields at Rennes, Bordeaux and Istres. The same day, two other aircraft took off with Horsas in tow, heading for Istres on the first leg of a journey to Qastina.

By the middle of January 1946, disposal of surplus Hamilcars was in progress. Over four successive days, 190 Squadron towed twenty-seven of them to Honeybourne in Worcestershire, where they were eventually scrapped.

On 21 January 1946, the Stirling-equipped 295 Squadron disbanded at Rivenhall, and 190 Squadron was renumbered as 295 Squadron. With the RAF's post-war run-down now gathering speed, the 'new' 295 Squadron only continued in the Halifax transport role for another two months at Tarrant Rushton, before it was, in turn, disbanded.

At Great Dunmow, the 620 Squadron crews had been carrying out transport flights to Germany and Egypt during the early part of November 1945. They maintained their glider-towing proficiency, and took part in Exercise 'Felix' on 7 November, when the Dunmow Horsas were taken on a cross-country before being released to land at base. However, over the next few days, 620 Squadron helped to dispose of more than seventy of these gliders, as they were ferried to Brize Norton, Thruxton, and Broadwell, and to the nearby Essex airfields of Gosfield and Wethersfield. Later in the month there were transport flights to Italy and North Africa, as well as dropping of paratroops at Great Sampford as part of Exercise 'Share-out'. The crews also spent many hours practising let-downs and approaches using Gee and BABS radio aids. These procedures had become standardised throughout Transport Command, but required good R/T communications, which were not always obtainable from the ageing installations at Great Dunmow.

It had recently been decided that 620 Squadron would be moving to Aqir, in Palestine. On 1 December, most of the aircrew personnel were sent on leave, but a couple of days later the air gunners were told that there was no requirement for them in the Middle East, so they were to be posted to other units. Five crews of 'C' Flight

...e Officers' Mess, RAF Great Dunmow, Christmas 1945. In the centre is the Station Commander, Group Captain ...rry Purvis DFC AFC, and on his left (with party hat) the President of the Mess Committee, Squadron Leader ...e Patient DFC of 620 Squadron. First in the line of guests on the left is Group Captain Douglas Bader DSO and ...r, DFC and Bar. (*190 & 620 Sqns Archive*)

stayed at Great Dunmow to carry out some air tests and local flying over the next fortnight. By the time the others had returned from leave, many of the ground personnel, including those belonging to 4620 Servicing Echelon, had gone to No. 1 Personnel Dispatch Centre, at West Kirby on the Wirral, to await embarkation. Plans were made for a number of new Halifaxes to be collected from Kinloss and High Ercall just before Christmas, but these flights had to be postponed because of bad weather. On 28 December the personnel at West Kirby travelled by rail to Southampton. There they joined the MV *Capetown Castle*, which set sail for Port Said during the afternoon of 29 December.

Since the move to the Middle East marked the end of 620 Squadron's time in 38 Group, the AOC, AVM Ivelaw-Chapman, sent the following message to Wg Cdr Alexander on 29 December:

> On your departure overseas I wish to send to you and to all ranks of your Squadron my thanks for all the excellent work you have put in for 38 Group. Coming to the Group after a period of strenuous operations in Bomber Command you quickly and effectively became part of the spearhead of Airborne Forces, a position you held with distinction in all the major airborne operations. All ranks, ground crew and air crew alike, have every reason to be proud of this record, which I know you will carry on in your new sphere of action. Good luck and Godspeed.

After 620 Squadron left Great Dunmow, there were no flying units based there. Few of the wartime buildings ha~ survived at the site of the airfield, but one that lasted longer than most was this unusual building, used by t~ parachute section. (*190 & 620 Sqns Archive*)

As dawn broke on 30 December, 620 Squadron's first wave of aircraft took off for Palestine. The weather was excellent for the first leg of their journey, to El Aouina in Tunisia. Fog meant that the departure of the second wave, planned for 31 December, was delayed, but these aircraft were able to leave on New Year's Day 1946, heading for Luqa airfield on Malta. During the first week of January 1946, most of the remaining aircraft completed the journey to Aqir, also via Malta, though some of the later ones ran into very stormy weather over the Mediterranean, as they headed for Aqir on the second leg.

WO Allan Schofield, 620 Squadron, recalled:

By January 1946 the rumours of an impending move of 620 Squadron from Great Dunmow to the Middle East had become a reality. Five aircraft each day were scheduled to take off for our new base at Aqir, in Palestine, which was under British mandate.

We were heading into a situation in which the Jews, homeless after the European upheaval, had decided that Palestine was their rightful home, and were migrating there across the Mediterranean Sea in large numbers. This was causing the Palestinian Arabs great concern, and Britain was obliged to send personnel to protect their interests. Little did we know that we were seeing the infancy of a conflict that still goes on, so many years later.

We were to have only one refuelling stop on our journey, at the island of Malta, and we duly arrived there, out of the chill of an English winter into

292

welcoming warm sunshine. I decided that this life would suit me well until my 'demob' date, which I was informed would be quite soon. Having refuelled, ready for the final leg, we became aware that our navigator had contracted a bad dose of influenza, and as it turned out we remained in Malta for eight days.

Our prolonged stay meant that as the other crews in the squadron came through we were expected to act as unofficial tour directors. We had, by this time, fully acquainted ourselves with the high (and low!) spots of the area. In particular, a certain section of Valetta, known affectionately as 'The Gut', was a great attraction for many servicemen.

However, one evening we were escorting a group that included a less than sober Scots NCO, who took exception to a decorative 'Officers Only' illuminated sign and proceeded to hurl a large stone, which shattered the glass display. The result was immediate and obviously pre-planned, as mean-looking men emerged from doorways along the alley, blocking thoughts of any rapid departure. We were saved by the arrival of the Maltese Police, who took us in for our protection and after some discussions let us go.

The mailship *Capetown Castle*, passing Gibraltar, *en route* for the Middle East with personnel of 620 Squadron and 4620 Servicing Echelon. (*W. Longhurst, via 190 & 620 Sqns Archive*)

The personnel making the sea voyage disembarked at Port Said in Egypt on 6 January, and reached Aqir, approximately 20 miles from Tel Aviv, a day later. Aqir airfield, which is now the Israeli Air Force's Tel Nof air base, had been con-

e rail transport from Port Said to Aqir was very basic. (*190 & 620 Sqns Archive*)

The 620 Squadron aircrews at RAF Aqir. *(190 & 620 Sqns Archive)*

structed for the RAF in 1941. It was an important staging post, used by aircraft flying to and from stations further east.

With the exception of one Halifax, which was unserviceable at Luqa, 620 Squadron's transfer to Palestine was complete by the end of the second week of January. There was then a spell of heavy rain, which grounded the aircraft, but also presented an opportunity to catch up with servicing work. As soon as conditions improved, there were air tests and other local flights to be carried out. Practice runs were made over a nearby DZ at Yibna, because the aircrews needed to maintain their proficiency in the parachute and glider-towing roles, so that they could still provide tactical air support, as well as a transport service. 620 Squadron also took on the responsibility of mail flights to the UK, usually via Luqa to Tarrant Rushton. These trips often gave the crews a chance to spend a few days' leave at home before returning to Aqir.

Allan Schofield recalled:

> I see from my Flying Log Book that during our stay at Aqir our main role was that of ferrying freight, mail, and the odd passenger. These flights took us to many countries, including Cyrenaica and Tripolitania within Libya, Malta and Greece, plus many places in Egypt, and we finally got the most coveted trip of all, the mail run to England. On one mail run stopover, I was especially pleased to be able to surprise my family by walking in and announcing that I was home on weekend leave from the Middle East! It was still January, and we discovered that English beer is not as warm as the Australians make out, certainly not after the heat of Palestine!

The 620 Squadron flight engineers roll out the barrel at Aqir. Warrant Officer Allan Schofield is at the back, far right. (*190 & 620 Sqns Archive*)

The cinema at RAF Aqir. (*190 & 620 Sqns Archive*)

We found that, on the whole, facilities at Aqir were very reasonable. We had a cinema and a decent-sized swimming pool, and who could forget the fruit shop? Unrelated to this, I am sure, was an outbreak of dysentery. I believe it was due to a fractured sewage pipe. Quite a few people were very ill, and some were sent home, but none of our crew or friends were affected.

Although the weather in Palestine made a pleasant change (most of the time) from the British winter climate, the personnel at Aqir accepted that they were highly unpopular among Jewish settlers, in what was a very unstable political situation. The British mandate to govern Palestine, which had been in force since 1920, allowed for the eventual establishment of a Jewish homeland. However, after the

The fruit shop. (*190 & 620 Sqns Archive*)

An Aqir billet, where mosquito nets were a necessity. (*190 & 620 Sqns Archive*)

A swimming gala in progress at RAF Aqir. (*190 & 620 Sqns Archive*)

A 'Donkey Derby' at Aqir. In the striped shirt is 620 Squadron's 'A' Flight Commander, Squadron Leader Patient DFC. (*J. Patient, via 190 & 620 Sqns Archive*)

'NAAFI up!' at Aqir. (*190 & 620 Sqns Archive*)

cessation of hostilities in Europe, survivors of the Holocaust were coming to Palestine in numbers that were difficult to regulate. At the same time, Zionist extremists were increasing their support for terrorist groups, of which Irgun and the Stern Gang were the most prominent. These groups regarded the British forces in Palestine as their targets.

Official station and squadron records make practically no mention of the tension that existed at Aqir and other RAF stations in Palestine, but those who served there with 620 Squadron well remember that they spent much of their time on guard duties, and went off the camp at their own risk. During January 1946, a number of airmen were badly beaten up after they had ventured into the nearby town of Rehovot, from where the sound of gunfire was heard at night. Soldiers of the British-trained Arab Legion were posted as guards at Aqir, but language difficulties often caused problems when trying to deploy them around the airfield.

Even without the difficulties associated with postings in hostile situations, morale was not good among many of the conscripted airmen stationed overseas, some of whom had been away from home for several years. Now that the war was over, they considered their duty had been done. They wished to be demobilised from the service as quickly as possible, or at least posted back to the UK. The government had failed to make clear its release policy for these men, whose dissent was about to be turned into direct action.

On 25 January, there were co-ordinated strikes by ground personnel at RAF stations all the way from the Middle East to Singapore. These put a stop to all transport flights from the UK to airfields east of Suez. The next day, everyone was back at work at Aqir, but there were still some forthright discussions going on between the CO of 620 Squadron and his airmen, who were also demanding that some local grievances be addressed.

All ranks at Aqir had been issued with weapons, and the terrorist threat was countered, or so they thought, when three saboteurs were apprehended at night, as they approached some parked aircraft. However, a few days later, on 28 January, a group of about ten terrorists drove a jeep and a truck into the station, in broad daylight. Disguised in RAF uniforms, they entered the armoury of 160 Maintenance Unit, where RAF personnel were held up at gunpoint. Arab civilian workers were then forced to load approximately 600 guns and a large quantity of ammunition onto the truck. The terrorists made off with their haul, but their getaway was foiled when the truck became stuck in the soft surface of the track they were following. By this stage, the alarm had been raised, but the terrorists managed to escape using the jeep, leaving the weapons and ammunition behind.

Allan Schofield recalled:

> The closest I came to contact with the terrorists was one evening, when I was informed that, because of some activity in the vicinity by these gangs, I was to be in charge of a truckload of personnel, to go out and do battle. Though I had a revolver strapped to my side, I was more than relieved when the operation was called off. Nothing of the John Wayne about me!

Following the short spell of heavy rain during the second week of January, the weather in Palestine was excellent for a while. The 620 Squadron crews enjoyed spectacular views as they flew on practice cross-countries, which took them through the Jordan Valley, over the Sea of Galilee, and in and out of the mountains to the west of these. A particularly novel experience was achieved by adjusting the aircraft's altimeter to the QNH (sea-level pressure setting), then flying just above the surface of the Dead Sea, where it read *minus* 1,200 feet.

During the first week of February, the squadron took part in Exercise 'Kick-Off III'. This comprised a drop of 6th Airborne Division paratroops at Yibna, followed by a short cross-country, with the aircraft formed into 'vics' of three. There were 'Snatch' exercises a few days later, the aim of these being to practise rapid loading and unloading of troops at various airfields, so as to keep to a minimum the time spent by the aircraft on the ground.

The weather broke again in the middle of February, this time with a vengeance. Gales, rain and hail put a stop to flights out of Aqir, while there were several inches of snow on the high ground surrounding Jerusalem. Heavy rain over the plains was followed by flooding, and the aerodrome at Aqir became unusable because of runway subsidence. Finally, there were thunderstorms, accompanied by more heavy rain.

The bad weather seriously disrupted transport flights to and from Palestine, and resulted in a backlog of airmail. 620 Squadron also had the responsibility of carrying out meteorological flights, but a good many of these had to be cancelled, or ended in diversions to other airfields, because of the conditions at Aqir. The purpose of these flights, which usually took about six hours, was to make observations for the Lydda Met Office, situated a few miles from Aqir. Two basic patterns were flown, each of them twice daily, with take-offs at 0400 and 1600 hrs. The first route extended 500 miles out over the Mediterranean, while the second went eastwards and passed overhead RAF Habbaniya, an airfield about 50 miles south-east of Baghdad. The aircraft flew out below the cloud base, if present, before their crews went on oxygen as they climbed to 20,000 feet for the return journey.

Beneath a cloudless sky, a 620 Squadron Halifax carries out a mail drop. (*190 & 620 Sqns Archive*)

at a contrast to the previous photograph: some of 620 Squadron's Halifax aircraft, seen in silhouette during a dle Eastern thunderstorm. (*190 & 620 Sqns Archive*)

As soon as the weather improved, 620 Squadron resumed its transport tasks throughout the Middle East Air Force area, and also brought RAF Regiment personnel from Italy to strengthen the airfield defences in Palestine. Allan Schofield recalled that one of these flights to Italy ended dramatically:

> One flight, to Bari in Italy, gave us a bit of excitement. On preparing to land it appeared that we had no brake pressure, and the Control Tower advised us that if the brakes failed on landing we should veer off the runway, as there happened to be a quarry at the far end! We were obliged to do so, and discovered that once off the runway we met a surface that distinctly resembled a close-up of the Moon; after a very bumpy ride our tailwheel was torn off and the main undercarriage was damaged. We never found out what eventually happened to 'D4-M', but later on, people returning from Bari reported that it was still there, and I believe it was written off.

There were paratroop-dropping exercises during February 1946, which involved the Halifaxes of both 620 and 644 Squadrons, plus a number of Dakotas. The latter aircraft are believed to have been sent initially as a detachment from 78 Squadron, based at Almaza, but records from June 1946 refer to a 'Dakota Flight' as part of 620 Squadron.

During the night of 25/26 February, British aircraft at Qastina, Petah Tiqva and Lydda were damaged by explosions, only a few days after an RAF radar installation on Mount Carmel had been attacked. The terrorists' targets at Qastina were eleven of 644 Squadron's Halifax aircraft. At least five of these were so badly damaged they were not worth repairing.

The continuing threat posed by the terrorist organisations was the main reason behind the decision to send 620 Squadron to the airfield at Cairo West in March

Warrant Officer Al Schofield (left) and his pilot, Flying Officer Ron Clement, with Halifax NA454 'D4-M', after their accident at Bari in Italy. This aircraft was eventually struck off charge in September 1946. (*190 & 620 Sqns Archive*)

1946. This airfield, situated a fair distance outside the Egyptian capital, was relatively safe, yet still within reasonable flying distance of the Palestinian airfields and DZs. Eleven of the squadron's aircraft left for Cairo West on 3 March, carrying the advance party, and were followed by the rest of the personnel within a week or so.

By the time 620 Squadron moved to the Middle East, none of the aircrews from Chedburgh or Leicester East remained. On the other hand, quite a number of the ground crew personnel saw continuous service with the squadron, at Chedburgh, Leicester East, Fairford, Great Dunmow, Aqir and Cairo West. One of them was Ray Seeley, a Flight Mechanic (Engines), who had joined 620 Squadron on its

This 644 Squadron Halifax, PN306, was one of those written off after the terrorist attack at Qastina on the nig 25/26 February 1946. (*190 & 620 Sqns Archive*)

A Halifax of 644 Squadron at Qastina, still standing, but badly damaged by a terrorist bomb placed in its starboard wheel-well on the night of 25/26 February 1946. (*190 & 620 Sqns Archive*)

formation in 1943, and stayed with it until September 1946, when it was renumbered. He recalled what happened upon their arrival at Cairo West:

> In March 1946, the activities of the 'Stern Gang' gave increased cause for concern and we moved to Cairo West until things settled down. We arrived at Cairo fairly late and then erected out tents, but during the night a severe sandstorm developed. We awoke to find all tents had been blown down and everything was covered in sand. The next few hours were spent in atrocious conditions, filling sandbags to anchor the tents. Of course in those days we had no personal protective kit (such as face masks) to help us, and we had to use handkerchiefs to keep some of the sand out of our mouths.

Allan Schofield recalled:

> It was decided to move us out of Palestine, and the squadron became based at Cairo West, which was about 20 miles out in the desert. In spite of its remoteness, the facilities were adequate, and certainly more modern in appearance than those at Aqir. We also had a house-boy to keep things tidy. His name was Abdul, and he liked to call me 'Sidky Pash'. Apparently, he saw in me some

Flying Officer Ron Clement, flying over Egypt. (*190 & 620 Sqns Archive*)

...s photograph, taken at Cairo West, gives a vivid impression of the scale and ferocity of a sandstorm. *...) & 620 Sqns Archive*)

...scene at Cairo West on 10 March 1946, as sandbags are used to anchor the tents. (*190 & 620 Sqns Archive*)

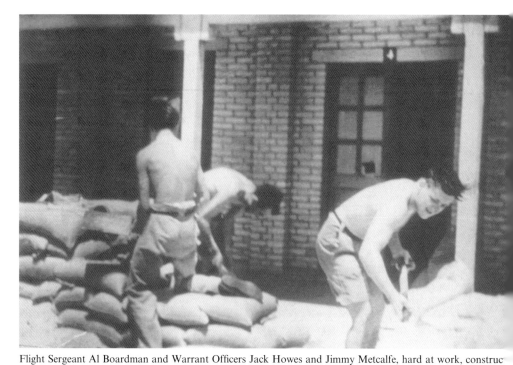

Flight Sergeant Al Boardman and Warrant Officers Jack Howes and Jimmy Metcalfe, hard at work, construc‑ walls of sandbags to protect a building at Cairo West from the sandstorm. (*190 & 620 Sqns Archive*)

resemblance to a certain Egyptian official. I never did find out whether or not this was flattering.

Being based in Egypt gave us the opportunity in our time off to visit the Pyramids and Sphinx at Giza, which was a marvellous experience. We made the 480-foot climb of the Great Pyramid of Cheops; not the safest of journeys, and I am not surprised that it is no longer permitted. In May, we were involved in an exercise which took us to Khartoum in the Sudan. The heat was stifling as we left the aircraft.

Things were not going well for the British in Egypt at that time. In Cairo itself anti-British feelings were apparent, and we were sometimes unable to safely walk the streets due to riots being in progress. After some four weeks or so of our transport duties at Cairo West I had to say farewell to 620 Squadron, having received a posting to a Personnel Transit Camp nearby, there to await my turn for the welcome boat home.

620 Squadron aircraft operated out of Cairo West on various transport and mail flights, but sent detachments to Aqir for paratroop exercises, which used the Yibna DZ. On 13 March, a large airborne exercise was staged. As part of this, 620 Squadron provided eleven aircraft to transport troops from Aqir to Habbaniya, the scenario being that an 'uprising' had started in Iraq. Unfortunately, one of the flight engineers, Sgt Francis Tarry, was killed the following day, when a lorry crashed while carrying crews on a 'liberty run' from Habbaniya to Baghdad.

At the beginning of April 1946, preparations were being made to transfer 620 Squadron from Cairo West to Shallufa, just north of Suez. Confusion reigned for

Pyramids, viewed from the gun turret of a 620 Squadron Halifax. (*190 & 620 Sqns Archive*)

...aring their Best Blues in the spring sunshine, 620 Squadron ground crew personnel visit the Pyramids. *& 620 Sqns Archive*)

A 620 Squadron Halifax, high above Egypt. (*190 & 620 Sqns Archive*)

the rest of the month. By 9 April, the aircraft had started to move to Shallufa, only for the squadron to be told that it had been decided to go back to Aqir. An advance party, carried in ten aircraft, flew to Aqir on 18 April, but on 28 April they were ordered to return to Cairo West.

Over the next few weeks, the flying programme at Cairo West settled down to the usual assortment of transport duties and training flights. On 11 June, 620 Squadron did move back to Aqir, where it was to remain for the rest of its existence. The squadron's Dakota Flight assisted by collecting personnel and kit from Cairo, before continuing with other tasks. These included the ferrying of aircraft spares between airfields in the Middle East, as well as taking part in weekly air landing exercises, flying troops to Cyprus.

In July 1946, the 620 Squadron Halifaxes flew to Kabrit, to tow Horsas on air tests. These gliders were then brought to Aqir, where they practised circuits and landings. On 22 July, a total of six crews from 620 Squadron left Qastina for St Mawgan in Cornwall, flying in four Halifax VIIs that had belonged to 644 Squadron. From St Mawgan, four of the crews flew on to Edzell in Scotland, where they exchanged the old aircraft for Halifax Mk IXs, which they ferried to Qastina. The two spare 620 Squadron crews collected two Halifax IXs from Pershore, also for delivery to Qastina. Towards the end of July, more Horsas were towed from Kabrit to Aqir. These glider movements continued throughout August 1946, during which there were further collections of Halifax IX aircraft from the UK.

The security situation in Palestine was now deteriorating rapidly. Irgun terrorists blew up the King David Hotel in Jerusalem on 22 July, killing ninety-one people,

Halifax PP344, after its undercarriage collapse at Aqir. This was the last accident to befall a 620 Squadron aircraft. *(190 & 620 Sqns Archive)*

twenty-eight of whom were British. In August, terrorists attacked two British ships being used for the deportation of immigrants, from Haifa to Cyprus. No. 620 Squadron was then called upon to fly out of Ein Shemer airfield on 'Sunburn' operations, searching for ships bringing further immigrants to Palestine. These sorties lasted up to twelve hours at a time. The squadron was also standing by in case it needed to assist in the rapid deployment of airborne troops, and on 14 August took part in an exercise, 'Staff Coll'. This involved glider towing and supply-dropping flights to Ramat David. On 21 August, Halifax PP344 'D4-Q' swung as a

Personnel of 113 Squadron, the short-lived successor to 620 Squadron. (*190 & 620 Sqns Archive*)

tyre burst on take-off at Aqir, causing the undercarriage to collapse. The aircraft was written off, but WO McKay and his crew were unhurt.

The varied tasks of August 1946 were the final ones carried out by 620 Squadron. Without ceremony, and remaining under the command of Wg Cdr Alexander, it became 113 Squadron on 1 September 1946.

As 113 Squadron, the unit's role was largely unchanged. Its transport tasks included the evacuation of British civilians from Palestine during Operation 'Polly', a few weeks before it was disbanded on 1 April 1947. A year later, the British forces left Palestine and the State of Israel came into being, in a part of the world that has yet to achieve lasting peace.

# Epilogue

B y the autumn of 1946, 190 and 620 Squadrons were no more. Their numbers are unlikely to be used again by Royal Air Force squadrons, but 620 (Duffield) Squadron of the Air Training Corps proudly upholds one tradition, by including the 'pegasus with lightning' in its crest. Some of the personnel who served with 190 and 620 Squadrons stayed in the RAF, RAAF, RCAF or RNZAF, but most returned to civilian life and pursued careers that had little or no connection with their wartime duties. These men considered they had 'done their bit' and looked forward to a time of peace, yet many of them retained the bonds of comradeship that had been forged as they faced the dangers and uncertainties of war. For those wishing to stay in touch, there were a few reunions during the late 1940s and 1950s, mainly in the guise of spirited gatherings in London pubs. The first

presentation of the 620 Squadron Roll of Honour to RAF Fairford. Left to right: Flight Lieutenant A.T. ʌble RAF Retd (Keeper of the 620 Squadron Register), Major M. Harris USAF (Base Chaplain), Group tain A.F. Wallace CBE DFC RAF Retd (former Flight Commander, 620 Squadron) and Squadron Leader A. ʌson RAF (Senior RAF Officer, Fairford). (*190 & 620 Sqns Archive*)

formal reunion, in 1993, was to mark the fiftieth anniversary of 620 Squadron's formation. This was followed by a further reunion for 620 Squadron in 1996, and a joint reunion for 190 and 620 Squadrons in 1999.

RAF Fairford, the home of 190 and 620 Squadrons in 1944, is now used by the United States Air Force as a base for occasional detachments by B-1 and B-52 bombers. The base's first occupants were recognised in 1985, when a new transit accommodation building was named 'Stirling House', with veterans from 190 and 620 Squadrons in attendance for its official opening.

In 1997, RAF Fairford was chosen as the place for the laying up of the 620 Squadron Roll of Honour. This was dedicated by the USAF Base Chaplain, Major M. Harris, in the presence of many former members of 620 Squadron. 190 and 620 Squadrons have been commemorated jointly at the other airfield from which they flew together, Great Dunmow. The memorial there takes the form of an avenue of trees in the grounds of Easton Lodge, and was dedicated in the year 2000.

The following Roll of Honour lists the names of Air Force personnel who were killed on operations, or in accidents, while serving with 190 and 620 Squadrons. Most of the casualties with known graves are commemorated by headstones erected and maintained by the Commonwealth War Graves Commission, while the names of those without known graves are recorded on the Runnymede Memorial. The Roll of Honour also includes the names of Army passengers who lost their lives in crashes involving Stirling aircraft of the two squadrons. There were no Halifax accidents that resulted in fatalities among crews or passengers. The names of soldiers killed on operations with 190 and 620 Squadrons, and who have no known graves, are recorded on either the Bayeux Memorial in Normandy, or the Groesbeek Memorial, near Nijmegen, according to the area in which they were posted as missing. May they all rest in peace.

# Roll of Honour

## 190 Squadron 1944–5

**11 April 1944 – Stirling LJ822**

Flight Sergeant Peter CROUDIS RNZAF
Flight Sergeant Douglas John SAMPSON RNZAF
Flight Sergeant Leslie Ernest ZIERSCH RAAF
Sergeant John Willie MITCHELL
Flight Sergeant Kenneth Stanley NUNN RAAF
Flying Officer Robert Stewart HADLEY RCAF

**6 June 1944 – Stirling LJ818**

Sergeant Clifford Owen BEVAN

**23 July 1944 – Stirling LJ882**

Flying Officer Leonard Alfred Arthur KILGOUR RNZAF
Flight Sergeant Henry Lester GUY
Sergeant Albert William SWINDELL
Flying Officer Blake Gordon FOY RCAF
Pilot Officer Frank COPLAND

Also on board LJ882, and killed on 23 July 1944, were soldiers of the following units:

2nd Special Air Service Regiment

Major Felix John Stewart SYMES
Lieutenant Ian Maxwell GRANT
Sergeant Douglas Hays McKAY
Private Leonard William CURTIS
Private James SIMPSON
Private James William Beattie REILLY

GHQ Liaison Regiment

Signalman Lachlan TAYLOR
Signalman Wilfred LEACH

**26 August 1944 – Stirling LJ827**

Flying Officer Norman Harry PORT RAAF
Pilot Officer Cyril Martin ROSAY
Pilot Officer Frank Cecil NEWMAN

Sergeant William Thomas BUSSELL (on detached duty from 1665 HCU)
Flight Sergeant Kenneth Charles GARNER
Flight Sergeant Ernest Thomas CORNELIUS

### 19 September 1944 – Stirling LJ939

Squadron Leader John Philip GILLIARD DFC
Flying Officer Norman Sutherland McEWEN

Also on board LJ939, and killed on 19 September 1944, were dispatchers of:

253 (Airborne) Composite Company, Royal Army Service Corps

Driver Denis BREADING
Driver Frederick TAYLOR

### 19 September 1944 – Stirling EF263

Warrant Officer Stanley Herbert COESHOTT
Flight Sergeant Stanley Vincent DAVIS
Flight Sergeant John Garfield JEFFREY
Sergeant George Lancelot WOOD
Flight Sergeant William Charles MOSS
Flight Sergeant George Stanley BRECKELS RCAF

Also on board EF263, and killed on 19 September 1944, were dispatchers of:

253 (Airborne) Composite Company, Royal Army Service Corps

Private George Cyril CADLE
Private James COURTNEY

### 20 September 1944 – Stirling LJ829

Flying Officer Roderick James MATHESON RCAF
Pilot Officer Reginald Austin DAVIS BEc RAAF
Pilot Officer Keith WILLETT RAAF
Sergeant Edward Francis KEEN
Sergeant Stanley James COOKE
Warrant Officer I Thomas William ALLEN RCAF
Warrant Officer I David Lorne BROUSE RCAF

Also on board LJ829, and killed on 20 September 1944, were dispatchers of:

253 (Airborne) Composite Company, Royal Army Service Corps

Driver Joseph Francis LEECH
Lance Corporal Frederick REXSTREW

### 21 September 1944 – Stirling LJ982

Wing Commander Graeme Elliott HARRISON DFC
Warrant Officer Thomas Barry BRIERLEY RNZAF
Warrant Officer Donald Meldrum MATHEWSON RNZAF
Flying Officer Neil MACKAY
Flight Sergeant Robert PERCY

Flight Lieutenant Norman Edward SKINNER DFC
Pilot Officer Comte Jacques Fernand de CORDOUE RCAF

Also on board LJ982, and killed on 21 September 1944, were dispatchers of:

253 (Airborne) Composite Company, Royal Army Service Corps

Lance Corporal Leslie H. CALDECOTT
Driver Harold GREGORY

### 21 September 1944 – Stirling LJ833

Flight Lieutenant Alexander ANDERSON
Flight Sergeant George Felix CONRY-CANDLER
Flying Officer Alexander Dalgety ADAMSON
Flight Sergeant William George TOLLEY
Flight Sergeant Arthur George Oliver BELLAMY

Also on board LJ833, and killed on 21 September 1944, was a dispatcher of:

253 (Airborne) Composite Company, Royal Army Service Corps

Driver Albert Edward ABBOTT

### 21 September 1944 – Stirling LJ830

Flying Officer John Russell THOMAS RCAF

Also killed on 21 September 1944, and possibly on board LJ830, were dispatchers of:

253 (Airborne) Composite Company, Royal Army Service Corps

Driver James Francis JOHNSTON
Driver Sydney L. CHURCHYARD

### 21 September 1944 – Stirling LJ943

Pilot Officer Robert Blair HERGER RCAF
Flying Officer Otto Hjalmar ANTOFT MA RCAF
Flying Officer John Kenneth MACDONNELL RCAF
Warrant Officer II Leslie Innes WHITLOCK RCAF
Flying Officer Harold Albert THORNINGTON

Also on board LJ943, and killed on 21 September 1944, were dispatchers of:

253 (Airborne) Composite Company, Royal Army Service Corps

Driver Ernest NOBLE
Driver Colin PARKER

### 21 September 1944 – Stirling LJ881

Flying Officer Brian Arthur BEBARFALD RNZAF
Pilot Officer Malcolm James YARWOOD RNZAF
Flight Sergeant Garnet Arthur PHILLIPS RAAF
Sergeant Charles Frederick BRANSON

One of the dispatchers of 253 (Airborne) Composite Company, Royal Army Service Corps, on board LJ881 was:

Driver George Evan JONES (died of wounds 22 September 1944)

### 21 September 1944 – Stirling LJ823

Flight Sergeant William Louis Pretsell CAIRNS
Flight Sergeant William Henry SKEWES
Warrant Officer Leslie John BILLEN (died 22 September 1944)

It is not known whether the date of Warrant Officer's Billen's death was recorded incorrectly or he survived the crash of LJ823 but died the next day.

### 6 November 1944 – Stirling LK195

Flying Officer Edwin Davis HODGSON RCAF
Flying Officer Elmer Joshua RUSENSTROM RCAF
Flying Officer George Langley TOWNS
Sergeant Reginald Henry George NEVARD
Warrant Officer William KING
Flying Officer Henry Edward EVANS

### 21 November 1944 – Stirling LK276

Flying Officer James Ian KIDGELL RAAF
Flying Officer William Walter D'Arcy BRAIN RNZAF
Flying Officer Ernest Douglas WOODS
Flight Sergeant Ronald David PAYNE
Sergeant Hugh HOLT
Flight Sergeant Reginald Matthew DAUNCEY
Flight Sergeant Arthur George REID (from Jamaica)

### 1 February 1945 – Stirling LJ832

Pilot Officer Robert Emmett MACDONALD RCAF

### 22 February 1945 – Stirling LK566

Warrant Officer Stanley Bernard CURRIE
Flight Sergeant Donald HOLLINRAKE
Flight Sergeant Kenneth Frank NEWMAN
Flight Sergeant Lewis George BALDOCK
Flight Sergeant Thomas James Alexander GRANT
Flight Sergeant Robert Edwin DAVIES

### 3 April 1945 – Stirling PK227

Flying Officer Sir Chandos WREN HOSKYNS
Flying Officer Sydney CARPENTER
Flying Officer Alan FISKEN
Sergeant Russell Ernest CHAPMAN

Warrant Officer Clifford BUCKLEY
Flying Officer Peter John Rupert VINEY

Also on board PK227, and killed on 3 April 1945, were dispatchers of:

223 Air Dispatch Company, Royal Army Service Corps

Driver Norman SMITH
Driver Frederick EVANS


**15 April 1945 – Stirling TS265**

Flying Officer Arthur James LEWIS
Flying Officer Ronald WELDON
Flight Sergeant Thomas William BOOKER
Flight Sergeant Anthony Peter Walter Ernest HILLIER
Sergeant Harry Victor BARROW
Flight Sergeant John CARTMELL
Flight Sergeant Walter Henry OGILVIE


**20 April 1945 – Stirling LJ930**

Wing Commander Richard Henry BUNKER DSO DFC and Bar
Sergeant Frederick Charles KING
Flying Officer George Robert Thompson TAYLOR
Sergeant Kenneth Gerald GARDINER
Flight Sergeant Ronald Lewis BAGLEY
Pilot Officer Samuel Alfred SULSH
Sergeant Jeffrey ALDRED


**10 May 1945 – Stirling LK297**

Squadron Leader Douglas Raymond ROBERTSON DFC RCAF
Flight Lieutenant Lemuel Ernest PROWSE RCAF
Flight Lieutenant Norman Leslie ROSEBLADE DFC RCAF
Flight Sergeant Ronald ALDERSON
Warrant Officer George Edward THOMPSON DFM
Flight Sergeant Arthur Gwynne DAVIES

Also on board LK297, and killed on 10 May 1945 were:

Air Vice-Marshal James Rowland SCARLETT-STREATFEILD CBE
    (AOC No. 38 Group)
Major Petter Kato JULIEBØ (Liaison Officer, Royal Norwegian Army)

and soldiers of the following units:

HQ 1st Airborne Division Defence Platoon

Private David William COOPER
Private Walter William ELLIOTT
Private Walter Robert LOVETT
Private Frank George McGLYNN
Private Edmund Charles MONK

The Commonwealth War Graves plot at the Western Civil Cemetery, Oslo, is the final resting place of the crew and passengers of Stirling LK297, which crashed on 10 May 1945. Their graves are marked by the close-spaced headstones to the left of the Cross of Sacrifice. (*Author's photograph*)

Corporal Sidney George RAYNER
Private William RODGER
Private John SHANNON
Private Clarence SUTHERLAND
Private Francis Gerard TRAINOR
Private George WALTON
Private Kenneth John WATTS
Private Michael Mullen WADE

2nd (Airborne) Battalion, Ox. & Bucks. Light Infantry

Private Frederick SAINTY
Sergeant Herbert William WOODWARD
Private Edward WABY

**10 May 1945 – Stirling LJ899**

The following soldiers of the 7th Battalion, King's Own Scottish Borderers were on board LJ899, and died when it ditched in Sweden:

Corporal James McAra DAVIDSON
Corporal John PEARL

318

Lance Serjeant John MULHOLLAND
Private Duncan Anthony CONNOLLY

## 11 May 1945

The following 190 Squadron personnel were killed as passengers in Wellington NC489:

Flying Officer John Henry VANULAR, RCAF
Flight Sergeant Wallace DEXTER
Warrant Officer II Joseph Arthur HAY RCAF
Warrant Officer John COGHLAN (from the Irish Republic)

# 620 Squadron 1943–6

### 23 June 1943 – Stirling EE875

Sergeant Thomas NICHOLSON
Sergeant Kenneth William READ
Flying Officer William Henry BOUNDY
Sergeant Ralph Owen JASPER
Sergeant Amos Alfred Thomas WOODARD
Sergeant Roy JACKSON (from the Irish Republic)
Sergeant Harold James WELLS

### 25 June 1943 – Stirling BK800

Flight Sergeant Richard Patrick REYNOLDS
Sergeant John GARBUTT
Sergeant John Douglas CRESSWELL
Sergeant John LINDLEY
Flying Officer Reginald Joseph BURKE RCAF
Sergeant Patrick James COURT

### 2 July 1943 – Stirling EF394

Sergeant Wilfred Martin COOPEY
Sergeant Douglas Menzies THOMSON
Sergeant Roderick Henry RICHARDS
Sergeant Richard William HEWITT
Flight Sergeant Robert Elmer ATKINSON RCAF
Sergeant Robert George LANCELOTT
LAC Hugh ROONEY
AC2 Thomas Alexander McLOUGHLIN

### 2 July 1943 – Stirling BK724

Flight Sergeant Thomas CORLESS
Sergeant Leslie Gordon TURVILLE
Sergeant Ralph Charles YOUNG
Sergeant William SHEARER

AC1 Arthur HAIGH
LAC Charles Storey FORSTER
LAC James Alexander MACDONALD

### 26 July 1943 – Stirling BF511

Pilot Officer John Grant PATTESON RCAF

### 26 July 1943 – Stirling EE906

Flight Sergeant Joseph Roderick Gerald MACDONALD RCAF
Sergeant Joseph Ballard LAMONT
Sergeant Howard HADFIELD
Sergeant Gwynfryn JONES
Sergeant John McLAUCHLAN

### 26 July 1943 – Stirling EH924

Sergeant John Desmond RATHBONE
Sergeant Robert WILD
Flying Officer John Frederick SHEPHERD
Sergeant John Horix WALLACE
Sergeant James Franklin WELLS
Sergeant Albert SIMONS

### 31 July 1943 – Stirling EE905

Sergeant William John FORD
Sergeant Robert Charles BROADBENT RCAF

### 7 August 1943 – Stirling BK690

Flying Officer John Arthur ROGERS
Pilot Officer Dixon David DONKIN
Sergeant Robert Ronnie BAIRD
Sergeant Colin Edward RASHLEY

### 12 August 1943 – Stirling BK713

Flight Lieutenant Leslie Kenneth WILLIAMS
Pilot Officer Gordon Harvey CLARKE ACA
Flight Sergeant Hugh MAITLAND
Sergeant Cyril HARRISON BSc
Sergeant Kenneth Ernest MOULDING
Sergeant Ronald THORNTON
Sergeant George Robert CUTTER
Sergeant Kenneth Neville DONALD (from Southern Rhodesia)

### 18 August 1943 – Stirling EF457

Flying Officer Leslie George KENNETT
Sergeant Dennis John CARRINGTON
Sergeant Ronald Ernest THOMPSON

**24 August 1943 – Stirling BK801**

Flying Officer George William MACDONALD
Sergeant Leslie RICHARDSON
Sergeant Ronald Henry COLE
Sergeant Philip James SAUNDERS
Sergeant Percy William Charles HIGGS

**28 August 1943 – Stirling EF451**

Sergeant William Henry DUROE
Flying Officer Romeo Dominick Louis VIETTO RCAF
Sergeant Albert TASKER
Sergeant Richard Patrick Michael MULLARKEY
Sergeant George McGREGOR

**28 August 1943 – Stirling BF576**

Sergeant Frank EELES
Flight Sergeant William Harrison THOMPSON
Sergeant Patrick Joseph CRUMMEY
Flight Sergeant George KARCZA RCAF

**28 August 1943 – Stirling EE942**

Flight Sergeant John Francis NICHOLS
Sergeant Stanley George BOND
Flying Officer Neville Sladen MITCHELL
Sergeant Maurice MEAKIN
Flight Sergeant James Patrick DONNELLY RNZAF
Sergeant George Charles BURTON
Sergeant Stephen George COYNE

**1 September 1943 – Stirling EH946**

Flying Officer Macquarie James CAMPBELL RAAF
Sergeant William Dennis WHITFIELD
Flight Sergeant Sydney Edmund BIRKETT
Sergeant Albert Edward TAYLOR
Sergeant Thomas Harold LOKE

**6 September 1943 – Stirling EH931**

Pilot Officer Peter Geoffrey QUAYLE
Sergeant Frederick Arthur JONES
Flight Sergeant Michael Joseph Thomas FINN
Sergeant Bernard Robert GILES

**27 September 1943 – Stirling EH945**

Sergeant Herbert William Ralph KERSLAKE
Sergeant William HOWES
Sergeant James Leo PARRY

Also from this crew was:

Flight Sergeant Frank Edward REED
(died 9 December 1944 while a prisoner-of-war)

### 4 October 1943 – Stirling EH894

Flight Sergeant Keith Albert LANGLEY RAAF

### 20 October 1943 – Stirling BK802

Warrant Officer II Victor Keith HARRIS RCAF
Sergeant James HARGREAVES

### 4 February 1944 – Stirling LK395

Squadron Leader Edward Creighton FYSON
Flying Officer George SALTER
Sergeant Eric BENNETT
Sergeant Alfred Victor Ronald EDWARDS
Flight Sergeant Leslie DARLINGTON
Sergeant Frederick William Christian DEAN
Sergeant George Harold KENT

### 12 April 1944 – Stirling LJ867

Flight Sergeant Alec David BARNETT

### 13 April 1944 – Stirling LJ475

Flight Sergeant Huia Nelson BURNS RAAF
Flight Sergeant Edmund Christopher WILLARD
Flying Officer John Alfred AMY
Sergeant George Whitton LEWIS
Sergeant Ernest William TOOTILL

### 8 May 1944 – Stirling LJ866

Flying Officer Archie Campbell SWAN RAAF
Flight Sergeant James Henry Bennison LISTER
Flying Officer William Joseph TAY
Sergeant Aubrey Louis Arthur ASH-SMITH
Sergeant Donald JONES
Sergeant Eric George SWALLOW

### 19 May 1944 – Stirling LJ880

Flight Lieutenant Richard Owen FRANCIS RCAF
Flying Officer Keith Alexander HILLS RCAF
Flying Officer Llewellyn Quinlan JENKINS BA
Sergeant Norman Harry FLACK

Flight Sergeant Richard KENNEDY
Flight Sergeant Antony Edmund HILL

## 19 May 1944 – Stirling EF244

Flight Sergeant Arthur Bruce HAYNES RAAF
Flight Sergeant Gwilym POWELL
Sergeant Robert Max COTTERELL LLB
Sergeant James Walter TAYLOR
Sergeant Albert Thomas FRANKS
Sergeant Garmon Peter JONES

## 6 June 1944 – Stirling EF295

Squadron Leader Wilmot Reginald PETTIT DFC OBE RCAF
Flying Officer Richard George WATKINS
Flight Sergeant Edward Harry Frederick ATKINSON RNZAF
Sergeant Geoffrey Albert MAUND

Soldiers of the following units were on board EF295 and also died on 6 June 1944. Some perished in the aircraft crash, and others were executed while prisoners-of-war:

HQ 6th Airborne Division, Royal Engineers

Sapper Peter GUARD

591st Parachute Squadron, Royal Engineers

Sapper Albert Edwin AUSTIN
Lance Corporal Kenneth William BRANSTON
Sapper John Joseph EVANS
Lance Corporal Thomas Andrew FRASER
Corporal William Alexander KELLY
Driver George THOMSON
Sapper David Henry WHEELER
Sapper Frank WOLFE
Sapper John YOUELL
Lance Corporal John REARDON-PARKER
(Died 7 June 1944, from injuries sustained in the crash)

## 6 June 1944 – Stirling EJ116

Pilot Officer Albert Hamilton BARTON
Flight Sergeant Henry Mark BITTINER
Sergeant Donald REID
Sergeant Geoffrey CROSSE
Sergeant William Eric WALLIS
Sergeant John Gillies SMITH

Also on board EJ116, and killed on 6 June 1944, were soldiers of the following units:

6th (Airborne) Armoured Regiment, Reconnaissance Corps, RAC

Lieutenant Raymond Charles BELCHER

The Commonwealth War Graves Commission Cemetery at Ranville. The graves of the RAF and Army casual from Stirlings EJ116 and EF295 (lost on D-Day) are in the foreground. (*Author's photograph*)

Trooper Michael Percy DONE
Corporal Peter Thomas EARWICKER
Trooper George Wilson LAMONT
Trooper Arthur Harry WILSON

7th Battalion, Parachute Regiment

Private Geoffrey COPSON
Private Reginald Albert Edward FRANCIS
Private Vincent Patrick Cole FROST
Lance Corporal John GASCOIGNE
Craftsman George William HUNT
Company Sergeant Major John Edward Philip HUTCHINGS
Corporal Alfred Ronald KEMP
Corporal George Henry LEAMER
Lance Corporal Robert Laurence MITCHELL
Private Walter SCOTT
Private Dennis SHUTT
Private Robert William STOBBART
Lance Corporal Robert TWIST
Corporal Albert Van RYNEN

**6 June 1944 – Stirling EF268**

Flying Officer Irvine Nathaniel CASKEY RCAF
Flying Officer Thomas Frederick BARKER RCAF
Flight Sergeant Arthur Welch JACKSON
Sergeant Alan Lacy SMITH
Flight Sergeant James HEWITT
Flight Sergeant Robert Alfred SPARKES

Also on board EF268, and killed on 6 June 1944, were soldiers of the:

7th Battalion, Parachute Regiment

Lance Corporal Alfred Henry James BEARD
Sergeant Joseph Albert BEECH
Private John CAVEY
Corporal Henry DENHAM
Private Peter Sidney FINCH
Private Frederick GARNETT
Private William HEK
Private Patrick HUGHES
Sergeant Ernest William JARVIS
Private Dennis KERR
Private Robert KINGSLEY
Lance Corporal Leslie Henry PHILLIPS
Private John William SMITH
Private Charles Kenneth STRINGER
Private Cyril Cooper STUBBINS
Private Cyril John SURMAN
Private Montague James TRUEMAN
Private John WALKER
Private Leslie Charles WEY
Sergeant Ernest Sidney HOUNSLOW

**18 June 1944 – Stirling LJ850**

Pilot Officer Robert William CRANE RAAF
Flight Sergeant Frank Norman JOHNSON
Warrant Officer II John Percy CLASPER RCAF
Sergeant David Wynne EVANS
Flight Sergeant Granville William STOPFORD
Flight Sergeant Benjamin James PROFIT RCAF

Also on board LJ850, and killed on 18 July 1944, were soldiers of the:

1st Special Air Service Regiment

Private John Seymour BOWEN
Lance Corporal Harold BROOK
Corporal William BRYSON
Lieutenant Leslie George CAIRNS MA
Private William John CREANEY
Private Donald Maurice GALE
Private George Malgwyn HAYES

Private George Dalton LAW
Corporal William LEADBETTER
Private Charles MACFARLANE
Private Dominic McBRIDE (from the Irish Republic)
Sergeant Ronald MILLER
Private James O'REILLY (from the Irish Republic)
Private John Kenneth ROGERS
Sergeant Reginald Josiah WORTLEY

## 23 July 1944 – Stirling LJ864

Flying Officer Ernest Cameron OKE RCAF
Flight Sergeant Thomas Michael GALVON RCAF
Flight Sergeant Luke Anthony HIGGINS RCAF
Sergeant Ronald Alfred WILKINS
Flying Officer Angus Sutherland MIDDLETON
Flight Sergeant Robert George CARROTHERS RCAF

## 4 August 1944 – Stirling LJ920

Pilot Officer Edward Grigg ROBINSON RNZAF
Flying Officer Ramsay McKenzie HABKIRK RCAF
Flight Sergeant James Frederick LEWIS
Warrant Officer Ihaia William TRAINOR RNZAF
Sergeant Richard George GLANVILLE
Flight Sergeant Kenneth Jefferies JOHNSON
Warrant Officer Peter STURGES RAAF

Also on board LJ920, and killed on 4 August 1944, were dispatchers of the:

Royal Army Service Corps

Corporal J.E. SMITH
Driver Ralph WRIGHT

## 10 August 1944 – Stirling EF256

The following soldiers of the 3rd Special Air Service Battalion were on board EF256, and died when it ditched in the sea:

Trooper Daniel SELLES
Trooper Roger DASTIS

## 20 September 1944 – Stirling LK127

Flying Officer Athol Richard SCANLON RAAF
Pilot Officer Raymond Joseph LAMONT RCAF
Warrant Officer Edward Joseph McGILVRAY RAAF
Sergeant John William MARSHALL

Also on board LK127 and killed on 20 September 1944, were dispatchers of:

253 (Airborne) Composite Company, Royal Army Service Corps

Corporal George Andrew FOWLER
Driver John Thomas HADLEY

## 20 September 1944 – Stirling LK548

Pilot Officer Maurice McHUGH RAAF
Flight Sergeant Eric Arthur BRADSHAW
Sergeant Thomas VICKERS

Also on board LK548, and killed on 20 September 1944, were dispatchers of:

398 (Airborne) Divisional Composite Company, RASC

Lance Corporal John WARING
Driver Ernest Victor HECKFORD

## 28 December 1944 – Stirling LJ970

Flying Officer John Henry McNAMARA RAAF
Warrant Officer David Wise JONES RAAF
Sergeant Raymond POOLE
Flight Lieutenant Kenneth James HARRIES
Flight Sergeant Sidney Walter Charles RODMAN
Sergeant George Lyon MITCHELL
Flight Sergeant Wilfred HUGHES

## 31 December 1944 – Stirling LJ914

Flying Officer Frederick George WARING
Warrant Officer Thomas Anthony LEYDEN
Flight Sergeant Graham Leslie OSMOND-JONES
Flight Sergeant Denis Carnaby FOSTER
Sergeant Kenneth CALLABY
Flight Sergeant Norman Arthur WHITE

## 20 March 1945 – Stirling LK116

Squadron Leader George Oliver Samuel WHITTY DFC
Warrant Officer John George Joseph WILLIAMS
Flight Sergeant George Robert DOUGLAS
Pilot Officer George Edward AMES
Warrant Officer I Andrew Paul BELL RCAF

Also on board LK116, and killed on 20 March 1945, was:

Captain George Frederick SLATER (Parachute Regiment, serving with the SAS)

## 14 March 1946

Sergeant Francis Ivens TARRY (killed in a road accident in Iraq)

# Index

Aachen 5

Ain 141

Aircraft types

Airspeed Horsa *25, 38, 43, 64, 87*

  delivered to Leicester East 15

  glue deterioration 54, 221

  structural failure 53

Airspeed Oxford 54, 72, 154

Armstrong Whitworth Albemarle

  dropping Pathfinder paratroops 59, 73

  glider tugs 55, 206

Armstrong Whitworth Whitley 18–19, *19*

Avro 504K 1

Avro Anson 176, 180

Avro Lancaster 3

BE2c and BE2e 1

Boeing B-17 Flying Fortress 51–2, 208, *209*, 230

Bristol Beaufighter 5

Bristol Bombay 36

Consolidated B-24 Liberator 32, 126

Consolidated Catalina 1, *2*

Curtiss C-46 251, 269, 278

DH6 1

DH Mosquito 63, 73, 212, 242

Douglas C-47 (USAAF) 32, 37, 50, 176, 181, 245, 249, 251

Douglas Dakota (RAF) 73, 96, 154, 167, 181, 244, 249, 251, 279

  620 Squadron 'Dakota Flight' 301

  SAS operation from Fairford 118

Focke-Wulf 190 102, 171

General Aircraft Hamilcar *91, 92*, 249, 290

Handley Page Halifax 13, 75, 77, 242, 249, 251, *281, 300, 308*

  replacing Stirling in air support role 256

Hawker Tempest 282

Heinkel 111 222

Junkers 188 275, *276*

Junkers 88 124, 125, 210, 242, 251, 275, 279, *279*

Martin B-26 Marauder 203

Messerschmitt 163 233

North American Mustang 90, 221

Republic P-47 Thunderbolt 167, 178, 285

Short Stirling Mk III *4, 25, 31*

  dropping supply containers 13, 27

  modified for glider towing 15

  withdrawn from main bomber force 12

Short Stirling Mk IV *28, 29*

  produced for air support role 27–8

Supermarine Spitfire 60, 90, 221, *226*

Supermarine Walrus 90

Vickers Warwick 90, 152

Vickers Wellington 278

Waco Hadrian 32, 108, 249

Airfields

Acklington 257

Aldergrove 288

Aldermaston 32

Almaza 301

Aqir 290, 293, *296–8*, 306

  620 Squadron moves to 292–3

  620 Squadron returns to 308

  personnel on strike 299

  station raided by terrorists 299

Aston Down 50, 60

B108 (Rheine) 259, 261, 263

B116 (Hannover/Wunstorf) 259, 261

B120 (Hannover/Lanenburg) 259

B14 (Amblie) 118

B50 (Vitry-en-Artois) 263

B56 (Brussels/Evere) 176

B58 (Brussels/Melsbroek) 259, 261, 263, 279, 280, 281, 284, 285, 286–8

B77 (Gilze-Rijen) 263

Bari 301

Barkston Heath 269

Bayonne 198

Blackbushe 262

Blakehill Farm 32, 118, 244

Bordeaux 290

Boscombe Down 44, 45–6, 60

Bourn 134

Brawdy 124

Brize Norton 32, 37, 38, 43–4, 134, 140, 290

Broadwell 32, 244, 290

Bungay 228

Cairo West 301
  620 Sqn moves to 302
  sandstorms at *305–6*
Carnaby 228, 230
Chedburgh
  620 Squadron forms at 2
  RAF Memorial *11*
Chilbolton 212, 279, 288
Chivenor 108
Ciampino 198, 200
Colerne 50, 289
Coltishall 5
Deelen 146, 152, 167
Deenethorpe 208
Down Ampney 32, *150*, 152, 244
Dunsfold 263, 280, 284, 285
Earls Colne 209, 285, 289
Edzell 308
Eggemoen 269–71
Ein Shemer 309
Eindhoven 269, 278
El Aouina 292
Fairford *36*
  190 Squadron moves to 37–8
  620 Squadron moves to 35
  flying accidents at 43, 49, 50, 59, 60–3,
    99–101, 137–9, 141–2
  'Opening-up' party 35
  'Stirling House' 312
Fairwood Common 124, 288
Foggia 287
Ford 105, 113, 115
Gardermoen 210, 269, 272, *273–7*, 275–9,
  285
  620 Squadron machine-gun found at 276,
  *277*
Gosfield 290
Great Dunmow *201*, *223*
  190 and 620 Squadrons move to 200–3,
    206
  fire in bomb dump 266
  flying accidents at 208, 212–16, 226, 237,
    *239*, 248, 266, *267*, 288
  gale damage to aircraft 230
  poor state of airfield 208
  Stirling shot down near 242–3
  VE Day celebrations at 267–8
  VJ Day celebrations at 287
Great Sampford 221, 226, 238, 242, 290
Greenham Common 32
Habbaniya 300, 306
Hampstead Norris 73, 140
Harrington 126
Harwell 32, 44, 111, 119
Hassani 287

Hawarden 289
Hawkinge 249
High Ercall 289, 291
Holmsley South 288
Honeybourne 290
Honiley 232–3
Hunsdon 12
Hurn 45
  SOE operations from *28–32*
Hutton Cranswick 230
Istres 198, *199*, 287, 290
Kabrit 308
Keevil 32, 44, 45, 107, 130, 145
Kelmscott, Local DZ 39, 47
Kinloss 210, 236–7, 289, 291
Lakenheath 2, 33, 50
Langham 257
Leicester East 14, *15*, *33*
  190 Squadron re-forms at 15
  620 Squadron moves to 14
  Horsa gliders delivered to 15–16
Long Marston 73
Luqa 292, 295
Lydda 301
  Meteorological Office 300
Madley 257
Maghaberry 279
Manston 9, 169, 201, 208, 289
Marston Moor 226
Matching 233, 284
Methwold 134
Middle Wallop 45–6, 89
Netheravon 15
  Divisional DZ 44, 53
  HQ 38 Group 14
  investiture parade at 178
Newmarket Heath 1, 134
North Weald 242
Northolt 166
Odiham 261
Pershore 113, 289, 308
Petah Tiqva 301
Peterhead 269, 271
Pomigliano 198, 200, *200*
Qastina 290, 301, *303*, 308
Rennes 290
Rivenhall 208, 263, 285, 290
Rochford 1
Rufforth 227
St Athan 137
St Mawgan 287, 308
Schleswig 285
Shallufa 306
Shepherd's Grove
  Stirling shot down at 236, 243

Sleap 18, 20
South Cerney 151, 154
Southrop 37, 38
Stansted 222
Steenwijk 254
Tangmere 140
Tarrant Rushton 32, 197, 212, 218, 232, 284, 285
  190 Sqn moves to 290
  196 Sqn moves to 16
  diversions to 108, 130, 257
  Fairford Stirlings operating from 40, 42–8, 53–5, 57–8, 60, 65
  mail flights to 295
Tempsford 13, 134, 266
Thruxton 282–3, 284, 290
Tilstock 18–20, *19*
Upwood 1
Vaaler 269, 275
Versailles 200
Warmwell 285, 286
Waterbeach 134
Welford
Westcott 230, 259, 263, *264*
Weston Zoyland 137
Wethersfield 208, 290
Wing 259, 261
Witchford 14, 78
Wittering 242
Woodbridge 141, 154, 169
Woolfox Lodge 12, 16
Yibna 295, 300, 306
Air Forces Memorial, Runnymede 312
Air Training Corps,
  620 (Duffield) Squadron 311
Airspeed Ltd 54
Aldeburgh 148
Alençon 45
Alexander, Wg Cdr 310
  assumes command of 620 Squadron 288
Alington, Wg Cdr 1
Allan, Fg Off *246, 265*, 265–6
Allen, Flt Sgt *129*
Altengrabow 265–6
Ames, Plt Off 243
Amsterdam 197, 198
Anchor Inn (Eaton Hastings) 51
Andelst 172
Anderson, Fg Off (later Flt Lt) A. 16, 172
Anderson, Flt Sgt I.A. *287*
Anderson, WO J.S. *235*
Andrews, Fg Off 168, *168*, 252, 266
Angers 115
Angus, Plt Off *171*
Anzex 48

Apeldoorn canal 254
Arab Legion 299
Argentan 45
Armstrong, WO I.S. *154*
Armstrong, WO L.N. 174, *175*
Arnesen, WO 78
Arnhem, see Operation 'Market'
  SOE DZs near 197
Arsbeck 231
Athens 287–8, *287*
Atkinson, Fg Off E. 266, 272
Atkinson, Flt Sgt E.H.F. 78–9
Atkinson, Plt Off J.H. 157
Aube 141
Auxerre 140
Avison, Bessie 51
Axe and Compass (Kempsford) 51


BABS (Beam Approach Beacon System) 290
Back, Plt Off (later Fg Off) 12, 29, 40, *41*, 42
Bagley, Flt Sgt 263
Bailey, Flt Sgt 257, 269
Bantoft, Sqn Ldr 158
Barnett, Plt Off 48
Barton, Flt Sgt 77
Bartram, Wg Cdr
  assumes command of 190 Squadron 284
Bate, Flt Sgt 176
Batten, Sgt *47*, 89
Battle of Britain air displays 234
Bayeux Memorial 312
Bebarfald, Plt Off (later Fg Off) 154, 157, 172
Beck, Flt Sgt *171*
Bedford River 16
Bedford, Sgt 61, *61*
Belgium, special operations 141, 145
Bell, Fg Off (later Flt Lt) W.P. 96, 132–3, *207*
Bell, Flt Sgt (later WO) A.P. 115, 243
Bennekom 176
Bennett, SSgt 251
Bénouville 73, 76, 77, 92
Berlin 8
Berridge, Sqn Ldr 231
Besançon 145
Bevan, Sgt 93
Bickford, Fg Off 236, 265
Billen, WO 172
Bishops Stortford 207, 214, 219, 221
Bliss, Flt Off (USAAF) 179–80, *180*, 187, 237
Bloomfield Dvr 172
Boardman, Flt Sgt 167, *306*
Bognor Regis 75–6, 89, 93
Booth, Plt Off M. 173
Booth, Sgt J.E. 168

Bordeaux  48, 55, 118, 139
Bordeaux-Tours railway  103
Boreham, Pte  115
Bossley, Fg Off  *171*
Bourges  30, 132, 145
Braathen, Fg Off  *94*
Bradbrook, Flt Sgt  *265*
Bradbury, Sgt  *47*
Bradshaw, Fg Off  133
Brain, Fg Off  115, 120, 212, *214*
Breading, Dvr  158
Brecon  55
Brest  109, 126
Bridges, Flt Sgt  133
Bridport  130
Briggs, Wg Cdr  271–2
    assumes command of 190 Squadron  264
    assumes command of 620 Squadron  284
Brillac  116
Brinson, LAC  *125*
British Army units
    1 Air Landing Brigade  43, 50, 149
    1 Parachute Brigade  50, 149
    1 and 2 SAS, see Special Air Service Brigade
    12th (Airborne) Battalion, The Devonshire
        Regiment  90
    1st Airborne Division  50, 143, 178, 182, 265,
        269
    1st Parachute Battalion  154, 156
    21st Independent Parachute Company  37,
        145, *147*
    225 Parachute Field Ambulance  82
    22nd Independent Parachute Company  49,
        73, 75
    2nd Parachute Battalion  154
    3 Parachute Brigade  38, 59, 73, 245
    3rd Parachute Battalion  154, 156
    4 Parachute Brigade  50
    5 Parachute Brigade  37, 59, 73, 245
    6 Air Landing Brigade  70, 87, 240, 246
    6th Airborne Division  13, 66, 212, 245, 300
    7th Parachute Battalion  73, 76
    GHQ Liaison Regiment  96
        'Phantom' signals teams  96, 104, 136
    Glider Pilot Regiment
        crews at Fairford  *88*
        C Squadron  290
        D Squadron  15
        G Squadron  39, 221, 290
        M Squadron  282, 284
        RAF pilots posted to  222
    Royal Engineers  73
        591 Parachute Squadron, RE  78
    Second Army  143, 156, 233, 245, 251

XVIII Airborne Corps
    (British/US, under command of Second
        Army)  245
    XXX Corps  178
Brittany  96, 109, 112, 126
Britten, Fg Off  286
Brive  114
Brown, Flt Sgt A.J.H.  173
Brown, Flt Sgt (later WO) L.J.S.  48–9, *49*,
    178
    awarded Military Medal  49
Brown, Sgt (dispatcher)  133
Brown, Sgt F.C.  53
Browning, Lt Gen  124
Brussels  166, 176
Bryce, Sgt  *42*
Buchan, Sgt  *94*
Buckley, Flt Sgt  173
'Bullseye' exercises  5
Bunce, Plt Off (later Fg Off)  30, 124, 126–7,
    129, *129*, 218
    awarded DFC  218
Bunker, Sqn Ldr (later Wg Cdr)  146, 197, 236,
    248, 254
    assumes command of 190 Squadron  197
    awarded DSO  218
    killed in flying accident  261–3
Burgess, Flt Sgt  *94*
Burnham-on-Sea  50
Burns, Flt Sgt  49
Bury St Edmunds  14, 242
Bussell, Sgt  140
Butcher, Flt Lt  135, 184
Byam, Mr G. (War Correspondent)  74
Byrne, Flt Sgt  158


Cabourg  43, 75, 109, 141,
Caen  91
Caen Canal  73, 92, 105
Cairns, Flt Sgt  172
Campbell, Plt Off  8
Canadian First Army  143, 233, 254
Carey, Plt Off  104, 176
'Carpetbagger' missions (US)  126
Caskey, Fg Off  77, *77*
Castle Eaton  152
Central Band of the Royal Air Force  239
Chaffey, Sgt (later Fg Off)  18, *18*, 51, 57, *58*,
    60, *71*, 92, 120, 124, 127, 178, 201, 219, *223*,
    225, 227, *258*, 259, 279, *280*, 284
Channel Islands  141
Chappell, Fg Off  *98*, 136
Charente  113
Chartres  130

Château de Grangues 79–80, *79*, *81*, 82, 84
Châteauroux 113, 145
Châtellerault 105, 130
Chaumont 115, 145
Chelmsford 219, 268, 287
Cherbourg 130, 133
Chesterton, Fg Off (later Flt Lt) 38, 45, *46*, 131, 145, 155, 158, 209, 226
Chipping Norton 60
Chrissop, Sqn Ldr (Chaplain) 63
Clark, Flt Sgt S.P., awarded DFM 9
Clark, SSgt W. 50
Clarke, Flt Sgt 184
CLE supply containers 27, *27*
Cleaver, Flt Sgt 169
Clement, Flt Sgt (later Fg Off) 42, *42*, 97, 152, *195*
Clun 109
Coeshott, Sgt (later Flt Sgt) 93, 123, 158
Coevordon 254
Coghlan, Flt Sgt (later WO) 244, 278
Coles, Sgt *49*
Cologne 3, 5
Combe Hill (Berks), Horsa accident at 53
'Comet', Operation Order for 144
Compiègne 140
Conley, Sgt 124
Connell, Fg Off 105, *105*, 124, 154, 248, 256, 259
Cook, Lt Col 271, *271*
Cook, Sgt (Army) 152
Copland, Plt Off 115
Copping, Sgt *217*
Côtes du Nord 114–15
Cotterell, Sgt *62*
Couch, Flt Sgt 174, *175*
Cox, Plt Off (later Fg Off) *121*, 122, 141
Coysh, Flt Sgt 178
Cramp, Flt Sgt 243
Crane, WO 106
Cretney, WO *171*
Crocker, Fg Off *58*, *107*, *258*
Croot, Maj 53–4
Crossman, Plt Off *98*
Croudis, Flt Sgt 48
Cullen, Fg Off 158
Cummins, Fg Off *235*
Cunningham, WO *265*
Currie, WO 237
Cutts, Plt Off *133*
Cyprus 308

Danby, Pte 161
Dane, Fg Off 162

Dann, Flt Sgt *217*, 261, *263*
Dastis, Tpr 133
Dauncey, Lt 39, 53, 59, 87, 151
Davidson, Flt Lt 131
Davies, Flt Sgt I. *270*
Davies, Sgt D.W. *9*
Dawe, WO *112*, 113, 136
Dawson, Flt Lt W.J. *41*
D-Day preparations and operations
 briefings at Fairford 73
 camp sealed at Fairford 66
 conference at HQ 38 Group 69
 'Fortitude' 71
 'invasion stripes' on aircraft 70–1
 landings postponed for 24 hours 72
 'Mallard' 85
 'Titanic' 75
 'Tonga' 73, 144
de Noblet family 79
de Rome, Flt Sgt (later Fg Off) 19, 57, *58*, 60, 92, *107*, 126–7, 129–30, *258*
Deacon, Fg Off 140, 169, *170*
Dead Sea 300
Deauville 125
Dengie Flats bombing range 231
Denmark, SOE operations 256
Derbyshire, Flt Sgt 54, 57
Dexter, Flt Sgt 278
Dickens, Flt Sgt 228
Diersfordter Wald 246
Dijon 140, 141, 145,
Dives-sur-Mer 77–8
Dolan, Air Fitter (E) 59
'Doomsday', Operation 269
Doorwerth 160
Dordogne 55
Douglas, Flt Sgt 243
Downham Market 16
Dowsett, Sgt, awarded DFM 9
Driel 176, 178
Driscoll, Flt Sgt 254
Drury, Sgt *171*
*Dulag Luft* interrogation centre 172
Dunkley, Flt Sgt *98*
Dunstan, Dvr 82
Durance 48
Duroe, Sgt 8
Düsseldorf 233
Dutch Resistance 197
Dutton, Flt Sgt 133, *134*
Duveen, Fg Off 16

East Hatley bombing range 231
Eastcote 145

Easton Lodge  200, *202*, *204–5*

Edgecombe, Fg Off  252

Edwards, Sgt  *103*

Eeles, Sgt  8

Eindhoven  143, 166, 176, 178, 278

Eisenhower, Gen  73

Elizabeth, HRH Princess  60

Elizabeth, HM Queen  60

Ellis, WO  59

Elst  160–1, 172

Emery, Flt Sgt  8

Emmen  145

Emmerich  245

Enkhuizen  209

Épinal  145, 197

'Eric' exercises  5

Essen  6

Etkin, Sgt (later Plt Off)  *100*, *224*

'Eureka'  43, 50, 53, 59, 73, 75, 92, 97, 109, 145, 148, 158, 198, 228, 230, 238, 251, 256

Evans, Sgt  101, 110, 124, 149, 162, 164

Everitt, Flt Sgt  169, *170*

Exercises

  Amber  266

  Angus  285

  Barry  285

  Bear  212

  Bizz I  37

  Bizz II  38

  Castle  218

  Confirmation  55

  Cru  218

  Dingo I  55

  Dingo II  58–9

  Doofah  289

  Dreme  43–4

  Drongo  59

  Essex  208

  Exeter  60–3

  Felix  290

  Find-it  109

  Flint  63

  Flot  240

  Hog I  44

  Kick-Off III  300

  Kingo  65

  Meteor  244

  Mush  50

  Posh  49–50

  Quiver  230

  Recurrent  221

  Release  285

  Renaissance  282

  Residue  284

  Riff Raff I  238

  Riff Raff II  239

  Rookie  289–90

  Share-out  290

  Snatch  300

  Staff Coll  309

  Token  240

  Tour  44

  Trap  63

  Turnround  63, *64*

  Vigour  221

  Vulture  240

  Womnud  289

Fairfax, Flt Sgt  17, 87, 184, 203

Fairweather, Sgt  179

Fargues  48

Farmer, Flt Sgt  *129*

Farren, Plt Off (later Fg Off)  43, 154, 172–3

Fauillet  130

FIDO (fog dispersal system)  169, 229

Fijnaart  152

Finistère  115, 118, 119

Fisher, Sqn Ldr  265

Fitzhugh, Dvr  173

Fletcher, Sgt (later Flt Sgt)  *65*, 89, 180, 208, 243, *276*

Fletcher, SSgt  99

Flying boat stations

  Calshot  133

  Hamworthy  2

  Pembroke Dock  1

  Sullom Voe  1, 2

Fogarty, Flt Sgt (later Plt Off)  105, *105*, 106, 178

Fontainebleau  96

Ford, Capt (US)  127

Fowler, Cpl (Army)  162

France, Sgt  *112*

Francis, Flt Lt  46, 60

Frankfurt  8

Franklin, Flt Sgt  137, 162

Franks, Sgt  *62*

French, Sgt (later Flt Sgt)  *65*, *276*

Frost, Sgt  6

Fryksände  272

Fulcher, Flt Sgt  140

Fyson, Sqn Ldr  30

'Gardening' (mine laying)  6

Gale, Maj Gen  239

Gamble, Sgt (later Flt Lt)  *4*, 5, *311*

Gardiner, Flt Lt  43, 99, 171, 243

Garwood, Sgt (later Flt Sgt)  *56*, *58*, *258*

Gascoyne, Flt Sgt  162
Gawith, Fg Off  *103*, 104, 152, *199*
'Gee'  16, 105, 130, 231, 233, 255, 257, 290
   enemy jamming of  34, 75
   Southern Chain  75
Gelsenkirchen  3
George VI, HM King  60
German Army units
   II SS *Panzer* Corps  154
   711th Coastal Defence Division  79
Ghent  156, 161
Gibb, Sqn Ldr  93
Gibson, Sgt  231
Gien  140
Gilliard, Sqn Ldr  109, 131, 158
Gillis, Mr B., KC  288
Gironde estuary  7
Gloucestershire Constabulary  65
Gosson, Plt Off  169
Gould, Flt Sgt A.  *41*
Gould, Sgt R.  282–4
Graham, Sgt  30
Grangues Memorial  85
Granville, Sgt  *125*
Grave  144, 173, 180
Greenslade, Flt Sgt  *41*
Grevenbroich  233
Griffin, Plt Off C.G.  48
Griffin, Sgt (later Flt Sgt) P.  *24*, *58*, *120*, *258*, 284
Griffiths, Fg Off  103
Groesbeek Memorial  312
Groningen  254
Guimiliau  129


Hadley, Dvr  162
Haifa  309
Haig, Sgt  176
Hall, LAC  *125*
Hall, Sgt (later Flt Sgt) W.  *100*, 101, *224*
Halliday, Plt Off  49
'Halophane' lights  55, 75
Hamburg  6, 7
Hamley, Sgt  *42*
Hamminkeln  245–6
Hampreston, Stirling accident at  48
Hannah, Flt Lt (later Sqn Ldr)  30, 131, 193
Hannover  8, *260*
Hanstein, Gen (Norwegian)  239
Haren  173
Hargreaves, Sgt J.  5, 12
Hargreaves, Flt Sgt H.  48
Harris, AM Sir Arthur  3
Harris, Flt Sgt V.K.  9

Harris, Maj M. (USAF Chaplain)  *311*, 312
Harris, Sgt J.W.  *217*
Harrison, Fg Off J.  *287*
Harrison, Wg Cdr G.E.  *16*, 74, 103, 130–1, *153*, 170
   assumes command of 190 Squadron  16
   awarded DFC  50
   killed near Arnhem  172
Hartt, Maj  272
Hatfield  146
Haute-Savoie  29, 141
Haute-Vienne  114, 130
Hawkstone Park  *26*
Hay, Fg Off J.S.  16, 173
Hay, WO J.A.  278
Haynes, Flt Sgt  60, *62*
Heald, LAC  186
Hebberd, SSgt  99
Heelsum  146
'Hellas', Operation  286
Herbert, WO (later Plt Off)  60, 65, *65*, *187*, *193*
Herger, Flt Sgt  55, 154, 172
Heteren  162
Higgins, Flt Off (USAAF)  33, 52, 54, 59, 63, 69, 72, 73, 85, 93, 95, 97, *98*, 102, 104, 105, 107, 108, 109, 110, 111, 114, 117, 118, 119, 122, 125, 126, 136
Hill, AM Sir Roderick  240
Hill, Flt Sgt C.G.  *154*
Hill, Sgt H.W.  *4*
Hillier, Sgt (later Flt Sgt)  60, *61*, *65*, 243
Hillyard, Sgt  172
Hilton, Fg Off  *34*
Hirtz Lt (US)  129
Hobbs, Fg Off  *4*
Hodge SSgt  *246*
Hodgson, Fg Off  209,
Holder, Dvr  59
Hollinghurst, AVM  14, 59, 80, 114, 124, 141
Hollinrake, Flt Sgt  237
Home Guard  65
Hønefoss  236, 238, 270–1
Hooper, Flt Sgt (later WO)  16, *41*, 91, 218
Hoorn  227
Houlgate coastal battery  77
Hoult, Flt Sgt  *5*
Howes, WO  270, *306*
Hughes, Dvr  172
Hughes, Flt Sgt P.E.  *287*
Hughes, Sgt M.  173, 175
Hughes, Sgt (later Flt Sgt) W.  30, 276
Hume, Flt Sgt  162
Husband, Flt Sgt  *270*

'Identification Friend or Foe' (IFF)  21, 57–8, 131
Indre  130
Insley, Fg Off  257, 269, 278
Irgun  299, 308
Isaacson, Flt Sgt (later Plt Off)  46, *47*, 53, 230, 249
Ivelaw-Chapman, AVM  288, 291
Jack, Flt Lt A.  104, *104*, 109, 154, 178

Jack, Sgt G.J.  *49*
Jacklin, Dvr  78
James, Fg Off  *170*
'Jedburgh' teams
  deployed in France  103
Jefferies, Mr J.  35, 61
Jervis, Flt Sgt  *103*
Johnson, Flt Sgt K.  *125*
Johnson, Sgt (later Flt Sgt) G.A.  *65, 276*
Johnson, Sgt D.J.  *112*
Johnson, WO W.S.  263
Jones, Dvr G.E.  172
Jones, Plt Off C.N.  257, *257*
Jones, Sgt G.P.  *62*
Jordan Valley  299
Jordan, Flt Sgt (later Plt Off)  100, *100*, 201, 255
'Jubilant', Operation  264
Jura mountains  142

Kalkar  233
Kassel  8
Kay, Flt Sgt W.C.  169
Kay, Plt Off (later Fg Off) J.H.  30, 104
Kebbell, Flt Sgt  78, 80, 84–5
Keenan, Sgt  *133*
Keiller, Sgt  *170*
Kelly, Cpl  83
Kempsford, Stirling accident at  49
Kempster, Flt Sgt  *170*
Kempton, Sgt  *154*
Kendrew, Flt Sgt  *246, 265*
Kennedy, Gp Capt  290
Keogh, Flt Sgt (later WO)  46, 136, 140, 141
Kern, Lt (US)  129
Kershaw, Flt Sgt  160, 212
Kidgell, Fg Off  152, 212, *213*
Kidner, Lt  234
King's Own Scottish Borderers  44, 272
Kilgour, Fg Off  53, 65, 115
King David Hotel, Jerusalem  308
King, Fg Off  176
Kitchener, Fg Off  *287*
Koenig, General (French)  178, 284

Krefeld  3
Kristiansand  226, 229, 237
Kviberg Cemetery  272

Lady Frances Ryder Scheme  120
Lambert, Sgt  *4*
Lambert, Sqn Ldr  7
Lamont, Flt Sgt  *162*
Landivisiau-Morlaix railway  126
Lane, Plt Off  158
Langang  237
Langdon, Fg Off  *103*
Langley, Sgt  8
Larroque  48
Lavadac  48
Lawton, Fg Off  158
le Bouvier, Fg Off (later Flt Lt)  16, 45–6, 160, 212, 216, 227, 236, 238
Le Creusot  3
Le Havre  75, 76, 93, 117
Le Mans  57, 113
Le Port  77
Lee, Wg Cdr  15, *69*, 73, 87, 131, 166, 180
  assumes command of 620 Squadron  3
  awarded DFC  16
  posted to Tilstock  198
  shot down near Arnhem  180
Leigh-Mallory, ACM Sir Trafford  55, 72
Leipzig  9
Leverkusen  12
Lewis, Fg Off A.J.  238, 248, 251, 257
Lewis, Flt Sgt J.B.  *235*
Lewis, Flt Sgt J.F.  *125*
Leysdown bombing range  231
Limoges  104, 113, 114, 131
Limoges-Vierzon railway  103
Little Easton  200
Littlehampton  75, 92
Loman, Fg Off  282–3
Long, Fg Off  272
Longhurst, LAC  *125*
Lot *département*  118
Lower Rhine river  143
Ludwigshafen  12
*Luftwaffe* units
  II/KG 26  275
  III/KG 26  275
  IV/NJG 3  275, 278
  *Nachtjagerstaffel Norwegen*  226, 229, 237, 275
Luxembourg, special operations  140, 142
Lydon, Sgt  *235*
Lynch, Cpl  *125*
Lyngved, Laura  *270*, 271

Macdonald, Fg Off F.C. *4*
Macdonald, Plt Off R.E. 232–3
Macdonald, Plt Off G.W. *7*, 8
Macdonald, Sgt J.R.G. 6
Macmillan, WO 180
Maloney, Fg Off 104
Malta 292–3
Mannheim 8
*Maquis* (French Resistance) 13, 29, 44, 46, 48–9, 96, 103, 105, 119, 126, 129, 136
Marcham bombing range 130
Marciac 57
Marçon 57
'Market', Operation 143
  air routes 146, *146*
  camp sealed at Fairford 145
  first lift 145
  Operation Order for 145
  resupply flights 157
  second lift 154
  selection of DZs and LZs
  third lift 157
Marriott, WO 57, 255, *256*, 257
Marshall, Fg Off J.R. (later Flt Lt) 141, 149, 153, 157, *157*, 167, 255, 275, *277*
Marshall, Sgt J.W. *133*, 162
Martin, Flt Sgt D. 160, 212
Martin, Flt Sgt J.C. *42*
Martin, Sgt J *4*
Mason, WO (later Plt Off) 66, 74, 120, 121, *121*, 123
Matheson, Fg Off 113, 160
Mathieson, WO *235*
Maund, Sgt 78–9
McDougall, LAC 50
McEwen, Fg Off 158
McGilvray, WO 162
McHugh, Plt Off 124, 162
McIlroy, Sgt *4*
McIntyre, Gp 200, 264, 272, 285
McKay, WO 310
McKearney, Mr A. 37
McKenzie, Plt Off (later Fg Off) D.S. 140, 234
McKenzie, Sgt R.C. *217*
McLeod, Fg Off H.M. 115, *116*, 176
McLeod, Sgt (later Flt Sgt) N.J. *100*, *224*
McMahon, Fg Off *94*, *113*
McMillan, Flt Sgt 53
McNamara, Flt Sgt (later Fg Off ) 30, 103, 114, 178, 226, *227*, 276
Metcalfe, WO *306*
Metz 115
Middleton Plt Off 151, 171, *171*, 236, 251
*Milice* (Vichy paramilitary force) 48

Miller, Flt Sgt (later WO) 137, *137*, 141, 269–71, *270*
*Milorg* (Norwegian Resistance) 209
Missaubie, Sgt 179
Mitchell, Sgt 46, *47*, 73, 116, 149, 159, 160, 199, 210, 249, 259, 275, 278, 288
Modane 8
Moissac 60
'Molten', Operation 198
Mönchen-gladbach 8, 231
Montaner 55
Montgomery, Field Marshal Sir Bernard 143
Montluçon 8
Moody, Sgt 168, *169*
*Moonlight to Gascony* (book) 48
Morgan, Sgt 50
Morris, WO 172
Morvan 96, 103, 140
Moss, Fg Off *49*
Mount Carmel (radar station) 301
Mowat, Fg Off *154*
Mülheim 3
Munro, Flt Lt 172
Murdoch, SSgt 39
Murray, Fg Off G.C. 16, 29–30, 31, *41*, 104, 124, 126–7, 129
Murray, Flt Sgt W.J. 162
MV *Capetown Castle* 291, *293*

Nantes 7
Naples 198–9
Neale, Fg Off 66, 72, 132, *133*, 162
Neder Krüchten 231
Needleman, SSgt 53
Nevers 140
Newcombe, Flt Sgt 232–3
Newton Green, Stirling crash at 212
Newton, Fg Off 176
Nicholls, Pte 93
Nichols, Flt Sgt 8
Nicholson, Sgt 3
'Nickels' (propaganda leaflets) 118
Nijmegen 143–4, 159, 181
Nogent-le-Rotrou 46
Norman, Sgt 48
North Foreland 156
Northfield, Sgt 133
Notre-Dame-de-Livaye 125
Nürnburg 7, 8

Obolensky, Lt Col (US) 126–7, *126*, *127*, 130
O'Connell, Sgt 3, 7
Office of Strategic Services (US) 13, 104, 118

Oke, Fg Off  115
Old, Plt Off  *112*
Oosterbeck  156, 158, 159, 171–2
Orange, Flt Sgt  172
Orléans  115
Orléans gap  106
Osgood, LAC  137–8
Oslo  209, 226, 236, 237, 269, 271, 272
Oslo Fjord  217, 226
Oss  180
Ostend  156, 159, 167
Ouistreham  91–2
'Overlord', Operation (see also D-Day)  11
Owen, Flt Lt  226
Ox and Bucks Light Infantry  76
Oxley, Flt Sgt  *98*

Palmer, Pte  93
Palmer, WO R.M.  *154*
Parry, Capt (Chaplain) 74, 77
Parsonage Down  50
Pas de Calais  76
Pascoe, Fg Off  130, 151, 159, 173
    awarded DFC  218
Patient, Sqn Ldr  *291, 298*
Patteson, Sgt  6
Payne, Fg Off  *103*
Pearman, Sgt (later Flt Sgt)  *58, 120, 258, 280*
Pearson, Sqn Ldr  *311*
Peenemünde (rocket establishment)  7
Pelletier, WO  159, 173, *175*
Pepperell, Plt Off  215
Petersen, WO  *112*
Petersfield  44
Pettit, Sqn Ldr  *69*, 77–9
Plumetot  93
'Plunder', Operation  245
Poisson  55
Poitiers  104, 116, 140
Polish Parachute Brigade  153, 176
    1st Polish Paratroop Battalion  50
'Polly', Operation  310
Pontivy  109
Pool, Plt Off  *98*
Poole, Dvr  173
Port Said  291, 293
Port, Fg Off  140
Porter, Flt Sgt (later Plt Off) F.E.  53, 115
Porter, Mr J.  85
Pountney, Sgt (later Flt Sgt)  *100, 224*
POW camps
    *Oflag* 79  84
    *Stalag Luft* III  172
    *Stalag Luft* VII  172

*Stalag* XIA  265
Powell, Fg Off R.  49
Powell, Sgt G.  *62*
Prague, bullion flown to  286, 289
Pratt, Flt Sgt  180–1, *182*
Price, Fg Off *94*
Pryce, Mr P.  77, 84–5
Pryce, Sgt A.  77–8, *78*, 80–2, 84–5
Purvis, Gp Capt  285, *291*
Pyramids  306, *307*

Quayle, Flt Sgt  8

Ramat David  309
Randall, WO  *265*
Ranville  73–4
Ranville War Cemetery  84
Rathbone, Sgt  6
Ravenstein  172
Reardon-Parker, LCpl  83
'Rebecca' (see also 'Eureka')  40, 53, 269, 272
Rees  236
Rehovot  299
Reid, Flt Sgt  213
Reims  218
Remfry, Cpl  5, 51, 74, 268
Remscheid  6
Renkum  176
Reynolds, Flt Sgt  3
Rhône Valley  123
Richardson, Dvr  173
Riddell, WO  *57*
Riddle, Flt Sgt  137
Ringenberg  245
*Ringerikes Blad* (newspaper)  271
River Dives  73, 77
River Dordogne  118
River Garonne  131
River Issel  245
River Loire  30
River Maas  143–4, 172
River Orne  73, 74–5, 77, 91
River Waal  143, 172
'Rob Roy' resupply operations  96–7, 102
Robertson, Fg Off (later Sqn Ldr)  16, 54, 161,
    178, 272
    awarded DFC  218
Robinson, Flt Sgt (later Plt Off) E.G.  53, 125,
    *125*
Robinson, LAC  *125*
Robson, Elizabeth  219, *220*
Rockall  230
Røgden Lake, Stirling ditches in  272
Rogers, Fg Off  7

Rome 198–9
Roscoff 129
Rosenblade, Flt Lt 161
Ross, Flt Sgt 173
Rostron, Fg Off *287*
Rowland, Sgt (Army) 152
Royal Air Force units
  1 Personnel Dispatch Centre 291
  11 Personnel Dispatch and Reception
    Centre 18
  113 Squadron *309*, 310
  115 Squadron 9
  138 Squadron 237
  149 Squadron 2, 3, 50
  160 Maintenance Unit 299
  1665 Heavy Conversion Unit 12, 16, 18, *25*,
    26, 37, 100, 140, 145, 242
  18 Group, Coastal Command 1
  190 Squadron
    aircrews *67*
    converting to Halifax 267
    disbands 1919 1
    disposing of Stirlings 279, 280
    forms as 190 (Depot) Squadron, RFC 1
    forms as a Catalina squadron 1
    moves to Fairford 37–8
    moves to Great Dunmow 202
    moves to Tarrant Rushton 290
    receives squadron crest 254
    re-forms at Leicester East 15
    renamed 190 (Night) Training Sqn, RFC
      1
    renumbered as 210 Squadron 2
    renumbered as 295 Squadron 290
    takes delivery of Stirlings 16
  196 Squadron 12, 14, 16, 30, 44, 104, 107,
    126, 236
  199 Squadron 33
  210 Squadron 1, 2
  214 Squadron 2, 3
  2706 Squadron, RAF Regiment 50, 52
  2886 Squadron, RAF Regiment 52
  295 Squadron 30, 290
  296 Squadron 30
  297 Squadron 30
  298 Squadron 197, 264, 280
  299 Squadron 44, 104, 107, 126, 145
  2nd Tactical Air Force 16, 249
  3 Glider Servicing Echelon 39, 202
  3 Group, Bomber Command 2, 12, 13, 14
  32 Air Sea Rescue Unit 133
  38 Group
    AOC's message to ground crews 141
    established by upgrading 38 Wing 14
    forms part of 2nd Tactical Air Force 14
    HQ at Netheravon 14
    HQ moves to Marks Hall 197
    placed in Fighter Command 240
    transfers to ADGB 16
    transfers to AEAF 14
    transfers to Transport Command 281
  4 Glider Servicing Echelon 39, 206
  4 Group, Bomber Command 2
  4190 Servicing Echelon 290
  46 Group, Transport Command 32, 44, 50,
    92, 96, 244
  4620 Servicing Echelon 289, 291
  513 Squadron 14, 78
  54 Operational Training Unit 187
  570 Squadron 30, 232, 286
  6190 Servicing Echelon 141, 184, 202, 246,
    254
  620 Squadron
    aircrews *68*, *294*
    converting to Halifax 267
    'Dakota Flight' 301, 308
    disposing of Stirlings 256, 284–5
    first SOE operations 28
    forms at Chedburgh 2
    moves to Aqir 292–4
    moves to Cairo West 301–2
    moves to Fairford 35
    moves to Leicester East 14
    receives squadron crest 288
    re-equips with Stirling IV 32
    renumbered as 113 Squadron 310
    returns to Aqir 308
    transfers to 38 Group 15
  644 Squadron 197, 280, 290, 301
  6620 Servicing Echelon 141, 184, 206, 246
  69 Squadron 278
  75 Squadron 33
  78 Squadron 301
  81 Operational Training Unit 18–20, 114
  83 Group, 2nd TAF 259
  92 Group, Bomber Command 18
  93 Group, Bomber Command 14
  Air Defence of Great Britain (ADGB) 16
  Allied Expeditionary Air Force (AEAF) 12,
    14
  Marine Craft Units 90
  Mediterranean Allied Air Force 198
  Operational and Refresher Training Unit
    284
  RAF Hospital, Wroughton 173
Ruhr 3

St Catherine's Point 43
St Michielsgestel 158

St-Brieuc 109
Salisbury 60
Salisbury Plain 49
Sande 226
Sanders, Flt Sgt 161
Saône-et-Loire 132, 136
Saracen's Head (Great Dunmow) 243
Scanlon, Fg Off 137, 139, *139*, 152, 162
Scarlett-Streatfeild, AVM 239, 254, 271
  killed in Stirling crash, Norway 272
'Schnapps', Operation 267
Schofield, Sgt (later WO) *42*, 292, 295, *295*,
  299, 301, *302*, 303
Schouwen 148
Scott, LAC 191
Sea of Galilee 299
SEBRO (Short Bros Repair Organisation) 31
Seeley, LAC 302
Seine Valley 140
Sellars, Plt Off 154, *154*, 180, 255
Selles, Tpr 133
Seymour, Flt Lt 272
Shaffer, Sgt *217*
Sharp, Flt Sgt 278
Shaw, Flt Sgt R.G. 131
Shaw, Sgt W.G. 48
's-Hertogenbosch 148, 152, 178
Shields AC1 *125*
Shinner, Lt 82–4
Siegert, Fg Off 54, 130, 148, 170–1, 212, 215,
  229, 233
  awarded DFC 218
Simmins, Fg Off *129*
Simpson, Fg Off 286
Sims, Sgt *49*
'Simulators' (dummy paratroops) 255
Sinclair, Sir Archibald 102
Skaggerak 210, 229
Skewes, Flt Sgt 172
Slater, Capt G.F. 242–3
Slater, Mr A. 82, 85
Slater, Wg Cdr K.R.
  assumes command of 620 Squadron 286
Smith, Flt Sgt A.H. 8
Smith, Fg Off G.E. 169–70, *170*
Smith, Flt Sgt H. 263
Smith, Sgt A.J. 172
Smith, Cpl J.R. 17, 38, 66, 204
Soissons 140
Special Air Service Brigade
  British Regiments (1 and 2 SAS) 96
  French Battalions (3 and 4 SAS) 96
  Belgian Company (5 SAS) 96
Special Air Service operations
  Abel 142, 145

  Amherst 254–5
  Barker 132, 135–6
  Bulbasket 96, 97, 104–5, 109, 111, 113,
    115–16
  Dickens 114, 145
  Dingson 96, 102, 104, 105, 107, 109, 120,
    124, 125
  Dopey 255, 257
  Dunhill 123, 124
  Fabian 208, 212, 230, 235, 236
  Gain 96, 106, 109, 115, 124, 136
  Gobbo 230
  Grog 109, 112, 113, 114, 118, 119, 120, 123,
    125
  Haft 113, 118
  Haggard 140, 145
  Hardy 139–40
  Harrod 132, 136, 140
  Houndsworth 96, 103, 105–6, 111, 112, 113,
    118, 125, 137, 139, 140
  Jockworth 136
  Keystone 254–6
  Kipling 140
  Lot 103–4
  Loyton 135–6, 139, 140, 141, 142, 145
  Moses 116, 140
  Rupert 115, 140
  Ruskin 235, 236
  Samwest 96, 102, 103, 109, 112, 113,
  Spenser 145
  Sunflower 96, 102–3, 105–7, 109
  Titanic 75
  Wallace 140
  Wash 112, 113, 114, 115, 118, 123, 125
  Wolsey 140
Special Allied Airborne Reconnaissance Force
  265
Special Duties squadrons 13
Special Forces HQ, London 103
Special Operations (US) 13
Special Operations Executive (SOE) 13
  SOE and Jedburgh operations
    Actor 118
    Bit 216, 228, 237, 259
    Black Widow 208
    Blinkers 257
    Bluebottle 208
    Bob 137, 145, 182
    Checkers 238
    Criena 208
    Crop 236–7
    Crupper 216, 227, 228–9, 236, 237, 238,
      251, 254, 259
    Cubbing 235, 238, 254, 255
    Dick 45, 130, 136

Digger 118
Diplomat 141
Director 141
Ditcher 132
Donald 118, 123
Donkeyman 118
Draughts 198, 207, 208, 209, 212, 216, 227, 235, 255
Dudley 208, 209, 212, 216, 233, 235, 236
Event 208, 212
Felix 114
Fireman 114, 118
Flank 227, 236, 237, 251
Footman 118
Francis 114, 118
Frederick 115
Gilbert 118
Giles 119, 134
Glover 115, 141, 145
Halter 209
Hamish 114, 118, 119
Harry 45
Hilary 126
Hippodrome 134
Historian 105, 118
Hugh 103, 131
Ian 113, 118, 123, 131
Jacob 136
John 134, 136, 137, 140
Luke 95
Mark 130
Marksman 141
Marmosette 198, 212
Medico 255
Messenger 136, 182
Mongoose 171
Mongrel 55, 137, 140,
Necking 216, 255
Nico 208, 254
Osric 145
Paul 57, 140
Percy 114–15, 130, 136, 140
Peter 118, 137
Pimento 123, 130
Podex 209, 212, 230
Pommel 227, 236
Puffin 227
Reins 209, 216, 237
Rummy 145, 207, 208, 221, 227, 230, 238, 254
Rupert 113
Salesman 130
Sculling 212
Shipwright 113, 130
Snaffle 228, 237

Stationer 113, 115
Stirrup 254
Tablejam 256
Tail 216, 226
Thrush Red 216, 226
Trainer 43, 55
Ventriloquist 115, 118
Vet 237
Wheelwright 48, 57, 114
Whimper 255, 256
Wrestler 113, 145
Stanley, Sgt 90
Stansfield, Stirlings crash at 5
Stern Gang 299
Stert Flats firing range 50
Steven, Sec Off *119*
Stewart, Sgt 257
Stone, Flt Sgt 173
Stow-on-the-Wold 240
Sturges, WO *125*
Sudbury 266
Summers, Fg Off *265*
'Sunburn' sea searches 309
Sutherland, Flt Sgt (later Plt Off) 55, 105
    awarded DFC 218
Sutton, Sgt *47*
Svensson, Plt Off *129*
Swan, Fg Off 55
Sykes, Sgt *100*
Symes, Maj 115

Tarn-et-Garonne 123
Tarry, Sgt 306
Taylor, Dvr 158
Taylor, Sgt J.W. *62*
Tetbury 60
The Hague (Den Haag) 288
The Railway Inn (Fairford) 38
Thomas, Fg Off J.R. 176, *177*
Thomas, Fg Off M. 217, *217*
Thomas, WO J.G. 172
Thompson, Flt Sgt G.E. 161–2
    awarded DFM 218
Thompson, Sgt N.S. *133*
Thomson, WO 171
Thornington, Fg Off 172
Thring, Fg Off (later Flt Lt) 94, *94*, *113*
    awarded DFC 113
Tibberton 233
Tilburg 173
Titterton, LAC 51, 137, 184, 191, 193
Tod, Flt Sgt 132–3
Tonneins 131
Torsby 272

Touffréville 73
Tours 30, 57, 60
'Townhall' resupply operations 105, 107
Townsend, Mr E. (War Correspondent) 160–1
Trainor, WO 125
Tranter, Mr D. 216
Troop Carrier Command Post 145
Trout Inn (Lechlade) 51
Turin 7
Turvey, SSgt 90
Tyler, Sgt 18

Uden 165
Uedem 233
Urquhart, Gen 271–2
US Army units
  101st Airborne Division 143
  13th Airborne Division 265
  17th Airborne Division 245, 246
  43rd Infantry Division 178
  501st Parachute Regiment 265
  508th Parachute Regiment 265
  82nd Airborne Division 32, 143, 159
  First Army 143
  Ninth Army 245, 251
  Operational Groups
    Donald 126–30
    Patrick 130
  Third Army 143
USAAF units
  401st Bomb Group 208
  492nd Bomb Group 126
  53rd Troop Carrier Wing 37
  801st Bomb Group 126
  IXth Troop Carrier Command 50, 143, 251
US Office of Strategic Services (OSS) 13, 82
Utrecht 197, 198, 227, 238

V1 'Flying Bomb' 162, 220, 222
V2 rocket 220, 222, 233
Val de Loire 114
Valberg 161, 172
Valetta 293
Vannes 109
Vanular, Fg Off 278
Varaville 73
'Varsity', Operation 245
  camp sealed at Great Dunmow 244
  Exercise 'Meteor' 244
  'Spoof' flights before 244
Veitch, Flt Sgt 270
Venning, Flt Sgt 287
Verrières 115

Vestre Gravlund, Oslo 272
Vesuvius 200
'Vicarage', Operation 265–6
Vickers, Sgt 164
Vienne 96, 113
Villebougis 140
Vincent, Fg Off 47, 210
Vinet, Fg Off 115
Vinoy, Flt Sgt 132
'Violet', Operation 265–6
Vogt, Hauptmann 276–7
Vorstenbosch 162
Vosges 136, 142

Wadman LAC 187, 189, 202, 206, 213, 218,
  220, 222, 231, 242, 246, 248,
Waite, WO 121
Wales, HRH the Prince of (later HM King
  Edward VII) 200
Walker, Plt Off R.T. 173, 175
Walker, Plt Off C.W. 112, 192
Wallace, Sqn Ldr (later Gp Capt) 69, 126,
  127, 128, 311
Walters, Anne-Marie 48
Waring, Fg Off 229
Warner, WO 129
Warnford 44
Warwick, Countess of 200
Watkins, Fg Off 78–9
Watson, Sgt (later Flt Sgt) 103, 231
Weeze 233
Weldon, Fg Off 248
Wells, Sgt 3
Welton, Flt Sgt 171
Wesel 233, 245–6
West Kirby 291
Wheeler, Fg Off E. 133
Wheeler, Gp Capt A.H. 35, 74, 130, 153
Whelford 36
White, Flt Sgt 198, 269, 270
Whitehead, Flt Sgt 286
Whiteley, Fg Off 237
Whitty, Sqn Ldr 238, 242–3
Williams, Flt Lt L.K. 7
Williams, WO J.G.J. 243
Willis, Fg Off 178, 215
Wills, Pte 59
Wilsdon, Fg Off 232–3
Wilson, Fg Off 182, 229, 234, 235, 237, 251,
  252, 252, 288
'Window' (radar jamming foil) 6, 75
Windlesham, Stirling accident at 262
Windsor, Stirling accident near 9
Winter, WO 121

Winterbourne  59
Withers, Cpl  184
Wood, Maj  84
Woodgates End  216
Woodley, Cpl (Army)  173
Worthing  75
Wren Hoskyns, Fg Off  233, 254
Wright, Flt Sgt (later WO) G.C.  168, *169*, 252
Wuppertal  3
Wynne-Powell, Wg Cdr  *219*
  assumes command of 620 Squadron  198

Yonne  118
Ypreville-Biville  76
Yvetot  75

Zetten  172
Zimmerself, Sgt (US)  61
Zuider Zee (Ijsselmeer)  209, 227, 254
Zwolle  254